2 KINGS

WISDOM COMMENTARY

Volume 12

2 Kings

Song-Mi Suzie Park

Ahida Calderón Pilarski
Volume Editor

Barbara E. Reid, OP
General Editor

A Michael Glazier Book

LITURGICAL PRESS
Collegeville, Minnesota

www.litpress.org

1   2   3   4   5   6   7   8   9

Library of Congress Cataloging-in-Publication Data

Names: Park, Song-Mi Suzie, author.
Title: 2 Kings / Song-Mi Suzie Park ; Ahida Calderón Pilarski, volume editor ; Barbara E. Reid, OP, general editor.
Other titles: Second Kings
Description: Collegeville : Liturgical Press, 2019. | Series: Wisdom commentary ; Volume 12 | "A Michael Glazier book." | Includes bibliographical references and index.
Identifiers: LCCN 2019019581 (print) | LCCN 2019022046 (ebook) | ISBN 9780814681367 (eBook) | ISBN 9780814681114 (hardcover)
Subjects: LCSH: Bible. Kings, 2nd—Commentaries. | Bible. Kings, 2nd.—Feminist criticism.
Classification: LCC BS1335.53 (ebook) | LCC BS1335.53 .P37 2019 (print) | DDC 222/.5407082—dc23
LC record available at https://lccn.loc.gov/2019019581

Contents

Acknowledgments   vii

List of Abbreviations   ix

List of Contributors   xiii

Foreword: *"Tell It on the Mountain"—or, "And You Shall Tell Your Daughter [as Well]"*   xv
    Athalya Brenner-Idan

Editor's Introduction to Wisdom Commentary:
    "She Is a Breath of the Power of God" (Wis 7:25)   xix
    Barbara E. Reid, OP

Author's Introduction: Women Among Kings   xxxix

2 Kings 1:1-18   Feminine Powers and Masculine Rivalries   1

2 Kings 2:1-25   Feminine Powers and Masculine Reproduction   11

2 Kings 3:1-27   War, Death, and Sacrifice: A Colonial Enterprise   27

2 Kings 4:1-44   Fecundity, Reproduction, and Life   39

2 Kings 5:1-27   The Powerless as Conduits of YHWH's Power   59

2 Kings 6:1–7:20   Women, Children, and the Sick as Victims
                            of War   75

2 Kings 8:1-29   The Remaining Deeds of Elisha   93

2 Kings 9:1-37   The Murder of Queen Jezebel   109

2 Kings 10:1-36   Regime Change and the Final Desecration
of Queen Jezebel   135

2 Kings 11:1-21   The Rise, Fall, and Delegitimation
of Queen Athaliah   143

2 Kings 12:1-21   The Reign and Mysterious Death of King Joash
in Judah   161

2 Kings 13:1-25   The Reigns of Jehoahaz and Jehoash in Israel,
and the Death of Elisha   173

2 Kings 14:1-29   The Reigns of Amaziah in Judah and Jeroboam II
in Israel   185

2 Kings 15:1-38   Political Instability and Voiceless Victims   197

2 Kings 16:1-20   The Reign of Ahaz in Judah   207

2 Kings 17:1-41   The Destruction of the Northern Kingdom
of Israel   223

2 Kings 18:1–20:21   The Reign of Hezekiah in Judah   239

2 Kings 21:1-26   The Reign of Manasseh in Judah   269

2 Kings 22:1–23:37   The Prophecy of Huldah and the Reign of Josiah
in Judah   283

2 Kings 24:1–25:30   The End of Judah and the Deconstruction
of Androcentrism   303

Afterword   317

Works Cited   319

Index of Scripture References and Other Ancient Writings   335

Index of Subjects   347

Acknowledgments

Several people were instrumental to the completion of this commentary. First and foremost, I am indebted to my editor, Ahida Pilarski, who read and reviewed all the drafts of this commentary with care, attention, and insight. Her astute questions, corrections, and suggestions undoubtedly improved and refined this work. I am also indebted to Barbara Reid for careful attention to detail, her general support, and her masterful work as general editor of this series. I could not have asked for better editors than Barbara Reid and Ahida Pilarski.

I would like to thank my student aids, Stephen Milburn and Reba Balint, for their speedy work in the formulation of the many indexes for this commentary.

I am grateful to the president and trustees of Austin Presbyterian Theological Seminary for granting me a needed sabbatical to write and complete this monograph.

My wonderful and supportive colleagues at Austin Seminary as well as in the Austin area make it a congenial and fun place to work. I am thankful for their suggestions, advice, and friendship.

I am appreciative of the contributors who wrote prompt and illuminating essays. Their insights have added a level of richness and complexity to this commentary.

And finally, I am grateful to Kevin Lam, who diligently and kindly offers feedback on nearly everything I write despite having much work of his own.

Abbreviations

AB	Anchor Bible
ABD	*Anchor Bible Dictionary*
ABS	Archaeology and Biblical Studies
AJSL	*American Journal of Semitic Languages and Literature*
AOTC	Abingdon Old Testament Commentaries
ATANT	Abhandlungen zur Theologie des Alten und Neuen Testaments
BA	*Biblical Archaeologist*
BAR	*Biblical Archaeology Review*
BASOR	*Bulletin of the American Schools of Oriental Research*
BBR	*Bulletin for Biblical Research*
Bib	*Biblica*
BibInt	*Biblical Interpretation*
BibInt	Biblical Interpretation series
BJS	Brown Jewish Studies
BRev	*Bible Review*
BR	*Biblical Research*
BTB	*Biblical Theology Bulletin*

BZAW	Beihefte zur Zeitschrift für die alttestamentliche Wissenschaft
CBET	Contributions to Biblical Exegesis and Theology
CBQ	*Catholic Bible Quarterly*
CBQMS	Catholic Bible Quarterly Monograph Series
CC	Continental Commentaries
CTQ	*Concordia Theological Quarterly*
CurTM	*Currents in Theology and Mission*
CV	*Communio Viatorum*
DCLS	Deuterocanonical and Cognate Literature Series
EBib	*Études bibliques*
FCB	Feminist Companion to the Bible
FOTL	Forms of the Old Testament Literature
GBS	Guides to Biblical Scholarship
HAR	*Hebrew Annual Review*
HCS	Hellenistic Culture and Society
HS	*Hebrew Studies*
HSM	Harvard Semitic Monographs
HTR	*Harvard Theological Review*
HUCA	*Hebrew Union College Annual*
IBC	Interpretation: A Bible Commentary for Teaching and Preaching
IEJ	*Israel Exploration Journal*
IFT	Introductions in Feminist Theology
Int	*Interpretation*
IOSOT	International Organization for the Study of the Old Testament
JAOS	*Journal of the American Oriental Society*
JBL	*Journal of Biblical Literature*
JBQ	*Jewish Bible Quarterly*
JCS	*Journal of Cuneiform Studies*

JES	*Journal of Ecumenical Studies*
JETS	*Journal of the Evangelical Theological Society*
JFSR	*Journal of Feminist Studies in Religion*
JHS	*Journal of Hebrew Scriptures*
JNES	*Journal of Near Eastern Studies*
JQR	*Jewish Quarterly Review*
JSJSup	Journal for the Study of Judaism Supplement Series
JSOT	*Journal for the Study of the Old Testament*
JSOTSup	Journal for the Study of the Old Testament Supplement Series
LXX	Septuagint
MT	Masoretic Text
NCB	New Century Bible
NIB	New Interpreter's Bible
NIDB	New Interpreter's Dictionary of the Bible
NIBCOT	New International Bible Commentary on the Old Testament
OBT	Overtures to Biblical Theology
Or	*Orientalia*
OTL	Old Testament Library
OTS	Old Testament Studies
OtSt	*Oudtestamentische Studiën*
PBM	Paternoster Biblical Monographs
POS	Pretoria Oriental Series
Psychoanal Rev	*Psychoanalytic Review*
RelEd	*Religious Education*
RevExp	*Review and Expositor*
SBLMS	Society of Biblical Literature Monograph Series
SBLSBS	Society of Biblical Literature Sources for Biblical Study
SBT	Studies in Biblical Theology

SCM	Student Christian Movement
SJOT	*Scandinavian Journal of the Old Testament*
SJT	*Scottish Journal of Theology*
SO	Symbolae Osloenses
SwMT	*Swedish Missiological Themes*
SymS	Symposium Series
TynBul	*Tyndale Bulletin*
UF	*Ugarit Forschungen*
VTSup	Supplements to Vetus Testamentum
VT	*Vetus Testamentum*
WBC	Word Biblical Commentary
WTJ	*Westminster Theological Journal*
ZABR	*Zeitschrift für altorientalische und biblische Rechtsgeschichte*
ZAW	*Zeitschrift für die alttestamentliche Wissenschaft*
ZDMG	*Zeitschrift der Deutschen Morgenländischen Gesellschaft*

Contributors

Anna M .V. Bowden is a PhD candidate in New Testament at Brite Divinity School, expecting to graduate in May 2020. Her dissertation, titled "They Did Not Repent of the Work of Their Hands: A Reading of Revelation from the Cultural Context of Ephesian Marble-Workers," employs a people's history approach to explore the (im)practicalities of John's call for zero cultural participation. She has also served as adjunct faculty at Austin Presbyterian Theological Seminary.

Dr. M. L. Case earned her PhD in ancient Mediterranean religions and Hebrew Bible from the University of Texas at Austin. She is currently the postdoctoral fellow in Judaic studies at Virginia Polytechnic Institute and State University.

Rev. Dr. Gregory Cuéllar is assistant professor of Old Testament at Austin Presbyterian Theological Seminary in Austin, Texas. He has written numerous monographs and articles on borders and borderlands, postcolonial theory, migration studies, museum studies, and other topics. He is currently at work on a social justice art project called Arte de Lágrimas: Refugee Artwork Project.

Rev. Dr. Ginny Brewer-Boydston is an assistant professor of religion in Old Testament/Hebrew Bible at Wayland Baptist University, Plainview, Texas. She is the author of *Good Queen Mothers, Bad Queen Mothers: The*

Theological Presentation of the Queen Mother in 1 and 2 Kings (Catholic Biblical Association of America, 2016).

Dr. Hilary Lipka is an instructor in the Religious Studies Program at the University of New Mexico in Albuquerque. She is the author of *Sexual Transgression in the Hebrew Bible* (Sheffield Phoenix, 2006) and several articles related to women, gender, and sexuality in the Hebrew Bible.

Rev. Dr. Julie Faith Parker is associate professor of biblical studies at the General Theological Seminary in New York City. She has written numerous articles and is the author or editor of seven books, often focusing on the topics of children in the Bible and childist interpretation.

Dr. Christine Neal Thomas is assistant professor of Hebrew Bible at the Hebrew Union College Jewish Institute of Religion and Xavier University. She has a PhD from Harvard University's Department of Near Eastern Languages and Civilizations. Her dissertation, "Reconceiving the House of the Father: Royal Women at Ugarit," closely examines disputes between royal women and men in Hittite imperial legal texts from the Late Bronze Period.

Sudie Niesen Thompson serves as the associate pastor at Westminster Presbyterian Church in Wilmington, Delaware. She has a master of divinity from Austin Presbyterian Theological Seminary and a master of theology from Princeton Theological Seminary with a concentration in the Old Testament.

Foreword

"Tell It on the Mountain"—or, "And You Shall Tell Your Daughter [as Well]"

Athalya Brenner-Idan

Universiteit van Amsterdam/Tel Aviv University

What can Wisdom Commentary do to help, and for whom? The commentary genre has always been privileged in biblical studies. Traditionally acclaimed commentary series, such as the International Critical Commentary, Old Testament and New Testament Library, Hermeneia, Anchor Bible, Eerdmans, and Word—to name but several—enjoy nearly automatic prestige, and the number of women authors who participate in those is relatively small by comparison to their growing number in the scholarly guild. There certainly are some volumes written by women in them, especially in recent decades. At this time, however, this does not reflect the situation on the ground. Further, size matters. In that sense, the sheer size of the Wisdom Commentary is essential. This also represents a considerable investment and the possibility of reaching a wider audience than those already "converted."

Expecting women scholars to deal especially or only with what are considered strictly "female" matters seems unwarranted. According to Audre Lorde, "The master's tools will never dismantle the master's house."[1] But this maxim is not relevant to our case. The point of this commentary is not to destroy but to attain greater participation in the interpretive dialogue about biblical texts. Women scholars may bring additional questions to the readerly agenda as well as fresh angles to existing issues. To assume that their questions are designed only to topple a certain male hegemony is not convincing.

At first I did ask myself: is this commentary series an addition to calm raw nerves, an embellishment to make upholding the old hierarchy palatable? Or is it indeed about becoming the Master? On second and third thoughts, however, I understood that becoming the Master is not what this is about. Knowledge is power. Since Foucault at the very least, this cannot be in dispute. Writing commentaries for biblical texts by feminist women and men for women and for men, of confessional as well as non-confessional convictions, will sabotage (hopefully) the established hierarchy but will not topple it. This is about an attempt to integrate more fully, to introduce another viewpoint, to become. What excites me about the Wisdom Commentary is that it is not offered as just an alternative supplanting or substituting for the dominant discourse.

These commentaries on biblical books will retain nonauthoritative, pluralistic viewpoints. And yes, once again, the weight of a dedicated series, to distinguish from collections of stand-alone volumes, will prove weightier.

That such an approach is especially important in the case of the Hebrew Bible/Old Testament is beyond doubt. Women of Judaism, Christianity, and also Islam have struggled to make it their own for centuries, even more than they have fought for the New Testament and the Qur'an. Every Hebrew Bible/Old Testament volume in this project is evidence that the day has arrived: it is now possible to read *all* the Jewish canonical books as a collection, for a collection they are, with guidance conceived of with the needs of women readers (not only men) as an integral inspiration and part thereof.

In my Jewish tradition, the main motivation for reciting the Haggadah, the ritual text recited yearly on Passover, the festival of liberation from

---

1. Audre Lorde, "The Master's Tools Will Never Dismantle the Master's House," in *Sister Outsider: Essays and Speeches* (Berkeley, CA: Crossing Press, 1984, 2007), 110–14. First delivered in the Second Sex Conference in New York, 1979.

bondage, is given as "And you shall tell your son" (from Exod 13:8). The knowledge and experience of past generations is thus transferred to the next, for constructing the present and the future. The ancient maxim is, literally, limited to a male audience. This series remolds the maxim into a new inclusive shape, which is of the utmost consequence: "And you shall tell your son" is extended to "And you shall tell your daughter [as well as your son]." Or, if you want, "Tell it on the mountain," for all to hear.

This is what it's all about.

Editor's Introduction to Wisdom Commentary

"She Is a Breath of the Power of God" (Wis 7:25)

Barbara E. Reid, OP

General Editor

Wisdom Commentary is the first series to offer detailed feminist interpretation of every book of the Bible. The fruit of collaborative work by an ecumenical and interreligious team of scholars, the volumes provide serious, scholarly engagement with the whole biblical text, not only those texts that explicitly mention women. The series is intended for clergy, teachers, ministers, and all serious students of the Bible. Designed to be both accessible and informed by the various approaches of biblical scholarship, it pays particular attention to the world in front of the text, that is, how the text is heard and appropriated. At the same time, this series aims to be faithful to the ancient text and its earliest audiences; thus the volumes also explicate the worlds behind the text and within it. While issues of gender are primary in this project, the volumes also address the intersecting issues of power, authority, ethnicity, race, class, and religious belief and practice. The fifty-eight volumes include the books regarded as canonical by Jews (i.e., the Tanakh); Protestants (the "Hebrew Bible" and the New Testament); and Roman Catholic, Anglican, and Eastern

Orthodox Communions (i.e., Tobit, Judith, 1 and 2 Maccabees, Wisdom of Solomon, Sirach/Ecclesiasticus, Baruch, including the Letter of Jeremiah, the additions to Esther, and Susanna and Bel and the Dragon in Daniel).

A Symphony of Diverse Voices

Included in the Wisdom Commentary series are voices from scholars of many different religious traditions, of diverse ages, differing sexual identities, and varying cultural, racial, ethnic, and social contexts. Some have been pioneers in feminist biblical interpretation; others are newer contributors from a younger generation. A further distinctive feature of this series is that each volume incorporates voices other than that of the lead author(s). These voices appear alongside the commentary of the lead author(s), in the grayscale inserts. At times, a contributor may offer an alternative interpretation or a critique of the position taken by the lead author(s). At other times, she or he may offer a complementary interpretation from a different cultural context or subject position. Occasionally, portions of previously published material bring in other views. The diverse voices are not intended to be contestants in a debate or a cacophony of discordant notes. The multiple voices reflect that there is no single definitive feminist interpretation of a text. In addition, they show the importance of subject position in the process of interpretation. In this regard, the Wisdom Commentary series takes inspiration from the Talmud and from *The Torah: A Women's Commentary* (ed. Tamara Cohn Eskenazi and Andrea L. Weiss; New York: Women of Reform Judaism, Federation of Temple Sisterhood, 2008), in which many voices, even conflicting ones, are included and not harmonized.

Contributors include biblical scholars, theologians, and readers of Scripture from outside the scholarly and religious guilds. At times, their comments pertain to a particular text. In some instances they address a theme or topic that arises from the text.

Another feature that highlights the collaborative nature of feminist biblical interpretation is that a number of the volumes have two lead authors who have worked in tandem from the inception of the project and whose voices interweave throughout the commentary.

Woman Wisdom

The title, Wisdom Commentary, reflects both the importance to feminists of the figure of Woman Wisdom in the Scriptures and the distinct wisdom that feminist women and men bring to the interpretive process. In the Scriptures, Woman Wisdom appears as "a breath of the power of God, and a pure emanation of the glory of the Almighty" (Wis 7:25), who was present and active in fashioning all that exists (Prov 8:22-31; Wis 8:6). She is a spirit who pervades and penetrates all things (Wis 7:22-23), and she provides guidance and nourishment at her all-inclusive table (Prov 9:1-5). In both postexilic biblical and nonbiblical Jewish sources, Woman Wisdom is often equated with Torah, e.g., Sirach 24:23-34; Baruch 3:9–4:4; 38:2; 46:4-5; 2 Baruch 48:33, 36; 4 Ezra 5:9-10; 13:55; 14:40; 1 Enoch 42.

The New Testament frequently portrays Jesus as Wisdom incarnate. He invites his followers, "take my yoke upon you and learn from me" (Matt 11:29), just as Ben Sira advises, "put your neck under her [Wisdom's] yoke and let your souls receive instruction" (Sir 51:26). Just as Wisdom experiences rejection (Prov 1:23-25; Sir 15:7-8; Wis 10:3; Bar 3:12), so too does Jesus (Mark 8:31; John 1:10-11). Only some accept his invitation to his all-inclusive banquet (Matt 22:1-14; Luke 14:15-24; compare Prov 1:20-21; 9:3-5). Yet, "wisdom is vindicated by her deeds" (Matt 11:19, speaking of Jesus and John the Baptist; in the Lucan parallel at 7:35 they are called "wisdom's children"). There are numerous parallels between what is said of Wisdom and of the *Logos* in the Prologue of the Fourth Gospel (John 1:1-18). These are only a few of many examples. This female embodiment of divine presence and power is an apt image to guide the work of this series.

Feminism

There are many different understandings of the term "feminism." The various meanings, aims, and methods have developed exponentially in recent decades. Feminism is a perspective and a movement that springs from a recognition of inequities toward women, and it advocates for changes in whatever structures prevent full human flourishing. Three waves of feminism in the United States are commonly recognized. The first, arising in the mid-nineteenth century and lasting into the early twentieth, was sparked by women's efforts to be involved in the public sphere and to win the right to vote. In the 1960s and 1970s, the second wave focused on civil rights and equality for women. With the third wave, from the 1980s forward, came global feminism and the emphasis on the contextual nature of interpretation. Now a fourth wave may be emerging, with a stronger emphasis on the intersectionality of women's concerns with those of other marginalized groups and the increased use of the internet as a platform for discussion and activism.[1] As feminism has matured, it has recognized that inequities based on gender are interwoven with power imbalances based on race, class, ethnicity, religion, sexual identity, physical ability, and a host of other social markers.

Feminist Women and Men

Men who choose to identify with and partner with feminist women in the work of deconstructing systems of domination and building structures of equality are rightly regarded as feminists. Some men readily identify with experiences of women who are discriminated against on the basis of sex/gender, having themselves had comparable experiences; others who may not have faced direct discrimination or stereotyping recognize that inequity and problematic characterization still occur, and they seek correction. This series is pleased to include feminist men both as lead authors and as contributing voices.

Feminist Biblical Interpretation

Women interpreting the Bible from the lenses of their own experience is nothing new. Throughout the ages women have recounted the biblical stories, teaching them to their children and others, all the while interpreting them afresh for their time and circumstances.[2] Following is a very brief sketch of select foremothers who laid the groundwork for contemporary feminist biblical interpretation.

One of the earliest known Christian women who challenged patriarchal interpretations of Scripture was a consecrated virgin named Helie, who lived in the second century CE. When she refused to marry, her

---

1. See Martha Rampton, "Four Waves of Feminism" (October 25, 2015), at http://www.pacificu.edu/about-us/news-events/four-waves-feminism; and Ealasaid Munro, "Feminism: A Fourth Wave?," https://www.psa.ac.uk/insight-plus/feminism-fourth-wave.

2. For fuller treatments of this history, see chap. 7, "One Thousand Years of Feminist Bible Criticism," in Gerda Lerner, *Creation of Feminist Consciousness: From the Middle Ages to Eighteen-Seventy* (New York: Oxford University Press, 1993), 138–66; Susanne Scholz, "From the 'Woman's Bible' to the 'Women's Bible,' The History of Feminist Approaches to the Hebrew Bible," in *Introducing the Women's Hebrew Bible*, IFT 13 (New York: T&T Clark, 2007), 12–32; Marion Ann Taylor and Agnes Choi, eds., *Handbook of Women Biblical Interpreters: A Historical and Biographical Guide* (Grand Rapids: Baker Academic, 2012).

parents brought her before a judge, who quoted to her Paul's admonition, "It is better to marry than to be aflame with passion" (1 Cor 7:9). In response, Helie first acknowledges that this is what Scripture says, but then she retorts, "but not for everyone, that is, not for holy virgins."[3] She is one of the first to question the notion that a text has one meaning that is applicable in all situations.

A Jewish woman who also lived in the second century CE, Beruriah, is said to have had "profound knowledge of biblical exegesis and outstanding intelligence."[4] One story preserved in the Talmud (b. Berakot 10a) tells of how she challenged her husband, Rabbi Meir, when he prayed for the destruction of a sinner. Proffering an alternate interpretation, she argued that Psalm 104:35 advocated praying for the destruction of sin, not the sinner.

In medieval times the first written commentaries on Scripture from a critical feminist point of view emerge. While others may have been produced and passed on orally, they are for the most part lost to us now. Among the earliest preserved feminist writings are those of Hildegard of Bingen (1098–1179), German writer, mystic, and abbess of a Benedictine monastery. She reinterpreted the Genesis narratives in a way that presented women and men as complementary and interdependent. She frequently wrote about feminine aspects of the Divine.[5] Along with other women mystics of the time, such as Julian of Norwich (1342–ca. 1416), she spoke authoritatively from her personal experiences of God's revelation in prayer.

In this era, women were also among the scribes who copied biblical manuscripts. Notable among them is Paula Dei Mansi of Verona, from a distinguished family of Jewish scribes. In 1288, she translated from Hebrew into Italian a collection of Bible commentaries written by her father and added her own explanations.[6]

Another pioneer, Christine de Pizan (1365–ca. 1430), was a French court writer and prolific poet. She used allegory and common sense

---

3. Madrid, Escorial MS, a II 9, f. 90 v., as cited in Lerner, *Feminist Consciousness*, 140.

4. See Judith R. Baskin, "Women and Post-Biblical Commentary," in *The Torah: A Women's Commentary*, ed. Tamara Cohn Eskenazi and Andrea L. Weiss (New York: Women of Reform Judaism, Federation of Temple Sisterhood, 2008), xlix–lv, at lii.

5. Hildegard of Bingen, *De Operatione Dei*, 1.4.100; PL 197:885bc, as cited in Lerner, *Feminist Consciousness*, 142–43. See also Barbara Newman, *Sister of Wisdom: St. Hildegard's Theology of the Feminine* (Berkeley: University of California Press, 1987).

6. Emily Taitz, Sondra Henry, Cheryl Tallan, eds., *JPS Guide to Jewish Women 600 B.C.E.–1900 C.E.* (Philadelphia: Jewish Publication Society of America, 2003), 110–11.

to subvert misogynist readings of Scripture and celebrated the accomplishments of female biblical figures to argue for women's active roles in building society.[7]

By the seventeenth century, there were women who asserted that the biblical text needs to be understood and interpreted in its historical context. For example, Rachel Speght (1597–ca. 1630), a Calvinist English poet, elaborates on the historical situation in first-century Corinth that prompted Paul to say, "It is well for a man not to touch a woman" (1 Cor 7:1). Her aim was to show that the biblical texts should not be applied in a literal fashion to all times and circumstances. Similarly, Margaret Fell (1614–1702), one of the founders of the Religious Society of Friends (Quakers) in Britain, addressed the Pauline prohibitions against women speaking in church by insisting that they do not have universal validity. Rather, they need to be understood in their historical context, as addressed to a local church in particular time-bound circumstances.[8]

Along with analyzing the historical context of the biblical writings, women in the eighteenth and nineteenth centuries began to attend to misogynistic interpretations based on faulty translations. One of the first to do so was British feminist Mary Astell (1666–1731).[9] In the United States, the Grimké sisters, Sarah (1792–1873) and Angelina (1805–1879), Quaker women from a slaveholding family in South Carolina, learned biblical Greek and Hebrew so that they could interpret the Bible for themselves. They were prompted to do so after men sought to silence them from speaking out against slavery and for women's rights by claiming that the Bible (e.g., 1 Cor 14:34) prevented women from speaking in public.[10] Another prominent abolitionist, Sojourner Truth (ca. 1797–1883), a former slave, quoted the Bible liberally in her speeches[11] and in so doing challenged cultural assumptions and biblical interpretations that undergird gender inequities.

---

7. See further Taylor and Choi, *Handbook of Women Biblical Interpreters*, 127–32.

8. Her major work, *Women's Speaking Justified, Proved and Allowed by the Scriptures*, published in London in 1667, gave a systematic feminist reading of all biblical texts pertaining to women.

9. Mary Astell, *Some Reflections upon Marriage* (New York: Source Book Press, 1970, reprint of the 1730 edition; earliest edition of this work is 1700), 103–4.

10. See further Sarah Grimké, *Letters on the Equality of the Sexes and the Condition of Woman* (Boston: Isaac Knapp, 1838).

11. See, for example, her most famous speech, "Ain't I a Woman?," delivered in 1851 at the Ohio Women's Rights Convention in Akron, OH; http://www.fordham.edu/halsall/mod/sojtruth-woman.asp.

Another monumental work that emerged in nineteenth-century England was that of Jewish theologian Grace Aguilar (1816–1847), *The Women of Israel*,[12] published in 1845. Aguilar's approach was to make connections between the biblical women and contemporary Jewish women's concerns. She aimed to counter the widespread notion that women were degraded in Jewish law and that only in Christianity were women's dignity and value upheld. Her intent was to help Jewish women find strength and encouragement by seeing the evidence of God's compassionate love in the history of every woman in the Bible. While not a full commentary on the Bible, Aguilar's work stands out for its comprehensive treatment of every female biblical character, including even the most obscure references.[13]

The first person to produce a full-blown feminist commentary on the Bible was Elizabeth Cady Stanton (1815–1902). A leading proponent in the United States for women's right to vote, she found that whenever women tried to make inroads into politics, education, or the work world, the Bible was quoted against them. Along with a team of like-minded women, she produced her own commentary on every text of the Bible that concerned women. Her pioneering two-volume project, *The Woman's Bible*, published in 1895 and 1898, urges women to recognize that texts that degrade women come from the men who wrote the texts, not from God, and to use their common sense to rethink what has been presented to them as sacred.

Nearly a century later, *The Women's Bible Commentary*, edited by Carol Newsom and Sharon Ringe (Louisville: Westminster John Knox, 1992), appeared. This one-volume commentary features North American feminist scholarship on each book of the Protestant canon. Like Cady Stanton's commentary, it does not contain comments on every section of the biblical text but only on those passages deemed relevant to women. It was revised and expanded in 1998 to include the Apocrypha/Deuterocanonical books, and the contributors to this new volume reflect the global face of contemporary feminist scholarship. The revisions made in the third edition, which appeared in 2012, represent the profound advances in feminist biblical scholarship and include newer voices. In both the second and third editions, *The* has been dropped from the title.

---

12. The full title is *The Women of Israel or Characters and Sketches from the Holy Scriptures and Jewish History Illustrative of the Past History, Present Duty, and Future Destiny of the Hebrew Females, as Based on the Word of God.*

13. See further Eskenazi and Weiss, *The Torah: A Women's Commentary*, xxxviii; Taylor and Choi, *Handbook of Women Biblical Interpreters*, 31–37.

Also appearing at the centennial of Cady Stanton's *The Woman's Bible*
were two volumes edited by Elisabeth Schüssler Fiorenza with the assistance of Shelly Matthews. The first, *Searching the Scriptures: A Feminist Introduction* (New York: Crossroad, 1993), charts a comprehensive
approach to feminist interpretation from ecumenical, interreligious,
and multicultural perspectives. The second volume, published in 1994,
provides critical feminist commentary on each book of the New Testament as well as on three books of Jewish Pseudepigrapha and eleven
other early Christian writings.

In Europe, similar endeavors have been undertaken, such as the one-
volume *Kompendium Feministische Bibelauslegung*, edited by Luise Schottroff and Marie-Theres Wacker (Gütersloh: Gütersloher Verlagshaus,
2007), featuring German feminist biblical interpretation of each book of
the Bible, along with apocryphal books, and several extrabiblical writings. This work, now in its third edition, has recently been translated into
English.[14] A multivolume project, *The Bible and Women: An Encylopaedia of
Exegesis and Cultural History*, edited by Irmtraud Fischer, Adriana Valerio,
Mercedes Navarro Puerto, and Christiana de Groot, is currently in production. This project presents a history of the reception of the Bible as embedded
in Western cultural history and focuses particularly on gender-relevant
biblical themes, biblical female characters, and women recipients of the
Bible. The volumes are published in English, Spanish, Italian, and German.[15]

Another groundbreaking work is the collection The Feminist Companion to the Bible Series, edited by Athalya Brenner (Sheffield: Sheffield
Academic, 1993–2015), which comprises twenty volumes of commentaries on the Old Testament. The parallel series, Feminist Companion

14. *Feminist Biblical Interpretation: A Compendium of Critical Commentary on the Books
of the Bible and Related Literature*, trans. Lisa E. Dahill, Everett R. Kalin, Nancy Lukens,
Linda M. Maloney, Barbara Rumscheidt, Martin Rumscheidt, and Tina Steiner (Grand
Rapids: Eerdmans, 2012). Another notable collection is the three volumes edited by
Susanne Scholz, *Feminist Interpretation of the Hebrew Bible in Retrospect*, Recent Research
in Biblical Studies 7, 8, 9 (Sheffield: Sheffield Phoenix, 2013, 2014, 2016).

15. The first volume, on the Torah, appeared in Spanish in 2009, in German and
Italian in 2010, and in English in 2011 (Atlanta: Society of Biblical Literature). Five more
volumes are now available: *Feminist Biblical Studies in the Twentieth Century*, ed. Elisabeth
Schüssler Fiorenza (2014); *The Writings and Later Wisdom Books*, ed. Christl M. Maier and
Nuria Calduch-Benages (2014); *Gospels: Narrative and History*, ed. Mercedes Navarro
Puerto and Marinella Perroni; English translation ed. Amy-Jill Levine (2015); *The High
Middle Ages*, ed. Kari Elisabeth Børresen and Adriana Valerio (2015); and *Early Jewish
Writings*, ed. Eileen Schuller and Marie-Theres Wacker (2017). For further information,
see http://www.bibleandwomen.org.

to the New Testament and Early Christian Writings, edited by Amy-Jill Levine with Marianne Blickenstaff and Maria Mayo Robbins (Sheffield: Sheffield Academic, 2001–2009), contains thirteen volumes with one more planned. These two series are not full commentaries on the biblical books but comprise collected essays on discrete biblical texts.

Works by individual feminist biblical scholars in all parts of the world abound, and they are now too numerous to list in this introduction. Feminist biblical interpretation has reached a level of maturity that now makes possible a commentary series on every book of the Bible. In recent decades, women have had greater access to formal theological education, have been able to learn critical analytical tools, have put their own interpretations into writing, and have developed new methods of biblical interpretation. Until recent decades the work of feminist biblical interpreters was largely unknown, both to other women and to their brothers in the synagogue, church, and academy. Feminists now have taken their place in the professional world of biblical scholars, where they build on the work of their foremothers and connect with one another across the globe in ways not previously possible. In a few short decades, feminist biblical criticism has become an integral part of the academy.

Methodologies

Feminist biblical scholars use a variety of methods and often employ a number of them together.[16] In the Wisdom Commentary series, the authors will explain their understanding of feminism and the feminist reading strategies used in their commentary. Each volume treats the biblical text in blocks of material, not an analysis verse by verse. The entire text is considered, not only those passages that feature female characters or that speak specifically about women. When women are not apparent in the narrative, feminist lenses are used to analyze the dynamics in the text between male characters, the models of power, binary ways of thinking, and the dynamics of imperialism. Attention is given to how the whole text functions and how it was and is heard, both in its original context and today. Issues of particular concern to women—e.g., poverty, food, health, the environment, water—come to the fore.

---

16. See the seventeen essays in Caroline Vander Stichele and Todd Penner, eds., *Her Master's Tools? Feminist and Postcolonial Engagements of Historical-Critical Discourse* (Atlanta: Society of Biblical Literature, 2005), which show the complementary of various approaches.

One of the approaches used by early feminists and still popular today is to lift up the overlooked and forgotten stories of women in the Bible. Studies of women in each of the Testaments have been done, and there are also studies on women in particular biblical books.[17] Feminists recognize that the examples of biblical characters can be both empowering and problematic. The point of the feminist enterprise is not to serve as an apologetic for women; it is rather, in part, to recover women's history and literary roles in all their complexity and to learn from that recovery.

Retrieving the submerged history of biblical women is a crucial step for constructing the story of the past so as to lead to liberative possibilities for the present and future. There are, however, some pitfalls to this approach. Sometimes depictions of biblical women have been naïve and romantic. Some commentators exalt the virtues of both biblical and contemporary women and paint women as superior to men. Such reverse discrimination inhibits movement toward equality for all. In addition, some feminists challenge the idea that one can "pluck positive images out of an admittedly androcentric text, separating literary characterizations from the androcentric interests they were created to serve."[18] Still other feminists find these images to have enormous value.

One other danger with seeking the submerged history of women is the tendency for Christian feminists to paint Jesus and even Paul as liberators of women in a way that demonizes Judaism.[19] Wisdom Commentary aims to enhance understanding of Jesus as well as Paul as Jews of their day and to forge solidarity among Jewish and Christian feminists.

---

17. See, e.g., Alice Bach, ed., *Women in the Hebrew Bible: A Reader* (New York: Routledge, 1998); Tikva Frymer-Kensky, *Reading the Women of the Bible* (New York: Schocken Books, 2002); Carol Meyers, Toni Craven, and Ross S. Kraemer, *Women in Scripture* (Grand Rapids: Eerdmans, 2000); Irene Nowell, *Women in the Old Testament* (Collegeville, MN: Liturgical Press, 1997); Katharine Doob Sakenfeld, *Just Wives? Stories of Power and Survival in the Old Testament and Today* (Louisville: Westminster John Knox, 2003); Mary Ann Getty-Sullivan, *Women in the New Testament* (Collegeville, MN: Liturgical Press, 2001); Bonnie Thurston, *Women in the New Testament: Questions and Commentary*, Companions to the New Testament (New York: Crossroad, 1998).

18. Cheryl Exum, "Second Thoughts about Secondary Characters: Women in Exodus 1.8–2.10," in *A Feminist Companion to Exodus to Deuteronomy*, FCB 6, ed. Athalya Brenner (Sheffield: Sheffield Academic, 1994), 75–97, at 76.

19. See Judith Plaskow, "Anti-Judaism in Feminist Christian Interpretation," in *Searching the Scriptures: A Feminist Introduction*, ed. Elisabeth Schüssler Fiorenza (New York: Crossroad, 1993), 1:117–29; Amy-Jill Levine, "The New Testament and Anti-Judaism," in *The Misunderstood Jew: The Church and the Scandal of the Jewish Jesus* (San Francisco: HarperSanFrancisco, 2006), 87–117.

Feminist scholars who use historical-critical methods analyze the world behind the text; they seek to understand the historical context from which the text emerged and the circumstances of the communities to whom it was addressed. In bringing feminist lenses to this approach, the aim is not to impose modern expectations on ancient cultures but to unmask the ways that ideologically problematic mind-sets that produced the ancient texts are still promulgated through the text. Feminist biblical scholars aim not only to deconstruct but also to reclaim and reconstruct biblical history as women's history, in which women were central and active agents in creating religious heritage.[20] A further step is to construct meaning for contemporary women and men in a liberative movement toward transformation of social, political, economic, and religious structures.[21] In recent years, some feminists have embraced new historicism, which accents the creative role of the interpreter in any construction of history and exposes the power struggles to which the text witnesses.[22]

Literary critics analyze the world of the text: its form, language patterns, and rhetorical function.[23] They do not attempt to separate layers of tradition and redaction but focus on the text holistically, as it is in

20. See, for example, Phyllis A. Bird, *Missing Persons and Mistaken Identities: Women and Gender in Ancient Israel* (Minneapolis: Fortress, 1997); Elisabeth Schüssler Fiorenza, *In Memory of Her: A Feminist Theological Reconstruction of Christian Origins* (New York: Crossroad, 1984); Ross Shepard Kraemer and Mary Rose D'Angelo, eds., *Women and Christian Origins* (New York: Oxford University Press, 1999).

21. See, e.g., Sandra M. Schneiders, *The Revelatory Text: Interpreting the New Testament as Sacred Scripture*, rev. ed. (Collegeville, MN: Liturgical Press, 1999), whose aim is to engage in biblical interpretation not only for intellectual enlightenment but, even more important, for personal and communal transformation. Elisabeth Schüssler Fiorenza (*Wisdom Ways: Introducing Feminist Biblical Interpretation* [Maryknoll, NY: Orbis Books, 2001]) envisions the work of feminist biblical interpretation as a dance of Wisdom that consists of seven steps that interweave in spiral movements toward liberation, the final one being transformative action for change.

22. See Gina Hens-Piazza, *The New Historicism*, GBS, Old Testament Series (Minneapolis: Fortress, 2002).

23. Phyllis Trible was among the first to employ this method with texts from Genesis and Ruth in her groundbreaking book *God and the Rhetoric of Sexuality*, OBT (Philadelphia: Fortress, 1978). Another pioneer in feminist literary criticism is Mieke Bal (*Lethal Love: Feminist Literary Readings of Biblical Love Stories* [Bloomington: Indiana University Press, 1987]). For surveys of recent developments in literary methods, see Terry Eagleton, *Literary Theory: An Introduction*, 3rd ed. (Minneapolis: University of Minnesota Press, 2008); Janice Capel Anderson and Stephen D. Moore, eds., *Mark and Method: New Approaches in Biblical Studies*, 2nd ed. (Minneapolis: Fortress, 2008).

its present form. They examine how meaning is created in the interaction between the text and its reader in multiple contexts. Within the arena of literary approaches are reader-oriented approaches, narrative, rhetorical, structuralist, post-structuralist, deconstructive, ideological, autobiographical, and performance criticism.[24] Narrative critics study the interrelation among author, text, and audience through investigation of settings, both spatial and temporal; characters; plot; and narrative techniques (e.g., irony, parody, intertextual allusions). Reader-response critics attend to the impact that the text has on the reader or hearer. They recognize that when a text is detrimental toward women there is the choice either to affirm the text or to read against the grain toward a liberative end. Rhetorical criticism analyzes the style of argumentation and attends to how the author is attempting to shape the thinking or actions of the hearer. Structuralist critics analyze the complex patterns of binary oppositions in the text to derive its meaning.[25] Post-structuralist approaches challenge the notion that there are fixed meanings to any biblical text or that there is one universal truth. They engage in close readings of the text and often engage in intertextual analysis.[26] Within this approach is deconstructionist criticism, which views the text as a site of conflict, with competing narratives. The interpreter aims to expose the fault lines and overturn and reconfigure binaries by elevating the underling of a pair and foregrounding it.[27] Feminists also use other post-modern approaches, such as ideological and autobiographical criticism. The former analyzes the system of ideas that underlies the power and

24. See, e.g., J. Cheryl Exum and David J. A. Clines, eds., *The New Literary Criticism and the Hebrew Bible* (Valley Forge, PA: Trinity Press International, 1993); Edgar V. McKnight and Elizabeth Struthers Malbon, eds., *The New Literary Criticism and the New Testament* (Valley Forge, PA: Trinity Press International, 1994).

25. See, e.g., David Jobling, *The Sense of Biblical Narrative: Three Structural Analyses in the Old Testament*, JSOTSup 7 (Sheffield: University of Sheffield, 1978).

26. See, e.g., Stephen D. Moore, *Poststructuralism and the New Testament: Derrida and Foucault at the Foot of the Cross* (Minneapolis: Fortress, 1994); *The Bible in Theory: Critical and Postcritical Essays* (Atlanta: Society of Biblical Literature, 2010); Yvonne Sherwood, *A Biblical Text and Its Afterlives: The Survival of Jonah in Western Culture* (Cambridge: Cambridge University Press, 2000).

27. David Penchansky, "Deconstruction," in *The Oxford Encyclopedia of Biblical Interpretation*, ed. Steven McKenzie (New York: Oxford University Press, 2013), 196–205. See, for example, Danna Nolan Fewell and David M. Gunn, *Gender, Power, and Promise: The Subject of the Bible's First Story* (Nashville: Abingdon, 1993); David Rutledge, *Reading Marginally: Feminism, Deconstruction and the Bible*, BibInt 21 (Leiden: Brill, 1996).

values concealed in the text as well as that of the interpreter.[28] The latter involves deliberate self-disclosure while reading the text as a critical exegete.[29] Performance criticism attends to how the text was passed on orally, usually in communal settings, and to the verbal and nonverbal interactions between the performer and the audience.[30]

From the beginning, feminists have understood that interpreting the Bible is an act of power. In recent decades, feminist biblical scholars have developed hermeneutical theories of the ethics and politics of biblical interpretation to challenge the claims to value neutrality of most academic biblical scholarship. Feminist biblical scholars have also turned their attention to how some biblical writings were shaped by the power of empire and how this still shapes readers' self-understandings today. They have developed hermeneutical approaches that reveal, critique, and evaluate the interactions depicted in the text against the context of empire, and they consider implications for contemporary contexts.[31] Feminists also analyze the dynamics of colonization and the mentalities of colonized peoples in the exercise of biblical interpretation. As Kwok Pui-lan explains, "A postcolonial feminist interpretation of the Bible needs to investigate the deployment of gender in the narration of identity, the negotiation of power differentials between the colonizers and the colonized, and the reinforcement of patriarchal control over spheres where these elites could exercise control."[32] Methods and models from sociology and cultural anthropology are used by feminists to investigate

28. See Tina Pippin, ed., *Ideological Criticism of Biblical Texts: Semeia* 59 (1992); Terry Eagleton, *Ideology: An Introduction* (London: Verso, 2007).

29. See, e.g., Ingrid Rosa Kitzberger, ed., *Autobiographical Biblical Interpretation: Between Text and Self* (Leiden: Deo, 2002); P. J. W. Schutte, "When *They, We,* and the Passive Become *I*—Introducing Autobiographical Biblical Criticism," *HTS Teologiese Studies / Theological Studies* 61 (2005): 401–16.

30. See, e.g., Holly Hearon and Philip Ruge-Jones, eds., *The Bible in Ancient and Modern Media: Story and Performance* (Eugene, OR: Cascade, 2009).

31. E.g., Gale Yee, ed., *Judges and Method: New Approaches in Biblical Studies* (Minneapolis: Fortress, 1995); Warren Carter, *The Gospel of Matthew in Its Roman Imperial Context* (London: T&T Clark, 2005); *The Roman Empire and the New Testament: An Essential Guide* (Nashville: Abingdon, 2006); Elisabeth Schüssler Fiorenza, *The Power of the Word: Scripture and the Rhetoric of Empire* (Minneapolis: Fortress, 2007); Judith E. McKinlay, *Reframing Her: Biblical Women in Postcolonial Focus* (Sheffield: Sheffield Phoenix, 2004).

32. Kwok Pui-lan, *Postcolonial Imagination and Feminist Theology* (Louisville: Westminster John Knox, 2005), 9. See also, Musa W. Dube, ed., *Postcolonial Feminist Interpretation of the Bible* (St. Louis: Chalice, 2000); Cristl M. Maier and Carolyn J. Sharp,

women's everyday lives, their experiences of marriage, childrearing, labor, money, illness, etc.[33]

As feminists have examined the construction of gender from varying cultural perspectives, they have become ever more cognizant that the way gender roles are defined within differing cultures varies radically. As Mary Ann Tolbert observes, "Attempts to isolate some universal role that cross-culturally defines 'woman' have run into contradictory evidence at every turn."[34] Some women have coined new terms to highlight the particularities of their socio-cultural context. Many African American feminists, for example, call themselves *womanists* to draw attention to the double oppression of racism and sexism they experience.[35] Similarly, many US Hispanic feminists speak of themselves as *mujeristas* (*mujer* is Spanish for "woman").[36] Others prefer to be called "Latina feminists."[37] Both groups emphasize that the context for their theologizing is *mestizaje* and *mulatez* (racial and cultural mixture), done *en conjunto* (in community), with *lo cotidiano* (everyday lived experience) of Hispanic women as starting points for theological reflection and the encounter with the divine. Intercultural analysis has become an indispensable tool for working toward justice for women at the global level.[38]

Prophecy and Power: Jeremiah in Feminist and Postcolonial Perspective (London: Bloomsbury, 2013).

33. See, for example, Carol Meyers, *Discovering Eve: Ancient Israelite Women in Context* (New York: Oxford University Press, 1991); Luise Schottroff, *Lydia's Impatient Sisters: A Feminist Social History of Early Christianity*, trans. Barbara and Martin Rumscheidt (Louisville: Westminster John Knox, 1995); Susan Niditch, *"My Brother Esau Is a Hairy Man": Hair and Identity in Ancient Israel* (Oxford: Oxford University Press, 2008).

34. Mary Ann Tolbert, "Social, Sociological, and Anthropological Methods," in *Searching the Scriptures*, 1:255–71, at 265.

35. Alice Walker coined the term (*In Search of Our Mothers' Gardens: Womanist Prose* [New York: Harcourt Brace Jovanovich, 1967, 1983]). See also Katie G. Cannon, "The Emergence of Black Feminist Consciousness," in *Feminist Interpretation of the Bible*, ed. Letty M. Russell (Philadelphia: Westminster, 1985), 30–40; Renita Weems, *Just a Sister Away: A Womanist Vision of Women's Relationships in the Bible* (San Diego: Lura Media, 1988); Nyasha Junior, *An Introduction to Womanist Biblical Interpretation* (Louisville: Westminster John Knox, 2015).

36. Ada María Isasi-Díaz (*Mujerista Theology: A Theology for the Twenty-First Century* [Maryknoll, NY: Orbis Books, 1996]) is credited with coining the term.

37. E.g., María Pilar Aquino, Daisy L. Machado, and Jeanette Rodríguez, eds., *A Reader in Latina Feminist Theology* (Austin: University of Texas Press, 2002).

38. See, e.g., María Pilar Aquino and María José Rosado-Nunes, eds., *Feminist Intercultural Theology: Latina Explorations for a Just World*, Studies in Latino/a Catholicism (Maryknoll, NY: Orbis Books, 2007).

Some feminists are among those who have developed lesbian, gay, bisexual, and transgender (LGBT) interpretation. This approach focuses on issues of sexual identity and uses various reading strategies. Some point out the ways in which categories that emerged in recent centuries are applied anachronistically to biblical texts to make modern-day judgments. Others show how the Bible is silent on contemporary issues about sexual identity. Still others examine same-sex relationships in the Bible by figures such as Ruth and Naomi or David and Jonathan. In recent years, queer theory has emerged; it emphasizes the blurriness of boundaries not just of sexual identity but also of gender roles. Queer critics often focus on texts in which figures transgress what is traditionally considered proper gender behavior.[39]

Feminists also recognize that the struggle for women's equality and dignity is intimately connected with the struggle for respect for Earth and for the whole of the cosmos. Ecofeminists interpret Scripture in ways that highlight the link between human domination of nature and male subjugation of women. They show how anthropocentric ways of interpreting the Bible have overlooked or dismissed Earth and Earth community. They invite readers to identify not only with human characters in the biblical narrative but also with other Earth creatures and domains of nature, especially those that are the object of injustice. Some use creative imagination to retrieve the interests of Earth implicit in the narrative and enable Earth to speak.[40]

Biblical Authority

By the late nineteenth century, some feminists, such as Elizabeth Cady Stanton, began to question openly whether the Bible could continue to be regarded as authoritative for women. They viewed the Bible itself as

39. See, e.g., Bernadette J. Brooten, *Love between Women: Early Christian Responses to Female Homoeroticism* (Chicago and London: University of Chicago Press, 1996); Mary Rose D'Angelo, "Women Partners in the New Testament," *JFSR* 6 (1990): 65–86; Deirdre J. Good, "Reading Strategies for Biblical Passages on Same-Sex Relations," *Theology and Sexuality* 7 (1997): 70–82; Deryn Guest, *When Deborah Met Jael: Lesbian Feminist Hermeneutics* (London: SCM, 2011); Teresa Hornsby and Ken Stone, eds., *Bible Trouble: Queer Readings at the Boundaries of Biblical Scholarship* (Atlanta: Society of Biblical Literature, 2011).

40. E.g., Norman C. Habel and Peter Trudinger, *Exploring Ecological Hermeneutics*, SymS 46 (Atlanta: Society of Biblical Literature, 2008); Mary Judith Ress, *Ecofeminism in Latin America*, Women from the Margins (Maryknoll, NY: Orbis Books, 2006).

the source of women's oppression, and some rejected its sacred origin and saving claims. Some decided that the Bible and the religious traditions that enshrine it are too thoroughly saturated with androcentrism and patriarchy to be redeemable.[41]

In the Wisdom Commentary series, questions such as these may be raised, but the aim of this series is not to lead readers to reject the authority of the biblical text. Rather, the aim is to promote better understanding of the contexts from which the text arose and of the rhetorical effects it has on women and men in contemporary contexts. Such understanding can lead to a deepening of faith, with the Bible serving as an aid to bring flourishing of life.

Language for God

Because of the ways in which the term "God" has been used to symbolize the divine in predominantly male, patriarchal, and monarchical modes, feminists have designed new ways of speaking of the divine. Some have called attention to the inadequacy of the term *God* by trying to visually destabilize our ways of thinking and speaking of the divine. Rosemary Radford Ruether proposed *God/ess*, as an unpronounceable term pointing to the unnameable understanding of the divine that transcends patriarchal limitations.[42] Some have followed traditional Jewish practice, writing *G-d*. Elisabeth Schüssler Fiorenza has adopted *G*d*.[43] Others draw on the biblical tradition to mine female and non-gender-specific metaphors and symbols.[44] In Wisdom Commentary, there is not one standard way of expressing the divine; each author will use her or his preferred ways. The one exception is that when the tetragrammaton, YHWH, the name revealed to Moses in Exodus 3:14, is used, it will be without vowels, respecting the Jewish custom of avoiding pronouncing the divine name out of reverence.

41. E.g., Mary Daly, *Beyond God the Father: A Philosophy of Women's Liberation* (Boston: Beacon, 1973).

42. Rosemary Radford Ruether, *Sexism and God-Talk: Toward a Feminist Theology* (Boston: Beacon, 1983).

43. Elisabeth Schüssler Fiorenza, *Jesus: Miriam's Child, Sophia's Prophet; Critical Issues in Feminist Christology* (New York: Continuum, 1994), 191 n. 3.

44. E.g., Sallie McFague, *Models of God: Theology for an Ecological, Nuclear Age* (Philadelphia: Fortress, 1987); Catherine LaCugna, *God for Us: The Trinity and Christian Life* (San Francisco: Harper Collins, 1991); Elizabeth A. Johnson, *She Who Is: The Mystery of God in Feminist Theological Discourse* (New York: Crossroad, 1992). See further Elizabeth A. Johnson, "God," in *Dictionary of Feminist Theologies*, 128–30.

Nomenclature for the Two Testaments

In recent decades, some biblical scholars have begun to call the two Testaments of the Bible by names other than the traditional nomenclature: Old and New Testament. Some regard "Old" as derogatory, implying that it is no longer relevant or that it has been superseded. Consequently, terms like Hebrew Bible, First Testament, and Jewish Scriptures and, correspondingly, Christian Scriptures or Second Testament have come into use. There are a number of difficulties with these designations. The term "Hebrew Bible" does not take into account that parts of the Old Testament are written not in Hebrew but in Aramaic.[45] Moreover, for Roman Catholics and Eastern Orthodox believers, the Old Testament includes books written in Greek—the Deuterocanonical books, considered Apocrypha by Protestants.[46] The term "Jewish Scriptures" is inadequate because these books are also sacred to Christians. Conversely, "Christian Scriptures" is not an accurate designation for the New Testament, since the Old Testament is also part of the Christian Scriptures. Using "First and Second Testament" also has difficulties, in that it can imply a hierarchy and a value judgment.[47] Jews generally use the term Tanakh, an acronym for Torah (Pentateuch), Nevi'im (Prophets), and Ketuvim (Writings).

In Wisdom Commentary, if authors choose to use a designation other than Tanakh, Old Testament, and New Testament, they will explain how they mean the term.

Translation

Modern feminist scholars recognize the complexities connected with biblical translation, as they have delved into questions about philosophy of language, how meanings are produced, and how they are culturally situated. Today it is evident that simply translating into gender-neutral formulations cannot address all the challenges presented by androcentric texts. Efforts at feminist translation must also deal with issues around authority and canonicity.[48]

---

45. Gen 31:47; Jer 10:11; Ezra 4:7–6:18; 7:12-26; Dan 2:4–7:28.

46. Representing the *via media* between Catholic and reformed, Anglicans generally consider the Apocrypha to be profitable, if not canonical, and utilize select Wisdom texts liturgically.

47. See Levine, *The Misunderstood Jew*, 193–99.

48. Elizabeth Castelli, "*Les Belles Infidèles*/Fidelity or Feminism? The Meanings of Feminist Biblical Translation," in *Searching the Scriptures*, 1:189–204, here 190.

Because of these complexities, the editors of the Wisdom Commentary series have chosen to use an existing translation, the New Revised Standard Version (NRSV), which is provided for easy reference at the top of each page of commentary. The NRSV was produced by a team of ecumenical and interreligious scholars, is a fairly literal translation, and uses inclusive language for human beings. Brief discussions about problematic translations appear in the inserts labeled "Translation Matters." When more detailed discussions are available, these will be indicated in footnotes. In the commentary, wherever Hebrew or Greek words are used, English translation is provided. In cases where a wordplay is involved, transliteration is provided to enable understanding.

Art and Poetry

Artistic expression in poetry, music, sculpture, painting, and various other modes is very important to feminist interpretation. Where possible, art and poetry are included in the print volumes of the series. In a number of instances, these are original works created for this project. Regrettably, copyright and production costs prohibit the inclusion of color photographs and other artistic work. It is our hope that the web version will allow a greater collection of such resources.

Glossary

Because there are a number of excellent readily available resources that provide definitions and concise explanations of terms used in feminist theological and biblical studies, this series will not include a glossary. We refer you to works such as *Dictionary of Feminist Theologies*, edited by Letty M. Russell with J. Shannon Clarkson (Louisville: Westminster John Knox, 1996), and volume 1 of *Searching the Scriptures*, edited by Elisabeth Schüssler Fiorenza with the assistance of Shelly Matthews (New York: Crossroad, 1992). Individual authors in the Wisdom Commentary series will define the way they are using terms that may be unfamiliar.

A Concluding Word

In just a few short decades, feminist biblical studies has grown exponentially, both in the methods that have been developed and in the number of scholars who have embraced it. We realize that this series is limited and will soon need to be revised and updated. It is our hope that Wisdom Commentary, by making the best of current feminist biblical scholarship available in an accessible format to ministers, preachers, teachers, scholars, and students, will aid all readers in their advancement toward God's vision of dignity, equality, and justice for all.

Acknowledgments

There are a great many people who have made this series possible: first, Peter Dwyer, director of Liturgical Press, and Hans Christoffersen, publisher of the academic market at Liturgical Press, who have believed in this project and have shepherded it since it was conceived in 2008. Editorial consultants Athalya Brenner-Idan and Elisabeth Schüssler Fiorenza have not only been an inspiration with their pioneering work but have encouraged us all along the way with their personal involvement. Volume editors Mary Ann Beavis, Carol J. Dempsey, Amy-Jill Levine, Linda M. Maloney, Ahida Pilarski, Sarah Tanzer, Lauress Wilkins Lawrence, and Gina Hens-Piazza have lent their extraordinary wisdom to the shaping of the series, have used their extensive networks of relationships to secure authors and contributors, and have worked tirelessly to guide their work to completion. Two others who contributed greatly to the shaping of the project at the outset were Linda M. Day and Mignon Jacobs, as well as Barbara E. Bowe of blessed memory (d. 2010). Editorial and research assistant Susan M. Hickman has provided invaluable support with administrative details and arrangements. I am grateful to Brian Eisenschenk and Christine Henderson who have assisted Susan Hickman with the Wiki. I am especially thankful to Lauren L. Murphy and Justin Howell for their work in copyediting; and to the staff at Liturgical Press, especially Colleen Stiller, production manager; Angie Steffens, production assistant; and Tara Durheim, associate publisher.

Author's Introduction

Women Among Kings

Second Kings, the last book in a group of writings known as the Deuteronomistic History (Joshua through 2 Kings), does not initially appear to be particularly suited to feminist biblical criticism. Considering that the book details the history of the ruling monarchs of Israel and Judah, nearly all of whom are male, and the complex relationships these rulers had with their people, their political neighbors, and, most important, their male god, YHWH, the androcentrism of this text is undeniable. Women and members of other marginalized groups, as is so often the case in ancient literature, rarely are front and center. When they do make an appearance in the narrative, they are, for the most part, noted in passing[1] or as part of the supporting cast. As Renita Weems puts it: "Women like Deborah, Jael, the wise woman of Tekoa, Tamar, Bathsheba, Rizpeh, and Huldah come across as subordinate characters, supporting actresses, bit players in a larger plot that revolves around the unpredictable passions of men."[2]

The few female characters whose stories are narrated in detail are sometimes more unlucky than those who are merely ignored. Used as

1. Phyllis Bird, *Missing Persons and Mistaken Identities: Women and Gender in Ancient Israel* (Minneapolis: Fortress, 1997), 34.

2. Renita J. Weems, "Huldah, the Prophet: Reading a (Deuteronomistic) Woman's Identity," in *A God So Near: Essays on Old Testament Theology in Honor of Patrick D. Miller*, ed. Brent A. Strawn and Nancy R. Bowen (Winona Lake, IN: Eisenbrauns, 2003), 332.

ciphers for the biblical writers' fears or as tools for their "androcentric ideological agendas,"[3] these women are rarely allowed a voice of their own. And the stories told about them would hardly be the ones they would choose to tell about themselves. To put it succinctly, 2 Kings, as the title so aptly denotes, is not a "history" of a people as such, and certainly not that of women, but of kings—male monarchs—whose stories were recorded, edited, and imbued with theological meaning by groups of elite male scribes.

As is so often the case, however, the undeniable androcentrism—especially the kind of theologically tinted androcentric focus so clearly present in 2 Kings—cannot help but convey illuminating (albeit biased) views and visions of women and other people whom the biblical writer regarded as the Other.[4] The purpose of this commentary is to expose and uncover these underlying visions, some of which are unfavorable and some of which are sympathetic, so as to elucidate and, at points, to deconstruct and interrogate them. Following Elisabeth Schüssler Fiorenza, this commentary explores "the liberating or oppressive values and visions inscribed in the text by identifying the androcentric patriarchal character and dynamics of the text."[5] In so doing, this work attempts to mitigate to some small degree the absent and missing voices of women and other marginalized figures even if a full remedy for their absence remains out of reach.

This particular focus will not likely generate the meanings that the ancient male biblical writer/editors intended to convey from their writings. Indeed, the meaning intended by the original authors or editors, whatever it might be, is likely impossible to ascertain.[6] Instead, the pur-

---

3. Shelly Matthews, "Feminist Biblical Historiography," in *Feminist Biblical Studies in the Twentieth Century: Scholarship and Movement*, ed. Elisabeth Schüssler Fiorenza, Bible and Women 9.1 (Atlanta: Society of Biblical Literature, 2014), 246.

4. There are numerous studies on the subject of the Other. To name just a few: Jonathan Z. Smith, "Differential Equations: On Constructing the Other," in *Relating Religion: Essays in the Study of Religion* (Chicago: University of Chicago Press, 2004), 230–50; idem., "What a Difference a Difference Makes," in *Relating Religion*, 251–302; Richard Wentz, *The Contemplation of Otherness: The Critical Vision of Religion* (Macon, GA: Mercer University Press, 1984); Lawrence M. Wills, *Not God's People: Insiders and Outsiders in the Biblical World* (Lanham, MD: Rowman & Littlefield, 2008).

5. Elisabeth Schüssler Fiorenza, *But She Said: Feminist Practices of Biblical Interpretation* (Boston: Beacon Press, 1992), 57.

6. Mention must be made here of the groundbreaking essay by Roland Barthes, "The Death of the Author," in *Image-Music-Text*, trans. Stephen Heath (New York: Hill and Wang, 1977), 142–48.

pose of this commentary is to uncover and bring out through a variety of means and methods the ways in which women and other people on the margins were portrayed, characterized, and narrated. In short, it is to shine a light on some of the androcentric messages, views, and visions that emerge from the narratives in 2 Kings so as to explore their meaning and significance. In so doing, this work seeks to recover "from historical silences the trace of the lives and faint echoes" of the voices of women who "suffered and resisted patriarchal oppression."[7]

Approaches to Feminist Biblical Interpretation

The research in this volume exemplifies a broad understanding of feminist biblical interpretation. A multitude of methods and approaches is used to uncover views of women and other marginalized people and to explore and recover, when possible, the stories, feelings, and experiences of these figures. Jacqueline Lapsley and Patricia Tull best sum up the kind of feminist exegesis employed in this volume:

> We engage in a complex, often dialogical process of acquainting ourselves with the "other" whose authorship underlies the text, seeking in sympathy to understand before responding. As we construct our reading of an ancient text, our work may be compared to home remodeling: having examined the materials available, we highlight what has been hidden from view, reclaim everything we can, repurpose or recycle what we must, and carefully refuse what we can no longer consider appropriate to the project of life-affirming inquiry—recognizing full well that other readers in other places or times may beg to differ.[8]

In line with this useful description and applying the various avenues of feminist interpretation as outlined by Alice Ogden Bellis,[9] this commentary examines 2 Kings through a feminist lens. In some instances, such as with the analyses of 2 Kings 13 and 2 Kings 17, historical, epigraphic, and archaeological evidence are employed to elucidate the lives, roles, and experiences of women during times of ancient warfare. At other points, such as with the pericopes about the deaths of the infamous queens Jezebel and Athaliah in 2 Kings 9 and 2 Kings 11, the work reassesses and deconstructs traditional interpretations of these reviled

---

7. Schüssler Fiorenza, *But She Said*, 101.

8. Jacqueline E. Lapsley and Patricia K. Tull, eds., *After Exegesis: Feminist Biblical Theology* (Waco, TX: Baylor University Press, 2015), 2.

9. Alice Ogden Bellis, *Helpmates, Harlots, and Heroes: Women Stories in the Hebrew Bible* (Louisville: Westminster John Knox, 2007), 229.

figures. These chapters, as well as others in this commentary, explore the ways in which biblical interpretations supported (and still support) the continued delegitimation of women, especially those who dared to assert and obtain a measure of political and religious authority. Relatedly, this research also searches the spaces between the words or the silences in the biblical text in order to uncover partially erased and hidden, and thereby overlooked, biblical traditions about women. Through this exposure and deconstruction, this commentary attempts to offer a counter-narrative to the one presented in the biblical text.

More generally, the depiction and presence of feminine images of the divine as well as the existence of folk religion as practiced by ancient women in Israel (e.g., 2 Kgs 13) are evaluated in this work. Also reviewed and discussed are literary and translational concerns, including an assessment of the translations of certain words and phrases as well as an exploration of recurrent themes and motifs related to the feminine. Finally, certain portions of this research attempt to look beyond the text, speculating and trying to create anew the lives of these marginalized figures who exist *sous rature.*

Masculinity of YHWH

While the approaches are many and while 2 Kings is a complicated text with many different motifs and foci, this work will highlight and trace a particular theme concerning gender that runs throughout the book as a whole. Namely, the commentary will show that one of the central issues of 2 Kings is the construction and assertion of the masculinity of Israel's god, YHWH. Narrating the various masculine contests and challenges faced by YHWH, 2 Kings aims to defend and assert the prowess, power, and virility of this deity. The most potent and important of these conflicts is the contest between YHWH and other gods, usually Baal, for the religious fidelity of Israel and Judah who are envisioned and portrayed as women. Maleness is thus bound up with YHWH's singularity and demand for exclusive worship. By examining how the masculinity of YHWH as well as that of other monarchic figures in 2 Kings is depicted, this commentary hopes to decipher and elucidate the ways in which the feminine was imagined and constructed in contradistinction.

Gendered meanings and messages conveyed by 2 Kings are not monolithic and univocal, however. The text at points admits that the dichotomous constructions and dualities that it asserts are indeed too simplistic to capture the complex relationship between a people and its deity. Thus, as I will argue, while the biblical text proclaims the masculinity and prowess of YHWH, it also simultaneously deconstructs and upends this assertion at the conclusion of the book when it describes Israel and Judah's destruction by foreign nations. Hence, though the narrative attempts at points to salvage and rescue the masculinity of the god YHWH, the dissonant ending to this book, concluding with the exile and desolation of both Israel and Judah, cannot help but elicit a counter-reading, not just of the preceding narratives, but also of the masculinity of YHWH, which is so aggressively avowed and defended in them. Hence, as strongly as the masculinity of YHWH is proclaimed so in equal measure the narrative admits of doubts and insecurities to this claim—doubts that are exposed and explored at the end of 2 Kings as Israel and Judah are exiled and desolated and as the temple of YHWH in Zion is ruined and demolished.

Because this work focuses on the construction, assertion, and finally deconstruction of YHWH's masculinity in 2 Kings, I will not use a gender-neutral term to refer to God in this commentary. Doing so would undermine and muddle the claim posited in this research that the masculine depiction of YHWH is purposeful and significant. Moreover, it would take away from the argument made at the end of this commentary that the description of Israel and Judah's, and thus possibly YHWH's, downfall works to undermine, question, and challenge the assertion of the indisputable masculinity and power of YHWH. Hence, I deliberately utilize the masculine pronoun.

Preceding Research

In the analysis of the depiction and characterization of YHWH, this work has much benefited from Cynthia Chapman's important work on the gendered significance of warfare in the ancient Near East.[10] Especially useful has been her careful elucidation of the ways in which gender, especially the masculinity of ancient Near Eastern monarchs including YHWH, was imagined and constructed in the ancient Near East. Her work has been crucial in uncovering the gendered lens through which ancient Israelite writers viewed their deity and their kings.

Aside from Chapman's research, this work has been informed by *The Women's Bible Commentary*, especially the commentary on 1 and 2 Kings

---

10. Cynthia Chapman, *The Gendered Language of Warfare in the Israelite-Assyrian Encounter*, HSM 62 (Winona Lake, IN: Eisenbrauns, 2004).

by Claudia Camp,[11] as well as the essays presented in a series of feminist companions to different portions of the Hebrew Bible, which was edited by Athalya Brenner.[12] Along with these works, two other commentaries, different in tone and focus, must also be mentioned as particularly helpful to the formulation of this work. The first is the commentary on 1 and 2 Kings by Gina Hens-Piazza.[13] Though her research is centered on a theological reading of 1 and 2 Kings, her voice provided a much-needed perspective on a text that has usually been read and studied by male scholars. Her comments about the ethical and theological concerns that are undeniably present and struggled with in 2 Kings have been instrumental to my theological engagements with and understanding of this particular text.

Also insightful and helpful but in a different manner is the historically and archaeologically centered commentary on 2 Kings by Mordechai Cogan and Hayim Tadmor.[14] Just as Hens-Piazza's work provided a much-needed theological perspective on 2 Kings, so Cogan and Tadmor's commentary provided equally valuable historical and archaeological insights into the ancient Near Eastern background of this particular text. Cogan and Tadmor's work reminds us with special urgency that the figures in 2 Kings are located in a particular social and historical context. Though certainly the stories of ancient women and men can be (and have been) used as a useful lens through which to reflect on the situations and problems in the modern world, a better understanding of the ancient world in which these characters were supposed to have lived and breathed, and from which these writings emerged, is equally important. Cogan and Tadmor's research helped to fill out the ancient Mediterranean universe that forms and informs the literary and historical contextual background of the stories in 2 Kings.

Social Location

Speaking of context, knowing my social location will help readers gain a better understanding of my reading. Undoubtedly, my background influences the questions, issues, and concerns that I bring to 2 Kings and

11. Claudia Camp, "1 and 2 Kings," in *The Women's Bible Commentary*, ed. Carol A. Newsom and Sharon H. Ringe (Louisville: Westminster John Knox, 1992), 102–16.

12. Especially useful was Athayla Brenner, ed., *A Feminist Companion to Samuel and Kings*, FCB 5 (Sheffield: Sheffield Academic, 2000).

13. Gina Hens-Piazza, *1–2 Kings*, AOTC (Nashville: Abingdon, 2006).

14. Mordechai Cogan and Hayim Tadmor, *II Kings: A New Translation with Introduction and Commentary*, AB 11 (New York: Doubleday, 1988).

thus shapes my interpretation. As a 1.5-generation Korean American female scholar of the Hebrew Bible, I am largely the product of two different contexts. The first is that of a patriarchal, structured, and religiously conservative immigrant community in which I was raised. And the second is the mostly white colleges and universities in the Northeastern parts of the United States where I received my training.

Both contexts shape what I find interesting and important about the biblical text. In particular, the social location of my upbringing makes me especially sensitive to issues pertaining to women and to those whom society regards as unimportant and marginal. Indeed, I believe that my Korean American background played a crucial role in my decision to pursue the study of the Hebrew Bible. In hindsight, pursuing doctoral studies was an act of rebellion against a context that favored men as the only appropriate pupils for the study of all things related to God. The second context was similarly influential, though in a different manner. My scholarly training in a Near Eastern program taught me that the knowledge of the ancient Near East is critical for an understanding of the Hebrew Scriptures. As a result, classical historical-critical approaches still remain important tools in my toolbox.

Aside from my own voice and reading, this commentary, as well as others in the Wisdom Commentary series, aims to provide a variety of voices and perspectives through the addition of shorter, discrete essays on topics related to the 2 Kings text written by other authors from a variety of backgrounds. This commentary on 2 Kings has been enriched by these other viewpoints and interpretations.

Composition and Redaction of the Deuteronomistic History

Finally, a brief discussion must be had about a much-debated issue concerning the compositional and redactional history of the Deuteronomistic History[15] (DtrH), a term coined by German scholar Martin Noth.[16] The writers/editors who assembled, composed, and edited the Deuteronomistic History are designated as the Deuteronomistic Historian (DH).

---

15. For a good, readable summary, see Richard Elliott Friedman, *Who Wrote the Bible?* (New York: HarperOne, 1997), esp. 101–16. For a more detailed overview, see Thomas Römer and Albert de Pury, "Deuteronomistic Historigraphy (DH): History of Research and Debated Issues," in *Israel Constructs Its History: Deuteronomistic Historiography in Recent Research*, ed. Albert de Pury, Thomas Römer, and Jean-Daniel Macchi (Sheffield: Sheffield Academic, 2000), 24–141.

16. Martin Noth, *The Deuteronomistic History*, JSOTSup 15 (Sheffield: JSOT, 1981).

Like many American scholars, I generally assent to the double redaction of the Deuteronomistic History associated with Frank Moore Cross,[17] which has been further refined by other scholars.[18] I maintain that there were at least two redactions of the DtrH:[19] a first preexilic redaction of the DtrH that likely stemmed from the reign of King Josiah, and a second, later redaction that occurred after the destruction of Judah, during the exile. Many European scholars, especially of the Göttingen school, have argued that there were additional redactions beyond these two and that the redactions should be categorized and understood differently.[20]

17. Frank Moore Cross, *Canaanite Myth and Hebrew Epic: Essays in the History of the Religion of Israel* (Cambridge, MA: Harvard University Press, 1973), 274–89.

18. Robert G. Boling, *Judges: Introduction, Translation, and Commentary*, AB 6A (Garden City, NY: Doubleday, 1975), 29–38; idem, "Levitical History and the Role of Joshua," in *The Word of the Lord Shall Go Forth: Essays in Honor of David Noel Freedman in Celebration of His Sixtieth Birthday*, ed. Carol L. Meyers and M. O'Connor (Winona Lake, IN: Eisenbrauns, 1983), 241–61; Mordechai Cogan, "Israel in Exile—The View of a Josianic Historian," *JBL* 97 (1978): 40–44; Richard Friedman, *The Exile and the Biblical Narrative: The Formation of the Deuteronomistic History and Priestly Codes* (Atlanta: Scholars Press, 1981); Steven L. McKenzie, *The Trouble with Kings: The Composition of the Book of Kings in the Deuteronomistic History*, VTSup 42 (Leiden: Brill, 1991), 135–44; Richard D. Nelson, *The Double Redaction of the Deuteronomistic History* (Sheffield: JSOT Press, 1981); Jon D. Levenson, "From Temple to Synagogue: 1 Kings 8," in *Traditions in Transformation: Turning Points in Biblical Faith*, ed. Jon D. Levenson and Baruch Halpern (Winona Lake, IN: Eisenbrauns, 1981), 143–66; idem, "Who Inserted the Book of the Torah?" *HTR* 68 (1975): 203–33.

19. In my work, I also argued for an earlier redaction during the reign of King Hezekiah. See Song-Mi Suzie Park, *Hezekiah and the Dialogue of Memory* (Minneapolis: Fortress, 2015), 73–77, 192–95. So also W. Boyd Barrick, "On the Removal of the 'High Places' in 1–2 Kings," *Bib* 55 (1974): 257–59; Baruch Halpern and D. S. Vanderhooft, "The Editions of Kings in the 7th–6th Centuries B.C.E.," *HUCA* 62 (1991): 179–224; Ian Provan, *Hezekiah and the Book of Kings: A Contribution to the Debate about the Composition of the Deuteronomistic History* (Berlin: de Gruyter, 1988), 133–56; Manfred Weippert, "Fragen des israelitischen Geschichtsbewusstseins," *VT* 23 (1973): 437–38; Francolino J. Gonçalves, *L'expédition de Sennachérib en Palestine dans la littérature hébraïque ancienne*, EBib 7 (Paris: Gabalda, 1986), 73–76.

20. The Göttingen School proposes (at least) three layers of redaction of the DtrH. See Rudolf Smend, "The Law and the Nations: A Contribution to Deuteronomistic Tradition History," in *Reconsidering Israel and Judah: Recent Studies on the Deuteronomistic History*, ed. Gary N. Knoppers and J. Gordon McConville, trans. P. T. Daniels (Winona Lake, IN: Eisenbrauns, 2000), 95–111; trans. of "Das Gesetz und die Völker: Ein Beitrag zur deuteronomistischen Redaktionsgeschichte," in *Probleme biblischer Theologie: Gerhard von Rad zum 70. Geburtstag*, ed. H. W. Wolff (Munich: Kaiser, 1971), 494–509. See also Walter Dietrich, *Prophetie und Geschichte: Eine redaktionsgeschichtliche*

These ideas have been challenged,[21] and the discussion of the composition and editing of the DtrH has grown complex and technical. This study will not delve into the intricacies of the authorship and redactional history of 2 Kings. Not only is this commentary intended to be accessible to a wide audience, but the focus of this work is centered on different queries and concerns. Namely, the purpose of this research is to read the individual narratives in 2 Kings with an eye toward issues of gender. As such, I have tried to interpret the narratives in 2 Kings largely without much recourse to editorial or redactional matters. Though historical issues are discussed in the commentary, this research has largely focused on literary aspects of 2 Kings.

Untersuchung zum deuteronomistischen Geschichtswerk (Göttingen: Vandenhoeck & Ruprecht, 1972); Timo Veijola, *Die Ewige Dynastie: David und die Entstehung seiner Dynastie nach der deuteronomistischen Darstellung* (Helsinki: Suomalainen Tiedeakatemia, 1975); idem, *Das Königtum in der Beurteilung der deuteronomistischen Historiographie: Eine redaktionsgeschichtliche Untersuchung* (Helsinki: Suomalainen Tiedeakatemia, 1977).

21. Römer and de Pury, "Deuteronomistic Historigraphy (DH)," 129–41; John Van Seters, *The Edited Bible: The Curious History of the "Editor" in Biblical Criticism* (Winona Lake, IN: Eisenbrauns, 2006).

2 Kings 1:1-18

Feminine Powers and Masculine Rivalries

The book of 2 Kings begins with a seemingly inconsequential tale about an unhappy accident of Ahaziah, the king of Israel, and his subsequent demise following his attempt to consult the foreign god, Baal-zebub, about his healing. The message of the narrative seems straightforward: seeking other deities instead of YHWH, the god of Israel, will lead to death and destruction. The pericope at the beginning of 2 Kings reveals several masculine rivalries—between YHWH and the human king, between YHWH's messengers and those of the monarch, and, finally, between YHWH and Baal as the ultimate deity of life and healing—that add nuance to this message about YHWH's singularity. These rivalries, which are found throughout 2 Kings, elucidate the central theme of the book as whole: the masculine contest for the loyalty and fidelity of Israel and Judah—nations that are personified in the biblical text in female categories as daughters, wives, or lovers of YHWH (see Hos 1–3; Isa 54; Jer 3, 14; Ezek 16, 23). As Jan Tarlin correctly notes, the Elijah cycle and perhaps also 2 Kings in its entirety can thus, "quite convincingly, be read as a manifesto of patriarchal Yahwism."[1]

---

1. Jan Tarlin, "Toward a 'Female' Reading of the Elijah Cycle: Ideology and Gender in the Interpretation of 1 Kings 17–19, 21 and 2 Kings 1–2.18," in *Feminist Companion to Samuel and Kings*, ed. Athalya Brenner, FCB 5 (Sheffield: Sheffield Academic, 1994), 208.

Ahaziah's Fall and the Fight for Masculine Power (1:1-8)

The division between the First and Second Books of Kings is an artificial one, first introduced into the codices of the Septuagint.[2] Second Kings immediately begins where 1 Kings left off—in the immediate aftermath of the death of King Ahab of Samaria. Right after the enthronement of Ahab's son Ahaziah as king, 2 Kings states that Moab, which had been under Israel's subjugation since the time of King David (2 Sam 8:12), took advantage of the country's political transition by rebelling against its Israelite colonizer (2 Kgs 1:1). The story of Moab's rebellion will find its conclusion in 2 Kings 3.

Some commentators view 2 Kings 1:1 as an insertion due to its succinctness and haphazard nature and also because the note about Moab is repeated in 2 Kings 3:5.[3] Moab foreshadows and colors the story of Ahaziah, king of Israel, and Elijah, YHWH's prophet, found in 2 Kings 1. Second Kings 1:1 shows that the reign of King Ahaziah, like all the monarchs in Samaria, will be judged negatively by the biblical writer. Moreover, it also sets the scene for the larger demonstration of YHWH's power through his prophet Elijah at the conclusion of this first chapter.

The end of 2 Kings 1 should be viewed as a theologically gendered response to the notification of the loss of Moab's vassalage mentioned in the first verse (2 Kgs 1:1). Moab's successful overthrow of Israel's powers would certainly have raised doubts about the power and, hence, the masculinity of Israel's deity, YHWH.[4] The narrative that follows 2 Kings 1, which speaks about the apostasy of and subsequent illness and death of the northern king Ahaziah, addresses these doubts by explicating the reasons why God allowed Israel to lose part of its colonial territories: because of the impiety and faithlessness of Israel's king. The story thus

---

2. Mordechai Cogan and Hayim Tadmor note that the line concerning Moab's rebellion is repeated as a catch-line at the end of the Third Kingdom and the beginning of the Fourth Kingdom in the LXX Vaticanus manuscript in order to show the connection between the two books (Mordechai Cogan and Hayim Tadmor, *II Kings: A New Translation with Introduction and Commentary*, AB 11 [Garden City, NY: Doubleday, 1988], 22).

3. Volkmar Fritz, *1 & 2 Kings*, trans. Anselm Hagedorn, CC (Minneapolis: Fortress, 2003), 229.

4. On masculinity, warfare, and kingship, see Cynthia Chapman, *The Gendered Language of Warfare in the Israelite-Assyrian Encounter*, HSM 62 (Winona Lake, IN: Eisenbrauns, 2004).

¹:¹After the death of Ahab, Moab rebelled against Israel.

²Ahaziah had fallen through the lattice in his upper chamber in Samaria, and lay injured; so he sent messengers, telling them, "Go, inquire of Baal-zebub, the god of Ekron, whether I shall recover from this injury." ³But the angel of the LORD said to Elijah the Tishbite, "Get up, go to meet the messengers of the king of Samaria, and say to them, 'Is it because there is no God in Israel that you are going to inquire of Baal-ze-bub, the god of Ekron?' ⁴Now therefore thus says the LORD, 'You shall not leave the bed to which you have gone, but you shall surely die.'" So Elijah went.

⁵The messengers returned to the king, who said to them, "Why have you returned?" ⁶They answered him, "There came a man to meet us, who said to us, 'Go back to the king who sent you, and say to him: Thus says the LORD: Is it because there is no God in Israel that you are sending to inquire of Baal-zebub, the god of Ekron? Therefore you shall not leave the bed to which you have gone, but shall surely die.'" ⁷He said to them, "What sort of man was he who came to meet you and told you these things?" ⁸They answered him, "A hairy man, with a leather belt around his waist." He said, "It is Elijah the Tishbite."

works to shift the blame for this loss of territory from YHWH to King Ahaziah, whose apostasy is clearly evident in his desire to consult Baal-zebub after his fall. Questions about the masculine colonizing power of YHWH raised by Moab's successful rebellion are fueled by the account of the apostate northern king, Ahaziah.

From a postcolonial perspective, subtle justifications of and explanations for Israel's subjugation and colonization of Moab are present throughout the biblical corpus. The story about the origins of the Moabites, who are depicted as distant relatives of the Israelites through Abraham's nephew Lot, as well the offspring of the incestuous relationship between Lot and his daughter after the destruction of Sodom and Gomorrah (Gen 19:30-38), serve to defend Moab's subjugation and colonialization by Israel: Moab is related to Israel, and, thus, Israel has a right to rule over it. Indeed, it might be that the Davidic genealogy in Ruth 4 served as a rationale for David's conquest of Moab. Moreover, considering their incestuous origins and past, the Moabites are said to be impure, not part of the chosen elect, and thus justifiably lesser. Indeed, Deuteronomy 23:3 seems to hint that Moab's illegitimate birth has something to do with their perpetual disqualification from admittance into the assembly of God. Hence, Moab's vassalage to Israel is explained as proper and natural: The better, purer country and people rightfully will rule over its lesser relations. Sexuality, genealogy, and foundation narratives are utilized to validate colonial power and conquest as well as to shore up and subtly address possible suspicions about the loss of power and masculinity of YHWH. Politics, such as the loss of colonial rule over Moab by Israel during the reign of Ahaziah, thus intersects with issues of ethnicity, sexuality, and theology.

The power of YHWH, which is undermined with the notice of Moab's rebellion, is reasserted in the next verse (1:2), which tells of King Aha-ziah's accident. The king of Israel falls through the lattice window on the upper chamber and is injured. According to John Gray, these windows refer to entire upper-story balconies that were closed by screen-work.[5] Interestingly, lattice windows will reappear in the story of Elisha and the Shunammite woman later in the book, in 2 Kings 4. Besides leading to his subsequent death, as well as signifying spiritual descent, Ahaziah's fall from the top of the house to the bottom constitutes the first of many physical movements, both vertical and horizontal, described in this chapter.[6] These movements, as Jan Tarlin shows in her work on the Elijah narratives, are significant. Particular movements, she argues, take on a gendered meaning and are intimately related to issues of power, as we will see in the following narratives about the prophet Elijah in 2 Kings.[7]

As a result of the injuries caused by his sudden physical movement downward, Ahaziah sends messengers horizontally (וישלח מלאכים) and in so doing makes a religious mistake: he sends envoys to Ekron (*Khirbet al-Muqanna*), one of the five cities of the Philistines (see 1 Sam 6:18; 18:30; 29:3, 4, 9), to inquire of or consult (דרש)—a "technical term for oracular inquiry"[8]—the local god of the city, Baal-zebub. Though the name of this deity is not found in extrabiblical texts, according to several commentators, Baal-zebub appears to be a compound name consisting of the name for the Canaanite deity בעל, *Baal*, and the Hebrew term זבוב, *zebub*, meaning "flies." As such, it probably refers to a local manifestation of this deity. Greek versions and Josephus also render the name of the deity that Ahaziah consults as *Baal muion* ("Lord of the Flies"). Most

---

5. John Gray, *I and II Kings*, OTL (Philadelphia: Westminster, 1970), 463.

6. Robert Cohn, "Convention and Creativity in the Book of Kings: The Case of the Dying Monarch," *CBQ* 47 (1985): 605–10.

7. Tarlin, "Toward a 'Female' Reading," 208.

8. Cogan and Tadmor, *II Kings*, 24. Also, Gray, *I & II Kings*, 463.

likely, *zebub* is a parody of *zebul* ("prince"), which, as the Ugaritic texts from Ras Shamra show, was an epithet of Baal. Interestingly, according to John Gray, some of the earliest New Testament texts also support reading Beelzebul instead of Beelzebub/Baal-zebub (Matt 10:25; 12:24; Mark 3:22; and Luke 11:15-19).[9]

Explaining the meaning of this deity's name, Gray notes that flies were seen as bearers of disease. If so, the deity appears to have been associated with death and, hence, related to the recovery from death or to healing. This would explain why Ahaziah seeks out this foreign deity after his fall. Karel van der Toorn argues that Baal-zebub was probably a Syrian storm god who "had power to revitalize the sick."[10] Van der Toorn, using Arvid Tangberg's work,[11] suggests that sculpted flies, which served or signified the apotropaic or healing function, might have adorned the statue of this deity.[12] F. Charles Fensham, however, posits instead that Ahaziah sent messengers to Baal Zebub, which he translates as "Baal, the Flame," for magical advice.[13] Considering the technical nature of the verb (דרש), it could be that Ahaziah sent messengers to the deity whom he deemed was in charge of death and revitalization to find out whether he would die or live from his accident. Richard Nelson argues that, similar to the oracle of Zeus at Dodona where rustling leaves were utilized, Baal-zebub may refer to an oracle at Ekron "where messages were interpreted from the sound of buzzing flies."[14]

The movement of Ahaziah's messengers, however, is stopped in its tracks or reversed as Elijah, the prophet of God, is sent by an angel of the Lord to confront the king's messengers shortly after they are dispatched to the Philistine town.[15] Meeting the messengers on their way to Ekron, Elijah tells them to go to their king and ask a rhetorical question, implying that he has no need to go to a foreign deity to discern the outcome of his injury. Rather, according to YHWH, the king will not recover but die (v. 3). Repetition

9. Gray, *I & II Kings*, 463.

10. Karel van der Toorn, "Ba'al-Zĕbūb," in *NIDB*, ed. Katharine Doob Sakenfeld et al. (Nashville: Abingdon, 2009), 1:374.

11. Arvid Tangberg, "A Note on Ba'al-Zebub in 2 Kgs 1:2, 3, 6, 16," *SJOT* 6 (1992): 293–96.

12. Van der Toorn, "Baal-Zebub," 1:373.

13. F. Charles Fensham, "A Possible Explanation of the Name Baal-Zebub of Ekron," *ZAW* 70 (1967): 363.

14. Richard Nelson, *First and Second Kings*, IBC (Atlanta: John Knox, 1987), 155.

15. Cohn, "Convention and Creativity," 609.

and movement abound in this passage: the divine message is first given ostensibly from God to an angel who then delivers it to Elijah (1:3-4). The message is then passed from Elijah to Ahaziah's messengers who are forced to reverse their journey, a boomerang back to Ahaziah to deliver Elijah's oracle of death. In so doing, the messengers of the king are inverted into becoming messengers for Elijah who will deliver "a message the king did not request."[16] This, in turn, leads to Ahaziah's triple commission of military officials to bring Elijah to him. At the end, Ahaziah's attempt to get back up, to recover from his fall, through horizontal motion seems to have failed utterly as he is destined to never recover and get back up again. According to Robert Cohn, all of these movements serve "to drive the power of YHWH ever nearer to the apostate king"[17] as well as to demonstrate the triumph of divine power over human monarchic power. Moreover, it confirms the authority of Elijah, the prophet,[18] whose name is mentioned eight times in the narrative in contrast to the single mention of King Ahaziah.

From a feminist perspective, the emphasis on prophetic and divine power has important gendered meanings and implications. The power of YHWH as conveyed through YHWH's prophet, Elijah, is manifested through and intertwined with depictions and demonstrations of masculine authority. For example, when his messengers return to the king after their aborted mission to Ekron to relay Elijah's message, Ahaziah is able to identify the prophet who they met on their journey because of their description of Elijah as a hairy man—literally, as the lord (*baal*) of hair, an evident wordplay on the word "baal"—who wears a leather belt around his waist (vv. 5-8). Paranomasia is used to show how the messengers who are sent to the "Lord of Flies" (*Baal-zebub*) are stopped and met on the road by the "Lord of Hair" whose personal name translates to "YHWH is my God" (*Elijah*). Or to put it differently, the God of the "Lord of Hair" is YHWH.

The emphasis on Elijah's hair is significant. Not only does his hair indicate Elijah's status as a Nazirite (Num 6:1-21)[19] and his religious affiliation as a true prophet of YHWH, but, as Susan Niditch has shown,

---

16. Ibid.

17. Ibid., 610.

18. So also Nelson, *First and Second Kings*, 158.

19. On the Nazirite vow and hair, see Susan Niditch, *My Brother Esau Is a Hairy Man: Hair and Identity in Ancient Israel* (New York: Oxford University Press, 2008), esp. 81–94.

hair has gendered meanings.[20] The hairy aspect of Elijah, similar to that of Samson, symbolizes the feral, wild, masculine nature of this prophet.[21] Like Enkidu, Elijah is outside society, uncultured, and, hence, unfeminized.[22] The hairiness of Elijah emphasizes the wildness and masculinity of the prophet and thus the wild masculinity of the God whom he serves—the masculinity of whom, as we noted earlier, is threatened with the successful rebellion of Moab and the subsequent consultation of a rival deity, Baal-zebub, by the Israelite king, Ahaziah.

The Masculinity of YHWH and the Feminine Powers of Life (1:9-18)

This threat to YHWH's masculinity and power is further addressed in the conclusion of 2 Kings 1, which describes the confrontation between Elijah and the military personnel sent by Ahaziah.

After King Ahaziah identifies the prophet who sent his messengers back to him with the oracle about his coming demise, the king tries to talk to Elijah face-to-face. To do so, he dispatches a series of military officials to coerce the prophet to come before him. The first two officials fail to convince the prophet to leave the top of the hill and are promptly consumed by fire, which Elijah calls down from the sky (2 Kgs 1:9-12). The third and last official is more successful. After begging and kneeling before Elijah, the prophet is told by an angel to follow this last official back to the palace to see the king (1:13-15). Anticlimactically, however, when Elijah reaches the king, he merely repeats the oracle of doom, which he stated earlier to the king's traveling messengers. The narrative quickly and neatly ends by telling the reader that Elijah's oracle came to pass and that Ahaziah died (1:16-17).

A certain circularity is evident in this chapter. As 2 Kings 1 begins with Ahaziah's unsuccessful dispatch of messengers to Baal-zebub, so the chapter concludes with a series of unsuccessful dispatches of Ahaziah's messengers to Elijah, who sits atop a mountain, unwilling to come at the

---

20. Ibid., esp. 66–67, 96–99, 112–18, 121–32.

21. Gregory Mobley, *Samson and the Liminal Hero in the Ancient Near East* (New York: T&T Clark, 2006), esp. 19–53, 85–108; idem., "The Wild Man in the Bible and the Ancient Near East," *JBL* 116 (1997): 217–33. Also Niditch, *My Brother Esau Is a Hairy Man*, 63–114.

22. Mobley, *Samson and the Liminal Hero*, esp. 19–53, 85–108; Mobley, "The Wild Man in the Bible," esp. 220–23.

2 Kgs 1:9-18

[9]Then the king sent to him a captain of fifty with his fifty men. He went up to Elijah, who was sitting on the top of a hill, and said to him, "O man of God, the king says, 'Come down.'" [10]But Elijah answered the captain of fifty, "If I am a man of God, let fire come down from heaven and consume you and your fifty." Then fire came down from heaven, and consumed him and his fifty.

[11]Again the king sent to him another captain of fifty with his fifty. He went up and said to him, "O man of God, this is the king's order: Come down quickly!" [12]But Elijah answered them, "If I am a man of God, let fire come down from heaven and consume you and your fifty." Then the fire of God came down from heaven and consumed him and his fifty.

[13]Again the king sent the captain of a third fifty with his fifty. So the third captain of fifty went up, and came and fell on his knees before Elijah, and entreated him, "O man of God, please let

summons of the king. Oddly, even though the third and last messenger is successful in getting the prophet to visit Ahaziah, he is ultimately unsuccessful as this leads to another declaration of Ahaziah's impending death. Hence, the healing power of Baal-zebub is nullified even before it can be authenticated, as YHWH's messenger interrupts the movement toward Ekron. Indeed, the power of YHWH seems to center around movement in this chapter: YHWH is shown as having the ability to interrupt or stop movement, including that toward life or toward death. As we will see in other stories about Elijah and Elisha, YHWH can cause death to reverse itself (2 Kgs 2; 4:8-37, 38-41).

YHWH's authority over movement, which is related to his authority over life and death, is emphasized in the repetitive narrative about the interaction between Ahaziah's messengers and the prophet who has ascended a hill. Nelson discusses the tightly wound narrative pattern of this pericope, which once again emphasizes directions for the purposes of highlighting divine power.[23] He notes that the three encounters between Elijah and Ahaziah's messengers each follow a tripartite pattern: the captain of the fifty speaks, first demanding and then asking and finally entreating Elijah to descend (1:9, 11, 12-14); this is followed in each case by Elijah's response (1:10a, 12a, 15a); finally, the narrator provides an assessment (1:10b, 12b, 15b). Moreover, each of the three scenes begins with an upward movement of the captains and ends with the down-

23. Nelson, *First and Second Kings*, 155–56.

my life, and the life of these fifty servants of yours, be precious in your sight. [14]Look, fire came down from heaven and consumed the two former captains of fifty men with their fifties; but now let my life be precious in your sight." [15]Then the angel of the LORD said to Elijah, "Go down with him; do not be afraid of him." So he set out and went down with him to the king, [16]and said to him, "Thus says the LORD: Because you have sent messengers to inquire of Baal-zebub, the god of Ekron,—is it because there is no God in Israel to inquire of his word?—therefore you shall not leave the bed to which you have gone, but you shall surely die."

[17]So he died according to the word of the LORD that Elijah had spoken. His brother, Jehoram succeeded him as king in the second year of King Jehoram son of Jehoshaphat of Judah, because Ahaziah had no son. [18]Now the rest of the acts of Ahaziah that he did, are they not written in the Book of the Annals of the Kings of Israel?

ward movement of either fire or, finally, Elijah himself. Movement thus is linked to power.

Moreover, the authority and power of YHWH as the true giver of life and death is further accentuated by the downward descent of the fire (אֵשׁ, *'ēsh*) of God, which consumes and kills the first two captains sent by Ahaziah to Elijah, or in another evident wordplay, "the man" or אִישׁ, *'îsh*, "of God" (1:7). The function of YHWH as the source of life (i.e., the giver and provider of food) is symbolized in his portrayal as a storm or thunder god who brings rain and, therefore, rejuvenation of the fields and crops.[24] This ability to provide food, as Cynthia Chapman has shown, is again intimately linked to visions of royal masculinity. She writes that the credentials of royal masculinity in the ancient Near East were defined by military prowess, ability to provide for his subjects, and royal status.[25] All three are asserted in the description of the annihilation of the first two captains by fire from heaven: The descent of fire and the death of Ahaziah's messengers affirms YHWH's military prowess or divine power over that of human royal power. Moreover, by depicting YHWH as the source of the fire from heaven or thunder, the text shows YHWH as the true storm god over against the false storm deity, Baal. As such, YHWH is shown to be the real source of rain, food, and thus life and also death; hence, YHWH's authority is affirmed. Correspondingly, the authority of

24. Leah Bronner, *The Stories of Elijah and Elisha as Polemics Against Baal Worship*, POS 6 (Leiden: Brill, 1968), esp. 50–85.

25. Chapman, *The Gendered Language of Warfare*, 30–39.

Elijah as the true and authentic messenger and servant of this true storm god, YHWH, is also emphasized by depicting the horrifying end of the first two military officials who fail to treat Elijah with the proper respect.

The assertion of YHWH as a storm/thunder god and thus as life-giver and creator has a gendered meaning. Though not wholly surprising considering the patriarchal nature of this literature, a male god is said to be the origins of and the producer of creation, crops, and thus life. The natural creative feminine powers of life-giving and creating are thwarted and replaced in the biblical text as emanating from a male god,[26] whose masculinity as well as that of his prophet is asserted in a variety of ways: the description of Elijah as hairy and wild and the assertion of YHWH as the true storm god, the master of movements, and the lord of life and death. Hence, this chapter is not only about Elijah and YHWH's authority and power but about the depiction of this authority as manifested in God's masculine attributes. As we will see, 2 Kings will frequently depict YHWH's procreative, reproductive, and healing powers as intimately intertwined with his masculinity.

Interestingly, though this pericope strongly asserts that YHWH, the wild, male, storm god, is master over life and death, in a deconstructionist move, the text depicts this deity and his servant as mainly inducing or proclaiming death in 2 Kings 1. While the narrative proclaims that YHWH is the god of life and healing, it shows YHWH and his messengers as the god of death. As such, perhaps we can see here a subtle undermining of the idea that correlates life, procreation, and reproduction with masculinity, not femininity. By aligning masculinity with death and not life in 2 Kings 1, the message might be that life is more associated with the power of the feminine. The chapter appropriately ends with the notice of more death, that of Ahaziah, the apostate king, who is further damned and emasculated in the text with the notice that he left no progeny (v. 17).

26. On the assertion of sacrifice as a patriarchal means by which to overcome natural, female birth, see Nancy Jay, *Throughout Your Generations Forever: Sacrifice, Religion, and Paternity* (Chicago: Chicago University Press, 1992).

2 Kings 2:1-25

Feminine Powers and Masculine Reproduction

Concluding the cycle of stories about the prophet Elijah, 2 Kings 2 depicts the continuation of this prophet's work in the figure of his successor, Elisha. Similar to the story of the call of Joshua after Moses' death, this narrative, which constitutes one of the few descriptions of prophetic succession in the Hebrew Bible,[1] serves to validate Elisha's prophetic ministry and leadership by directly connecting it to the authority and power of his mentor, Elijah. In so intimately linking Elijah and Elisha, this chapter is less about the end of Elijah's ministry on earth as it is about the ways in which Elijah, as a valid and true prophet of YHWH, defies death in order to continue his earthly mission.

Elijah lives on in two ways according to 2 Kings 2: First, he never undergoes a physical, mortal death as he is taken to the heavens in a whirlwind. Elijah's death-defying conclusion leads to his transformation as a precursor to the messiah in the New Testament and postbiblical

---

1. Robert P. Carroll, "The Elijah-Elisha Sagas: Some Remarks on Prophetic Succession in Ancient Israel," *VT* 19 (1969): 403. Note that Moses, whom Elijah imitates, is also considered a prophet in the biblical tradition and, as such, there are not one but two prophets who get to appoint a successor, Moses and Elijah (Rachel Havrelock, *The River Jordan* [Chicago: Chicago University Press, 2011], 138).

traditions.[2] Second, Elijah's ministry carries on in that of Elisha, his successor, who confirms Elijah's perpetuation by doubling and repeating many of the same miracles that Elijah performed earlier in Kings.[3] In depicting those associated with YHWH, such as the prophet Elijah, as overcoming and not being subject to death, 2 Kings 2 offers a strong contrast to the preceding chapter, which depicted the early demise of the apostate king, Ahaziah, for his consultation of the foreign god, Baalzebub.[4] As in the preceding chapter, 2 Kings 2 is also intent on showing the ways in which YHWH equals life while associating Baal and the other gods with death. In so doing, the text again closely connects life-giving abilities with YHWH's masculinity and power. The natural, normative reproductive powers associated with the feminine are thus replaced and subverted by a more androcentric vision of procreation and regeneration.

Elijah's Goodbye and Gendered Meanderings (2:1-6)

This pericope describes how Elijah, before he is taken by YHWH, makes his final visitation rounds to the various Israelite prophetic groups with his protégé, Elisha.

Elisha insists on accompanying his master despite several attempts by Elijah to dissuade him (2 Kgs 2:1-2). That this is Elijah's farewell tour seems to be known to all the prophetic colleagues the two encounter (v.

---

2. In later Jewish traditions, Elijah is expected to return as the forerunner of the Messiah, and at the Passover Seder, an extra cup of wine—Elijah's Cup—is always placed on the table in anticipation of his return. Moreover, in the New Testament, Elijah, in the form of John the Baptist, is presented as Jesus' forerunner (Matt 11:14; Mark 9:11-13; Luke 1:17) and also appears with Moses at Jesus' transfiguration (Mark 9:2-8 // Matt 17:1-9 // Luke 9:28-36). Elijah also, along with Enoch, makes an appearance in Revelation 11, which tells of two unnamed prophets who will appear on earth just after the mysterious Seventh Seal is opened and just before the day of God's wrath. For more on the fascinating *Nachleben* of Elijah and the Elijah traditions, see J. Edward Wright, "Whither Elijah? The Ascension of Elijah in Biblical and Extrabiblical Traditions," in *Things Revealed: Studies in Early Jewish and Christian Literature in Honor of Michael E. Stone*, ed. Esther G. Chazon, David Satran, and Ruth A. Clements, JSJSup 89 (Leiden: Brill, 2004), 595–608.

3. See n. 11 in this chapter.

4. For other connections between 2 Kings 1 and 2 Kings 2, see Judith A. Todd, "The Pre-Deuteronomistic Elijah Cycle," in *Elijah and Elisha in Socio-Literary Perspective*, ed. Robert B. Coote (Atlanta: Scholars Press, 1992), 1–35; Joel S. Burnett, " 'Going Down' to Bethel: Elijah and Elisha in the Theological Geography of the Deuteronomistic History," *JBL* 129 (2010): 281–97.

2:1Now when the LORD was about to take Elijah up to heaven by a whirlwind, Elijah and Elisha were on their way from Gilgal. 2Elijah said to Elisha, "Stay here; for the LORD has sent me as far as Bethel." But Elisha said, "As the LORD lives, and as you yourself live, I will not leave you." So they went down to Bethel. 3The company of prophets who were in Bethel came out to Elisha, and said to him, "Do you know that today the LORD will take your master away from you?" And he said, "Yes, I know; keep silent."

4Elijah said to him, "Elisha, stay here; for the LORD has sent me to Jericho." But he said, "As the LORD lives, and as you yourself live, I will not leave you." So they came to Jericho. 5The company of prophets drew near to Elisha, and said to him, "Do you know that today the LORD will take your master away from you?" And he answered, "Yes, I know; be silent."

6Then Elijah said to him, "Stay here; for the LORD has sent me to the Jordan." But he said, "As the LORD lives, and as you yourself live, I will not leave you." So the two of them went on.

3). The conclusion to Elijah's earthly ministry, Mordechai Cogan and Hayim Tadmor note, perfectly fits the movement and elusiveness that characterized the stories of his career in 1 Kings.[5] Jan Tarlin puts it more directly, calling the Elijah narrative cycle in that book a "labyrinthine journey of a moving target."[6] Interestingly, this wandering, according to Tarlin, has a gendered significance. She maintains that the nonteleological journeying of Elijah undermines the "discursive authority within the text," and, in so doing, the Elijah cycle can be read as characterizing a "'female' narrative."[7]

Though Tarlin's argument is enticing, the narratives of Elijah's and later Elisha's flitting and aimless movements better fit the trajectory and structure associated with the "epic of the losers" as outlined in David Quint's monumental study.[8]

5. Mordechai Cogan and Hayim Tadmor, *II Kings: A New Translation with Introduction and Commentary*, AB 11 (Garden City, NY: Doubleday, 1988), 33.

6. Jan Tarlin, "Toward a 'Female' Reading of the Elijah Cycle: Ideology and Gender in the Interpretation of 1 Kings 17–19, 21 and 2 Kings 1–2.18," in *Feminist Companion to Samuel and Kings*, FCB 5, ed. Athalya Brenner (Sheffield: Sheffield Academic, 1994), 213.

7. Ibid., 214.

8. David Quint, *Epic and Empire: Politics and General Form from Virgil to Milton* (Princeton, NJ: Princeton University Press, 1993).

*Excursus on
the Epic of the Losers
and the Epic of the Winners*

Focusing on the "politicization of epic poetry," David Quint, in his work *Epic and Empire*,[9] argues that two narrative models are evident in classical literature. The first is the epic of the winners. Exemplified by the *Iliad*, the epic of the winners consists of a narrative that is linear, teleological, and closed. In contrast to this model, the epic of the losers, which is exemplified by the *Odyssey*, is meandering, endless, repetitive, and aimless. Some texts, such as the *Aeneid*, utilize both models to make a political point. The first six books of the *Aeneid*, with its description of the pointless wanderings of Aeneas and the Trojans, initially follow the model of the epic of the losers. At the end of the poem, however, the *Aeneid* reverts to the model of the epic of the winners as it concludes with a lengthy description of a battle in which the Trojans emerge as victors over the Latins. This victory sets the context for the coming reign of Augustus.

As evident, these narrative models not only convey political meanings but also coexist in dialectical tension. Though Quint does not touch on biblical literature, the aimless wanderings of Elijah and later Elisha seem to embody the trajectory of the losers. Considering the intertwined relationship between the two models, however, these initial wanderings stress a future inversion in which these prophets and their deity, YHWH, will emerge as the true winners.

The aimlessness that characterizes Elijah's (and later Elisha's) story does not so much as undermine authority—and, therefore, should not be considered "feminine" *per se*—as it depicts the movements of outsiders looking for and in search of a teleology and, hence, power. In other words, the Elijah and Elisha cycle can be read as an attempt by underdogs, losers, or outsiders to transform their story into that of the winner through the maximization and emphasis on the masculine powers of their god, YHWH, the source of their own prophetic prowess. As in the preceding chapter, a strong sense of insecurity about the status and masculine power of YHWH can also be detected in this chapter and indeed in the entire cycle of stories about these two prophets.

9. Quint, *Epic and Empire*.

The Female Spirit and Masculine Procreation (2:7-9)

After refusing to leave the side of his mentor Elijah a third time, Elisha follows Elijah, and they cross the Jordan while fifty of the "company [literally 'sons'] of the prophets"—perhaps a reference to a guild, order, or class of prophets[10]—watch them (on the "sons of the prophets," see discussion on 2 Kgs 4). In a repetition of the exodus event, Elijah splits the waters of the Jordan by striking it with his mantle so that he and Elisha can cross over (2 Kgs 2:8).

Later in this chapter, immediately on the heels of Elijah's ascendance into heaven, Elisha, in mimicry of his master, will again divide the waters of the Jordan with Elijah's mantle, thus confirming his status as Elijah's prophetic heir (2 Kgs 2:14-15). Indeed, the sons of the prophets, who are witnesses to the double water demonstration, reconfirm the succession by saying: " 'The spirit of Elijah rests on Elisha. 'They came to meet him and bowed to the ground before him" (2 Kgs 2:15).

Elisha, like Joshua, affirms his position by mimicking the predecessor's water-splitting miracle. A strong emphasis on doubling and repetition can be detected. Worth noticing is that the doubling is itself doubled as Elisha repeats Elijah's early action, which in itself mimics Joshua's imitation of Moses.[11] David Zucker points out that the placement of this episode at Gilgal further analogizes Elisha and Joshua. Gilgal is the site of Joshua's first encampment after Israel crossed over the Jordan (Josh 4–5).[12] As noted earlier, the significance of the doubling, in part, lies in the fact that the narrative asserts the continuation of Elijah's ministry in the form of Elisha and, hence, the continual presence of YHWH and his power in Israel.

From a feminist perspective, however, the doubling also works to assert and stress the masculine forms of regeneration and procreation. Like the previous chapter, 2 Kings 2 is also centered on male relationships. For example, the all-male group of prophets—the sons of the prophets—who serve the male deity, YHWH, is mentioned four times in the narrative (2 Kgs 2:3, 5, 7, 15-16). Some scholars speculate that the

10. Cogan and Tadmor, *II Kings*, 31.

11. David Zucker states that Elijah is "Moses *redivivus*" and notes the similarities between the Elijah/Elisha and Moses/Joshua narratives ("Elijah and Elisha: Part I; Moses and Joshua," *JQR* 40 [2012]: 225); see also Carroll, "The Elijah-Elisha Sagas," 410–14; Dale Ralph Davis, "The Kingdom of God in Transition: Interpreting 2 Kings 2," *WTJ* 46 (1984): 388.

12. Zucker, "Elijah and Elisha," 229.

2 Kgs 2:7-9

[7]Fifty men of the company of prophets also went, and stood at some distance from them, as they both were standing by the Jordan. [8]Then Elijah took his mantle and rolled it up, and struck the water; the water was parted to the one side and to the other, until the two of them crossed on dry ground.

[9]When they had crossed, Elijah said to Elisha, "Tell me what I may do for you, before I am taken from you." Elisha said, "Please let me inherit a double share of your spirit."

sons of the prophets were those whom Elijah had emboldened in his religious battle against Jezebel. It was then appropriate for them to appear during Elijah's departure. Yet the gender composition of this farewell party seems strikingly one-sided. Where are all the women during this mixed farewell/promotion celebration? Where are the daughters of the prophets? Where are the wives of these sons of the prophets? Second Kings 4 mentions that some of these prophets were married. Are there no women who came into contact with Elijah or who were touched by his ministry? What about the widow at Zarephath (1 Kgs 17:9-24)? The context for this reference was the description of the desperate economic situation of the widow of one of these prophets.

Some scholars have argued that women prophets might have been part of this cohort (see commentary on 2 Kgs 21)[13] and that the correct designation for this group is the "children of the prophet" (see commentary on 2 Kgs 4). Though the ambiguities of the language make it impossible to ascertain whether this cohort was gender inclusive, in this case, 2 Kings 2:7 specifies that Elijah's colleagues were all men. More important, the complete absence of women better fits the theme and message of this pericope. The utter absence of women stresses the fraternal bond of this prophet and his group and, in so doing, emphasizes the masculinity of YHWH—to whom the service of all these prophets is bound. Therefore, the narrative also asserts the masculine forms of procreation associated with YHWH, which eschews, undermines, and replaces the natural, feminine modes of reproduction. Elijah does not die so much as spawn or split off like a

13. Mercedes L. García Bachmann, *Women at Work in the Deuteronomistic History* (Atlanta: Society of Biblical Literature, 2013), esp. 161–76, 174; Wilda C. Gafney, *Daughters of Miriam: Women Prophets in Ancient Israel* (Minneapolis: Fortress, 2008), 15.

tendril of a starfish in the form of Elisha, who embodies within himself a substantial portion of Elijah in the reception of a double share of his spirit.[14] Thus, it is through the masculine energy and power of Israel's patriarchal God, YHWH, that these prophets derive their energy and power, even the power to double themselves, defying the very logic of natural death and female childbirth. The message of the pericope is clear: This is how the prophets of the male God, YHWH, reproduce and live on. No children or women are needed.

Excursus:
The Various Occupations
of Women in the Ancient World

Although often unrecognized, proximity of women to blood, birth, sickness, and death makes it very likely that the same women who helped as midwives were also healers and advisors, prepared the dead for burial, and perhaps even directed the burial rites, especially since corpses were polluting. . . . Whether more emotional, more unprotected by the social system, more flexible to perform in different circumstances, or more barred from the official ritual practices—for whatever reason, women seem to have occupied this niche throughout cultures and times, being needed, respected and also feared and suspected. What we call in general "sorcerers" (health practitioners and religious specialists) belonged probably to every social stratum and served those around them: examples range from King Saul seeking a medium he himself had banned to Rebekah seeking an oracle to understand what was going on in her womb.[15]

Mercedes L. García Bachmann

After following his master around Israel on his goodbye tour, Elisha is allowed a final gift request from Elijah for his demonstration of loyalty (v. 9). Elisha requests to receive a double share of Elijah's spirit. Elijah responds that this is a difficult request (v. 10). Most scholars explain that Elisha's request is an indication of his position as Elijah's rightful

---

14. On the "spirit of the Lord," see Robert B. Chisholm, Jr., "The 'Spirit of the Lord' in 2 Kings 2:16," in *Presence, Power, and Promise: The Role of the Spirit of God in the Old Testament*, ed. David G. Firth and Paul D. Wegner (Downers Grove, IL: Intervarsity Press, 2011), 306–17.

15. García Bachmann, *Women at Work*, 12–13.

heir; firstborn sons would have traditionally received a double portion of the inheritance.[16]

Though certainly plausible, this explanation makes little sense of the ambiguity and oddity of Elisha's request. Aside from once again emphasizing the doubling motif, what is Elisha asking for? What exactly constitutes a "double share" of Elijah's spirit? Can someone be twofold more spiritually infused? Moreover, why does Elijah say this is a difficult request, only possible if Elisha witnesses Elijah's wondrous ascent into heaven (v. 10)? What does the seeing have to do with the reception of this gift? Finally, what is the evidence of this double spirit? Though Judith Todd argues that Elisha's passage of the "seeing" test (vv. 10 and 12), the parting of the Jordan (v. 14), and the affirmation of the prophetic community (v. 15) validate his reception of the double spirit, there seems to be little evidence of it elsewhere in the remaining account of Elisha's activities.[17] In other words, though the text tells us that Elisha did indeed receive the double portion, it does not depict very clearly the ways in which this gift was later manifested in Elisha's career.

Classical rabbinic tradition explains this mysterious request by attributing to Elisha double the *number* of miracles compared to Elijah.[18] Though a clever suggestion, the obvious problem is that sheer quantity or number is not what seems to be implied in the narrative. Indeed, the request of double the spirit stresses something, which seems to be the very opposite of numbers. It is a request for something more essential, more qualitative, something that is by definition unquantifiable—something spiritual. Can something without a physicality be doubled? And if so, how so and where is the proof?

The meaning of Elisha's final request seems to lie, not in the numbers, but again in the identity and function of Elisha as a double—a mimic—of Elijah. In other words, Elisha's strange request stresses this mimetic function. Not only does Elisha continue Elijah's ministry and thus act as his symbolic double, but succeeding narratives will depict him as repeating, literally doubling, the miracles performed earlier by his predecessor, Elijah. Cogan and Tadmor write that "several deeds told of Elisha—the

16. Joseph Blenkinsopp, *A History of Prophecy in Israel* (Louisville: Westminster John Knox, 1996), 62; Cogan and Tadmor, *II Kings*, 32; John Gray, *I and II Kings*, OTL (Philadelphia: Westminster, 1970), 475.

17. Todd, "The Pre-Deuteronomistic Elijah Cycle," 29.

18. For the list of miracles by David Pyles, "A Double Portion of Thy Spirit." http://www.bcbsr.com/survey/eli.html.

multiplication of oil (vv. 4-5) and bread (vv. 43-44), and the revival of the woman's son (vv. 33-35)—have their counterpart in the Elijah cycle of stories; cf. 1 Kgs. 17:14-16, 17:20-22."[19]

The language of רוח or "spirit" again seems to allude to Joshua and Moses, stressing the identity of Elisha as Elijah's reflection and continuation. David Zucker writes that the term "spirit" is used by God to describe Joshua to Moses (Num 27:18) as a איש אשר־רוח or "inspired man." It will be used again to describe Joshua after Moses' death as filled with the spirit (רוח) in Deuteronomy 34:9.[20] It thus appears that being filled, or doubly filled, with the spirit is a way to emphasize and legitimate the prophetic successor. The emphasis on the double portion points to Elisha's role as a double of Elijah. Elijah is a prophet so powerful that he is depicted as being able to double a more potent form of himself in the figure of his successor Elisha.

The Female Spirit and the Sight of YHWH's "Weapons" (2:10-18)

The requirements for the reception of this gift of the double spirit—the need for Elisha to witness Elijah's ascendance (v. 10)—add an element of quality to the doubling theme.

The final act of gazing between Elijah and Elisha, two figures who, as we noted, are remarkably similar, creates a mirroring effect. The scene of Elijah's ascendance paints a picture of a twin gazing into a mirror. As this is a requirement for Elisha's reception of a double portion of his spirit, it seems that the mirroring not only stresses the doubling theme but also is a necessary component of this miracle. Only by keeping his eyes on his mirrored twin can Elisha effectively spawn from Elijah into a distinct yet similar, almost parallel, figure who will continue and indeed repeat much of the work done by his predecessor. The double spirit thus seems less about anything quantifiable as about the quality of Elisha as a twin or mirrored reflection of Elijah. He received double of Elijah's spirit because Elisha is Elijah xeroxed and duplicated. With Elijah in heaven, Elisha remains both the only "surviving" original and also its copy—he embodies, in essence, Elijah doubled.

---

19. Cogan and Tadmor, *II Kings*, 59; see also Gray, *I & II Kings*, 467.
20. Zucker, "Elijah and Elisha," 229.

[10]He responded, "You have asked a hard thing; yet, if you see me as I am being taken from you, it will be granted you; if not, it will not." [11]As they continued walking and talking, a chariot of fire and horses of fire separated the two of them, and Elijah ascended in a whirlwind into heaven. [12]Elisha kept watching and crying out, "Father, father! The chariots of Israel and its horsemen!" But when he could no longer see him, he grasped his own clothes and tore them in two pieces.

[13]He picked up the mantle of Elijah that had fallen from him, and went back and stood on the bank of the Jordan. [14]He took the mantle of Elijah that had fallen from him, and struck the water, saying, "Where is the LORD, the God of Elijah?" When he had struck the water, the water was parted to the one side and to the other, and Elisha went over.

By utilizing the seeing test for the reception of this gift, the text also stresses the divine vision necessary to be a true prophet of YHWH—the extrasensory ophthalmological prophetic gift that is to be passed on, continued, and perhaps even increased in some form in Elisha. Or to put it differently, it is by seeing that Elisha truly learns to see and thus truly becomes a seer and a prophet.[21] Only by viewing and understanding the true movements of the heavenly sphere during Elijah's ascent as evident by Elisha's cry of, "My father! My father! The chariots and horsemen of Israel" (v. 12), does the text make clear that Elisha has earned and thus inherited his new divine vision. Indeed, Elisha's new gift will be reverified in 2 Kings 6:17, where the account shows him again seeing the "horses and chariots of fire." Thus, it is by seeing the departure of his reflected, mirror image, Elijah, that Elisha is given the gift of divine sight. And it is only by obtaining this gift of divine sight that Elisha can be truly declared Elijah's mirror image or double.

But what does Elisha's cry about the chariots and horsemen mean? What exactly does Elisha see? Robert Chisholm, as well as some medieval Jewish commentators, such as Rashi, Abarbanel, and Gersonides, suggests that Elisha's cry indicates a correspondence between the heavenly armies and the prophet.[22] Elijah (and later Elisha) symbolizes or stands for the "chariot and horseman of Israel." Joseph Blenkinsopp,

---

21. P. Kyle McCarter notes that prophets were earlier designated as seers (*I Samuel: A New Translation, Introduction, and Commentary*, AB 8 [Garden City, NY: Doubleday, 1980], 177).

22. Chisholm, "The 'Spirit of the Lord,'" 316.

¹⁵When the company of prophets who were at Jericho saw him at a distance, they declared, "The spirit of Elijah rests on Elisha." They came to meet him and bowed to the ground before him. ¹⁶They said to him, "See now, we have fifty strong men among your servants; please let them go and seek your master; it may be that the spirit of the Lord has caught him up and thrown him down on some mountain or into some valley." He responded, "No, do not send them." ¹⁷But when they urged him until he was ashamed, he said, "Send them." So they sent fifty men who searched for three days but did not find him. ¹⁸When they came back to him (he had remained at Jericho), he said to them, "Did I not say to you, Do not go?"

using evidence from Psalm 68:5, 18 goes farther and maintains that it is YHWH who is the master charioteer of the hosts of heaven. Thus, the mentioning of chariots and horsemen emphasizes the image of the prophet as the "devotee of the chariot god."[23] The Aramaic Targum also sees a connection between Elijah and the armies as indicative of Elijah's greater importance to the defense of Israel than those offered by earthly chariots or horsemen. Similarly, Martinus Adrianus Beek, noting the appearance of the phrase "horses and chariots of fire" later in 2 Kings 6, also states that this phrase might be a title of the prophet, which contrasts human weapons, such as chariots and horses, with the word of a prophet.[24]

From a feminist perspective, the cry of Elisha at the departure of his mentor, Elijah, seems to indicate that he witnesses a scene that is militaristic in nature. Most likely, Elisha sees not only a whirlwind—a manifestation of YHWH as a storm god—but also the presence of a heavenly convoy of some sort, sent to transport his master, his reflection, to the divine realm. In short, what Elisha sees with his newly given divine gaze are divine weapons and military equipment (i.e., chariots, horsemen, wind) and the heavenly armed forces. In having Elisha see these particular things, what the text again stresses is the martial prowess and power—i.e., the masculinity—of YHWH. Hence, only by seeing and thus understanding the true extent of YHWH's martial abilities and the power

23. Blenkinsopp, *History of Prophecy*, 61.

24. Martinus Adrianus Beek, "The Meaning of the Expression the Chariots and the Horsemen of Israel (2 Kings ii 12)," *OtSt* 17 (1972): 1–10; also Cogan and Tadmor, *II Kings*, 32.

of his armed forces can Elisha be empowered to carry on the ministry of Elijah. Or to put it differently, it is by *seeing* (and thus understanding) the masculine power of their deity, YHWH, that the prophets of YHWH can truly be reproduced and regenerated. Thus, in order to carry on the ministry of their masculine god, the prophets must obtain true, divine—that is, masculine—sight and insight about YHWH's masculinity.

As in the preceding chapter, the assertive emphasis on virility of YHWH in 2 Kings 2 has theological significance. As we noted earlier, many narratives in 2 Kings focus on masculine contests. Like 2 Kings 1, chapter 2 also concerns the rivalry between YHWH and Baal. Leah Bronner notes, for example, that the ascent of Elijah via the "chariot of fire and the horses of fire" is another way to repudiate Baal's storm-god control over fire and lightening. According to Bronner, 2 Kings 2 asserts the identity of YHWH as the true storm god over against the false god, Baal.[25] Moreover, 2 Kings 2 seems to continue and respond to another rivalry, that between the human king and YHWH, which was present in the preceding chapter. For example, the downward descent of divine fire, which devours Ahaziah's soldiers in 2 Kings 1, is inverted and matched by the upward ascent of Elijah, the prophet of YHWH, by or through a chariot of fire in 2 Kings 2.[26] As the text so clearly demonstrates, YHWH's military forces easily overpower those of the human Israelite king. YHWH, as evident in the literary display of his virility and divine weaponry, is thus depicted as the ultimate masculine king and god.

Yet is the feminine wholly erased in this narrative? This pericope, after all, centers on themes of reproduction, doubling, and continuation. We argue that though diminished and undermined by the overtly masculine portrayal of YHWH, a whisper of the gynocentric voice can be detected in the emotional parting scene between Elijah and Elisha where Elisha requests a double measure of Elijah's spirit. Though the term for spirit (רוח) is sometimes used with a masculine verb (2 Sam 23:2; 1 Kgs 18:12; 22:24; 2 Chr 18:23; Hos 13:15; and Mic 2:7), it is most often found with a feminine singular verb (Judg 3:10; 6:34; 11:29; 13:25; 14:6, 19; 15:14; 1 Sam 10:6; 16:13-14; 19:9; 2 Chr 20:14; Isa 11:2; 40:7; 59:19; 63:14; Ezek 11:5).[27] Though it is best not to read too much into the gender of a particular

25. Leah Bronner, *The Stories of Elijah and Elisha as Polemics against Baal Worship*, POS 6 (Leiden: Brill, 1968), 64, 125–27, 132–33.

26. For intertextual connections of directions and movements in 2 Kings 1 and 2 Kings 2, see Burnett, "'Going Down' to Bethel," 281–97.

27. Chisholm, "The 'Spirit of the Lord,'" 512.

Hebrew term, perhaps a nod to the feminine powers of reproduction can be subtly discerned in Elisha's request for a double portion of the female רוח, "spirit." Perhaps Elisha's request for the spirit is a request for the powers of regeneration, life, and procreation—things that are usually and more naturally associated with the feminine. If so, lurking beneath this masculine tale about the brotherhood and masculine twinning of prophets, a gynocentric presence can be faintly detected. Hence, though the overt emphasis of this story remains on masculine, female-less reproduction and procreation of prophets, the more natural female power of reproduction is not wholly erased, especially as this pericope centrally concerns prophetic reproduction and doubling.

Rejuvenation of the Waters at Jericho (2:19-22)

Episodes involving Elisha and water follow on the heels of Elijah's ascent into heaven. Immediately after Elijah's departure, the people of the city of Jericho come to Elisha to tell him about the unusable water in the city, which the prophet purifies by throwing salt into it so that "neither death nor miscarriage shall come from it" (2 Kgs 2:21).

Gina Hens-Piazza notes that this miracle is another reference linking Elisha to Joshua, in particular his curse over Jericho (Josh 6:26; 1 Kgs 16:34).[28] In alluding to Moses' successor, Joshua, this episode reaffirms Elisha as the Joshua to Elijah. The fact that this initial miracle of Elisha concerns water is significant.

Water not only symbolizes fertility and life but also brings to mind the preceding splitting of it by Moses and Elijah. Hence, Elisha's miracle concerning water stresses the continuation of YHWH's life-giving, pro-creative, healing powers in Elisha. Moreover, John Gray maintains that the mentioning of salt in this miracle, an agent used to purify and sepa-rate an object from the profane world, is important because it indicates a rite of separation for which Elisha might have been known.[29] Perhaps the presence of water and the purifying element of salt is meant to bring to mind a dedication ritual, perhaps even a gendered one, whereby Elisha is established as Elijah's rightful heir. Gray, who also believes that some sort of ritual is reflected in this scene, mentions that newborn babies were rubbed with salt to signify their emergence into society.[30] Likewise,

---

28. Gina Hens-Piazza, *1–2 Kings*, AOTC (Nashville: Abingdon, 2006), 236.
29. Gray, *I & II Kings*, 478.
30. Ibid.

[19]Now the people of the city said to Elisha, "The location of this city is good, as my lord sees; but the water is bad, and the land is unfruitful." [20]He said, "Bring me a new bowl, and put salt in it." So they brought it to him. [21]Then he went to the spring of water and threw the salt into it, and said, "Thus says the LORD, I have made this water wholesome; from now on neither death nor miscarriage shall come from it." [22]So the water has been wholesome to this day, according to the word that Elisha spoke.

water, as seen in baptisms and mikvehs, is also utilized in purification, initiation, and conversion rituals. Both substances—water, as evident in the portrayal of the saltwater deity, Tiamat, in the great Babylonian creation epic *Enuma Elish*, and salt, with its links to Aphrodite[31]—are intimately related to the feminine. Considering the various symbolisms associated with water and salt, some sort of gendered ritual might be alluded to in this scene.

She-Bears, Taunting Children, and YHWH's Reproductive Powers (2:23-25)

The concluding verses about Elisha's confrontation with the taunting lads further asserts and authenticates Elisha's status as Elijah's prophetic successor. While the preceding pericope affirmed Elisha's authority by the demonstration of YHWH's life-giving abilities, this second pericope, in contrast, does so by showing YHWH's aggressive and violent masculine powers as enacted and channeled through his servant, Elisha. The strangeness and ethical dubiousness of this tale is evident in commentaries that try to lessen the horror of this tale by arguing that the children were not children but young men.[32]

Regardless of age, these young men are shown as questioning Elisha's authority as Elijah's successor by subtly contrasting Elijah with Elisha. This was a great offense, considering that these two figures are depicted as doubles or reproductions of each other in the preceding part of the

31. Bernard M. Moinier and Tilman B. Drueke, "Aphrodite, Sex and Salt—From Butterfly to Man," *Nephrology Dialysis Transplantation* 23 (2008): 2154–61, esp. 2154–55.

32. E.g., Fred E. Woods, "Elisha and the Children: The Question of Accepting Prophetic Succession," *BYU Studies* 32 (1992): 48.

²³He went up from there to Bethel; and while he was going up on the way, some small boys came out of the city and jeered at him, saying, "Go away, baldhead! Go away, baldhead!" ²⁴When he turned around and saw them, he cursed them in the name of the LORD. Then two she-bears came out of the woods and mauled forty-two of the boys. ²⁵From there he went on to Mount Carmel, and then returned to Samaria.

narrative. The lads contrast Elijah and Elisha, first, by calling Elisha a baldy, a jab that evokes the oppositional image of the hirsute Elijah (2 Kgs 1:8). Fred Woods notes that by calling Elisha a "baldy," the lads also allude to the hairy mantle (אדרת) used by Elijah to call Elisha to the prophetic profession in 1 Kings 19:19. The mantle, which, incidentally, can also mean "glory," reappears in this chapter to authenticate Elisha as Elijah's successor. After Elijah's ascent into heaven, Elisha picks up and uses Elijah's mantle, which had fallen off him, to split the waters of the Jordan just as Elijah had done before he was taken up (2 Kgs 2:8, 13-14).[33] By calling Elisha a baldy, the lads are referring to more than what is on his head. Finally, adding insult to injury, the lads also cry out for Elisha to "go up." Though the command initially appears innocent, these young men are really taunting Elisha to go up just as his master did, that is, to prove himself as Elijah's true heir by mimicking the heavenly ascent of his master. In contrasting Elijah and Elisha, the youths thus express doubt about Elisha's authority.[34]

The questioning of Elisha's status as the successor and double of Elijah is not an insult to Elisha alone, however. Rather, these lads are insulting or questioning the very authority of YHWH, himself, and, in particular, his procreative ability—i.e., his ability to cause prophets to double themselves through succession. That this violent pericope is centrally about YHWH's masculine procreative powers is evident, not only in the use of *mother* bears as the weapon of choice against doubting children, but also in the presence of doublets. Joel S. Burnett notes that the lads taunt Elisha by twice calling him a baldhead and twice commanding him to go up—"Go up, baldy! Go up, baldy!" (2 Kgs 2:23).[35]

33. Woods, "Elisha and the Children," 52; Davis, "The Kingdom of God," 392–93.
34. Woods, "Elisha and the Children," 54; Davis, "The Kingdom of God," 392–93.
35. Burnett, " 'Going Down' to Bethel," 296.

As a result, two she-bears come out to maul forty-two children—that is two plus forty, which symbolizes completeness. Julie Faith Parker notes that it is ironic that two mother bears are used as the medium of divine aggression as their fearsomeness and aggression would have stemmed from their maternal status as producers and protectors of their own children or cubs.[36] Yet the use of mother bears further supports the reading that the insult targets the reproductive powers of YHWH. For doubting YHWH's masculine ability to double, the young men (and maybe some young women, Julie Faith Parker speculates)[37]—the products of normal, female reproduction—are mauled by a pair of mother bears. YHWH's masculine reproductive abilities are so powerful that even the mere hint of doubt, even by children, is immediately and violently squashed. In this case, he avenges the emasculating insult through the use of mother bears who, though female in gender, also represent the violent, uncontrolled masculine powers of the deity they serve.

36. Julie Faith Parker, *Valuable and Vulnerable: Children in the Hebrew Bible, Especially the Elisha Cycle*, BJS 355 (Providence, RI: Brown University Press, 2013), 101.

37. Ibid., 93.

2 Kings 3:1-27

War, Death, and Sacrifice:
A Colonial Enterprise

The pericope in 2 Kings 3 about the battle between Israel and Moab draws out and concludes the story about Moab's rebellion, which was briefly mentioned in 2 Kings 1:1 as a somewhat disjunctive introductory sentence to the summary of Ahaziah's short-lived reign. With the heirless Ahaziah dead from his fall, his brother Jehoram assumes the throne of Israel and shortly thereafter goes after the rebellious Moabites who had been withholding tribute. Initially, Israel and Judah's joint campaign against Moab is successful, and they are able to demolish and destroy many of the Moabite towns. As Moab is about to fall, however, the tide of war suddenly turns as the Moabite king sacrifices his firstborn son, unleashing a great wrath upon Israel (2 Kgs 3:27). The narrative concludes with a surprise ending as Israel is forced to withdraw without reconquering Moab. The unexpected ending to this pericope raises important theological questions about the nature of war and the colonial enterprise. The Mesha Inscription or the Moabite Stone, a stela found in 1868 in modern Dhiban, Jordan (biblical Dibon), offers an interesting and important historical comparison to this narrative about the battle between Israel and Moab.[1]

---

1. For a comparison between the Mesha Inscription and the biblical account, see Joe M. Sprinkle, "2 Kings 3: History or Historical Fiction?" *BBR* 9 (1999): 247–70. For a fuller analysis of the Mesha Inscription, see the various essays in Andrew Dearman, ed., *Studies in the Mesha Inscription and Moab*, ABS 2 (Atlanta: Scholars Press, 1989).

The Summary of Jehoram's Reign (3:1-3)

The chapter begins with the usual Deuteronomistic assessment and summary of the king's reign. Typical of northern kings, Jehoram is given a negative overall rating. He is, however, designated as an improvement over his father and mother (Ahab and Jezebel) for having removed the pillar of Baal, most likely a stela of sorts, unattested in the description of Ahab's cultic activities in 1 Kings 16:31-33.

Although Jehoram is said to have "clung to the sin of Jeroboam son of Nebat," he seems to be initially assessed more positively than his brother Ahaziah. Unlike Ahaziah, who is introduced only to be immediately killed off, reigning only two short years, Jehoram (c. 849–842 BCE) is said to have ruled for a decade longer than his brother.

YHWH as God of Water and Life, and Violence and Death (3:4-19)

Shortly after the death of Ahab, 2 Kings 3 states that the neighboring country of Moab, which had been a vassal of Israel since the time of David, rebels against Israel. In response, King Jehoram of Israel quickly forms an alliance with Judah under King Jehoshaphat and with Edom, which, most likely, is a vassal of Judah (1 Kgs 22:47) in order to recapture Moab and to punish its king, Mesha, for the rebellion.

The joint coalition (Israel, Judah, and Edom) takes the route through the Edomite wilderness. All goes well until the alliance finds their water depleted and is unable to find a water source en route for their army and animals. Displaying the typical unfaithfulness exhibited by northern kings, Jehoram declares that he has been set up by the YHWH who desires to defeat him (v. 9). The Judahite king, Jehoshaphat, on the contrary, reacts more calmly to the water issue and inquires about the whereabouts of a prophet. The fact that the coalition has waited so long to consult a prophet about this military excursion speaks to Jehoram's impiety. Normally a deity would have been consulted *before* going to war (Judg 1:1-3; 6:36-40; 20:18-28; 1 Sam 23:2-4; 2 Sam 2:1; 5:19; 1 Kgs 22:5).[2]

Despite blaming YHWH for the water problem, by depicting Jehoram as remiss in getting the proper pre-battle oracle, the narrative squarely places the blame for the predicament on the Israelite king. Jehoram is

---

2. See Susan Niditch, *War in the Hebrew Bible: A Study of the Ethics of Violence* (New York: Oxford University Press, 1993), 137–44.

3:1In the eighteenth year of King Jehoshaphat of Judah, Jehoram son of Ahab became king over Israel in Samaria; he reigned twelve years. 2He did what was evil in the sight of the Lord, though not like his father and mother, for he removed the pillar of Baal that his father had made. 3Nevertheless he clung to the sin of Jeroboam son of Nebat, which he caused Israel to commit; he did not depart from it.

4Now King Mesha of Moab was a sheep breeder, who used to deliver to the king of Israel one hundred thousand lambs, and the wool of one hundred thousand rams. 5But when Ahab died, the king of Moab rebelled against the king of Israel. 6So King Jehoram marched out of Samaria at the time and mustered all Israel. 7As he went

he sent word to King Jehoshaphat of Judah, "The king of Moab has rebelled against me; will you go with me to battle against Moab?" He answered, "I will; I am with you, my people are your people, my horses are your horses." 8Then he asked, "By which way shall we march?" Jehoram answered, "By the way of the wilderness of Edom."

9So the king of Israel, the king of Judah, and the king of Edom set out; and when they had made roundabout march of seven days, there was no water for the army or for the animals that were with them. 10Then the king of Israel said, "Alas! The Lord has summoned us, three kings, only to be handed over to Moab." 11But Jehoshaphat said, "Is there no prophet of the Lord here, through whom we may

the one who, without inquiring of God, led the coalition into battle along this foolhardy, desiccated route. Adding to the northern monarch's negative portrayal, a servant has to inform the Israelite king of the presence of the prophet Elisha, who seems to be among the traveling group or an attendant group that is following along (v. 10). The narrative thus clearly contrasts the unfaithful northern king with his more pious and wise Judean counterpart, Jehoshaphat.

Though given a more balanced assessment at the beginning of this chapter, the narrative, as it progresses, increasingly dampens Jehoram's portrayal, especially in contradistinction to the southern king. When Elisha finally comes on the scene, the prophet vehemently exclaims that he would not have bothered if it were not for the presence of the Davidic monarch, Jehoshaphat (v. 14). While at the beginning of the narrative Jehoram is assessed as better than his parents, Elisha here parallels Jehoram with the hated Ahab and Jezebel by snidely advising Jehoram to go to his father or mother's prophets instead of coming to him (v. 13). Perhaps this increasingly negative vision of Jehoram is meant to subtly

inquire of the LORD?" Then one of the servants of the king of Israel answered, "Elisha son of Shaphat, who used to pour water on the hands of Elijah is here." ¹²Jehoshaphat said, "The word of the LORD is with him." So the king of Israel and Jehoshaphat and the king of Edom went down to him.

¹³Elisha said to the king of Israel, "What have I to do with you? Go to your father's prophets or to your mother's." But the king of Israel said to him, "No; it is the LORD who has summoned us, three kings, only to be handed over to Moab." ¹⁴Elisha said, "As the LORD of hosts lives, whom I serve, were it not that I have regard for King Jehoshaphat

of Judah, I would give you neither a look nor a glance. ¹⁵But get me a musician." And then, while the musician was playing, the power of the LORD came on him. ¹⁶And he said, "Thus says the LORD, 'I will make this wadi full of pools.' ¹⁷For thus says the LORD, 'You shall see neither wind nor rain, but the wadi shall be filled with water, so that you shall drink, you, your cattle, and your animals.' ¹⁸This is only a trifle in the sight of the LORD, for he will also hand Moab over to you. ¹⁹You shall conquer every fortified city and every choice city; every good tree you shall fell, all springs of water you shall stop up, and every good piece of land you shall ruin with stones."

set up and explain the problematic ending of the narrative whereby the Israelite coalition fails to subdue Moab as Elisha prophesized.[3]

As we have seen in previous chapters, 2 Kings 3, in stressing YHWH's ability to provide water, continues the portrayal of YHWH as the true procreative, life-giving, storm deity in comparison to the false storm god, Baal. Gina Hens-Piazza elucidates the variety of ways that water is used and stressed in this chapter. For example, when the servant of Jehoram mentions Elisha, he authenticates the prophet by stating that Elisha is the one who used to pour water over Elijah's hands, thus linking Elisha to the authority of his master, Elijah (v. 11), the prophet who earlier resolved the national drought crisis with his miraculous inducement of rain (1 Kgs 18).[4]

Another instance of the use of water is found in the previous chapter. Water is utilized to authenticate a prophet and thus to affirm the deity whom the prophet serves. In 2 Kings 2, Elisha's authority as Elijah's protégé and a true prophet of YHWH is confirmed when Elisha repli-

3. Robert B. Chisholm, Jr., "Israel's Retreat and the Failure of Prophecy in 2 Kings 3," *Bib* 92 (2011): 70–80.

4. Gina Hens-Piazza, *1–2 Kings*, AOTC (Nashville: Abingdon, 2006), 243.

cates Elijah's earlier splitting of the waters of the Jordan and when he purifies the waters of Jericho with the addition of salt. Similarly, this chapter also asserts YHWH as the ultimate source and master of life-giving water. YHWH's utter mastery over this substance is shown in the miraculous, nonnatural manner in which water is produced in this chapter. In contrast to Baal, the Canaanite deity of rain and storm, YHWH here works "miraculously outside the forces that some could confuse with the work of Baal"[5] by having the wadi fill up with water without the aid of wind or rain.

Second Kings 3 connects water and the power over it with the preservation of life. Hens-Piazza notes that though Jehoram complains that Moab will be victorious because of the coalition's lack of water, the opposite is announced by Elisha. He prophesizes that Israel will be made victorious through the "miraculous gift of water" at the end.[6] He also announces that Moab, not Israel, per Jehoram's complaint, will be handed over to be conquered (v. 18). Further emphasizing the contrast between life and death, the prophet concludes by calling for the utter decimation of Moab. Israel and its coalition, in violation of the Deuteronomic code for conduct during war (Deut 20:19-20), are told to chop down every good tree, stop up every water spring, and ruin the land with stones.[7] In other words, they are not only to kill the Moabites but to induce a kind of permanent death to the land itself. The land that YHWH fills with life-giving water for the Israelites and its alliance are to be ruined by the Israelite army so that their enemy can never again obtain life from it. As in the preceding pericope about Elisha and the she-bears, the prophet's oracle shows a darker side of YHWH. Even though YHWH will give life and healing to his devotees, the deity, or at least his messenger, does not hesitate to resort to violence, especially during war.

War and the Sacrifice of Children (3:20-27)

This narrative presents a series of shifting and stark images of life and death. For example, it begins with a scene of a frantic search for water by thirsty soldiers and animals in a desiccated land. This is followed by a scene of flowing streams that form large pools of water, which overwhelm

5. Ibid., 244.
6. Ibid., 245.
7. Patricia Berlyn, "The Wrath of Moab," *JBQ* 30 (2002): 222; Chisholm, "Israel's Retreat," 75.

²⁰The next day, about the time of the morning offering, suddenly water began to flow from the direction of Edom, until the country was filled with water.

²¹When all the Moabites heard that the kings had come up to fight against them, all who were able to put on armor, from the youngest to the oldest, were called out and were drawn up at the frontier. ²²When they rose early in the morning, and the sun shone upon the water, the Moabites saw the water opposite them as red as blood. ²³They said, "This is blood; the kings must have fought together, and killed one another. Now then, Moab, to the spoil!" ²⁴But when they came to the camp of Israel, the Israelites rose up and attacked the Moabites, who fled before them; as they entered Moab they continued the attack. ²⁵The cities they overturned, and on every good piece of land everyone threw a stone, until it was covered; every spring of water they stopped up, and every good tree they felled. Only at Kir-hareseth did the stone walls remain, until the slingers surrounded and attacked it. ²⁶When the king of Moab saw that the battle was going against him, he took with him seven hundred swordsmen to break through, opposite the king of Edom; but they could not. ²⁷Then he took his firstborn son who was to succeed him, and offered him as a burnt offering on the wall. And great wrath came upon Israel, so they withdrew from him and returned to their own land.

and fill the landscape. The scene dramatically switches again as these pools of life transform into pools of blood in the eyes of the Moabites, who, perhaps seeing the red tint of the Edomite soil or some kind of reflection (an evident wordplay on "Edom," אדמים כדם, "red as blood," v. 22),[8] think that the coalition has turned on and massacred each other. Rushing forward to finish them off, the Moabites meet their own death as they are confronted with the still-alive Israelite army. Water, the source of life for Israel and its coalition, will thus ironically become a source of death for Moab.[9] The scene ends with a final vision of utter decimation as the Israelites completely destroy Moab by cutting down trees, stopping up springs, and throwing stones on the land.

Had the text stopped here, the story would have ended with a neat yet bloody conclusion. In the verses that follow, however, we witness another shift from life to death as the Israelite victory is suddenly stopped by

---

8. Choon-Leong Seow, "The First and Second Book of Kings," in *NIB*, ed. Leander E. Keck et al. (Nashville: Abingdon, 1999), 3:184.

9. Hens-Piazza, *1–2 Kings*, 245.

King Mesha's sacrifice of his firstborn son. This dramatic and powerful act reverses the direction of battle as a קֶצֶף־גָּדל, "great wrath"—caused by whom the text leaves unstated[10]—descends upon the Israelites who then retreat and return to their own land. No matter how distasteful to the modern reader, the killing of the son, especially a royal firstborn son, appears to have worked.

Julie Faith Parker compares the sacrifice of Mesha's son to that of Jephthah's daughter in Judges 11.[11] As in Judges, so in 2 Kings 3 an unnamed child of a warrior is killed to benefit a military campaign. The key difference between the daughter and Mesha's son, however, is that the daughter is sacrificed after the battle is over and victory achieved, while Mesha's son is killed so as to induce victory. From a feminist perspective, this difference raises a question as to whether the sacrifice of a daughter is as effective to the success of a military campaign as the death of a son. Is the sacrifice of a male youth, especially that of a royal son, more significant and powerful than that of a female? Would the death of a daughter have aroused the same kind of divine wrath? If we compare the death of Mesha's son with that of Jephthah's daughter, the utter silence of God in Judges 11 offers a stark contrast to the undeniably effective and strong wrath induced by the sacrifice of the son in 2 Kings 3, though the source of the wrath remains unstated.[12]

The death of the firstborn son attests to a subtle emphasis on the gendered aspect of this violence. The masculine, military violence, which leads to death, can be compared to feminine forms of reproduction and life giving, as evident in the recurrence of the water theme. While scholars have noted the ways in which this chapter alludes to the Passover pericope, with its imagery of water, blood, and death of the firstborn (Exod 7:14-25, esp. v. 21),[13] what has not been noticed are the ways in which the presence of water, blood, and children (and also, presumably, the screaming and chaotic sounds of war) conjures up images of childbirth.

---

10. Patricia Berlyn states that usually divine wrath is meant by the term קֶצֶף. She argues, however, that the wrath might not have been an emotion but an unfortunate event of sorts that led to the defeat of the Israelite coalition ("The Wrath of Moab," 224–25).

11. Julie Faith Parker, *Valuable and Vulnerable: Children in the Hebrew Bible, Especially the Elisha Cycle*, BJS 355 (Providence, RI: Brown University Press, 2013), 117–18.

12. Baruch Margalit explains the sacrifice of a king's son as an essential part of the Canaanite tradition of holy war ("Why King Mesha of Moab Sacrificed His Oldest Son," *BAR* 12 [1986]: 62–63).

13. Seow, "The First and Second Book of Kings," 184.

The childbirth imagery in 2 Kings 3 thus sets up a powerful contrast between masculine powers, which induce death, violence, and the end of progeny, with the feminine powers that give water, life, and healing.

A subtle judgment might be detectable here as well. As scholars have noted, the narrative is ambiguous as to which deity's קֶצֶף, "wrath," is unleashed on the Israelites with the sacrifice of Mesha's son. Certainly, clearly identifying the powerful wrath as emanating from Chemosh, the rival god of the Moabites,[14] would have raised theological questions about the power of YHWH—namely, is Chemosh stronger than YHWH? Aside from theological issues, the text might not have clearly identified the source of the wrath so as to not directly associate YHWH, who at many points in 2 Kings is presented as the master of water and life, too strongly with child sacrifice and death. Jon Levenson has persuasively written about transformation and sublimation of the child sacrifice motif in the Hebrew biblical text by writers uncomfortable with this practice.[15] Perhaps the biblical writers felt that the earlier life-giving, almost birthing imagery of YHWH, with the deity depicted as drenching the land with water, did not fit well with the concluding image of a god who allows child sacrifice. Hence, by leaving the source of the wrath deliberately ambiguous, Chemosh, not YHWH, can be connected to death. By not clearly identifying the deity from which the powerful wrath emanates, however, YHWH's power can remain unquestioned.

The lack of desire to pinpoint the source of the unleashed divine rage might also explain why the conclusion of this pericope seems to contradict Elisha's earlier prophecy. Considering that the narrative ends with a lack of victory for Israel and its coalition, scholars have wondered about the veracity of Elisha's initial prophecy of victory.[16] Ian Provan argues that the prophecy was fulfilled, though there is "a certain economy with the truth," which led to "mistaken expectations" about total victory.[17]

---

14. Julie Faith Parker writes about the similarities between Chemosh and YHWH, such as the acceptance of child sacrifice in exchange for military victory (Judg 11:30-40) (Parker, *Valuable and Vulnerable*, 110).

15. Jon Levenson, *The Death and Resurrection of the Beloved Son: The Transformation of Child Sacrifice in Judaism and Christianity* (New Haven: Yale University Press, 1993).

16. Mordechai Cogan and Hayim Tadmor, *II Kings: A New Translation with Introduction and Commentary*, AB 11 (Garden City, NY: Doubleday, 1988), 51; Leon-Sofia Tiemeyer, "Prophecy as a Way of Cancelling Prophecy—The Strategic Uses of Foreknowledge," *ZAW* 117 (2005): 333.

17. Ian W. Provan, *1 and 2 Kings*, NIBCOT (Peabody, MA: Hendrickson; Carlisle: Paternoster, 1995), 183.

Raymond Westbrook maintains something similar when he states that Elisha's prophecy was *misunderstood* by Jehoram as wrongly ensuring final victory.[18] These conclusions are countered by Robert B. Chisholm, who argues that the expression "give into your hands" usually refers to total, not partial, victory (see Josh 10:32; Judg 3:28; 4:14; 7:2; 8:7; 1 Sam 28:19; Jer 44:30).[19] Chisholm maintains that the prophecy failed because of Israel's lack of faith in YHWH.

Yet regardless of the impiety of the king or people, the odd, anti-climactic ending raises important questions about the narrative. Why would the narrative end by describing the failure of Elisha's prophecy only two chapters after confirming his succession to Elijah? Would not such a depiction severely damage Elisha's authority and authenticity as a true prophet of YHWH? Why even describe the trials and tribulations of the Israelite army only to have them return home empty-handed at the end? What is the point of this narrative, exactly?

We posit that Elisha's prophecy is depicted as unfulfilled so as to dissociate YHWH with child sacrifice and perhaps even the horrors of war. Perhaps the biblical writers felt that it was theologically preferable to show the prophecy as failing to come to pass than it was to depict YHWH as allowing an Israelite victory in the face of a sacrifice of a child. Perhaps this deed and the unrelenting violence that preceded it, whereby the army engages in something akin to scorched-earth tactics, albeit in alignment with the directions given to them by Elisha, did not sit well with the biblical writers who wanted to portray YHWH as a water-provider and life-giver.

Joe Sprinkle argues something similar when he posits that Israel's defeat was likely caused by its violations of the Deuteronomic codes of conduct during war.[20] As Julie Faith Parker counters, however, there is no textual evidence that the writer knows of such regulations.[21] More generally, we posit that, considering the historicity of the event, which, as the Moabite Stone shows, ended with Israel's defeat—indeed, Israel was never again able to subjugate Moab—the biblical writers might have felt that it was more important to associate YHWH with water and

18. Raymond Westbrook, "Elisha's True Prophecy in 2 Kings 3," *JBL* 124 (2005): 530–32.

19. Chisholm, "Israel's Retreat," 72.

20. Joe M. Sprinkle, "Deuteronomic 'Just War' (Deut 20, 10-20) and 2 Kings 3,27," *ZABR* 6 (2000): 285–301.

21. Parker, *Valuable and Vulnerable*, 106.

life than it was to present an unhistorical story of Israel's success. In so doing, the theological problems caused by Elisha's earlier prophecy of Israelite success were left unresolved in the pericope.

Colonialism and the Abuses against Women and Children

From a postcolonial perspective, Elisha's unfulfilled prophecy remains a minor issue in comparison to the larger theological and ethical questions raised by this pericope. The story gruesomely portrays the violent decimation and destruction of a foreign land and populace—a destruction so severe that it violates Deuteronomic guidelines on war (Deut 20:10-20)—by a colonial army led by an unfaithful descendant of Ahab and Jezebel. Moreover, this violence is depicted as stemming from a desire to avenge Moab for its attempt to overthrow its subjugation. Adding to the disturbing picture, Parker argues that unnamed children and youth were probably part of the fighting Moabite group. Mesha's son was probably "not the only youth to die in this battle."[22] As we will see with other narratives in 2 Kings, the amount of violence committed by Israel and allowed by YHWH causes ambivalent feelings on the part of the reader. Considering the cruelty of the invading Israelite army, who is the reader supposed to side with in this story? Who exactly is the protagonist, and who is the antagonist? In raising these questions, the text perhaps unwittingly reveals the bloodshed, horror, and violence that lie at the heart of every colonial enterprise.

Interestingly, perhaps a subtle postcolonial critique can even be detected in the portrayal of the sacrifice of Mesha's son. Though this act of violence "works" and some sort of wrath is unleashed, the sacrifice uncomfortably shows the toll that colonialism takes on the colonized and colonizers alike. The armies of Israel and Judah nearly die of thirst on the way and are ultimately unsuccessful despite all their efforts. Moab suffers great human losses and is able to fend off the Israelite invaders only by murdering the royal heir. The narrative shows how the violence caused by colonialism induces more acts of violence.

Carol Delaney also argues that biblical tales of child sacrifice legitimate modern abuses of women and children.[23] Though she is correct about the potent power possessed by the biblical text, I posit that a more

---

22. Ibid., 107.

23. Carol Delaney, *Abraham on Trial: The Social Legacy of Biblical Myth* (Princeton, NJ: Princeton University Press, 1998), esp. 231–50.

critical message can be detected. As I noted earlier, it is significant that this pericope ends, in contradiction to Elisha's prophecy, with the lack of success for the Israelite coalition. That God does not allow Israel to have final victory, especially in the face of the killing of Mesha's son, seems to express not only dismay at the act of child sacrifice but also possibly ambivalence about the nature of wars and the colonial enterprise as a whole. After the onslaught of violence, God no longer seems to be on the side of the Israelite coalition, no matter the earlier prophecy of Elisha. What kind of victory can anyone have in the face of such violence? Who actually wins—the text seems to say!

The ambivalent voice becomes even more audible when we compare this passage to the plague and Passover narrative (Exod 8–12). During the plague and Passover event, the waters of the Nile are turned into blood and the firstborn children of Egypt are killed so that Israel can be freed from Egyptian rule. In this chapter in 2 Kings, we again have the images of the transformation of water into blood and the death of a firstborn child. As during the Passover event, so here, these events lead to the liberation of a group of people. This time, however, the liberation is from subjugation to Israel, not of Israel. The similarities between the Passover narrative and 2 Kings 3 suggest and lean toward a postcolonial reading. Both the foundational Exodus narrative and this story about the Moabite battle lucidly show the misery, violence, and bloodshed that follows on the heels of any forced oppression. Any oppression that stems from nothing more than human desire for power, domination, and riches is bound to fail.

2 Kings 4:1-44

Fecundity, Reproduction, and Life

Although the preceding chapters in 2 Kings are mainly concerned with the deaths of kings, people, and children, each of the four narratives that comprise 2 Kings 4, in contrast, centers on the themes of fecundity, reproduction, and life. The first story describes a poor widow's miraculous salvation and the rescue of her children through Elisha's gift of continually generating oil (2 Kgs 4:1-7). In contrast, the second narrative centers on a wealthy Shunammite woman's gift of material support to Elisha and his reciprocal gift to her of a child who subsequently dies and is revived by Elisha (4:7-37). Elisha's transformation of a poisonous soup consumed by a band of prophets during famine forms the plot of the third story (4:38-42). And finally, the chapter closes with a last pericope about Elisha's multiplication of barley and grain for the people (4:42-44).

The four episodes that comprise 2 Kings 4 all swing from death—as represented by economic, social, or reproductive starvation and deprivation—to life as manifested in the abundant reproduction of food, people, and health. Moreover, as Gina Hens-Piazza notes, all the narratives in this chapter center on nameless characters who lack social standing— in other words, those in need and those on the margins. In so doing, these stories celebrate "the power of God as the source of life among his people."[1] Thus, YHWH is once again celebrated as the fruitful provider and producer of life for his group.

---

1. Gina Hens-Piazza, *1–2 Kings*, AOTC (Nashville: Abingdon, 2006), 249–50.

The Economic Insecurities of Women and Children (4:1-7)

The narrative, which might be a variation of a similar tale concerning Elijah's multiplication of oil and meal for the widow at Zarephath (1 Kings 17),[2] begins dramatically with an unnamed woman crying out to Elisha for help because her husband, a member of the sons of the prophets,[3] had died, causing her and her family to become impoverished (2 Kgs 4:1).

Adding to the misery, the widow tells the prophet that creditors are about to show up to take her children as slaves because she has failed to pay back her loan. Mordechai Cogan and Hayim Tadmor write that early tradition identifies the nameless widow as the wife of Obadiah, the steward of Ahab, thus giving her a context and a relationship to a known male in the Deuteronomistic History.[4] Though she is anonymous, it is fitting that this chapter begins with the widow's cry, for it is the unnamed woman who, according to Julie Faith Parker, is the true star of the story, simultaneously juggling the roles of "widow, supplicant, mother, advocate, protector, worker, and reporter."[5]

Though the miraculous reduplication of oil is performed by Elisha, much of the tale's emotional core centers on the widow as she desperately tries to hang on to her children who would otherwise be sold into slavery. The reader cannot help but feel for this poor, hungry woman who, in the largely patriarchal setting, has to care for two children alone. Yet the brevity with which the widow's story is discussed in most modern commentaries speaks to the general disregard of such victims—both inside and outside of the text. Theologically speaking, this narrative urges readers to open their eyes to similarly desperate situations faced by the widow's modern-day twins. By beginning this chapter with her cry, the text makes the cries of this widow all the more immediate.

---

2. Yael Shemesh, "Elisha and the Miraculous Jug of Oil (2 Kgs 4:1-7)," *JHS* 8 (2008). http://www.jhsonline.org/Articles/article_81.pdf. On the authorship of the Deuteronomistic History, see the section, "Composition and Redaction of the Deuteronomistic History," in the introduction.

3. On "sons of the prophets," see commentary for 2 Kings 2 and 2 Kings 21.

4. Mordechai Cogan and Hayim Tadmor, *II Kings: A New Translation with Introduction and Commentary*, AB 11 (Garden City, NY: Doubleday, 1988), 57.

5. Julie Faith Parker, *Valuable and Vulnerable: Children in the Hebrew Bible, Especially the Elisha Cycle*, BJS 355 (Providence, RI: Brown University Press, 2013), 120.

2 Kgs 4:1-7

4:1Now the wife of a member of the company of prophets cried to Elisha, "Your servant my husband is dead; and you know that your servant feared the LORD, but a creditor has come to take my two children as slaves." 2Elisha said to her, "What shall I do for you? Tell me, what do you have in the house?" She answered, "Your servant has nothing in the house, except a jar of oil." 3He said, "Go outside, borrow vessels from all your neighbors, empty vessels and not just a few. 4Then go in, and shut the door behind you and your children, and start pouring into all these vessels; when each is full, set it aside." 5So she left him and shut the door behind her and her children; they kept bringing vessels to her, and she kept pouring. 6When the vessels were full, she said to her son, "Bring me another vessel." But he said to her, "There are no more." Then the oil stopped flowing. 7She came and told the man of God, and he said, "Go sell the oil and pay your debts, and you and your children can live on the rest."

Elisha is immediately attentive to the widow's cry (2 Kgs 4:2): "Elisha said to her, 'What shall I do for you? Tell me, what do you have in the house?'" The oddly sensitive and caring response by Elisha—the child/youth-slewing prophet of 2 Kings 2—to the widow's cry has also been noticed by other scholars. Parker writes that Elisha seems much more personable and human here.[6] A more cynical reading, however, suggests that it is the social location of the woman—a widow of one of the sons of the prophets (v. 1)—that may explain the real reason for Elisha's involvement. She is not just a poor woman, but the widow of a fellow prophet, a fact that she emphasizes twice by reminding Elisha that her deceased husband was his "servant" and that he feared the Lord.[7] Robert Wilson even suggests that these sons of the prophets were similar to "members of a peripheral possession cult."[8] Whatever the relationship between Elisha and this group, it appears that Elisha deems the woman's situation as worthy of his attention possibly because of her husband's membership in this group. As Volkmar Fritz more pointedly notes, it is not about the woman but the special care that Elisha "bestows on the community of prophets."[9]

6. Ibid., 122.

7. Hens-Piazza, *1–2 Kings*, 250.

8. Robert R. Wilson, *Prophecy and Society in Ancient Israel* (Philadelphia: Fortress, 1980), 202, also 140–41.

9. Volkmar Fritz, *1 & 2 Kings*, trans. Anselm Hagedorn, CC (Minneapolis: Fortress, 2003), 247.

Some scholars have argued that women prophets might have been part of this cohort (see commentary on 2 Kgs 21).[10] Though "children of the prophet" is a possible translation of בני־הנביאים, the emphasis in the stories about Elijah and Elisha, as I have tried to show, is on the masculine prowess of YHWH as reflected through his male messengers. Hence, though more female prophets probably existed in ancient Israel than the biblical text admits, it is difficult to imagine that a prophetic group associated with Elijah and Elisha, the archenemies of the pious Queen Jezebel, would include female religious officials. Hence, בני־הנביאים, especially the group that had a relationship with Elijah and Elisha, likely refers to an all-male cohort. I have thus translated בני־הנביאים as the "sons of the prophets."

Despite the likely all-male membership, what is remarkable about this narrative is the way in which it provides a window into a different group that is rarely mentioned or given voice in the Hebrew biblical text: the widows, wives, and family members of prophets. The widow's designation as the wife of one of the members of the sons of the prophets reveals several interesting things (2 Kgs 4:1). For instance, the text shows that the sons of the prophets were not just composed of a cohort of single, isolated, wandering males, like Elijah and Elisha. Indeed, Elisha's family relationships seem to impinge upon his call in 1 Kings 19:20. In contrast, this pericope informs us that some of the prophets were husbands, fathers, uncles, and grandfathers. That is, some were members of larger family households and groups. For some of these prophetic men (and maybe even women), prophecy seems to have been just a job like any other job, something to do to support the family.

By giving the reader a small glimpse into the hidden family life of the prophets, the narrative also forces the reader to reconsider the difficult lives of the women and children who exist in the shadow of these (largely) male prophetic figures. Viewed in this light, the holy wars waged between Elijah/Elisha and the various monarchs in the books of 1 and 2 Kings, such as Ahab and Jezebel, take on a more terrifying significance. The mention of the deaths of groups of prophets and cultic personnel, whether affiliated with Baal or YHWH, are not only about the demise of individual men. Rather, behind the male prophets lay the

10. Mercedes L. García Bachmann, *Women at Work in the Deuteronomistic History* (Atlanta: Society of Biblical Literature, 2013), esp. 161–76, 174; Wilda C. Gafney, *Daughters of Miriam: Women Prophets in Ancient Israel* (Minneapolis: Fortress, 2008), 15.

untold stories of socio-economic tribulation borne by the spouses and the children on the heels of the breadwinner's demise. The identification of the woman as a widow of a prophet thus reveals the tenuous situation of women and children who remain hidden in the background of various religio-political events.

The story elucidates the particular socio-economical vulnerability faced by women and children. As the pericope shows, even the spouses married to those in the prophetic, godly trade were not safe from economic insecurities. The protection of orphans, widows, and the poor—those who were deemed the most vulnerable in society—was common policy in the ancient Near East.[11] That this widow has to seek out Elisha, instead of a king, paints a damning portrait of the monarchy in Israel. The ones in charge who were supposed to help her had failed to do so.

With no help forthcoming from those in political power, the widow is in a desperate situation as a creditor is about to appear to seize her children as slaves. Hens-Piazza notes that slavery for unpaid debts was an accepted practice in Israel (Exod 21:7), frequently condemned by the prophets as an unethical act despised by God (Amos 2:6; 8:8; Mic 2:9).[12] Adding to the horrors, Parker notes that the widow's statement that a creditor has come to take away her *two* children in 2 Kings 4:1 hints that she may have had other children who were either earlier given away or died as infants for an unstated reason.[13] Moreover, as only a son is mentioned later in the narrative (v. 6), Parker posits that the other remaining child might have been a girl.[14] Unbetrothed girls who were sold into slavery, Carolyn Pressler writes, would have been subject to horrifying situations of rape and sexual abuse as they would have been purchased not just for labor but also for breeding children and for sexual use.[15]

---

11. F. Charles Fensham, "Widow, Orphan, and the Poor in the Ancient Near Eastern Legal and Wisdom Literature," *JNES* 21 (1962): 129–39. See also Mark R. Cohen, "Feeding the Poor and Clothing the Naked: The Cairo Geniza," *The Journal of Interdisciplinary History* 35 (2005): 407–21.

12. Hens-Piazza, *1–2 Kings*, 250.

13. Parker, *Valuable and Vulnerable*, 123.

14. Ibid., 124.

15. Carolyn Pressler, "Wives and Daughters, Bond and Free: Views of Women in the Slave Laws of Exodus 21.2-11," in *Gender and Law in the Hebrew Bible and the Ancient Near East*, ed. Victory H. Matthews, Bernard M. Levinson, and Tikva Frymer-Kensky (Sheffield: Sheffield Academic, 1998), 155.

*Excursus: Girls and Sexual
Abuse in the Ancient Near East*

We may assume that an unbetrothed girl's primary economic value is her sexual and reproductive capacity, and that she typically would be purchased for sexual use and for breeding children, as well as for general labor. A major concern of biblical and cuneiform legal texts having to do with unbethrothed daughters is the economic value of their sexuality. This is seen in Exod. 22.15,16 (Heb) and Deut. 22.28, 29, which require a man who seduces or rapes an unbetrothed girl to pay her father, and in Middle Assyrian Law (MAL) 48, which deals with whether a creditor can marry off a girl he holds as a pledge. It is especially obvious in the Nuzi "daughter and daughter-in-law" contracts that specify the sum the "adopter" pays in exchange for a claim to the girl's bridewealth, or, in the case of prostitution, her fees.[16]

Carolyn Pressler

Once Elisha is alerted to the problem, however, the resolution quickly follows. Elisha asks the widow to find as many vessels as she can and to shut the door and fill the containers with oil, the only thing that the widow has remaining in the house (4:4). The oil keeps flowing until all the vessels are filled, and Elisha tells the widow to use the oil to feed her children and to pay her debts (4:5-7). Harry Hoffner notes that oil in Hittite texts was "included among the elementary needs of the poor which compassionate people are enjoined to meet."[17]

Reproduction and life are doubly emphasized in this story. Not only is the oil continuously regenerated, but the widow's children, the "products" of her reproduction, are also saved from slavery. Though slavery is not the same as death, the children of the widow are allowed, like the oil, to reproduce freely and continually because of this miracle. As is evident, the prophet Elisha, like his master (Elijah) before him, is once again connected to the reproductive, regenerative, and procreative powers of the life-affirming God, YHWH. As we noted in preceding chapters, the emphasis on these particular powers of YHWH, in part, stems from the divine rivalry between YHWH and the Canaanite storm god, Baal. As the stories in 2 Kings keep reminding the reader, it is YHWH who truly possesses the powers of regeneration, reproduction, and life.

16. Pressler, "Wives and Daughters," 155–56.
17. Harry A. Hoffner Jr., "Oil in Hittite Texts," *BA* 58 (1995): 108–14.

The Great Woman of Shunem (4:8-37)

While 2 Kings 4:1-7 centers on Elisha's assistance to a poor, husband-less widow of one of the sons of the prophets, the story that follows (2 Kgs 4:8-36), in sharp contrast, concerns a wealthy, childless, married woman in Shunem, in need of nothing. Indeed, the story begins with the woman giving gifts *to* Elisha only to receive an unprompted gift of a child in return for his gratitude. Whether poor or rich, however, in this chapter, it is the women who are the focus of the stories and the center of all the subsequent actions.

At the beginning of the episode, the Shunammite woman suggests to her husband that they should provide Elisha, whom she identifies as a holy man of God, a little office or vacation room to use when he comes into town (vv. 9-10). Elisha seems to recognize that it is the woman who is his main benefactor and host and thus asks his servant Gehazi what he should give to the woman to thank her in return for her gift (v. 13). When her gift-child dies later in the tale, it is again the woman who, like the widow in the preceding narrative, steps in and saves her child by running to Elisha for help.

It is worth noting that the woman who is the main hero in this narra-tive is rarely directly addressed by Elisha in this pericope. Elisha uses his servant Gehazi as a constant go-between.[18] The oddity of these indirect exchanges is evident in several places in the narrative. For example, when Elisha wants to find out what he can do to reward the woman for her provision of a room, he calls for her to come before him (v. 12). Instead of talking to her directly, however, Elisha then tells Gehazi to ask the woman, who is presumably standing among them, whether Elisha can speak to the king or commander on her behalf (v. 13). When she answers Elisha and Gehazi (seemingly) by replying that she "lives among her own people," which Cogan and Tadmor take as a polite refusal connoting that she is well taken care of by her family[19]—indeed, the woman will speak directly to the king later in 2 Kings 8:6—Elisha again oddly turns to Gehazi, instead of the woman, to ask what other reward he should then offer. It is only after Gehazi informs him that the woman has no child and that her husband is old that Elisha tells Gehazi

---

18. Fokkelien van Dijk-Hemmes,"The Great Woman of Shunem and the Man of God: A Dual Interpretation of 2 Kings 4.8-37," in *A Feminist Companion to Samuel and Kings*, ed. Athalya Brenner, FCB 5 (Sheffield: Sheffield Academic, 1994), 226–27.
19. Cogan and Tadmor, *II Kings*, 57.

⁸One day Elisha was passing through Shunem, where a wealthy woman lived, who urged him to have a meal. So whenever he passed that way, he would stop there for a meal. ⁹She said to her husband, "Look, I am sure that this man who regularly passes our way is a holy man of God. ¹⁰Let us make a small roof chamber with walls, and put there for him a bed, a table, a chair, and a lamp, so that he can stay there whenever he comes to us."

¹¹One day when he came there, he went up to the chamber and lay down there. ¹²He said to his servant Gehazi, "Call the Shunammite woman." When he had called her, she stood before him. ¹³He said to him, "Say to her, Since you have taken all this trouble for us, what may be done for you? Would you have a word spoken on your behalf to the king or to the commander of the army?" She answered, "I live among my own people." ¹⁴He said, "What then may be done for her?" Gehazi answered, "Well, she has no son, and her husband is old." ¹⁵He said, "Call her." When he had called her, she stood at the door. ¹⁶He said, "At this season, in due time, you shall embrace a son." She replied, "No, my lord, O man of God; do not deceive your servant."

¹⁷The woman conceived and bore a son at that season, in due time, as Elisha had declared to her.

¹⁸When the child was older, he went out one day to his father among the reapers. ¹⁹He complained to his father, "Oh, my head, my head!" The father said to his servant, "Carry him to his mother." ²⁰He carried him and brought him to his mother; the child sat on her lap until noon, and he died. ²¹She went up and laid him on the bed of the man of God, closed the door on him, and left. ²²Then she called to her husband, and said, "Send me one of the servants and one of the donkeys, so that I may quickly go to the man of God and come back again." ²³He said, "Why go to him today? It is neither new moon nor sabbath." She said, "It will be all right." ²⁴Then she saddled the donkey and said to her servant, "Urge the animal on; do not hold back for me unless I tell you." ²⁵So she set out, and came to the man of God at Mount Carmel.

When the man of God saw her coming, he said to Gehazi his servant, "Look, there is the Shunammite woman; ²⁶run at once to meet her, and say to her, Are you all right? Is your husband all right? Is the child all right?" She answered, "It is all right." ²⁷When she came to the man of God at the mountain, she caught hold of his feet. Gehazi approached to push her away. But the man of God said, "Let her alone, for she is in bitter distress; the LORD has hidden it from me and has not told me." ²⁸Then she said, "Did I ask my lord for a son? Did I not say, Do not mislead me?" ²⁹He said to Gehazi, "Gird up your loins, and take my staff in your hand, and go. If you meet anyone, give no greeting, and if anyone greets you, do not answer; and lay my staff on the face of the child." ³⁰Then the mother of the child said, "As the LORD lives, and as you yourself live, I will not leave without you." So he rose up and followed her. ³¹Gehazi went on ahead and laid the staff on the face of the child, but there was no sound or sign of life. He came back to meet him and told him, "The child has not awakened."

³²When Elisha came into the house, he saw the child lying dead on his bed. ³³So he went in and closed the door on the two of them and prayed to the LORD. ³⁴Then he got up on the bed and lay upon the child, putting his mouth upon his mouth, his eyes upon his eyes, and his hands upon his hands; and while he lay bent over him, the flesh of the child became warm. ³⁵He got down, walked once to and fro in the room, then got up again and bent over him; the child sneezed seven times, and the child opened his eyes. ³⁶Elisha summoned Gehazi and said, "Call the Shunammite woman." So he called her. When she came to him, he said, "Take your son." ³⁷She came and fell at his feet, bowing to the ground; then she took her son and left.

to call the woman in again (where did she go?). While she stands in the doorway, the prophet finally declares to her directly—in mimicry of the promise to Abraham in Genesis 18:14—that in due season she will bear a son (2 Kgs 4:16). She responds to this promise by telling Elisha to not deceive her (v. 16).

The Shunammite Woman

"No" is the first word uttered by the Shunammite woman in 2 Kings 4:16 after Elisha tells her that she will embrace a son in due time, making her the only woman in the Bible to respond to the annunciation of a pending pregnancy with no. But what does she mean by no? The most common interpretation of her response is to overlook both the force of the no itself and the larger setting for the no, focusing instead on her subsequent plea not to be deceived. Her reply to Elisha is read as an appeal not to tell her that she will have a baby if it is not the truth. She is painted as a distressed, barren woman who has been deprived of the experience of motherhood. Her yearning for a child is agonizing, and a deceptive birth announcement would be unbearable.

But how do we know the Shunammite woman is barren? The text never describes her as barren, and the desire for a child never leaves her lips. In fact, she is not even the one who tells us that she does not have a son. It is Gehazi, Elisha's servant, from whom we learn: "she has no son" (v. 14). It is after Elisha tells her that she will have a son that she responds, "no . . . do not deceive me." But, why does this response have to mean that she is barren?

What if she does not want a child? I can imagine a woman in her doctor's office. She does not want a baby and is afraid of the results. When the doctor enters and tells her she is pregnant, she reluctantly asks, "Are you sure?" She too is not in the mood for deception. Given that the Shunammite woman never mentions wanting a child and that it is possible that she makes her request not to be deceived because she does not want a child, maybe we should be more willing to hear her say no when Elisha tells her she will embrace a child in due time. To take it a step further, there is yet another interpretation of her no. At the beginning of the scene, Elisha summons her to his chamber room where he has lain down. In this horizontal position he makes his announcement (proposition?) that she will be with child. In this scenario we might be able to imagine her two-letter response as a rejection to his rather presumptuous invitation to join him in his bedchamber.

In conclusion, the Shunammite woman's voice is at best ambiguous. Due to our cultural setting and a biblical emphasis on motherhood, we might think her response is clear—she is barren and aches for a child. Given the ambiguity of the text, however, and the ambiguity that often accompanies sexual encounters, perhaps we should be more willing to listen to what she has to say. As the slogan of sexual assault survivors and victim advocates reminds us, no means no!

Anna Bowden

The narrative concludes with an equally odd indirect conference. When the woman approaches the prophet after her child dies in her arms, instead of talking directly to her, Elisha again sends Gehazi to speak to the woman instead (vv. 25-26). Desiring to speak to the prophet directly, the woman lies and tells Gehazi that everything is fine, until she reaches Elisha, at which point she falls at his feet (v. 28). When Elisha again tries to put distance between them by once more sending Gehazi to act, this time as his intermediary healer, the woman insists on Elisha's direct intervention, stating that she will not leave him until he goes with her to her child whose body she has already placed in Elisha's office at her house (v. 30).

All these indirect interactions create an odd, tortuous narrative. More important, it raises the question as to why Elisha is so eager to put distance between himself and this woman. As Fokkelien van Dijk-Hemmes notes, Elisha addresses the woman only twice directly in the entire narrative and only in her capacity as a mother (vv. 16 and 36). Perhaps the prophet has a difficult time viewing this woman beyond her reproductive capacity.[20] Mary Shields observes that, by calling the woman a "great woman" (v. 8) and describing her as independent, wealthy, and active, the beginning part of this story unexpectedly flips the expected patriarchal power dynamics.[21] The presence of a wealthy, active, independent woman without the need of a son seems, however, to have been too much for the male-centric text to sustain—the "patriarchal perspective will and must inevitably return and predominate."[22]

The underlying patriarchal sentiments also explain why the story is so eager to give a child to a woman who, unlike most childless women in the Bible, never states that she seeks or desires one. Rather, by all indications in the narrative, she appears to be living a fulfilling life "among her people" with support from her family, husband, and community. It is the prophet and his assistant who decide in private conversation between themselves that a woman without a child cannot possibly be fulfilled, no matter what she says. It is telling, Shields writes, that, during the conversation about the gift-child when Elisha asks Gehazi about the woman, the prophet does not name her or call her the "great woman" but takes her down a notch by addressing her as simply "this Shunammite" (vv. 12, 36).[23] It appears that it is the men in the narrative who, uncomfortable with receiving gifts from a self-sufficient, childless woman, decide that the birth of a son would entail "the greatest fulfillment in the life of a woman."[24]

Shortly thereafter, the narrative further diminishes the woman's independence by promptly giving her a son, regardless of her stated desires. Once the son appears, the story refocuses around this child whom the mother appears to raise or care for alone. When the child falls dead, it is she who is forced to act to save her child while her husband remains oddly passive and unaware, merely getting a servant to return the child to his mother after he falls ill in a field (4:19-20). Indeed, the onus of this unrequested motherhood, the question of whether this was a gift or a

20. Van Dijk-Hemmes,"The Great Woman of Shunem," 226.

21. Mary E. Shields, "Subverting a Man of God, Elevating a Woman: Role and Power Reversals in 2 Kings 4," *JSOT* 58 (1993): 59–69, esp. 60.

22. Ibid., 66. See also Yairah Amit, "A Prophet Tested: Elisha, the Great Woman of Shunem, and the Story's Double Message," *BibInt* 11 (2003): 279–93.

23. Shields, "Subverting a Man of God," 61.

24. Fritz, *1 & 2 Kings*, 247.

burden, is poignantly present in the woman's reply to the prophet after her son's demise (v. 28): "Did I ask my lord for a son? Did I not say, do not mislead me?" Saddled with a child she did not ask for, she yet seems to be emotionally burdened with the child's care and wellbeing. In the face of an unaware, disengaged husband and an unresponsive prophet, the woman is the only one who seems intent on fighting for the life of her child.

It is difficult to dissent from van Dijk-Hemmes's summation of this narrative as an "extraordinary feast of patriarchal propaganda."[25] Not only does the narrative maintain that women should become mothers no matter their wishes or desires, but Elisha's subsequent revivification of the child further acts to diminish the woman's stature. When the boy falls ill and dies, Elisha clumsily revives him, first by laying a staff on his body and then, when that fails, by prayer and bodily contact whereby the prophet touches his mouth, eyes, and hands to those of the child (vv. 31, 34). Fritz suggests that through bodily contact, the life force of Elisha passes on to the dead child, who sneezes, indicating that life has returned to him.[26]

More eerily, the prophet seems to revive the child by mirroring and thus (re)spawning himself. As we saw earlier (see commentary on 2 Kgs 2:1-18), mimicry is also present in 2 Kings 2, where Elisha succeeds Elijah through an act of seeing, mirroring, and doubling. Considering the bodily touch and the twinning imagery in the scene of this boy's revivification, it is unsurprising that van Dijk-Hemmes sees in Elisha's act of resurrection a kind of male rebirthing. Van Dijk-Hemmes argues that the purpose of this narrative is to override and negate the mother's role in the procreation of the child by birthing the child anew through the body and spirit of Elisha, the prophet of YHWH: "Acting as father and mother combined, the man of God has now granted life to the child."[27] Van Dijk-Hemmes notes that, adding insult to injury, the narrative ends with the mother throwing herself at a man's feet for the rebirth/resurrection of a child,

25. Van Dijk-Hemmes,"The Great Woman of Shunem," 227.

26. Fritz, *1 & 2 Kings*, 252.

27. Van Dijk-Hemmes, "The Great Woman of Shunem," 227. Van Dijk-Hemmes likens the role of Elisha here—the one who rebirths the child—to modern-day male ministers, pastors, priests, or doctors. Burke Long writes that not only the biblical text, but interpreters and readers, for theological reasons, have also diminished the role of the Shunammite woman and heightened that of Elisha ("The Shunammite Woman: In the Shadow of the Prophet?," *BRev* 7 [1991]: 12–19).

whom she accepts anew and continues to care for, showing how fathers have more important things to tend to.

While the androcentric bias of the narrative is undeniable, there might, however, be another reason why the story oddly features an unrequested son, scenes of paternal rebirth, and cagey, indirect communications between Elisha and the Shunammite woman. As we noted earlier, the narrative rarely portrays Elisha and the woman speaking directly to each other without Gehazi acting as an intermediary. Indeed, the only two instances when they do speak directly concern the child. Some commentators argue that the strange relationship between Elisha and the woman stems from an attempt to cover up Elisha's unprofessional behavior. According to Gershon Hepner and Mary Shields, among others, there are hints in the text that indicate that Elisha might have been the father of the Shunammite woman's son.[28]

Hepner notes several double entendres in the story that speak of a sexual relationship between the woman and Elisha: (1) like Abishag, David's concubine, the woman is also said to be from Shunem; (2) the presence of the phrase "take a morsel of bread," among other phrases, implies sexual contact in both the story of Abraham and Sarah in Genesis 18:5 and also here in 2 Kings 4:8; (3) the use of the verb "seize" (חזק) in 2 Kings 4:8 has sexual connotations elsewhere in the biblical text (2 Sam 13:14; Jer 20:7; Prov 7:13; Deut 25:11); (4) the woman's offer to Elisha of an attic with a table and lampstand recalls the tabernacle, which in turn, according to Hepner, is defiled by Elisha and the woman's implied sexual act in the attic; and, finally, (5) there are similarities between this tale and the story of the possible adultery among Abimelech, Isaac, and Rebecca in Genesis 26.[29]

While some of Hepner's points are speculative, he is not the only scholar to have noticed hints of a possible relationship between the woman and Elisha. Aside from the strange indirect nature of their interactions, Shields, among others, notes the odd absence of the Shunammite's husband, who is never told about the birth of the child or mentioned as or ever behaves as the child's father, even when the boy falls ill and dies. Moreover, Shields notes that while the husband is explicitly stated to be too old for a child in verse 14, the woman is never said to be barren

28. Gerson Hepner, "There's a Crowd in Shunem: Elisha's Misconduct with the Shunamite Reflects a Polemic against Prophetism," *ZAW* 122 (2010): 387–400; Shields, "Subverting a Man of God," 63.

29. Hepner, "There's a Crowd in Shunem," 389–95.

or old.[30] Mark Roncace notes that the annunciation scene in 2 Kings 4 "completely subverts" and fails to follow the typical pattern of such a type scene in the Bible in that God is never mentioned as involved in the boy's miraculous birth.[31] Yairah Amit and Gerson Hepner observe that the conspicuous absence of the mention of God in Elisha's promise of a son seems to suggest that the "child is *Elisha's* gift to the woman."[32] To this, we can add the oddity of the woman's response after the death of her son, whereby she fails to tell her husband about the boy's demise and instead runs immediately to Elisha. Is she running to the real father? Also to be noted, as we stated earlier, is the strange resurrection scene in which Elisha lays his mouth, eyes, and hands on those of the child, thereby effectively twinning, spawning, and, as van Dijk-Hemmes posits, rebirthing the boy.

Hepner argues that the relationship between Elisha and the woman described here might even entail that of a tripartite breeding relationship whereby a third party, in this case Elisha, facilitates reproduction for a man who is infertile. Literarily, the possibility of Elisha's paternity make some sense to the larger, overall flow of the chapter as well. As we noted earlier, the first episode of this chapter about the destitute widow shows that these prophets were not celibate monks. Rather, some of them had families and children. Perhaps the first story—by showing the reader that prophecy, as a profession, was at times separate from a prophet's personal life—hints that such a double life was even a possibility for Elisha.

Added to these hints is the theme of reproduction and reduplication that runs throughout 2 Kings 4. By depicting Elisha at the center of all these rejuvenating actions, the text suggests that Elisha may be reproductive in more ways than one. Indeed, while Elijah "reproduced" his successor (Elisha), via the visually focused, doubling ascension scene, Elisha is depicted without a successor. Could it be that Elisha does not need a successor because he has produced one in the more profane and common manner? Interestingly, the woman's plea to Elisha when she approaches him about the child—"As the LORD lives, and as you yourself live, I will not leave without you" (2 Kgs 4:30)—is exactly the same

30. Shields, "Subverting a Man of God," 64 n. 9.

31. Mark Roncace, "Elisha and the Woman of Shunem: 2 Kings 4.8-37 and 8.1-6 Read in Conjunction," *JSOT* 91 (2000): 115.

32. Hepner, "There's a Crowd in Shunem," 393; Amit, "A Prophet Tested," 286. Emphasis added.

statement that Elisha says to Elijah during the succession narrative (2 Kgs 2:2, 4, 6).[33] Perhaps the repetition of this phrase further hints at Elisha's spiritual and profane paternity. As these words signified Elisha becoming Elijah's successor and spiritual son in the preceding narrative in 2 Kings 2, so the words spoken in 2 Kings 4 signify how the son of the Shunammite woman, who will soon be revived and reborn (and who might be Elisha's biological son), is Elisha's successor, especially through Elisha's act of rebirth.

While these hypotheses are fascinating, the nature of the relationship between the woman and Elisha is never clearly stated in the text. Certainly, it would have diminished Elisha's reputation as a holy and magical prophet of YHWH to be portrayed as behaving like a common, ordinary man. Nevertheless, clues of a possible relationship have led some commentators to argue that Elisha might be subtly disparaged in this narrative. Aside from the possibility of an intimate relationship between the prophet and the woman, there are other possible failures on the part of Elisha. Namely, he fails to hear about the boy's death from God (v. 27) and fails to revive the child when he instructs Gehazi to place a staff on the child's face (v. 30). These snafus are significant and indicate an attempt to discredit the prophet.[34] Van Dijk-Hemmes even argues that this story of Elisha in 2 Kings 4:8-37 parodies Elijah's interaction with the woman from Zarephath in 1 Kings 17:8-24.[35]

The rebukes, like the relationship between Elisha and the woman, are not clearly spelled out. It may be that the target of the criticism is Gehazi rather than Elisha. It is Gehazi who lays the staff on the boy's face and, hence, it is Gehazi who fails to revive the boy. The same Gehazi, as we will see in the next chapter, is depicted as less than ideal in his role as the prophet's assistant, lying and illegally taking clothes and money from an Aramean general. Moreover, the delay in Elisha's revivification of

33. Jopie Siebert-Hommes, "The Widow of Zarephath and the Great Woman of Shunem: A Comparative Analysis of Two Stories," in *A Feminist Companion to the Bible: Samuel and Kings,* ed. Athalya Brenner, FCB 7 (Sheffield: Sheffield Academic, 2000), 106.

34. Amit, "A Prophet Tested," 291–92; van Dijk-Hemmes, "The Great Woman of Shunem," 228; Hepner, "There's a Crowd in Shunem," 387–99; Roncace, "Elisha and the Woman of Shunem," esp. 124–25; Siebert-Hommes "The Widow of Zarephath and the Great Woman," 98–114.

35. Van Dijk-Hemmes, "The Great Woman of Shunem," 228. Jopie Siebert-Hommes offers a detailed comparison of the two stories ("The Widow of Zarephath and the Great Woman," 98–115).

the boy might not be a clear criticism either. Rather, it can be explained as showing the difficulties involved in resurrecting a human being. As 2 Kings 4 makes it clear, it is much easier to reduplicate food or oil or substances than it is to revive a person.

Some of Elisha's failures can also be interpreted as possible hints of Elisha's paternity. Perhaps the child will not waken unless he is rebirthed and twinned through bodily contact with his real father. According to van Dijk-Hemmes, the boy's cries of "My head, my head" in verse 19 might really be about wanting to know the identity of his father (or head).[36] The first failed attempt to revive the boy with the use of Elisha's staff, which according to van Dijk-Hemmes, symbolizes the phallus, is about the rejection and denial of Gehazi's spiritual paternity. The second attempt through bodily contact, in contrast, establishes Elisha's paternity.[37] What looks like failure, in other words, might be another hint of Elisha's personal involvement with the great woman from Shunem, something the text does not want to reveal outright. As we will see, this will not be the final indirect contact the two figures will have with each other (see 2 Kgs 8:1-6). Elisha will reemerge, albeit indirectly, when Gehazi helps the Shunammite woman to reacquire her land in 2 Kings 8.

From a feminist perspective, a better way to read Elisha's unsuccessful first attempt to revive the child is to see it as less about the prophet and his possible failure than about the woman and her triumph and reputation. In other words, commentators, by focusing on the prophet, have missed the activity and success of the great woman. What the text clearly shows is that she is the one who is ultimately proven correct and indeed prophetic in her actions concerning her child after he falls ill. She is the one who knows where to go, what needs to be done, and how to get it accomplished so that her son will live again. She knows that Elisha and only Elisha can revive her son and therefore gets her dead child ready by laying him on Elisha's bed before running to get Elisha for aid. She is the one who knows that only the direct intervention of Elisha and not an intermediary healer, like Gehazi, is necessary to successfully cause the miracle. Hence, she does not let Elisha go until he agrees to follow her back home to her child. She is the one who knows that telling Gehazi or her husband about the child's death only wastes valuable time and, hence, says nothing until she reaches the prophet. By

---

36. Van Dijk-Hemmes, "The Great Woman of Shunem," 227.
37. Ibid.

looking only at Elisha's actions and his lack of immediate success, we miss how prescient, active, and successful the woman and, indeed, the widowed woman before her are in protecting, saving, and supporting their children and family. No matter the reputation of the prophet, at the end of the narrative, it is the woman who emerges as the true hero. She is indeed the great person of Shunem!

The Child in the Refrigerator

The miraculous birth motif (a previously barren woman giving birth) appears frequently in the Hebrew Bible, such as with the births of Isaac (Gen 21), Samson (Judg 13), or Samuel (1 Sam 1). This motif highlights the child's significance, but in 2 Kings 4:8-37 the miracle child serves no function other than to be born, die, and be resurrected. This narrative focuses instead on the child's mother, the woman of Shunem, and her faithfulness, using the child only as a plot device. He is the Hebrew Bible's equivalent to the woman in the refrigerator.

Comic book writer Gail Simone first articulated the "Women-in-Refrigerator" syndrome in 1999 to describe a common comic book trope where female characters are injured, killed, or depowered for the sole purpose of developing the male protagonists' storylines. Simone named the trope after Alexandra DeWitt's death and literal refrigeration in *Green Lantern* #54 (1994). Not a fully developed character in her own right, her death serves as a plot device in the hero's story, providing the motivation for Green Lantern to confront the villain.[38]

In 2 Kings 4, the gender of the characters has been swapped, but the trope explains the purpose of the miracle child. This story resembles Elijah's resurrection of the widow's son in 1 Kings 17, with Elisha proving himself just as capable as his mentor, resurrecting the child when Gehazi cannot (2 Kgs 4:31). The text also portrays the woman of Shunem as even more faithful than Elijah's widow. While the widow simply berates Elijah, the woman of Shunem remains confident that Elisha can resurrect her son (vv. 22-30). Though his very birth was a miracle, she is assured of another. Thus, the "child in the refrigerator" serves as a plot device to illustrate the woman's faithfulness and Elisha's power as surpassing that of the widow and Elijah.

M. L. Case

---

38. For more information on the "Women in Refrigerators" motif and a list of such characters in comic books, see Simone's website, http://lby3.com/wir/index.html.

Famine, Poisonous Stew, and the Marginalized (4:38-41)

The third narrative returns to the sons of the prophets by describing Elisha as interceding on the group's behalf in a moment of need. Continuing the theme of reproduction and life, the story here concerns a pot of stew made for a group of prophets during famine into which is added a poisonous plant.

Similar to the first narrative of 2 Kings 4, this story reveals the desperate pecuniary state of the prophets (and their unmentioned families), especially during times of hardship. The prophets are hungry and starving, and in order to scrounge up enough food, the servant adds to the pot a plant that he finds, which unbeknownst to him is poisonous (2 Kgs 4:39). What is to provide desperately needed nourishment for the group suddenly shifts and morphs into a harbinger of death.

From a postcolonial perspective, this sudden change clearly elucidates the razor-thin line that separates life from death for those who live on the margins, especially during times of difficulty. In so doing, the narrative reminds the reader of similar situations of need and hunger currently faced by those on the periphery of society throughout the world, even in the richest of nations. Hens-Piazza, reflecting on the narratives in 2 Kings 4, writes that they reveal "the distressful conditions in which the peasants were forced to live, specifically under the Omrides, and perhaps more generally during most of the period of the monarchy," whereby the most economically, socially, and politically vulnerable are left defenseless, deserted, and hungry.[39]

The biblical narrative again shines a light on the unfortunate victims of an impious and unethical political system. Such systems, which induce starvation, sickness, misery, and death, are juxtaposed and contrasted to the procreative, fruitful life offered by YHWH. This contradistinction is evident in the sudden shift from death to life in this story as Elisha's addition of flour makes the soup suddenly edible. By showing the desperate situation of the prophets, the narrative aligns them with the poor and the desperate. In so doing, the God of these prophets, YHWH, is also placed on the side of those who are marginal and suffering.

The Multiplication of Food for the Hungry (4:42-44)

Similar sentiments underlie the last story of 2 Kings 4 about the man of God's multiplication of food. Reinforcing the idea of YHWH as the

---

39. Hens-Piazza, *1–2 Kings*, 255.

38When Elisha returned to Gilgal, there was a famine in the land. As the company of prophets was sitting before him, he said to his servant, "Put the large pot on, and make some stew for the company of prophets." 39One of them went out into the field to gather herbs; he found a wild vine and gathered from it a lapful of wild gourds, and came and cut them up into the pot of stew, not knowing what they were. 40They served some for the men to eat. But while they were eating the stew, they cried out, "O man of God, there is death in the pot!" They could not eat it. 41He said, "Then bring some flour." He threw it into the pot, and said, "Serve the people and let them eat." And there was nothing harmful in the pot.

42A man came from Baal-shalishah, bringing food from the first fruits to the man of God: twenty loaves of barley and fresh ears of grain in his sack. Elisha said, "Give it to the people and let them eat." 43But his servant said, "How can I set this before a hundred people?" So he repeated, "Give it to the people and let them eat, for thus says the LORD, 'They shall eat and have some left.'" 44He set it before them, they ate, and had some left, according to the word of the LORD.

source of abundance, life, and sustenance, this story describes how a man of God continually reproduces the firstfruits that he receives in order to feed a large group of hungry people.

For many readers in developed countries, surrounded by easily accessible comestibles, the significance of this narrative is lost. Yet in the ancient world, this act of food reproduction, especially if set in the same context as the preceding narrative—during famine—would be viewed as a powerful, awe-inspiring miracle; a testimony to YHWH's gracious providence and provision. This pericope asks the reader to imagine throngs of hungry and desperate men, women, and children surrounding a slightly bewildered and confused man. The man of God passes out food as fast as possible, and only after everyone has been fed does he discover the extent of the miracle of which he has been a part.

Here again, as in the preceding narrative about the poisonous stew, the narrative describes an instance where death is transformed into life. This shift, according to Jan Heller, has a theological significance, showing how the usual life cycle of nature has been upended and mismanaged by Baal and his worshipers, many of whom, the text accuses, are part of the monarchy. That this narrative is about the death and destruction caused by YHWH's rival deity, Baal, is evident in the name of the man who is offering food—he is described as someone from Baal-shalisha.[40] As we have seen in other parts of 2 Kings, this pericope too interprets the suffering in Israel through the lens of a larger religious and theological contest: as a fight between the two male storm deities, Baal and YHWH, to be recognized as the chief divinity possessing the feminine powers of life, fertility, and reproduction.

40. Jan Heller, "Tod in Topfe: 2 Kön 4:38-41," *CV* 10 (1967): 71.

2 Kings 5:1-27

The Powerless as Conduits of YHWH's Power

In this chapter, the text continues its focus on the restorative and productive power of YHWH as manifested through his prophet by describing Elisha's healing of Naaman's leprosy. Stressing YHWH's curative powers as extending to and effective for foreigners, this story again points to YHWH as the ultimate and true deity of life and healing. From a feminist point of view, though the narrative of 2 Kings 5 is centered on the healing and journey of Naaman, an Aramean military commander, the real star of this story is an anonymous, displaced servant girl who transforms Naaman's life with her statement about the existence of a healing prophet in Israel. While the preceding chapter depicted Elisha's aid to those hungry and suffering on the margins, this chapter focuses on the ways in which those on the margins function as significant and faithful conduits of YHWH's restorative gifts.

The Israelite Slave Girl and the Leprous General (5:1-4)

The story in 2 Kings 5 begins in Aram, a country located north of Israel (modern Syria), which is depicted as an enemy of Israel throughout Kings. In Aram, we are introduced to Naaman, a high-ranking, rich army commander with leprosy.[1] Gina Hens-Piazza comments that it is

---

1. There is some debate about the identity of the disease. W. Alan Smith argues that leprosy here is *leuke*, a whitening or discoloration of the skin pigment, and not Hansen's

2 Kgs 5:1-4

⁵:¹Naaman, commander of the army of the king of Aram, was a great man and in high favor with his master, because by him the LORD had given victory to Aram. The man, though a mighty warrior, suffered from leprosy. ²Now the Arameans on one of their raids had taken a young girl captive from the land of Israel, and she served Naaman's wife. ³She said to her mistress, "If only my lord were with the prophet who is in Samaria! He would cure him of his leprosy." ⁴So Naaman went in and told his lord just what the girl from the land of Israel had said.

odd that the chapter begins with such a positive appraisal of a member of an enemy nation of Israel, an Aramean who is said to have obtained the favor of both Aram's king and also the God of Israel (2 Kgs 5:1).² The mention of divine and royal regard stresses his illness—the one blight on his otherwise blessed life.

The statement that YHWH favored Naaman by allowing him to lead successful military campaigns, presumably even against Israel, is particularly significant (2 Kgs 5:1). By identifying the source of Naaman's military victories as YHWH, the text not only serves to introduce a key character of the drama that will follow—the Israelite girl who was taken and enslaved by the Arameans during one of their successful raids—but also sets up the theological trajectory of the narrative. In the story, with knowledge obtained from the Israelite girl, the foreigner Naaman will move from initial ignorance of the divine source of his success to a personal, intimate understanding of YHWH as he experiences the healing powers of the God of Israel. Considering this movement, it is unsurprising that this tale has been read as a conversion story by many commentators. From a meta-literary point of view, the reader, through the narrative, is also invited to experience and witness the restorative power of YHWH.

The statement that Naaman's military victory stems from YHWH raises the question as to why God presumably allowed his own country to be defeated by Aram. Adding to the mystery, Philip Satterthwaite writes that this is the only time in the Hebrew text that YHWH is said

---

disease (W. Alan Smith, "Naaman and Elisha: Healing, Wholeness, and the Task of Religious Education," *Religious Education* 89 [1994]: 206). On different meanings of leprosy in the Hebrew Bible, see Judith Z. Abrams, "*Metzora(at) Kashaleg*: Leprosy, Challenges to Authority in the Bible," *JBQ* 21 (1993): 41–45.

2. Gina Hens-Piazza, *1–2 Kings*, AOTC (Nashville: Abingdon, 2006), 258–59.

to "give victory" (נתן־יהוה תשועה) to another nation.[3] In this, we can detect a criticism of Israel's monarchy—a criticism that will get louder as the narrative progresses. Since military defeat is a sign of divine disfavor, YHWH seemingly has allowed Israel to be defeated by Aram because he is displeased with its kings. From a theological standpoint, this detail also hints toward a larger divine purpose or plan. Perhaps God has allowed Naaman to be militarily successful, even against his own country, so that a captured, unnamed slave girl can enter Naaman's home and become the conduit through which God can perform his healing and thus affect a theological shift in Naaman. If this text were edited during the exilic period of later times, as Walter Brueggemann argues, the idea of a larger divine universal plan would have been particularly meaningful for an exilic or postexilic community.[4]

While the chapter begins with the introduction of the Aramean general, many commentators consider the unnamed slave girl, who embodies the universal life-giving powers of YHWH,[5] to be the true protagonist of the narrative. As the only person explicitly designated a "little girl" (נערה) who has a speaking part in the Hebrew Bible, her uniqueness is evident.[6] She is said to have been taken by the Arameans on one of their raids and enslaved as a servant to Naaman's wife. Brueggemann speculates that the young girl might have been taken captive by the Syrians during one of their military engagements with Israel and might even have been used and abused before ending up as a servant to the commander.[7] The existence of Deuteronomic rules for conduct when dealing with seized enemy women during military campaigns indicate that the seizure of women during combat was not uncommon (Deut 20:14; 21:10-14).[8]

---

3. Philip Satterthwaite, "The Elisha Narratives and Coherence of 2 Kings 2–8," *TynBul* 49 (1998): 16 n. 42.

4. Walter Brueggemann, "A Brief Moment for a One-Person Remnant (2 Kings 5:2-3)," *BTB* 31 (2001): 56–58.

5. Brueggemann, "A Brief Moment," 53; Jean Kyoung Kim, "Reading and Retelling Naaman's Story (2 Kings 5)," *JSOT* 30 (2005): 53; Esther M. Menn, "A Little Girl Shall Lead Them: The Role of the Little Israelite Servant Girl (2 Kings 5:1-19)," *CurTM* 35 (2008): 243; Lai Ling Elizabeth Ngan, "2 Kings 5," *RevExp* 94 (1997): 594.

6. Julie Faith Parker, *Valuable and Vulnerable: Children in the Hebrew Bible, Especially the Elisha Cycle*, BJS 355 (Providence, RI: Brown University Press, 2013), 161.

7. Brueggemann, "A Brief Moment," 53.

8. For more on children and captivity in the Hebrew Bible and the ancient world, see Parker, *Valuable and Vulnerable*, 170–72.

This seemingly insignificant young woman whose name, age, background, and personality are unstated in the text drives the narrative forward with a single statement. She says to Naaman's wife that there is a prophet in Samaria, seemingly Elisha, who can cure Naaman of his leprosy (v. 3). Brueggemann writes that the girl's utterance is theologically significant, "an understated testimony to the God of Israel who authorizes this prophet and who is, as will be clear by the end of the narrative, the God to whom despairing Syrians will also submit."[9] More significant, the girl's statement reveals a glimpse into the family life of Naaman, as evident in the unrecorded conversations between the various characters of this pericope. Though the girl seems to say this single sentence out of the blue, we can safely assume that it comes in the middle of an unrecorded conversation with her mistress during which they are discussing Naaman's illness. Moreover, though also absent, Naaman's wife seems to have told her husband about the existence of this Israelite prophet, as the next verse depicts the commander talking to the Aramean king about the presence of a possible cure in Israel (2 Kgs 5:4). These unrecorded conversations provide a window into the characters' domestic life and, in particular, the disturbance that Naaman's affliction would have caused to his family and spouse. That his wife is depicted as talking about his ailment with her servant girl shows the extent to which she was distressed by her husband's illness. Also worth noting is that no sons or daughters are mentioned in the story; perhaps this ailment has something to do with it.

Considering the patriarchal background of the narrative, we are told very little about the wife or the family or even the Israelite slave girl who changes Naaman's life with her single statement. Though it is clear that many people—women, men, and children—are affected by Naaman's health, the story records only the deeds and actions of the principal male characters. We know little about the girl, what her background was, how she came to be in her current situation, how she was treated by Naaman's family, whether she was ever thanked for her advice, or whether she remained a slave after Naaman's return. She speaks and then disappears. Another detail in the narrative worth mentioning is what some commentators have noted in the description of Naaman's skin as that of a young boy after he is healed (v. 14). This might be another subtle reference to this young woman who initiated the commander's journey.[10]

9. Brueggemann, "A Brief Moment," 54.

10. Burke O. Long, *2 Kings*, FOTL 10 (Grand Rapids, MI: Eerdmans, 1991), 66–76; Brueggemann, "A Brief Moment," 56.

The Powerful Israelite Slave Girl

To speak of a "powerful slave" seems oxymoronic, especially if that slave is a young girl. Yet 2 Kings 5:10-14 presents a small girl (קטנה- נערה) with great influence. On the one hand, she is the picture of vulnerability: a small, young, foreign, captive, anonymous girl who serves. She stands in stark contrast to her master Naaman: a great, adult, commanding, revered man who conquers. All Naaman's power, however, does not spare him agony, for he is afflicted by a terrible skin disease. The marginalized and disenfranchised slave girl voices a simple and sincere hope that Naaman would be healed of the condition that afflicts him. In Hebrew she utters ten words: oh-that my-master [would-go] before the-prophet who is-in-Samaria then he-would-cure him of-his-leprosy. Amazingly, the Israelite slave girl's suggestion spurs action among the most powerful people in the land, including Naaman, the kings of Aram and Israel, and eventually the prophet Elisha. When Naaman is cured after following through on the girl's wish, his skin becomes like that of a little child (נער קטן, *na`ar qāṭān*), echoing the description of the Israelite slave girl (נערה-קטנה, *na`ărāh qĕṭannāh*). The great commander has become like the humble slave, not only in outward appearance, but also in knowledge of the power of the prophet in Samaria.

Despite her youth and lowly social status, clearly this child is respected for her suggestion to be taken so seriously. Moreover, she is the only girl explicitly called "little" who speaks in the entire Hebrew Bible. While other girls and young women speak and take action, such as Jephthah's daughter in Judges 11 or Moses' sister in Exodus 2, they are not called "little" and may well be pubescent or older. While she is a slave, the Israelite girl in 2 Kings 5 is also a pioneer. Her words, belief, and conviction extend the boundaries of our understanding of young girls in the Hebrew Bible.

Julie Faith Parker

The central concern of the narrative is clearly not focused on the girl or her story. As Brueggemann notes, none of the male characters in the story allude to, thank, or commend the girl even though "their more dramatic roles are all informed and made possible by her initial bold and compelling declaration that is pure gift without return."[11] A masculine-centered

---

11. Brueggemann, "A Brief Moment," 56.

reading shows that 2 Kings 5 is centered around the male body as a "textual site of contestation for male power and religious identity."[12] Unsurprisingly, most of the narrative remains fixated on the main male character and *his* physical and spiritual transformations.

As a result, it has been left to modern interpreters to give the young woman her deserved due. Short of rewriting the story to make the child the main actor—which Jean Young Kim does in her article[13]—the paucity of information on this figure compels the reader to search for the lingering strands of her story by juxtaposing her to other, more textually prominent characters. The girl has been thus compared to a variety of figures. Some commentators contrast the young girl to Naaman, for example.[14] While the girl is an Israelite, a "little" maiden, a captive servant, without fame or even a name, Naaman, conversely, is a "great" or "big" man, a commander who is regarded by the Aramean king as well as by YHWH.[15] This contradistinction, according to Robert Cohn, heightens the irony of the narrative whereby the "lowest of the low, a female Israelite captive, is heeded by the great king of Syria," as her statement travels via her mistress to her husband, to, finally, the Aramean king.[16] Brueggemann views the girl as an antithesis to Gehazi (Elisha's servant [2 Kgs 4]) and as a forerunner to what Naaman becomes, "both in skin and in faith."[17] Julie Faith Parker too contrasts the girl, not to Naaman, but to the Israelite king, who, though master over his land, remains impiously ignorant of the possessors of prophetic and divine powers that roam his domain.[18]

12. Cheryl Strimple and Ovidiu Creangă, "'And His Skin Returned Like a Skin of a Little Boy': Masculinity, Disability and the Healing of Naaman," in *Men and Masculinity in the Hebrew Bible and Beyond*, ed. Ovidiu Creangă (Sheffield: Sheffield Phoenix, 2010), 110–26.

13. Kim, "Reading and Retelling Naaman's Story," 49–61.

14. Robert L Cohn, "Form and Perspective in 2 Kings," *VT* 33 (1983): 171–84; Kim, "Reading and Retelling," 52; Menn, "A Little Girl," 342; Long, *2 Kings*, 70.

15. Cohn, "Form and Perspective," 174; Long, *2 Kings*, 70; Parker, *Valuable and Vulnerable*, 161.

16. Cohn, "Form and Perspective," 175.

17. Brueggemann, "A Brief Moment," 56–57.

18. Parker, *Valuable and Vulnerable*, 168.

A Powerful Girl

I was a stranger in a foreign land when I first found myself immersed in the story of Naaman. Hours after my fellow volunteers and I stepped off the plane to begin a year of service in India, our site coordinator summoned us to his kitchen table and drew our attention to this text. The story was an invitation for us to consider our privilege, particularly as white college graduates from the United States, and the legacy of colonization our presence recalled. It was an invitation to listen to voices from the margins, speaking truth to power. It was an invitation for us—like Naaman—to find transformation in a foreign land.

Throughout the narrative it is the lowly who facilitate Naaman's healing. The Aramean commander learns of the prophet who can cure his leprosy, not from society's elite, but from an Israelite captive who serves his wife. This child could not be more different from Naaman. While he is a mighty warrior, she is a spoil of war; while he is a great man, she is a powerless girl.

Yet, she is the one who plants a seed of hope for a commander suffering from leprosy. Though Naaman turns next to "proper" channels, it is the servants who continue to point toward healing. When Naaman arrives at Elisha's house with a parade of chariots bursting with riches, the prophet sends a messenger with instructions to wash in the Jordan. When the commander threatens to return to the "superior" rivers of Damascus, his servants encourage him to heed Elisha's command. It is only by listening to these voices from the margins and immersing himself in the waters of a foreign land that Naaman finds transformation. Interestingly, after he has washed seven times, his flesh becomes "like the flesh of a young boy [נער]." Healed of his disease, Naaman is now linked rhetorically to the young girl (נערה) who first pointed him to the man of God. Led by a child to healing, the childlike Naaman returns home with new understanding of God. Perhaps, we can imagine, he too will point others toward transformation.

Sudie Niesen Thompson

Commentators have recognized the little girl's significance in the narrative, especially the theological meanings she embodies. Esther M. Menn, for example, likens her to a young David and states that the point of the narrative is to show the deceptive nature of appearances. This story, according to Menn, "presents a sustained and ironic contrast between what appears big and important, and what appears small and insignificant" by inverting their expected valuation.[19] Brueggemann too takes the girl as a type of theological model and object lesson. Seeing parallels between the girl and modern people living in a bilingual existence, he argues that this character embodies, both to the modern reader and to the Israelites in the exilic or postexilic context, a way to responsibly and faithfully live in a displaced environment "marked by suffering and despair."[20] Parker sums up the importance of this character with her assessment that the girl, while poor, unnamed, and ignored by text and society, embodies those qualities esteemed by the biblical text: faith, knowledge, communication abilities, and kindness.[21]

Royal Reactions and the Reactions of the People at the Margins (5:5-7)

In the depiction of the unnamed girl, a sharp criticism of the northern kings and of the monarchy in general can be detected. This rebuke is evident in the description of the reactions of the Aramean and Israelite kings when the girl's message about the presence of a healing prophet reaches their ears. When Naaman tells his king the servant girl's news, the king of Aram sends Naaman to Israel with a reference letter. When the letter reaches the unnamed king of Israel, he reacts with despair and paranoia, believing that it is a trap by the Aramean king to corner him into a fight. The reaction of the Israelite king damns him as well as the monarchic system of Israel in several ways. First, as Menn has argued, the existence of an enslaved, captured, Israelite girl in a foreign land disparages the king by clearly displaying his inability to protect his country and its citizens.[22] As we have seen and will continue to see in other chapters of this book, the marginalized of society, such as children, widows, women, and the poor, are continually depicted as harmed and victimized by an uncaring, impious political system.

Parker goes further and argues that the king of Israel is purposefully portrayed as the antithesis of the Israelite girl. Indeed, one wonders whether both the king and the girl are deliberately unnamed in order to provide such a contrast. While the unnamed girl, forced into service in another land remembers the presence of a powerful prophet in her

19. Menn, "A Little Girl," 342.
20. Brueggemann, "A Brief Moment," 56–57.
21. Parker, *Valuable and Vulnerable*, 161.
22. Menn, "A Little Girl," 342.

---

2 Kgs 5:5-7

[5]And the king of Aram said, "Go then, and I will send along a letter to the king of Israel."

He went, taking with him ten talents of silver, six thousand shekels of gold, and ten sets of garments. [6]He brought the letter to the king of Israel, which read, "When this letter reaches you, know that I have sent to you my servant Naaman, that you may cure him of his leprosy." [7]When the king of Israel read the letter, he tore his clothes and said, "Am I God, to give death or life, that this man sends word to me to cure a man of his leprosy? Just look and see how he is trying to pick a quarrel with me."

---

home country, the king, with all his servants, armies, and retinue, who seemingly is in charge of the land, is oddly ignorant that such a prophet of YHWH exists.[23] This depiction shows, according to Parker, that "prodigious wisdom is not limited to outwardly impressive people."[24] Brueggemann and Cohn also argue that this negative depiction of the king is a *Leitmotiv* of prophetic narratives in general, which frequently depict the monarch as ineffective, idiotically unaware, and generally irrelevant.[25]

This depiction, aside from deriding the impotence and ridiculous posturing of monarchs, again sets up a contrast between the real, effective power of YHWH and the false, failing pretensions of power affected by the human kings, especially in the land of Israel. Moreover, the fact that the Aramean king sends a reference letter for Naaman to the Israelite monarch instead of to the prophet—the only person who can cure the commander, according to the little girl—shows his confusion about the divine origins of such a cure. What the narrative emphasizes is that healing powers do not reside with the kings and, hence, cannot be commanded by them. Rather, as Menn states, such restorative powers belong to YHWH alone.[26]

This lack of understanding on the part of the monarchs again emphasizes the physical and spiritual "journey" that Naaman takes in this narrative as he moves from a similar ignorance to a personal awareness and experience of the healing deity, YHWH. That a foreigner is able to realize the power of YHWH at the end of this narrative further adds to

---

23. Parker, *Valuable and Vulnerable*, 168.
24. Ibid.
25. Brueggemann, "A Brief Moment," 56; Cohn, "Form and Perspective," 176.
26. Menn, "A Little Girl," 343.

the criticisms of kings. W. Alan Smith sees a connection between Naaman's story and that of Ahaziah's sickness in 2 Kings 1. He argues that while 2 Kings 5 describes a foreigner, an Israelite enemy, who is made well because he seeks out a prophet of YHWH in the land of Israel, 2 Kings 1, in contrast, describes an Israelite monarch who dies as a result of seeking out a prophet of a foreign deity in a foreign land.[27] As is clear, foreigners—even foreign military commanders—and enslaved children are shown as wiser, more aware, and more pious than the kings of Israel.

The Marginalized and Powerless as Conduits of Healing (5:8-14)

Naaman's recognition of the divine origins of his healing is intimately linked to and facilitated by his realization of the true valuation of individuals. When Naaman arrives at the door of Elisha with his horses, chariots, and gifts—his "symbols of social status"[28]—to seek his healing, Elisha is remote, almost rude, not even greeting the visitor directly, but telling the commander through a servant to wash in the river Jordan seven times.[29] Seemingly, Naaman was expecting at least a personal greeting from the prophet and maybe even something more magical, grand, and demonstrative, so he is put off and enraged by Elisha's dismissive reception (v. 12).

This is not the first time, however, that Elisha has tried to perform his miracles remotely. For instance, when the son of the Shunnamite woman dies (2 Kgs 4), Elisha, at first, attempts to send along Gehazi to heal the child and is only persuaded to go with the Shunnamite woman because she clings to him and gives him little choice. The story about Naaman and that of the Shunnamite appear to be connected. Aside from the similarity of Elisha's reaction to both parties, Elisha's command to Naaman to rinse in the Jordan river seven times recalls the seven sneezes of the child of the Shunnamite woman when he is revived (2 Kgs 4:35).[30] Hens-Piazza states that the number seven conveys a sense of completion in the biblical text (Lev 14:7, 16, 27, 51).[31] This allusion to the preceding narrative in 2 Kings 4 compels the reader to compare Naaman and the Shunnamite

27. Smith, "Naaman and Elisha," 212.

28. Long, *2 Kings*, 71.

29. Long, *2 Kings*, 71; Volkmar Fritz, *1 & 2 Kings*, trans. Anselm Hagedorn, CC (Minneapolis: Fortress, 2003), 259; Hens-Piazza, *1–2 Kings*, 260–61.

30. Hens-Piazza, *1–2 Kings*, 260.

31. Ibid.

⁸But when Elisha the man of God heard that the king of Israel had torn his clothes, he sent a message to the king, "Why have you torn your clothes? Let him come to me, that he may learn that there is a prophet in Israel." ⁹So Naaman came with his horses and chariots, and halted at the entrance of Elisha's house. ¹⁰Elisha sent a messenger to him, saying, "Go, wash in the Jordan seven times, and your flesh shall be restored and you shall be clean." ¹¹But Naaman became angry and went away, saying, "I thought that for me he would surely come out, and stand and call on the name of the LORD his God, and would wave his hand over the spot, and cure the leprosy! ¹²Are not Abana and Pharpar, the rivers of Damascus, better than all the waters of Israel? Could I not wash in them, and be clean?" He turned and went away in a rage. ¹³But his servants approached and said to him, "Father, if the prophet had commanded you to do something difficult, would you not have done it? How much more, when all he said to you was, 'Wash, and be clean'?" ¹⁴So he went down and immersed himself seven times in the Jordan, according to the word of the man of God; his flesh was restored like the flesh of a young boy, and he was clean.

woman, especially their reactions to the initial disregard of the prophet. Expecting to be treated with more respect as befitting a powerful, rich, male military leader, Naaman is upset with the prophet's disregard. The Shunnamite woman, however, though she is rich, as a female not only is unruffled by the prophet's reaction but seems to expect it, as shown by her preparations. She gets the body of her child ready by laying him on the bed in Elisha's room, she lies to Gehazi saying that everything is all right until she comes face-to-face with Elisha, and then she refuses to leave without Elisha (2 Kgs 4:21, 24-30).

The difference in reaction between Naaman and the woman when faced with the same disregard of Elisha again highlights the message that runs throughout the first chapters of 2 Kings: it is the marginal and powerless—the children, the poor, women, widows, and orphans—who truly possess knowledge of YHWH. This message indeed is doubly emphasized in 2 Kings 5 by the reaction of Naaman's servant to his master's initial anger to Elisha's cold reception toward him. When Naaman reacts with rage at Elisha's instructions through a messenger, another unnamed servant wisely urges him to listen to the prophet, gently noting that a miracle does not have to be complex to be effective (v. 13). The servant's reasoning drives home the message repeated throughout the narrative that appearances are deceiving. As Smith notes, it is through those who appear insignificant—the girl and the unnamed servant—that Naaman's healing is accomplished. In contrast, those who seem powerful, such as the kings of Israel and Aram, are depicted as unable to help the commander.[32] As noted earlier, the description of Naaman's healed skin as like that of a young boy (נער) again alludes to the young Israelite servant girl (נערה) who initiated Naaman's journey. Thus, the text highlights the marginalized as the true servants and conduits of YHWH's miraculous deeds of healing and restoration.

The Advice of the Powerless Leads to Naaman's Transformation (5:15-18)

Listening to his servant's advice, Naaman goes and dips in the river seven times and is healed—his flesh transformed into that of a young boy (v. 14). So wowed and grateful is the Aramean commander that he goes back to the man of God and declares that now he knows there is no God except in Israel (v. 15). Naaman's reaction to his healing clearly shows that he now recognizes the identity of the true deity of restoration, healing, and life. Naaman is so cognizant and thankful of YHWH that he declares that he wants to continue worshiping the deity, even in Aram.

Many scholars have interpreted Naaman's declaration in verse 15—"Now I know that there is no God in all the earth except in Israel"—as indicative of his conversion. Some scholars, such as Walter Maier, Emmanuel Nwaoru, and D. P. O'Brien, argue that Naaman's story reflects his conversion to Yahwism and, hence, should be read as analogous to modern Christian mission trips.[33] Others scholars, however, maintain that Naaman does not convert as this act is understood in the modern vernacular. Rather, he merely indicates his desire to engage in a monolatrous worship of YHWH. Mordechai Cogan and Hayim Tadmor, however, argue that Naaman is a proselyte into the worship of YHWH. This story reflects an expression of "ancient Israelite universalism" wherein YHWH is recognized as the sole deity who is able to work outside of

32. Smith, "Naaman and Elisha," 211.

33. Walter A. Maier III, "The Healing of Naaman in Missological Perspective," *CTQ* 61 (1997): 177–96; Emmanuel O. Nwaoru, "The Story of Naaman (2 Kings 5:1-19): Implication for Mission Today," *SwMT* 96 (2008): 27–41; D. P. O'Brien, " 'Is This the Time to Accept. . . . ?' (2 Kings V 26B): Simply Moralizing (LXX) or an Ominous Foreboding of Yahweh's Rejection of Israel (MT)?" *VT* 46 (1996): 448–57.

[15]Then he returned to the man of God, he and all his company; he came and stood before him and said, "Now I know that there is no God in all the earth except in Israel; please accept a present from your servant." [16]But he said, "As the LORD lives, whom I serve, I will accept nothing!" He urged him to accept, but he refused. [17]Then Naaman said, "If not, please let two mule-loads of earth be given to your servant; for your servant will no longer offer burnt offering or sacrifice to any god except the LORD. [18]But may the LORD pardon your servant on one count: when my master goes into the house of Rimmon to worship there, leaning on my arm, and I bow down in the house of Rimmon, when I do bow down in the house of Rimmon, may the LORD pardon your servant on this one count."

Israel.[34] Hens-Piazza more broadly terms Naaman's transformation as a "spiritual conversion."[35] What Naaman means when he declares his knowledge of YHWH in verse 15 and whether this is indicative of his conversion remain ambiguous.[36]

Related to this question about Naaman's possible conversion is his request to the man of God for two mule-loads of Israelite soil to take back to Aram so that he can continue to worship YHWH (v. 16). Naaman not only wants the soil but also asks that the Lord forgive him when he worships in the House of Rimmon, the national deity of Aram (v. 18). John Gray argues that Naaman's request for forgiveness indicates a desire for the monolatrous worship of YHWH.[37] Though this might be the case, the problem is that there is a slight contradiction between Naaman's declaration of the universality of YHWH in verse 15—"there is no God except in Israel"—and his subsequent request for an amount of soil so that he can worship YHWH properly back home. Is YHWH the only universal God and, if so, why does Naaman require soil from the land of Israel?

34. Mordechai Cogan and Hayim Tadmor, *II Kings: A New Translation with Introduction and Commentary*, AB 11 (Garden City, NY: Doubleday, 1988), 67.

35. Hens-Piazza, *1–2 Kings*, 258.

36. On conversion during antiquity, see Shaye J. D. Cohen, *The Beginnings of Jewishness: Boundaries, Varieties, Uncertainties*, HCS 31 (Berkeley: University of California Press, 1999).

37. John Gray, *I and II Kings*, OTL (Philadelphia: Westminster, 1970), 507.

Some commentators argue that the request for the land indicates Naaman's belief in the "cultic sanctity of the land" whereby YHWH is seen as tied to the land of Israel. Other lands were envisioned as too polluted for the worship of this particular deity.[38] Scholars like Smith, following Gerhard von Rad, maintain that Naaman is confused and does not understand that YHWH's power is not limited to Israel.[39] Nwaoru usefully notes, however, that both ideas—that YHWH worship is limited to the land of Israel and also that YHWH is present and can be worshiped anywhere—can be found throughout the Hebrew corpus.[40] Naaman is depicted as reflecting both religious sentiments, albeit contradictory. Lai Ling Elizabeth Ngan sums it up best when she states that the text does not provide "a neatly worked-out theology, but a tangible expression of his newfound faith."[41]

Reversals of Fortune and Gehazi's Misdeed (5:19-27)

While the story begins with the statement of a faithful servant girl, the narrative concludes with a misdeed by a lying, unfaithful servant of Elisha, Gehazi.

After Elisha mysteriously refuses any payment from Naaman for his healing—Ngan speculates that Elisha deliberately refused Naaman's payment as a way to show how God's power and grace cannot be purchased by wealth or status[42]—Elisha's assistant, Gehazi, whose name Gray translates as "avaricious,"[43] chases after Naaman and lies to the commander about the sudden arrival of fellow prophets so as to receive two talents of silver and two changes of clothing from him. When Gehazi returns, Elisha confronts him and states that he is aware of Gehazi's misdeed since he traveled with him in spirit (v. 26), and he condemns him and his descendants with the same leprosy from which Naaman has

---

38. Cogan and Tadmor, *II Kings*, 67; Cohn, "Form and Perspective," 178.

39. Smith, "Naaman and Elisha," 207, 215.

40. Nwaoru, "The Story of Naaman," 36–37. He writes that the more particularistic view is found in Josh 22:19; Hos 9:3-5; Amos 7:17; 1 Sam 26:19; Ps 137:4 while the more universal idea is present in Gen 24:12; Judg 16:28; 1 Sam 30:6-8, 23, 26; 2 Sam 15:8 (ibid.).

41. Ngan, "2 Kings 5," 593.

42. Ibid., 592.

43. Gray, *I & II Kings*, 508.

[19]He said to him, "Go in peace."

But when Naaman had gone from him a short distance, [20]Gehazi, the servant of Elisha the man of God, thought, "My master has let that Aramean Naaman off too lightly by not accepting from him what he offered. As the LORD lives, I will run after him and get something out of him." [21]So Gehazi went after Naaman. When Naaman saw someone running after him, he jumped down from the chariot to meet him and said, "Is everything all right?" [22]He replied, "Yes, but my master has sent me to say, 'Two members of a company of prophets have come to me from the hill country of Ephraim; please give them a talent of silver and two changes of clothing.'" [23]Naaman said, "Please accept two talents." He urged him, and tied up two talents of silver in two bags, with two changes of clothing, and gave them to two of his servants, who carried them in front of Gehazi. [24]When he came to the citadel, he took the bags from them, and stored them inside; he dismissed the men, and they left.

[25]He went in and stood before his master; and Elisha said to him, "Where have you been, Gehazi?" He answered, "Your servant has not gone anywhere at all." [26]But he said to him, "Did I not go with you in spirit when someone left his chariot to meet you? Is this a time to accept money and to accept clothing, olive orchards and vineyards, sheep and oxen, and male and female slaves? [27]Therefore the leprosy of Naaman shall cling to you, and to your descendants forever." So he left his presence leprous, as white as snow.

just been cured (v. 27). Cohn writes that since Gehazi stole Naaman's possessions, so he now also inherits the disease.[44]

As Cohn notes, the portrayal of Gehazi in 2 Kings 5 does not fit stories of him found elsewhere in 2 Kings, which may indicate the independent nature of this particular pericope.[45] When we encounter Gehazi again in 2 Kings 8, there is no indication of the leprosy he receives as a result of his illegal interactions with Naaman. The question is why Gehazi is portrayed so negatively here. Though difficult to prove, perhaps this part of the narrative functions as an explanation of why Gehazi does not become the successor to Elisha in the same way that Elisha became Elijah's successor. It provides an explanation of why the spirit of Elijah ceases to exist in Israel, even though Gehazi leads a band of prophets after the death of Elijah's protégé, Elisha. In fact, Gehazi's story ends

44. Cohn, "Form and Perspective," 182.
45. Ibid., 171.

when Elisha's does. Perhaps the narrative of Gehazi's "sin" is subtly meant to supply the reason for Gehazi's mysterious disappearance.

Another possible explanation is that this story reflects larger concerns about the nature of prophecy. Considering that both the servant girl and Naaman's accompanying servant offer helpful information and advice without monetary inducement, and considering the rather emphatic refusal of payment by Elisha for Naaman's healing, the narrative appears to show that God's grace and healing are free and available to anyone who seeks them, regardless of wealth, status, or even ethnicity. The restoration offered by YHWH cannot be bought; nor are the human conduits, through whom YHWH chooses to offer rejuvenation, to seek material gain for these God-given abilities. Perhaps undergirding this message is some argumentation over the nature of the prophetic occupation. As we saw in the preceding chapter, prophecy, at times, is depicted as a relatively normal profession, performed by ordinary human beings with dependent spouses and children (2 Kgs 4). This chapter, in contrast, asserts a loftier vision of the prophetic profession and of the prophets of YHWH. Perhaps the preceding chapter had depicted the prophets of YHWH as too mundane and, hence, giving up too much of their divine authority. This chapter thus attempts a corrective, showing Elisha and YHWH's prophets as divinely unsullied, set apart, and therefore unconcerned with earthly things such as money.

The pericope of Gehazi's misdeed may also serve a literary purpose as it neatly draws the chapter to a close by depicting a final reversal in a series of reversals and contrasts: the rich, ruling unnamed kings are shown, at the end, to be actually powerless and uninformed; the unnamed slave girl and Naaman's nameless slave are depicted as the ones who are truly informed, wise, and important, especially in the fulfillment of divine healing; Naaman, the proud, rich, leprous "great man" (v. 1), at the end, is likened to a little boy and is depicted as becoming a humbled servant of Elisha (v. 15). Finally, Naaman, the ex-leper, becomes a servant of Elisha (v. 15) while Gehazi, the real servant of Elisha, is made to become a leper.[46] This final reversal again highlights the chapter's theme that looks are deceiving and that the knowledge and restorative power of YHWH can be manifest in even the lowliest or most unlikely of people.

46. Ibid., 183.

2 Kings 6:1–7:20

Women, Children, and the Sick as Victims of War

Second Kings 6–7 consists of several more episodes featuring Elisha, the prophet. The first part of the narrative concerns the recovery of a lost ax head by Elisha, while the second and third pericopes deal with the combative relationship between Samaria and Aram. Embedded within the two military episodes about Aram is a heartbreaking tale about the victims of warfare and violence: two women and two children, one of whom is killed and eaten during the ensuing famine. The harrowing tale of the cannibalism by desperate, starving mothers functions as the beating heart of these two chapters, overshadowing and bleeding into the stories that precede and follow. As a result, the message asserted in all four pericopes of 2 Kings 6–7—that YHWH is the powerful sovereign deity who reigns supreme over Israel—is undermined by this story. In the face of such a tale describing the horrors and desperation experienced by those most vulnerable in Israelite society, such as the poor, the sick, women, and children, the assertion of YHWH's life-giving power sounds tonally discordant. Renewed attention to such victims, both in the text and outside of the text, remains the only recourse left to the modern reader.

Elisha and the Fallen Ax (6:1-7)

The first episode about the fallen ax head presents another instance in which Elisha comes to aid the sons of the prophets (see discussion

2 Kgs 6:1-7

[6:1]Now the company of prophets said to Elisha, "As you see, the place where we live under your charge is too small for us. [2]Let us go to the Jordan, and let us collect logs there, one for each of us, and build a place there for us to live." He answered, "Do so." [3]Then one of them said, "Please come with your servants." And he answered, "I will." [4]So he went with them. When they came to the Jordan, they cut down trees. [5]But as one was felling a log, his ax head fell into the water; he cried out, "Alas, master! It was borrowed." [6]Then the man of God said, "Where did it fall?" When he showed him the place, he cut off a stick, and threw it in there, and made the iron float. [7]He said, "Pick it up." So he reached out his hand and took it.

in 2 Kgs 4). Seemingly unconnected to the preceding episode about Naaman's healing, Mordechai Cogan and Hayim Tadmor suggest that this legend about the ax succeeded the Naaman episode because of their shared context at the Jordan.[1] This pericope begins with the band of prophets running out of space—presumably because their numbers have increased under Elisha's leadership—and needing to relocate to a larger venue and abode. In the midst of their rebuilding, one of the prophets accidentally loses the head of a borrowed iron ax in the river. Gina Hens-Piazza explains that this would have been a serious matter because iron was valuable and costly in the ancient world.[2] The band of prophets again appears as impoverished and on the fringes, building their own hut with borrowed equipment. Gone are the portrayals of the prophets as salaried family men with dependents, which we saw in 2 Kings 4. Rather, in 2 Kings 6, they all appear to be single, unattached men who work and live together in a type of cooperative.

When Elisha finds out about the drowned ax head, he comes to the rescue. Cutting off a stick, he throws it into the river, miraculously causing the head of the ax to float so that it can be recovered. Medieval Rabbi Qimḥi, in his commentary on 2 Kings 6:6, opines that perhaps a new item—the newly broken stick—instead of the old wooden handle of the ax was needed to perform this miracle successfully.[3] John Gray,

---

1. Mordechai Cogan and Hayim Tadmor, *II Kings: A New Translation with Introduction and Commentary*, AB 11 (Garden City, NY: Doubleday, 1988), 70.

2. Gina Hens-Piazza, *1–2 Kings*, AOTC (Nashville: Abingdon, 2006), 267.

3. David Qimchi, also spelled Kimchi (1160–1235), was a biblical commentator, philosopher, and grammarian, who also went by the acronym RaDak (Rabbi David

however, posits that Elisha simply utilized a stick to swirl the water until he relocated the ax head in the river and that this simple scenario became inflated into a miraculous legend.[4] Regardless of the origins, this pericope again stresses Elisha as the head of the prophet group and depicts him as something more than just a prophet—as a miracle worker who helps those who are marginalized and poor, including the poor members of his guild. Theologically, as Hens-Piazza notes, this story also teaches the reader to notice the presence of God in everyday tasks. This neat ending, however, will become increasingly questionable as the chapter progresses and as we encounter stories about the hardships faced by those not in the guild of prophets.

Divine Sight and the Spying Prophet (6:8-14)

The second story of this chapter, which appears to be unconnected to that of the ax head, concerns the capture and release of Aramean soldiers by Elisha. This pericope centers on the theme of seeing and blindness,[5] in particular on the contradistinction between true, divine sight and human blindness.

The episode begins with a secondhand description of Elisha's amazing gift of "second sight,"[6] which allows him to secretly overhear the king's discussions in Aram concerning the country's military strategies against Israel (6:8-11). The text does not describe the nature of Elisha's extrasensory abilities—whether he is able to see and hear the happenings in Aram, or whether he merely receives messages outlining the enemy country's battle strategies. In either case, Elisha is depicted as possessing a higher, almost divine level of sensory skill, either visual or auditory or both. As usual, the prophet uses his ability to help his country by informing the Israelite king of Aram's surprise attacks and thus foiling them (2 Kgs 6:10).

Continuing the critique of human political systems that we have seen in preceding chapters of 2 Kings, the extraordinary vision of the prophet is juxtaposed to the blindness of the Aramean king. While Elisha can see

---

Kimchi). Cogan and Tadmor, *II Kings,* 70, quote his commentary in *Mikra'ot Gedolot* on 2 Kgs 6:6.

4. John Gray, *I and II Kings*, OTL (Philadelphia: Westminster, 1970), 511.

5. Rachelle Gilmour, "A Note on the Horses and Chariots of Fire at Dothan," *ZAW* 125 (2013): 311.

6. Cogan and Tadmor, *II Kings*, 74.

---

2 Kgs 6:8-14

⁸Once when the king of Aram was at war with Israel, he took counsel with his officers. He said, "At such and such a place shall be my camp." ⁹But the man of God sent word to the king of Israel, "Take care not to pass this place, because the Arameans are going down there." ¹⁰The king of Israel sent word to the place of which the man of God spoke. More than once or twice he warned such a place so that it was on the alert.

¹¹The mind of the king of Aram was greatly perturbed because of this; he called his officers and said to them, "Now tell me who among us sides with the king of Israel?" ¹²Then one of his officers said, "No one, my lord king. It is Elisha, the prophet in Israel, who tells the king of Israel the words that you speak in your bedchamber." ¹³He said, "Go and find where he is; I will send and seize him." He was told, "He is in Dothan." ¹⁴So he sent horses and chariots there and a great army; they came by night, and surrounded the city.

---

or hear inside the very "bedchamber" of the king, the Aramean monarch is ignorant of the existence of this prophet, thinking that Israel's knowledge of Aram's surprise attacks is due to the presence of a traitor in their midst (v. 11). When the king is informed by one of his officers that it is Elisha who is leaking the information, the Aramean king continues in his befuddlement, commanding that they locate the prophet (v. 12). When the location of Elisha is confirmed, a comedic scene ensues whereby the Aramean king attempts to put a stop to the prophet's spying simply by kidnapping him from Dothan (v. 13). The king naively seems to think that a prophet who can overhear the king's discussions and military plans in Aram would be ignorant of plans for his future kidnapping. Hens-Piazza notes the irony of the monarch's command to his soldiers, who will shortly become visually impaired by Elisha, to "go and see" in the Hebrew (v. 13) about this Israelite prophet.[7]

This plan of the Aramean king indicates that either he is a bad strategist or he is doubtful or too simpleminded to understand the extent of Elisha's abilities. The manifestation of the gifts of YHWH's prophet, especially to the Arameans, but also to the reader, thus appears to be one of the purposes of this pericope. Though the Arameans in this narrative appear to have no knowledge about Naaman,[8] both the earlier

---

7. Hens-Piazza, *1–2 Kings*, 269.

8. Hens-Piazza reads 2 Kings 5–6 as continuous, stating that Elisha should have been a household name in Syria by this point because of Naaman (ibid., 268).

story about the healing of the Aramean army commander's leprosy and this episode about prophetic spying share the theme of the revelation of YHWH's powers to foreigners.

Blindness, Hospitality, and Kidnapping the Kidnappers (6:15-23)

The readers must assume that Elisha has full knowledge of the foreign monarch's "devious" plans to abduct him. Indeed, this assumption is important to understanding Elisha's calm attitude when, shortly thereafter, his house is surrounded by the horses and chariots of the Aramean army.

The alarm of his attendant who asks, "Alas, master! What shall we do?" when he sees the coming soldiers is juxtaposed to Elisha's sedate response to not be afraid "for there is more with us than there are with them" (v. 16). The blindness of the servant is transformed into spiritual sight when Elisha then prays for the eyes of his servant to be opened, thus revealing the presence of the more numerous horses and chariots of fire that surround the prophet (v. 17). Rachelle Gilmour states that the fiery, divine army is closely connected to the theme of sight, pointing to a similar mention of horses and chariots of fire during Elijah's annunciation scene, which Elisha witnesses (2 Kgs 3).[9]

Vision is also the means by which Elisha foils the Aramean army that shows up and surrounds the city in which he is dwelling (v. 14). Right after asking for the eyes of his servant to be opened, Elisha, in reverse, prays that the sight of the Aramean army be closed or hampered in some way (v. 18). Though the word סנורים in 2 Kings 6:18, is usually translated as "blindness," possibly based on the Akkadian *sinlurma* (also spelled *sinuri*) meaning "blindness," Gilmour and Robert LaBarbera suggest instead that the Aramean army was struck with a blinding, bright light that distorted their vision.[10] In other words, the army was afflicted not with the lack of sight, as they do not act blind when they follow Elisha into Israel, but with a supernaturally confused vision. Indeed, the Aramean soldiers appear to be unaware of the fact that they are no longer seeing correctly. Taking Elisha to be their military leader,[11] they follow him back to Samaria (v. 19). Only after their arrival are their eyes opened again, and they realize that they are now in the midst of enemy territory.

---

9. Gilmour, "A Note," 312.

10. Gilmour, "A Note," 310; Robert LaBarbera, "The Man of War and the Man of God: Social Satire in 2 Kings 6:8–7:20," *CBQ* 46 (1984): 643.

11. LaBarbera, "The Man of War," 644.

[15]When an attendant of the man of God rose early in the morning and went out, an army with horses and chariots was all around the city. His servant said, "Alas, master! What shall we do?" [16]He replied, "Do not be afraid, for there are more with us than there are with them." [17]Then Elisha prayed: "O LORD, please open his eyes that he may see." So the LORD opened the eyes of the servant, and he saw; the mountain was full of horses and chariots of fire all around Elisha. [18]When the Arameans came down against him, Elisha prayed to the LORD, and said, "Strike this people, please, with blindness." So he struck them with blindness as Elisha had asked. [19]Elisha said to them, "This is not the way, and this is not the city; follow me, and I will bring you to the

The text never tells the reader why Elisha leads the army back to Samaria, and, indeed, his act also seems to confuse the Israelite king as he asks the prophet whether he should kill the captured Aramean soldiers (v. 22). Surprisingly, Elisha instead tells him to act hospitably, to give them food and drink before returning them to Aram. Indeed, the feast scene is the last in a series of ironies and reversals in this pericope. In order to stop Elisha's supernatural sight, the Aramean king decides to kidnap him, leading instead to his army "losing" its sight and being kidnapped by Elisha. The army shows up with physical weaponry, only to be captured through the use of a supernatural weapon;[12] and instead of death, the enemy soldiers are met with hospitality in Samaria. La-Barbera connects the blinding of the Aramean soldiers with the Sodom and Gommorah narrative in which the townspeople are also struck with confused vision for their lack of hospitality. He argues that in reverse of Genesis 19, the Aramean soldiers in 2 Kings 6 are visually impaired so that hospitality can be offered to them.[13]

The contradistinction between human and divine sight, and true and false security, is again stressed. True protection comes from Israel's God, YHWH. Human kings and their armies, in contrast, only offer a distorted vision, a false sense of security. A series of wordplays heighten the drama and more fully elucidate this theme. LaBarbera notes that the root שמר, *sh-m-r* ("to guard, protect"), is repeated throughout the narrative: in verses 8-10, Elisha warns the Israelites to be on their guard (השמר, *hishshamer*),

---

12. Gilmour, "A Note," 309.
13. LaBarbera, "The Man of War," 644.

man whom you seek." And he led them to Samaria.

²⁰As soon as they entered Samaria, Elisha said, "O Lᴏʀᴅ, open the eyes of these men so that they may see." The Lᴏʀᴅ opened their eyes, and they saw that they were inside Samaria. ²¹When the king of Israel saw them he said to Elisha, "Father, shall I kill them? Shall I kill them?" ²²He answered, "No! Did you capture with your sword and your bow those whom you want to kill? Set food and water before them so that they may eat and drink; and let them go to their master." ²³So he prepared for them a great feast; after they ate and drank, he sent them on their way, and they went to their master. And the Arameans no longer came raiding into the land of Israel.

putting them on alert (נשמר, *nishmar*) of the Arameans' surprise attacks; later, the Aramean troops, in order to capture the prophet who is warning Israel, themselves end up in Samaria (שמרון, *shomron*); and, finally, the "latest raiding party is contained by *šōmrôn* (root שמר, *šmr*) just as the previous raids were contained by Elisha's warning, *hiššāmer* (root שמר, *šmr*)."¹⁴ The purpose of the emphasis on שמר, *sh-m-r*, is apparent: the true military protector of Israel is not a human king or army but the heavenly forces commanded by Elisha, the prophet of YHWH.

From a feminist point of view, this pericope again stresses YHWH's divine ability to protect his country and people—an attribute centrally linked to ideas of masculinity and power in the ancient Near East. What is unusual about this pericope, however, is that this protection is depicted as partially resulting from an act of hospitality—from feeding Aramean troops to returning them unharmed to their country. In this, perhaps a subtle critique of usual notions of masculinity and power, especially as exemplified in human monarchs and their war games, is detectable. Human kings and the system that supports them lead to death and destruction, while the true monarch, YHWH, and his rule lead to life, health, and fecundity. Indeed, the show of peaceful power by YHWH through Elisha at the end of the narrative "overpowers and overshadows the acts of aggression and retaliation of both Aram's ruler and Israel's king,"¹⁵ bringing about a time of temporary peace, security, and life.

14. Ibid.
15. Hens-Piazza, *1–2 Kings*, 270.

Famine and Starving Mothers and Children (6:24-31)

The story about the capture of Aramean soldiers ends with an offer of food; the next narrative about the hungry mothers is about the lack of nourishment.[16] The cessation of Aramean attacks at the conclusion of the last pericope appears to have been short lived. The fragile peace ends when Ben-hadad, the king of Aram, begins attacking and putting Samaria under a siege. The famine caused by the siege is said to be quite severe, as items that were usually discarded or utilized by the very poor, such as a donkey's head and a *qab*—about one-sixth of a *seah* (1.2 liters)—of dove's dung, which Cogan and Tadmor take to be inedible husks of either a carob or another plant,[17] are sold for exorbitant prices (2 Kgs 6:25).

The desperation of the situation takes a personal and harrowing turn as the Israelite king, who many identify as Jehoram, is confronted by a woman who asks him for help while he is walking on the wall of the city. Perhaps thinking that she is asking him for something to eat, he curtly replies even before he hears her complaint—"No! Let the LORD help you. How can I help you?" (v. 27). Shirking responsibility, the Israelite king repeatedly throughout the pericope deflects blame for the dire situation. The ineptitude and irresponsibility of the king becomes more evident and repugnant as the woman tells him of her problem, which goes beyond mere hunger. In a possible allusion to the tale of Solomon and the prostitutes in 1 Kings 3:16-28,[18] the woman succinctly recounts for the king that she and another woman had planned to kill and eat both of their children. After her son was killed and eaten, the other woman hid her son in order to prevent him from the same fate (vv. 28-29).

16. Cogan and Tadmor, *II Kings*, 83–84.

17. Ibid., 79. It is unclear what is meant by this item. Josephus argued that the substance might have been used like salt (*Ant.* 9.62), while Qimḥi (commentary on 2 Kgs 6:25) thought it might have been used for kindling (as quoted by Cogan and Tadmor, *II Kings*, 79. See n. 3 above on Qimḥi). Hens-Piazza, however, believes that the dove's dung was used by the poor to plant a few stalks of wheat or corn (Hens-Piazza, *1–2 Kings*, 271).

18. Claudia Camp, "1 and 2 Kings" in *The Women's Bible Commentary*, ed. Carol A. Newsom and Sharon H. Ringe (Louisville: Westminster John Knox, 1992), 114; Stuart Lasine, "Jehoram and the Cannibal Mothers (2 Kings 6.24-33): Solomon's Judgement in an Inverted World," *JSOT* 50 (1991): 27–53; idem, "The Ups and Downs of Monarchical Justice," *JSOT* 59 (1993): 37–53; LaBarbera, "The Man of War," 646; Julie Faith Parker, *Valuable and Vulnerable: Children in the Hebrew Bible, Especially the Elisha Cycle*, BJS 355 (Providence, RI: Brown University Press, 2013), 187.

²⁴Some time later King Ben-hadad of Aram mustered his entire army; he marched against Samaria and laid siege to it. ²⁵As the siege continued, famine in Samaria became so great that a donkey's head was sold for eighty shekels of silver, and one-fourth of a kab of doves dung for five shekels of silver. ²⁶Now as the king of Israel was walking on the city wall, a woman cried out to him, "Help, my lord king!" ²⁷He said, "No! Let the LORD help you. How can I help you? From the threshing floor or from the wine press?" ²⁸But then the king asked her, "What is your complaint?" She answered, "This woman said to me, 'Give up your son; we will eat him today, and we will eat my son tomorrow.' ²⁹So we cooked my son and ate him. The next day I said to her, 'Give up your son and we will eat him.' But she has hidden her son." ³⁰When the king heard the words of the woman he tore his clothes—now since he was walking on the city wall, the people could see that he had sackcloth on his body underneath—³¹and he said, "So may God do to me, and more, if the head of Elisha son of Shaphat stays on his shoulders today."

With this short, horrifying summary, the unnamed woman is summarily dismissed from the narrative. As a result, we never discover the motivation for her conversation with the king. Does she want the king to force the other woman to give up her child so that he too can be killed and eaten? Or does she merely want to inform him about the dire effects of the famine on the population? Moreover, how does she feel about her son's death? Does she feel any remorse, regret, or even anger? Or in the face of such horrors and such hunger, does she view her desperate act rather dispassionately? Both the woman and her unnamed colleague remain silent throughout the narrative.[19] Like the woman, we are again left with more questions than answers about the other mother: What does this woman feel about eating the other woman's son? Does she feel remorse or regret, and is that why she changed her mind about her own child? Did she plan all along to renege on her promise? Or was it that after her hunger was sated she was finally able to think clearly about the horrifying plan that she suggested and therefore to decide otherwise?

Not only is the woman's story incompletely told, but the king never replies to her plea and does not attempt to resolve her situation. Rather, tearing his clothes and displaying the sackcloth he is wearing, he blames

19. Parker, *Valuable and Vulnerable*, 178.

Elisha for the famine and threatens to kill him (v. 30). The reason for his anger at the prophet is unstated. Perhaps the king is enraged because he feels that Elisha, who in preceding narratives magically reproduced food (2 Kgs 4:42-44), raised an ax head from water (2 Kgs 6:1-7), and overheard the enemy's plans in another country (2 Kgs 6:15-23), is not doing enough to lift the siege and alleviate the famine. Or perhaps the king is angry at the prophet for making him feed and release the captured Aramean soldiers earlier in 2 Kings 6:8-23 instead of killing them, thus allowing them to return later to besiege Samaria.[20] Whatever the reason, instead of addressing the woman, the king reacts to a situation of violence with another threat of violence by vowing to behead Elisha (2 Kgs 6:31).[21] Indeed, the king's tearing of his clothes not only displays his feelings of mourning and horror at the woman's situation but also appears to be a physical demonstration of what he wants to do to the prophet.

The rending of the king's clothes further contrasts the king with the hungry woman, poignantly juxtaposing those in power and those who are victims of power. Hens-Piazza notes that the sackcloth, which shows that the king is fasting, highlights the difference between the king who is optionally refusing to eat food with the starving woman who is forced to eat her own son—her future—because she had so little to eat.[22] In so doing, the story brings to the fore the true victims of wars and violence caused by kings and rulers: women, children, the elderly, the poor, and other figures on the margins.

The presence of this woman and other victims like her speaks to the general malaise of Israelite society. Though other parts of the Bible also mention famine in the context of a siege (Deut 28:56-57; Lam 2:20; Ezek 5:10), Hens-Piazza writes that cannibalism is never just about eating or not eating. Not all people resort to cannibalism when under duress. Rather, she argues that it is societies that already have in place an accepted system of control and domination—in other words, where abuse and victimization are part of the norm—that succumb to cannibalism.[23] Though this woman, like other female characters in the Bible, is given a few short lines, her story, like those of other marginalized victims, functions as a litmus test for the ethical and religious health of a particular

20. Ibid., 182.

21. Gina Hens-Piazza, "Forms of Violence and the Violence of Forms: Two Cannibal Mothers before a King (2 Kings 6:24-33)," *JFSR* 14 (1998): 99.

22. Hens-Piazza, *1–2 Kings*, 272; idem, "Forms of Violence," 100, 102.

23. Hens-Piazza, "Forms of Violence," 96–97.

society. This story thus clearly indicates that something is very rotten in Israel.[24]

Considering the important function that this character serves in so publicly exposing the illness of Israel's society, it is therefore unsurprising to detect attempts to suppress her story. Hens-Piazza remarks that the woman's voice is silenced in the text in a multitude of ways—by the king, by the text itself, and also by modern interpreters. Like the Israelite king, the text ignores the woman's plea, cutting her conversation short and quickly panning the camera away from her and her dire situation to focus again on the more important male protagonists—the king and the prophet—and the power struggle between them. Outlining the narrative's structure, Hens-Piazza writes that the text sandwiches her story between "contestants vying for domination and control," and, in so doing, the wrestling for power by the privileged overshadows and consumes the "life plans, identity, significance and well-being of mothers and children."[25] The woman is thus rendered insignificant. She is never again mentioned, and her situation is never addressed or resolved. She, like so many who are poor, suffering, or hungry, becomes mere background.[26]

Hens-Piazza argues that not just the text itself but also modern interpreters have diminished the woman's voice.[27] Some commentators attempt to explain away the cannibalism by contextualizing the practice. Other interpreters, similar to the king and the text, ignore the woman, quickly bypassing her story to focus on that of the king, the prophet, or the political situation as a whole. When the women are discussed, they are leered at, judged, condemned, and dismissed but rarely empathized with.[28] In such readings, these women are not mothers who produce and care for their children but monsters who, in an act of filial cannibalism, kill and consume their own offspring. Indeed, Claudia Camp states that "our expectations of self-sacrificing mother . . . turn us against the cannibal mothers here."[29] Their act is so lewd, so outrageous, that the narrative

24. On the complex ways in which the woman has been used as litmus test of social decay, see ibid., 101–2.

25. Ibid., 95.

26. Ibid., 96.

27. On the dismissal of the child's voice and story, see Parker, *Valuable and Vulnerable*, 183–89.

28. Hens-Piazza, "Forms of Violence," 100–103.

29. Camp, "1 and 2 Kings," 115.

should be considered a dark comedy.[30] Labeled by interpreters oxymo-
ronically as the "cannibalistic mothers," these women are thus viewed
as wholly unrelatable, totally Other.[31] As criminals, their fate is not a
matter of concern. They do not deserve our pity or our attention. Thus
they are treated accordingly—utilized and then summarily dismissed
from the narrative.

Elisha Foresees the End of the Famine (6:32–7:2)

The story moves quickly to the real action—the confrontation between
the angry king and the prophet. Yet the attuned reader is unable to forget these women so easily. Their harrowing story bleeds into the next
pericope about the encounter between king and prophet. As the royal
messenger of the enraged king approaches, Elisha, who is sitting with
the elders of the city, presciently replies that the angry monarch has sent
an assassin to kill him (2 Kgs 6:31).

The prophet is still in possession of his extraordinary gift of foreknowledge. Yet in light of what we have just heard about the desperate situation
in the city, this reminder of the prophet's stunning sensory abilities has
the opposite effect from the preceding narrative about Elisha's foiling of
the Arameans. Here, it compels the reader to condemn the prophet for
his apathy. Such a skilled prophet must surely be aware of the horrible
conditions faced by the women and the general populace in Samaria. He
must have known about the woman and her dead child. If he is aware
of the situation, troubling questions arise as to his character: Why has
Elisha done nothing to relieve some of the people's suffering? Why has
he not asked YHWH for some relief?

Equally damning is the prophet's measured response when the king
appears. Instead of confronting the prophet with a show of violent force
as he vowed earlier, the king, when he sees the prophet, dejectedly replies
that he has lost hope because this situation is from God (2 Kgs 6:33). To
this, Elisha calmly prophesies that the price of food will experience a
dramatic drop tomorrow and that the famine's end is imminent (2 Kgs
7:1). Yet, this oracle seems oddly coldhearted in light of the story we
just heard. Why did Elisha not inform the women about the looming

---

30. Lasine, "Jehoram and the Cannibalistic Mothers," 33; also Camp, "1 and 2
Kings," 115. For a critique of Lasine's article, see Laurel Lanner, "Cannibal Mothers
and Me: A Mother's Reading of 2 Kings 6.24–7.20," *JSOT* 85 (1999): 107–16.
    31. Hens-Piazza, "Forms of Violence," 87.

³²So he dispatched a man from his presence.

Now Elisha was sitting in his house, and the elders were sitting with him. Before the messenger arrived, Elisha said to the elders, "Are you aware that this murderer has sent someone to take off my head? When the messenger comes, see that you shut the door and hold it closed against him. Is not the sound of his master's feet behind him?" ³³While he was still speaking with them, the king came down to him and said, "This trouble is from the Lord! Why should I hope in the Lord any longer?"

⁷:¹But Elisha said, "Hear the word of the Lord: thus says the Lord, Tomorrow about this time a measure of choice meal shall be sold for a shekel, and two measures of barley for a shekel, at the gate of Samaria." ²Then the captain on whose hand the king leaned said to the man of God, "Even if the Lord were to make windows in the sky, could such a thing happen?" But he said, "You shall see it with your own eyes, but you shall not eat from it."

conclusion of the famine? Why did he not step in just one day earlier to stop the women from killing one of their children? Why does he wait until after a child has died to announce this oracle? Could it be that the prophet cares little about the child but is just sharing the prophecy at this moment so as to save his own neck from the violent reactions of a despondent king?

Equally incriminating is the prophet's volatile response to the comment of an officer accompanying the king. Indeed, what seems to get Elisha really worked up is not a situation in which a starving woman is forced to kill and eat her child but when doubts about the authenticity of his oracle are expressed. When a captain accompanying the king wonders aloud in response to Elisha's prophecy how such a miraculous lowering of food prices can occur so quickly, the ever-patient prophet lashes out. He angrily states that because of his disbelief, the commander will not partake of the miracle (7:2). He will die tomorrow. Dutifully, the narrative confirms the oracle as the unlucky commander is trampled to death moments after the city learns about the end of the siege (7:17-20).

It is difficult not to read this story cynically. Women might be forced to eat their children, but, according to the narrative, the true sin is to doubt the oracle of a prophet of YHWH. What matters is not the situation of the poor and hungry but the authority of Elisha! Theologically speaking, what we learn from this pericope is that all of us are prone to become accustomed and hardened to the suffering of those around us.

Even this visually skilled prophet, when daily surrounded by scenes of desperation and need, appears to have lost some of his empathetic insight. Perhaps he has become acclimated or grown cold to the horrors daily inflicted on the poor around him. If this is the case, then the story functions as a dire warning to readers to be ever vigilant against such easy desensitization. It reminds us to open our eyes so that we can truly see and empathize with those who are in need.

One could also argue that, to salvage Elisha, maybe the prophet is not as cold-hearted as he initially appears. Perhaps he was on the cusp of doing something about the dire situation. When the messenger of the king approaches, Elisha is said to be meeting with the elders of the city (2 Kgs 6:32). Could it be that this meeting was for the purpose of discussing ways to alleviate the suffering of the poor and desperate, especially in light of the woman's story? Could it be that that the woman's desperate deed reinvigorated both the prophet and his God to bring the famine to a quick end? Perhaps the child's death at the hands of his poor, starving mother finally compelled YHWH to act on behalf of his people through his prophet.

Excursus:
Who Is Doing the (B)eating?

When I read with the cannibal mother I find a story of betrayal and powerlessness. The only person she can access is a kindly, but peculiarly powerless king. Those that hold the real influence are shut away behind closed doors. The true cannibals in this story are those spoken of in Mic. 3.3 and Isa. 9.19-20. These are the rulers of Israel who eat the flesh of God's people, and God, the Cannibal Parent, who allows it. The most difficult aspect of the woman's experience is knowing that food was only a miracle away.

This story has a familiar ring to it, as does the response of the critics. At the time of writing (August 1997) there is a controversy in the news media surrounding a woman who killed her baby. Certainly, her position is not comparable to the cannibal mother in its extremity. Her diet, while minimal, would not have been below the level that would sustain life and she was not resident in a besieged city. However, on the issues of access to resources, lack of control of her own circumstances and hopelessness, comparison may be warranted. While the contemporary mother's circumstances were complex and her action cannot be condoned, her situation is shared by many women raising children alone and having to rely on the state for their income. At her trial, the defense showed that she had received only a third of the financial assistance to which she was entitled from the state to raise her four children.

Regardless of exactly how much money she had to live on—even the maximum state entitlement is undoubtedly low—her position of powerlessness is notably similar to that of the cannibal mother. She is surrounded by food and resources. The representatives of the state she approaches for help are often kindly, but not always. However, they too are similarly powerless to act without the authority of the men behind closed doors (Mic. 3.3). In the language of Micah they flay her skin and break her bones. But no, she broke the bones of her baby. Who is doing the (b)eating? Those in power place the responsibility squarely upon the woman. Certainly her hand struck the final blow, but the first blow was not hers.[32]

Laurel Lanner

The Sick Witness the End of the Famine (7:3-20)

If it is the case that the mother had some influence on the prophet or YHWH, then the famine is depicted as coming to an end because of a desperate act committed by those who exist on the margins. Fittingly, it is also those on the periphery of society who are the first to witness and bring back news of the city's salvation. Showing the immediate effectiveness of Elisha's prophecy, the scene swiftly moves from the confrontation between the prophet and the king to those at the other end of the socio-political hierarchy: four starving lepers sitting outside of the city gate (2 Kgs 7:3). Rather than dying of starvation in the city, these men decide that they have a better chance of survival if they desert to the Arameans (7:4). That those on the very far edges of society believe that it is better to risk death by surrendering to their enemies than remaining in their own city speaks to how dire the situation has become.

When the leprous men reach the Aramean camp, however, they find it miraculously deserted (7:5). YHWH has caused the Aramean army to hear the phantom sounds of a great army, growing nearer, which leads the soldiers to flee in such a haste that they have abandoned all their tents, provisions, and animals (7:6-7). Indeed, they were in such a great hurry to leave that they left a trail of possessions in their wake (7:15).

---

32. Lanner, "Cannibal Mothers and Me," 114–15.

³Now there were four leprous men outside the city gate, who said to one another, "Why should we sit here until we die? ⁴If we say, 'Let us enter the city,' the famine is in the city, and we shall die there; but if we sit here, we shall also die. Therefore, let us desert to the Aramean camp; if they spare our lives, we shall live; and if they kill us, we shall but die." ⁵So they arose at twilight to go to the Aramean camp; but when they came to the edge of the Aramean camp, there was no one there at all. ⁶For the Lord had caused the Aramean army to hear the sound of chariots, and of horses, the sound of a great army, so that they said to one another, "The king of Israel has hired the kings of the Hittites and the kings of Egypt to fight against us." ⁷So they fled away in the twilight and abandoned their tents, their horses, and their donkeys leaving the camp just as it was, and fled for their lives. ⁸When these leprous men had come to the edge of the camp, they went into a tent, ate and drank, carried off silver, gold, and clothing, and went and hid them. Then they came back, entered another tent, carried off things from it, and went and hid them.

In a dramatic reversal, those at the very bottom of society, the leprous men, are transformed into the first pillagers of the camp of the mighty Arameans. Ironically, the defeat of the Arameans comes at the sound of imaginary whisperings and their looting at the hands of starving lepers.

At the empty camp of the Arameans, these leprous men eat, drink, and pilfer gold, silver, and clothing from one tent and then proceed to do the same from a second tent. Yet their conscience quickly gets the better of them. Declaring the wrongness of their actions, and the guilt they would incur if they fail to share the good news, they decide to inform the king of the desertion: "What we are doing is wrong. This is a day of good news; if we are silent and wait until the morning light, we will be found guilty" (2 Kgs 7:9). It might be that their decision to share the good news is motivated by their social location. Unlike the king and the prophet who fail to act until faced with the devastating situation of the starving women, perhaps the hungry, desperate leprous men are more attuned to others who are also suffering in the city, having had firsthand experience of such hardships.

The leprous men quickly spread the news of the Arameans' abandonment to the gatekeepers, who in turn proceed to tell the king. The king, however, thinking the desertion is a trap and having promptly forgotten Elisha's oracle, sends out two men to verify the news brought by the lepers. Those dispatched shortly return to confirm the removal of the Arameans and the whole city goes out to plunder their camp (7:16). The

⁹Then they said to one another, "What we are doing is wrong. This is a day of good news; if we are silent and wait until the morning light, we will be found guilty; therefore let us go and tell the king's household." ¹⁰So they came and called to the gatekeepers of the city, and told them, "We went to the Aramean camp, but there was no one to be seen or heard there, nothing but the horses tied, the donkeys tied, and the tents as they were." ¹¹Then the gatekeepers called out and proclaimed it to the king's household. ¹²The king got up in the night, and said to his servants, "I will tell you what the Arameans have prepared against us. They know that we are starving; so they have left the camp to hide themselves in the open country, thinking, 'When they come out of the city, we shall take them alive and get into the city.'" ¹³One of his servants said, "Let some men take five of the remaining horses, since those left here will suffer the fate of the whole multitude of Israel that have perished already; let us send and find out." ¹⁴So they took two mounted men, and the king sent them after the Aramean army, saying, "Go and find out." ¹⁵So they

bounty first discovered by the four leprous men, at the end, is shared by all. All except the doubting commander, that is. The famine comes to an end along with the skeptical soldier who, in confirmation of Elisha's earlier oracle, is trampled to death by the eager populace exiting through the city gates, which he is guarding (7:17). The narrative twists the dagger into the poor fellow a bit further by repeating the earlier words of this doubting Thomas (7:18-20).[33] The reader is thus warned against similar offenses.

With this, the narrative comes to a neat, pedagogical end. The authenticity of Elisha's prophecy is confirmed. Moreover, the power, security, and life-giving abilities of YHWH are placed in contradistinction to the weak, violent, fatal rule of human kings. It is thus YHWH who is once again depicted as the true sovereign over Israel. This theological message might help us to figure out more precisely the reason for the Arameans' departure: because they heard the noises of an imaginary approaching army (7:6). This description of false sounds connects this pericope to the earlier episode about Elisha's foiling of the Arameans through his visual gifts (2 Kgs 6:17-23) as both stories share an emphasis on distorted sounds and sights. Both stories also emphasize Elisha's extrasensory abilities.

---

33. A doubting Thomas—or someone who is a skeptic—refers to Jesus' disciple, Thomas, who in John 20:24-29 does not believe that Jesus has been resurrected until Jesus offers to let Thomas feel his wounds.

went after them as far as the Jordan; the whole way was littered with garments and equipment that the Arameans had thrown away in their haste. So the messengers returned, and told the king.

¹⁶Then the people went out, and plundered the camp of the Arameans. So a measure of choice meal was sold for a shekel, and two measures of barley for a shekel, according to the word of the LORD. ¹⁷Now the king had appointed the captain on whose hand he leaned to have charge of the gate; the people trampled him to death in the gate, just as the man of God had said when the king came down to him. ¹⁸For when the man of God had said to the king, "Two measures of barley shall be sold for a shekel, and a measure of choice meal for a shekel, about this time tomorrow in the gate of Samaria," ¹⁹the captain had answered to the man of God, "Even if the LORD were to make windows in the sky, could such a thing happen?" And he had answered, "You shall see it with your own eyes, but you shall not eat from it." ²⁰It did indeed happen to him; the people trampled him to death in the gate.

The first episode stresses his "second sight" or ability to overhear private conversation while the second highlights his ability to foresee the approach of the angry king and the imminent end of the famine.

In light of these parallels, the two stories can be read in conjunction to provide a better understanding of the mysterious, fraudulent noises overheard by the Aramean army: the sounds of chariots, horses, and armies that the Lord causes the Arameans to hear are the noises of the horses and chariots of fire—the invisible yet audible heavenly army of YHWH. While the earlier narrative about the Arameans focuses on the removal of human blindness and the unveiling of the invisible army constantly surrounding Elisha, so this current episode emphasizes another "unveiling" of the heavenly army to the Arameans—this time, in an aural sense. In both cases, the message is clear: though invisible and, at times, inaudible, the true sovereign of Israel continues to look after and protect his country with his divine army.

Yet the earlier story of the starving women cannot help but edge into this happier pericope about the end of the famine and the siege, undermining the theological conclusion it puts forth. If YHWH is indeed the true monarch and if he does look out for his people, where was he when the starving mothers were forced to resort to their unimaginable deed? What use are the fiery chariots and horses in the face of starving children, women, and sick? As in the text, so also in life, the demonstration of divine power remains in tension with situations of human suffering.

2 Kings 8:1-29

The Remaining Deeds of Elisha

Concluding the stories about Elisha, 2 Kings 8 consists of both the last episodes related to or featuring the prophet as well as the account summaries of the reign of Jehoram (c. 849–842 BCE) and Ahaziah of Judah (c. 842–841 BCE). After this chapter, Elisha will reemerge once more in 2 Kings 9 to conclude the narrative cycle by anointing and crowning Jehu right before the commander assassinates Jezebel, the queen so hated by Elisha's mentor, Elijah. The prophet will breathe his last in 2 Kings 13. Chapters 8–9 of 2 Kings tie up the loose ends of the stories about this prophet and also transition from the Elijah/Elisha stories into the Deuteronomistic accounts of the regnal histories of Israel and Judah, which make up the bulk of the rest of 2 Kings. Interestingly, this transition has a gendered component. The story about the grisly demise of Jezebel, which we find in the next chapter, functions as a powerful, transformational passageway—a betwixt-and-between space—that bridges the concluding stories about Elisha/Elijah and the regnal histories of the kings of Israel and Judah. Though she will not die until the next chapter, Jezebel functions as a kind of temporal marker, demarcating one era from the next. In so doing, the hated foreign woman, Jezebel, subversively lingers in the very structure and ordering of the stories of 2 Kings.

The Return and Restoration of the Woman of Shunem (8:1-6)

The story of the rich, anonymous Shunnamite woman who is given a son by Elisha in 2 Kings 4:8-37 concludes in 2 Kings 8:1-6. The two narratives are intricately intertwined, sharing motifs and features, such as the emphasis on food and house.[1] For example, while 2 Kings 4 concerns the woman's acquisition of a metaphoric house through the birth of her son, 2 Kings 8 is about the woman's reacquisition of her literal house after her return.[2] The narrative begins with Elisha presciently warning the Shunnamite woman to leave her land and house because of a lengthy, coming famine (8:1). Unlike the starving women in 2 Kings 6, it seems that there were some women that Elisha did care enough about to forewarn about the impending disaster. The earlier commentary on 2 Kings 4 discussed a possible reason for the prophet's particular attention to the Shunnamite woman and her child. Moreover, it is telling and bespeaks her competency that the prophet tells her instead of her husband about this coming disaster.[3] Whether the famine predicted is the same one described in the preceding chapter, which stemmed from the Aramean siege, is unclear. As with other episodes concerning Elisha, the connections among and the chronology of the stories are ambiguous.

Heeding the prophet's warning, the Shunnamite woman, who earlier stated that she lived among her people (2 Kgs 4:13), leaves everything behind and flees to Philistia (2 Kgs 8:2). When the chapter begins, the famine has concluded, and she has returned to her land (8:3). While she was away, she seems to have lost possession of her house and her land. Perhaps her house was confiscated by the king or acquired illegally or legally by a neighbor or family.[4] She, however, has not only luck or divine fortune on her side but also the great energy she manifested earlier. As in 2 Kings 4, she is active and bold, going directly to the king to address the loss of her land. When she arrives to talk to the king, the monarch, coincidentally, is in the midst of a conversation with Elisha's assistant, Gehazi, who is telling him about the prophet's miraculous deeds, includ-

---

1. Mark Roncace, "Elisha and the Woman of Shunem: 2 Kings 4.8-37 and 8.1-6 Read in Conjunction," *JSOT* 91 (2000): 125.

2. Ibid., 122, 127.

3. Claudia Camp, "1 and 2 Kings" in *The Women's Bible Commentary*, ed. Carol A. Newsom and Sharon H. Ringe (Louisville: Westminster John Knox, 1992), 114.

4. Mordechai Cogan and Hayim Tadmor, *II Kings: A New Translation with Introduction and Commentary*, AB 11 (Garden City, NY: Doubleday, 1988), 88; Camp, "1 and 2 Kings," 114.

⁸:¹Now Elisha had said to the woman whose son he had restored to life, "Get up and go with your household, and settle wherever you can; for the LORD has called for a famine, and it will come on the land for seven years." ²So the woman got up and did according to the word of the man of God; she went with her household and settled in the land of the Philistines seven years. ³At the end of the seven years, when the woman returned from the land of the Philistines, she set out to appeal to the king for her house and her land. ⁴Now the king was talking with Gehazi the servant of the man of God, saying, "Tell me all the great things that Elisha has done." ⁵While he was telling the king how Elisha had restored a dead person to life, the woman whose son he had restored to life appealed to the king for her house and her land. Gehazi said, "My lord king, here is the woman, and here his her son whom Elisha restored to life." ⁶When the king questioned the woman, she told him. So the king appointed an official for her, saying, "Restore all that was hers, together with all the revenue of the fields from the day that she left the land until now."

ing the resurrection of the Shunnamite woman's son (8:5). The woman arrives just as her story is being relayed to the king, allowing a fateful introduction and reference: "Gehazi said, 'My lord king, here is the woman, and here is her son whom Elisha restored to life'" (8:6). After the king questions her and her story is confirmed, her land is restored to her as expected (8:6).

Excursus on Women and Land in the Ancient Near East

In the ancient Near East, property usually passed from father to legitimate sons. In special cases, however, daughters and wives were allowed to inherit land. For example, when there were no male heirs, unmarried women were permitted to receive property (Num 27:8-11). In the case of Zelophehad's daughters, who inherited their father's land, they were encouraged to marry their cousins so as to keep the holdings within the family (Num 27:8-11; 36:1-12). Indeed, Numbers 27:8-11, which delineates the line of inheritance, indicates a preference for the land to remain in the clan.⁵ Land

---

5. Raymond Westbrook and Bruce Wells, *Everyday Law in Biblical Israel: An Introduction* (Louisville: Westminster John Knox, 2009), 91–105.

might also be transferred to wives and daughters through a man's testament or will if the women were included as heirs (Job 42:15; Jer 3:19).

Women were also able to obtain their share of the family land as part of their dowry. Dowries, that is, part of the inheritance passed on from father to daughter at marriage, came with the bride (1 Kgs 9:16; Mic 1:14; Josh 15:18-19; Judg 1:13-15; Job 42:15) and were the primary ways by which women acquired land.[6]

The land belonging to the woman in 2 Kings 8:1-6, which she gets back when she returns to Israel, might have been inherited from her husband, who might have been deceased (2 Kgs 4:14). She might also have managed her husband's properties as a trustee or manager until her son came of age.[7] Considering that the text stresses that the land and house are hers (2 Kgs 8:3, 5, 6), the land might also have been part of her dowry, which returned to her possession after her husband's death. After her death, this property would likely be passed on to her son.

As in 2 Kings 4, the interaction between Elisha and the Shunnamite woman in 2 Kings 8 is indirect. Elisha is not actually present in the scene in 2 Kings 8. It is Gehazi who once again acts as an intermediary among the various figures. Or more precisely, in an inverse of the promise made by the prophet earlier to speak to the king on the woman's behalf (4:13), she actually finds Gehazi speaking on Elisha's behalf in 2 Kings 8. The woman even has to interrupt Gehazi's discussion so that she can speak on her own behalf.[8] Contrary to other commentators who maintain that Elisha is indirectly responsible for the reacquisition of the woman's house, Mark Roncace argues that it is actually the woman who reacquires the land by herself: "In the conspicuous absence of the prophet, it is the words of the woman that have the authority; she is the one who speaks with the king and it is her words that lead to her restoration."[9] Moreover, in reaffirming the previous resurrection of her son, the woman,

---

6. Ibid., 98.

7. Richard H. Hiers, "Transfer of Property by Inheritance and Bequest in Biblical Law and Tradition," *Journal of Law and Religion* 10 (1993): 133.

8. Roncace, "Elisha and the Woman of Shunem," 123.

9. Ibid., 125.

at the end, is the one "who speaks to the king on behalf of Elisha."[10] In both narratives about the Shunnamite, the woman is portrayed more positively—as more active, powerful, and primary—than the prophet Elisha.[11]

While it would be desirable to ascribe more voice and agency to this interesting character, as Roncace tries to do in his reading, the problem is that the woman is still diminished in the narrative in a variety of ways: she still remains anonymous; she never directly speaks; and she is remembered only in relation to other male figures—as the mother of her son (a son whom, we must recall, she did not request in 2 Kgs 4) and as the recipient of a miracle by the prophet Elisha (2 Kgs 8:5). These attempts to temper her regard in 2 Kings 8 make it difficult to agree with Roncace's position that she is portrayed more favorably in comparison to the prophet, especially since the prophet is wholly absent here. As before, it seems that Elisha prefers to do his bidding through a proxy, his servant Gehazi.

It remains unclear how much Elisha is to be credited for the fortuitous return of the Shunnamite woman's land and house. In the commentary on 2 Kings 4, it was discussed that even Elisha's initial gift to the woman of a son was an odd one as it was unrequested. It is even more difficult to attribute to the prophet any merit for the return of the woman's possessions as he is even less involved and active in this pericope. Elisha merely warns the woman to flee without ever addressing the situation she will find when she returns. Hence, while the pericope shows that the continuing blessings of a person can be received from contact with and by showing hospitality to a prophet of YHWH, it also communicates a need for the activity and engagement of the recipient in the reception of the benefits. In other words, it is not so much that the woman is shown to be better than Elisha, as Roncace argues, especially in his absence in 2 Kings 8, but that she is to be actively working toward her own goals regardless of any help from the prophet, her husband, or even her son.[12] Similar to the dynamics in 2 Kings 4, here it is because of and through the woman's own enterprising exertions that she receives the blessings of YHWH.

---

10. Ibid., 124.

11. Ibid., 125.

12. Roncace notes that the son that Elisha gives the woman is not very useful to her in requesting the return of her land and house ("Elisha and the Woman of Shunem," 122–23).

From a postcolonial perspective, the end of the woman's pericope sheds light on loss of property and possessions endured and suffered by modern-day refugees, who, like the woman, flee their homeland because of natural or human-made disasters. Unlike the woman, many such victims never get an opportunity to return to their country, and when they do, depending on the situation, they never reacquire their lost land or property. The woman's story in 2 Kings 8 functions as an optimistic and hopeful tale that shows how, with divine luck, human engagement, and some political influence, a refugee, even one who is female, can sometimes come back home.

The Illness and Death of Ben-hadad (8:7-15)

Abruptly switching to the situation in Damascus, the next part of the narrative discusses the illness and death of Aram's king, Ben-hadad. In direct contradistinction to King Ahaziah of Israel (2 Kgs 1),[13] the narrative depicts Ben-hadad sending his messenger, Hazael, to the prophet Elisha to inquire as to whether he will recover from his illness. Perhaps in an effort to induce a good prophecy, Ben-hadad also sends a gift to Elisha—forty camel loads (8:9)—in the hands of Hazael.

Condemnation of the northern kings of Israel is evident in the undeniable similarities between the story of Ahaziah in 2 Kings 1 and that of Ben-hadad. The Israelite king Ahaziah (850–849 BCE), when he is unwell, sends messengers to inquire of Baal-zebub in Ekron (2 Kgs 1). In contrast, the foreign king, Ben-hadad, when he is ill, sends a messenger to inquire of YHWH through his prophet, Elisha (2 Kgs 8). The question Ben-hadad tells Hazael (Ben-hadad's messenger) to ask Elisha—"Will I recover from this illness?"—is the same one Ahaziah asks in 2 Kings 1:2.[14] Ben-hadad, though a non-Israelite, seems to be more cognizant than Ahaziah of the identity of the true, life-giving deity, YHWH.

As with the other narratives concerning Elisha, the chronology and order of the pericopes is unclear. It is uncertain whether Ben-hadad is the same monarch who earlier tried to kidnap Elisha (2 Kgs 6:8-13) or the one who tells Naaman to seek his healing in Israel (2 Kgs 5:5). Even when a monarch is named, the relationship among the various stories remains opaque. Ben-hadad is said to be the same Aramean king who earlier

---

13. Cogan and Tadmor, *II Kings*, 90.
14. Ibid.

[7]Elisha went to Damascus while King Ben-hadad of Aram was ill. When it was told him, "The man of God has come here," [8]the king said to Hazael, "Take a present with you and go to meet the man of God. Inquire of the LORD through him, whether I shall recover from this illness." [9]So Hazael went to meet him, taking a present with him, all kinds of goods of Damascus, forty camel loads. When he entered and stood before him, he said, "Your son King Ben-hadad of Aram has sent me to you, saying, 'Shall I recover from this illness?'" [10]Elisha said to him, "Go, say to him, 'You shall certainly recover'; but the LORD has shown me that he shall certainly die." [11]He fixed his gaze and stared at him, until he was ashamed. Then the man of God wept. [12]Hazael asked, "Why does my lord weep?" He answered, "Because I know the evil that you will do to the people of Israel; you will set their fortresses on fire, you will kill their young men with the sword, dash in pieces their little ones, and rip up their pregnant women." [13]Hazael said, "What is your servant, who is a mere dog, that he should do this great thing?" Elisha answered, "The LORD has shown me that you are to be king over Aram." [14]Then he left Elisha, and went to his master Ben-hadad, who said to him, "What did Elisha say to you?" And he answered, "He told me that you would certainly recover." [15]But the next day he took the bed-cover and dipped it in water and spread it over the king's face, until he died. And Hazael succeeded him.

put Samaria under siege (2 Kgs 6:24). Yet if so, how do we explain this sympathetic, almost positive portrayal of this monarch in 2 Kings 8? Are we to read the stories together and assume that Ben-hadad, after failing to kidnap Elisha and to capture Samaria, came to recognize the power of YHWH? Adding to the confusion about the order of and relationship among the stories is the misalignment of Elisha's oracle about Hazael in 2 Kings 8:10-13 with 1 Kings 19:15-18, which records a variant tradition about the appointment of Hazael (and Jehu) wherein Elijah, not Elisha, is tasked with anointing Hazael as king of Damascus.[15]

As mentioned above, another element to consider in the first part of 2 Kings is that the narratives do not appear to be chronologically ordered. Rather, the best we can say is that these stories, aside from recording the various legends and miracle tales about Elisha and Elijah, reflect more broadly the heightened level of interactions between Aram and Israel during the monarchic period. A literary aspect worth noticing is that the

15. Ibid., 92.

confusing and chronologically misplaced accounts also show the different ways in which neighboring countries were utilized by the biblical
writer to convey a particular message.

Though the sequence of the narratives does not appear to be chronological, some of the ordering does seem deliberate and purposeful. For
example, there might be a theological reason why this pericope about
Ben-hadad's death was placed after that of his siege of Samaria. As commentators have noticed, Elisha gives a strange response to Ben-hadad's
question, which he sent through Hazael, as to whether he will live or die
from his illness. To this query, "Elisha said to him [Hazael], 'Go, say to
him, "You shall certainly recover" [תחיה, literally 'he will live']; but the
LORD has shown me that he shall certainly die'" (2 Kgs 8:10). Elisha's
answer appears both contradictory and dishonest. Why does the prophet
tell Ben-hadad that he will recover when the Lord has told the prophet
that the king will perish? More intriguing, is Elisha complicit in Ben-
hadad's murder as he tells Hazael to lie to Ben-hadad about his recovery?
Later scribes will attempt to "correct" Elisha's contradictory prophecy
by putting the *ketib*[16] לא, meaning "no" or "not," before the verb תחיה to
get the reading "you will not recover."[17] Moreover, other commentators
such as Casper J. Labuschagne[18] will attempt to salvage the prophecy by
arguing that "you will live" refers to Hazael, not to Ben-hadad.

The seemingly contradictory oracle is confirmed at the end of the
narrative when Ben-hadad does not die from his illness but is instead
assassinated by Hazael. Hazael, maybe because he realizes that his murderous plot has been discovered by Elisha or because his desire for power
has been validated by the prophet's oracle, lies and tells the king he will
recover only to smother him to death the next day (8:15).[19] Clarifying
Elisha's prophecy, the conclusion thus explains why the prophet tells
Hazael to tell the king he will recover though Elisha foresees his death.
The king would have recovered and lived had he not been murdered by
Hazael. In other words, the king does live and yet also, at the end, dies.

---

16. When there are differences in the text of the Hebrew Bible, *ketib* refers to that
which is written in the text versus the *qere*, which refers to what is read or said.

17. Cogan and Tadmor, *II Kings*, 90.

18. Casper J. Labuschagne, "Did Elisha Deliberately Lie? A Note on II Kings 8:10,"
ZAW 77 (1965): 327–28.

19. There are some questions as to what Hazael is attempting to do to Ben-hadad
by placing a cloth on his face. Josephus believes that this was suffocation (*Ant.* 9.92),
while Cogan and Tadmor note that medieval commentators, in order to exculpate
Elisha, favor the view that Hazael was merely applying a compress to the sick Ben-
hadad (Cogan and Tadmor, *II Kings*, 91).

Elisha's clever oracle—he will live but also will die—thus is ultimately proven true.

Nevertheless, the conclusion raises theological problems and queries. Why does Ben-hadad die even though he consulted the right prophet of the right God? The question is more problematic considering the contrast between Ben-hadad and Ahaziah, which we noted earlier. If Ahaziah never recovered from his sickness and was condemned to death because he consulted the wrong deity, then should not the monarch who consulted the right prophet and the right God, in contrast, be rewarded with recovery and life? As Naaman, the Aramean general, was healed because he sought out Elisha, should not Ben-hadad be similarly restored?

An initial explanation as to why Ben-hadad's recovery is depicted as ineffectual is that it better aligned with historical events. Assyrian evidence also alludes to Hazael's coup d'état (c. 842).[20] Indeed, what we know from biblical and ancient Near Eastern sources is that Hazael, whom the Assyrian sources call the "son of nobody," took over Aram[21] and that his reign led to increased hostility between Aram and Judah. Though debated, Hazael appears to have expanded Aram's territories, including colonizing parts of Israel and Judah (2 Kgs 13:3; 10:32-33). Israel was only able to fully regain its independence after Hazael's death (2 Kgs 13:22-25). This history of subjugation and colonization of Israel and Judah is probably what underlies Elisha's sorrowful prophecy to Hazael about the damage he will do to Israel—"Because I know the evil that you will do to the people of Israel; you will set their fortresses on fire, you will kill their young men with sword, dash in pieces their little ones, and rip up their pregnant women" (2 Kgs 8:12). Thus, Ben-hadad dies by the hands of Hazael even if he consulted the right prophet partly because the historical Hazael usurped the throne of Ben-hadad.

The historical evidence, however, does not fully address the literary and theological questions raised by the narrative. Indeed, what we know about the history leads to more questions about the literature and the theology underlying it. If the historical events belie the intent of the literature, why did the biblical writer depict Ben-hadad, in particular, as seeking and receiving this particular prophecy from YHWH's prophet, Elisha? Why, in other words, create a tension by portraying Ben-hadad undertaking the right actions only to have him be killed off at the end? Why not just leave the king anonymous as in other parts of 2 Kings?

---

20. Ibid., 92.
21. Ibid.

To these questions, some preliminary theological answers can be proposed. First, by depicting the king of Aram as consulting YHWH through Elisha, his prophet, the universality of YHWH can be asserted. Similar to the oracles against the nations found in the prophetic books,[22] Elisha's prophecy shows that YHWH is in control over the fate of all the nations, not just Israel.[23] In contrast to 2 Kings 5, which depicts Naaman, the healed Aramean general, requesting soil from Israel so that he can worship YHWH in Aram, 2 Kings 8 asserts that YHWH is not bound to any land mass or territory. YHWH knows what will happen anywhere and to anyone, even to a king in Aram.

Aside from proclaiming the universality of YHWH, another reason for Ben-hadad's death might be to exact literary punishment on the foreign king. Remember that Ben-hadad is named as the king who also puts Samaria under a siege, causing a horrifying famine in 2 Kings 6:24-33. For this deed, he is never punished. That Ben-hadad is specifically named as the Aramean king in both the siege/famine pericope in 2 Kings 6:24 and in this story about his illness is telling and speaks to a particular motivation for the identification. Perhaps the biblical writers wanted to right the earlier wrong of the famine and the siege caused by Ben-hadad by punishing the king with death, assassination, and usurpation a couple of chapters later. Hence, though Ben-hadad is depicted as turning to the right prophet and the right God, he, at the end, still gets his just desserts for his earlier offenses against Israel.

With Elisha's contradictory oracle—Ben-hadad will recover, and he will die—the narrator can have his cake and eat it too by both rewarding and punishing Ben-hadad. The Aramean king would have lived—the reward for consulting the right God—had not surrounding evildoers foiled this plan. The failure for the monarch to be healed is conveniently blamed on treasonous and violent machinations in Aram. In so doing, the narrative conveys the message that, unlike Ahaziah, Ben-hadad took the correct action in going to YHWH and Elisha, while simultaneously settling the score with Ben-hadad for his earlier wrongdoing by depicting his assassination—an assassination that is conveniently blamed on power-hungry traitors.

---

22. John Barton, *The Theology of the Book of Amos* (Cambridge: Cambridge University Press, 2012), esp. 58–59; G. R. Hamborg, "Reasons for Judgement in the Oracles Against the Nations of the Prophet Isaiah," *VT* 31 (1981): 145–59; John McKenzie, *A Theology of the Old Testament* (Eugene, OR: Wipf & Stock, 1974), 178–79.

23. Cogan and Tadmor, *II Kings*, 92.

The other part of Elisha's prophecy concerning the destiny of Hazael is more difficult to explain theologically. As we noted earlier, Elisha, after telling Hazael to tell Ben-hadad that he will recover, stares at Hazael and then sorrowfully lists the savage violence that he will unleash against the people of Israel, including dashing children into pieces and ripping up pregnant women (8:12). Elisha's brief, sorrowful statement elucidates the horrors suffered by those who are the most vulnerable, such as women and children, as a result of warfare or power struggles (see Amos 1:13; Hos 14:1). Moreover, if this is an allusion to Aramean colonization, it also shows the appalling violence that follows in the wake of a greedy colonial enterprise.

To this charge, Hazael replies that he is nothing, a "mere dog," incapable of doing these "great things" (v. 13). Elisha then presciently replies that he knows that Hazael will become king of Aram (v. 13). It is difficult to judge the veracity of Hazael's response. Is he lying to Elisha, deceptively acting humble and ignorant even though he has been caught red-handed by Elisha in planning to assassinate Ben-hadad?[24] Or is he genuinely surprised, not yet having a plan in place to take the throne? Whether authentic or feigned, Hazael's self-deprecating reference to himself as a dog is certainly meant to convey his humbleness and unimportance. His statement, however, conveys an important theological message: even an insignificant, unimportant person has the capacity to commit atrocities. One humble nobody, when given a certain amount of power, can utilize that power to spread terror and wreak havoc on those who are weak and vulnerable.

Aside from warning the reader again about the dangers of political and military power, the exchange between Hazael and the prophet also offers a model as to how the reader is supposed to react in the face of such violence. Different interpretations of this exchange lead to different views of the prophet and how he can serve as the model for the reader. If Hazael is lying to Elisha, then Elisha's response can be read as bolder and more confrontational. Instead of letting Hazael off with a comment about Ben-hadad, the prophet stares the Aramean down and then goes face-to-face with him about the evils that he is about to commit against Israel, tallying up his impending crimes.[25] In so doing, Elisha reveals the evils that lie deep inside Hazael's heart and divulges to Hazael that his

---

24. Gina Hens-Piazza, *1–2 Kings*, AOTC (Nashville: Abingdon, 2006), 281.
25. Ibid., 284.

misdeeds are indeed known to God. The prophet models behavior that should be followed by modern religious leaders as they confront the "ills of political forces," even those that seem inevitable.[26]

If we read the exchange between Elisha and Hazael slightly differently, a varying theological message emerges. If Elisha's response to Hazael is interpreted as less aggressive and more dejected and resigned—the prophet, "weeping," foretells Hazael's rise to power and the violence he will commit as king—a more human portrait of the prophet is revealed. Like with the starving mothers in 2 Kings 6, this reading stresses the constraints of the prophet—even a prophet of YHWH—when confronted with the evils of the world. Though the prophet can foresee some of the horrors that people will do or suffer, he does not always have the power to stop them. Rather, he can only warn, admonish, attempt to persuade, and, finally, serve as a witness. Discussions about the limitations of the prophet are undoubtedly related to those about God, and, hence, this interpretation cannot help but raise larger questions of theodicy: Is God just and if so, why does he or Elisha not stop Hazael, knowing the horrors he will inflict on his own people? Though there can never be a satisfactory answer to this query, perhaps some small comfort can be found in Elisha's oracle. Elisha, in foretelling what Hazael will do as king, clearly acknowledges that God knows of these evils. Though we will never know why YHWH chooses not to intervene, we do find out, however, that YHWH notices these horrible acts. This more constrained vision of the prophet offers a slightly different pedagogical message for modern religious leaders: if they cannot stop injustice, then they should, like Elisha, at least bear witness to it. At points, they may even need to serve as a witness against God when he fails to intervene on behalf of his own people.[27]

The Reign of Jehoram and Ahaziah of Judah (8:16-29)

Resuming the regnal accounts of the kings of Judah and Israel, 2 Kings 8:16-29 returns to the situation in Judah with two summaries of the reign of Jehoram and his successor, Ahaziah, in Judah. As typical of these reg-

---

26. Ibid.

27. For people bearing witness even against God, see the various works of Elie Wiesel (*Messengers of God: Biblical Portraits and Legends,* trans. Marion Wiesel [New York: Random House, 1976], esp. 211–35; idem, *The Trial of God,* trans. Marion Wiesel [New York: Schocken Books, 1979]).

¹⁶In the fifth year of King Joram son of Ahab of Israel, Jehoram son of King Jehoshaphat of Judah began to reign. ¹⁷He was thirty-two years old when he became king, and he reigned eight years in Jerusalem. ¹⁸He walked in the way of the kings of Israel, as the house of Ahab had done, for the daughter of Ahab was his wife. He did what was evil in the sight of the LORD. ¹⁹Yet the LORD would not destroy Judah, for the sake of his servant David, since he had promised to give a lamp to him and to his descendants forever.

²⁰In his days Edom revolted against the rule of Judah, and set up a king of their own. ²¹Then Joram crossed over to Zair with all his chariots. He set out by night and attacked the Edomites and their chariot commanders who had surrounded him; but his army fled home. ²²So Edom has been in revolt against the rule of Judah to this day. Libnah also revolted at the same time. ²³Now the rest of the acts of Joram, and all that he did, are they not written in the Book of the Annals of the Kings of Judah? ²⁴So Joram slept with his

nal summaries, it lists the name and regnal year of the corresponding monarch in Samaria, the king's age when he assumed the throne, his lineage, and a positive or negative assessment of his reign. Many chapters separate the regnal accounts of Jehoram and Ahaziah, and the last preceding one about Jehoram's father, Jehoshaphat, is found in 1 Kings 22:41-51. Most likely, the summaries restart here in order to preface the account of Jehu's rise in the next chapter. Jehu's rebellion will lead to the deaths of both Ahaziah of Judah and Joram of Israel as well as the decimation of Ahab's family (2 Kgs 9:1–10:28).[28]

That these pericopes serve as a prelude to the narrative about the decline and fall of the house of Ahab[29] is evident by the numerous repetitions of Ahab and Omri throughout the summaries (2 Kgs 8:16, 18 [2x], 25, 26, 27 [3x], 28, 29). Moreover, not only are Jehoram and Ahaziah both given negative assessments, but their sinfulness is explained as a result of their ties to the hated northern dynasty. Jehoram, for example, is said to have married the daughter of Ahab, Athaliah (see discussion in 2 Kgs 11), who is the daughter either of Ahab (2 Kgs 8:19) or of Omri

---

28. Cogan and Tadmor, *II Kings*, 97.

29. Cogan and Tadmor note that Assyrian texts consistently designate Israel as the *Bit-Humri* or "house of Omri," while the biblical text designates the lineage as the "house of Ahab" (2 Kgs 9:7-9; 10:10-11; 21:13) (ibid., 99).

ancestors, and was buried with them in the city of David; his son Ahaziah succeeded him.

²⁵In the twelfth year of King Joram son of Ahab of Israel, Ahaziah son of King Jehoram of Judah began to reign. ²⁶Ahaziah was twenty-two years old when he began to reign; he reigned one year in Jerusalem. His mother's name was Athaliah, a grand-daughter of King Omri of Israel. ²⁷He also walked in the way of the house of Ahab, doing what was evil in the sight of the Lord,

as the house of Ahab had done, for he was son-in-law to the house of Ahab.

²⁸He went with Joram son of Ahab to wage war against King Hazael of Aram at Ramoth-gilead, where the Arameans wounded Joram. ²⁹King Joram returned to be healed in Jezreel of the wounds that the Arameans had inflicted on him at Ramah, when he fought against King Hazael of Aram. King Ahaziah son of Jehoram of Judah went down to see Joram son of Ahab in Jezreel, because he was wounded.

(2 Kgs 8:26).³⁰ Blaming the wife as a bad influence on the king, Jehoram is said to have followed the ways of the kings of Israel and displeased the Lord. Though Judah survives because of YHWH's promises to David (8:19), God's displeasure is manifest in the loss of Judah's colonial territories. Edom, which was conquered by David (2 Sam 8:2, 12-14; cf. 1 Kgs 11:14-22), successfully revolts, sets up its own king, and fends off Jehoram's attack. Both Edom and the town of Libnah rebel against Judah during Jehoram's reign (8:20). The loss of these territories depicts Jehoram as a weak and powerless leader, unfavored by YHWH.

Jehoram's successor, Ahaziah, is as equally unsuccessful a king as his father. This again is blamed on his familial ties to Ahab. Ahaziah is not just the son of the hated Athaliah but also seems to have married another member of Ahab's family (8:25). With such a family, Ahaziah, as expected, is said to have displeased YHWH, acting in line with the detested Ahab clan (8:27). As a result, in what most scholars think is a secondary insertion,³¹ 2 Kings 8:28-29 tells of his alliance with Joram of Israel and his early demise. The displeasure of YHWH is evident in the short one-year reign of Ahaziah, during which he accomplished nothing but angering God.

30. The term for daughter (בת), however, can mean granddaughter, thus making her a granddaughter of Omri and a daughter of Ahab (ibid., 98).
31. Ibid., 99.

The narrative seethes with hatred of the house of Ahab, especially the women of that family. The hatred will gradually crescendo, reaching its apex in the next chapter wherein the Deuteronomistic writer will painstakingly detail the grisly death of the hated Queen Jezebel. Special animus is reserved by the biblical writer for foreign women who are both pious and powerful. Though they possess no official power, these women receive the lion's share of the blame for the political, sociological, and religious wrongdoings in the country. The mismanagement and inabilities of their husbands—the male kings—are excused as a result of the negative influence of their wives. Women, in the biblical text, are depicted as a gateway drug, luring unsuspecting kings and men into worship of foreign gods or other lewd, ungodly acts (see Prov 7; 1 Kgs 11).

The same patriarchal blame is evident in the two regnal summaries here in 2 Kings 8. The Judean monarchs' inabilities and failures as kings are blamed on their affiliation with the women of Ahab's family—in the case of Jehoram, his marriage to Athaliah (8:18), and, in the case of Ahaziah, his marriage to an unnamed member of Ahab's family (8:27). As with Ahab, so here with Jehoram and Ahaziah, the monarch's bad, impious behavior is excused as a result of their wives' influence. By not naming Ahaziah's wife and identifying her as an Omride, emphasis can be placed on Ahaziah's connection and thus similarity to the detested members of Ahab's family, particularly Jezebel.[32] Especially important is the mention of Athaliah, who is envisioned as a Jezebel redux and who will bravely try to take the throne for herself a few chapters later in 2 Kings 11. That she is mentioned here is important. As stated earlier, we can see in the account of Jehoram and Ahaziah's reigns, the biblical writer takes particular relish in describing the fall of the house of Ahab. Jezebel and, shortly thereafter, Athaliah will soon be dispatched with something approaching glee.

32. Robert Cohn, 2 Kings, Berit Olam (Collegeville, MN: Liturgical Press, 2000), 63–64; Johanna Stiebert, Fathers and Daughters in the Hebrew Bible (Oxford: Oxford University Press, 2013), 44.

2 Kings 9:1-37

The Murder of Queen Jezebel

The biblical writer gleefully tells of the demise of the house of Ahab at the hands of the usurper, Jehu, in chapters 9 and 10. Cycle after cycle of violence immediately follows on the heels of the anointing of Jehu as king over Israel. Everyone related to or associated with Ahab is killed off, including his reigning successor, Joram, the rest of his other sons, his hated wife, Jezebel, his friends, his supporters, and, finally, the royally supported religious personnel of Baal. Vividly told, with interesting touches of detail, the biblical writer's enjoyment of the literary murder of his hated antagonists is undeniable. Of special interest to feminist scholars is the evocative and exegetically loaded depiction of the grisly demise of Queen Jezebel. While the narrative concerns the end of Ahab and his dynasty, Jezebel is the main target of the biblical writer's venom. The narrative attempts not simply to erase Jezebel but to scapegoat, torture, and punish her so as to exorcise her powerful persona and spirit. Despite this attempt, however, the almost ghostly last images of her remaining palms, feet, and skull (2 Kgs 9:35) hint of her lingering presence in the text: fighting against the narrative and against the murdering pen of the scribe,[1] she endures as a shadowy poltergeist.

---

1. On literary murder of women in the biblical text, see J. Cheryl Exum, *Fragmented Women: Feminist (Sub)versions of Biblical Narratives*, JSOTSup 163 (Sheffield: JSOT Press, 1993), esp. 16–41.

Jehu Anointed as King (9:1-13)

The narrative begins with the prophet Elisha commanding one of the members of the sons of the prophets, בני הנבאים,[2] to go and secretly anoint Jehu, an Israelite army commander, as king over Israel (9:1). Oddly, both Jehu's father, Jehoshaphat, and his grandfather, Nimshi, are named (9:2)—maybe to differentiate his father from Jehoshaphat, the king of Judah, or perhaps because his grandfather was better known.[3] Why Elisha chooses a proxy instead of going himself is unstated. Perhaps Elisha is too old or maybe it would appear too suspicious if he were to undertake the task himself. As evident in Elisha's instructions to his proxy to act quickly and secretly—he is to gird up his loins, take Jehu into a private room, pour oil on him, and then immediately flee (9:2-3)—anointing a new king while another monarch was still alive and on the throne was fraught with danger. The prophet, if caught, would certainly have been charged with treason. David's secret anointing by Samuel during Saul's reign offers an apt parallel (1 Sam 16).

Immediately, Elisha's proxy, the young prophet, goes to work. He goes to Ramoth-gilead where Jehu and Israel's armies are stationed, finds Israel's commanders in a meeting (v. 4), singles out Jehu (v. 5), anoints him after getting him alone, and declares him king over Israel (v. 6). So far he has followed Elisha's directions precisely. At this point, however, the young prophet deviates from Elisha's instructions. Instead of immediately fleeing, he offers a long-winded explanation of his treasonous appointment of Jehu as monarch—i.e., this is YHWH's way to avenge Jezebel for her purge of the prophets and religious personnel of YHWH (v. 7). No longer in a hurry, the narrative tarries to draw out what YHWH will do to Jezebel and to the house of Ahab: God will kill every man related to Ahab (v. 8), and Ahab's house will suffer the same fate as those of Jeroboam and Baasha (v. 9), two Israelite kings who angered YHWH and were stripped of their crowns.

Special hatred, however, is reserved for Jezebel, the Phoenician wife of Ahab. The young prophet reiterates Elijah's earlier prophecy in 1 Kings 21, which foretells the grisly consumption of Jezebel's corpse by dogs in Jezreel, the location of Naboth's vineyard. Such a demise would have "brought horror to the ancients," as the spirit of a person without proper

---

2. On the "sons of the prophets," see the discussion in 2 Kings 2 and 4.

3. Mordechai Cogan and Hayim Tadmor, *II Kings: A New Translation with Introduction and Commentary*, AB 11 (Garden City, NY: Doubleday, 1988), 106; Choon-Leong Seow "The First and Second Book of Kings," in *NIB*, ed. Leander E. Keck et al. (Nashville: Abingdon, 1999), 3:217.

2 Kgs 9:1-13

⁹:¹Then the prophet Elisha called a member of the company of prophets and said to him, "Gird up your loins; take this flask of oil in your hand, and go to Ramoth-gilead. ²When you arrive, look there for Jehu son of Jehoshaphat, son of Nimshi; go in and get him to leave his companions, and take him into an inner chamber. ³Then take the flask of oil, pour it on his head, and say, 'Thus says the LORD: I anoint you king over Israel.' Then open the door and flee; do not linger."

⁴So the young man, the young prophet, went to Ramoth-gilead. ⁵He arrived while the commanders of the army were in council, and he announced, "I have a message for you commander." "For which one of us?" asked Jehu. "For you, commander." ⁶So Jehu got up and went inside; the young man poured the oil on his head, saying to him, "Thus says the LORD the God of Israel: I anoint you king over the people of the LORD, over Israel. ⁷You shall strike down the house of your

burial would be condemned to wander about forever.[4] Hence, not only is Jezebel predicted to die, but she is to be continually punished after her death. Not being properly buried, her spirit is condemned to never find peace. As in the preceding accounts of Jehoram and Ahaziah, blame is once again placed on the woman as Jezebel is almost singlehandedly said to be responsible for causing the end of Ahab's dynasty and the national increase in religious impiety. In receiving "one of the most damning of punishments," Jezebel thus serves as a narrative scapegoat.[5]

After damning Jezebel, Elisha's proxy suddenly seems to have realized that his actions put him in quite a bit of danger, and he flees out the door (v. 10). When Jehu returns to the meeting, the military commanders are, unsurprisingly, curious as to what that "madman" (מְשֻׁגָּע) wanted to tell Jehu (v. 11-12): "they said to him, 'Is everything all right? Why did that madman come to you?'" (2 Kgs 9:11). The reference to the young prophet as a madman alludes to a later description of Jehu who is said to drive his chariot like a madman (2 Kgs 9:20). Moreover, this reference also highlights the marginal, outsider status of the prophets in Israel, who do not behave according to conventions.[6] As we have noted

---

4. Cogan and Tadmor, *II Kings*, 108–9; see also Volkmar Fritz, *1 & 2 Kings*, trans. Anselm Hagedorn, CC (Minneapolis: Fortress, 2003), 284.

5. Gina Hens-Piazza, *1–2 Kings*, AOTC (Nashville: Abingdon, 2006), 288.

6. Thomas Overholt, *Prophecy in Cross-Cultural Perspective: A Sourcebook for Biblical Researchers*, SBLSBS 17 (Atlanta: Scholars Press, 1986); Robert Wilson, *Prophecy and Society in Ancient Israel* (Philadelphia: Fortress, 1980), 204–5.

master Ahab, so that I may avenge on Jezebel the blood of my servants the prophets, and the blood of all the servants of the LORD. ⁸For the whole house of Ahab shall perish; I will cut off from Ahab every male, bond or free, in Israel. ⁹I will make the house of Ahab like the house of Jeroboam son of Nebat, like the house of Baasha son of Ahijah. ¹⁰The dogs shall eat Jezebel in the territory of Jezreel, and no one shall bury her." Then he opened the door and fled.

¹¹When Jehu came back to his master's officers, they said to him, "Is everything all right? Why did that madman come to you?" He answered them, "You know the sort and how they babble." ¹²They said, "Liar! Come on, tell us!" So he said, "This is just what he said to me: 'Thus says the LORD, I anoint you king over Israel.'" ¹³Then hurriedly they all took their cloaks and spread them for him on the bare steps; and they blew the trumpet, and proclaimed, "Jehu is king."

earlier, two different pictures of the sons of the prophets are presented in 2 Kings: At points, the prophet is depicted as a normal, family man in the prophetic trade (2 Kgs 4:1-7); at other times, the prophet is pictured as part of a separate, religious community of men who live and work together in relative poverty (2 Kgs 6:1-7). Some scholars even posit that women might have been part of this group but were concealed under the masculine terminology (see discussion on 2 Kgs 21).[7]

The reference to the prophet as a "madman" is also derogatory and speaks to the general disrespect and disregard the military have for prophets in Israel. Showing the state of religious impiety in Israel, nobody in power seems to treat the prophets of YHWH with much respect or take them very seriously—that is, until a prophet tells them what they want to hear. In this case, when the other commanders ask Jehu what the madman has told him, Jehu lies and tries to skirt the question with an ambiguous reply about the usual babble of prophets (v. 11). Perhaps sensing he is lying or at least trying to cover up something more interesting, the commanders press Jehu until he tells them the truth (v. 12). When his anointing is revealed, the words of the madman are now wholly accepted by the army, and the soldiers spread out their cloaks to make a royal carpet, blow the trumpets, and publicly proclaim Jehu as king (v. 13).

7. Mercedes L. García Bachmann, *Women at Work in the Deuteronomistic History* (Atlanta: Society of Biblical Literature, 2013), esp. 161–76, 174; Wilda C. Gafney, *Daughters of Miriam: Women Prophets in Ancient Israel* (Minneapolis: Fortress, 2008), 15.

Like other usurpers with dubious legitimacy, Jehu's succession narrative is infused with political undertones and messages. By depicting the army commanders as pressuring Jehu into telling them about his secret anointing, Jehu can be depicted as somewhat reluctant to take the throne: Jehu wanted to keep his promotion quiet but was forced to tell his fellow commanders who, incidentally, are all part of Israel's militia, and when they find out, they are so excited that they declare him king immediately. Moreover, by repeatedly stating that Jehu's anointing came as a sudden command by YHWH to his legitimate prophet, Elisha—and thus as a complete surprise to Jehu and others in the army—the charge of treason can be modified. Jehu's usurpation was not planned. Rather, it came about at the insistence of YHWH. Yet reading between the lines, the jarring about-face of Jehu's commanders to the words of the "madman" prophet seems to indicate that his elevation to power was not entirely a surprise to the army. Rather, the "instant acclamation" of his kingship hints that the "seeds of revolt were likely sown long before the events."[8] Most important, the narrative tries to justify and excuse Jehu's treasonous grab for power by shifting the blame to a foreign woman, the ultimate Other.[9]

Excursus: Jezebel as the "Other"

If one accepts, with scholars such as Elisabeth Bronfen and Sarah Webster Goodwin, that a community's identity is intimately tied to those it chooses to kill, then what is clear is that this woman, who has been so clearly presented as "Other" in crucial respects such as ethnicity and religious belief, represents what Israel wants eliminated from its midst, or, at the very least, what a section of later Israel wants written as elimination. . . . The later writers needed this figure of Jezebel as a means of asserting their own sense of Israelite identity; she is to be the measure of what they are not, by definitions that carry divine sanction.[10]

Judith E. McKinlay

---

8. Hens-Piazza, *1–2 Kings*, 289.

9. On Jezebel as the ultimate Other, see Judith E. McKinlay, "Negotiating the Frame for Viewing the Death of Jezebel," *BibInt* 10 (2002): 305–23.

10. McKinlay, "Negotiating the Frame," 309–10.

Jezebel is said to be the real reason for Jehu's usurpation. She so angered YHWH that he was forced through his prophet Elijah to issue an oracle of judgment against her and Ahab in 1 Kings 21:21-23. It is only fitting that Elijah's protégé, Elisha, before he dies, would fulfill the oracle of his master. Jehu is, therefore, merely an "innocent" benefactor of a larger divine plan to rid Israel of the hated Phoenician queen and her family, the Omrides—a plan that was foretold by the esteemed prophet Elijah. Religious, sexist, and xenophobic disinformation and agitprop are thus neatly utilized to mask political ambitions and a bloodthirsty grab for power.

Jehu's Usurpation of the Throne (9:14-23)

The scene now shifts to the whereabouts of the sitting king of Israel, Joram (c. 849–842 BCE), who, unaware of the dramatic events unfolding in his army camp in Ramoth-gilead, is in Jezreel, recovering from wounds he received in a battle against Aram (2 Kgs 9:14-15). There, he is joined by his relative, King Ahaziah of Judah who is visiting him (v. 16).

The notice of Joram's affliction might explain the suspicious timing of Jehu's anointing. Indeed, it seems rather fortuitous that Jehu is suddenly anointed as king and immediately accepted by the army as such exactly at a point when Joram is sick and absent from the camp in Ramoth-gilead. Mordechai Cogan and Hayim Tadmor suggest that the king's illness may have provided the perfect moment of weakness for a usurpation, which would have been brewing for some time. They argue that the continuing war with Aram-Damascus, the extravagant lifestyle of the royal family, and the increasing class disparity between rich and poor, exacerbated by the illegal confiscation of Naboth's property, which became a *cause celebre*, created a perfect storm for an insurrection.[11]

Timing thus seems to be of crucial importance to Jehu in his plan to take the throne. Jehu relies on speed, surprise, and secrecy. Jehu needs to strike before Joram has returned to his full health and full power—that is, before Joram realizes that a coup is afoot and musters his loyalists. Hence, Jehu shrewdly tells his men to prevent anyone from leaving Ramoth-gilead lest news of his anointing reach Joram in Jezreel (v. 15). He then speeds off on his chariot toward Jezreel, most likely with a retinue of soldiers, to confront and assassinate Joram. That no large

---

11. Cogan and Tadmor, *II Kings*, 120.

¹⁴Thus Jehu son of Jehoshaphat son of Nimshi conspired against Joram. Joram with all Israel had been on guard against King Hazael of Aram; ¹⁵but King Joram had returned to be healed in Jezreel of the wounds that the Arameans had inflicted on him, when he fought against King Hazael of Aram. So Jehu said, "If this is your wish, then let no one slip out of the city to go and tell the news in Jezreel." ¹⁶Then Jehu mounted his chariot and went to Jezreel, where Joram was lying ill. King Ahaziah of Judah had come down to visit Joram.

¹⁷In Jezreel, the sentinel standing on the tower spied the company of Jehu arriving, and said, "I see a company." Joram said, "Take a horseman; send him to meet them, and let him say, 'Is it peace?'" ¹⁸So the horseman went to meet him; he said, "Thus says the king, 'Is it peace?'" Jehu responded, "What have you to do with peace? Fall in behind me." The sentinel reported, saying, "The messenger reached them, but he is not coming back." ¹⁹Then he sent out a second horseman, who came to them and said, "Thus says the

army is mentioned as accompanying Jehu appears to indicate that he is rather confident that the soldiers who are guarding Joram in Jezreel can be easily persuaded to turn against their current king and join him in the rebellion. This again hints that Jehu's plan, which seems to have been plotted in and by the military, was not as spontaneous as depicted in the narrative but something that had been formulated and planned for some time.

As Jehu draws near, Joram sends two soldiers to ask the approaching charioteer, whose identity remains unknown, whether it is השלום, *shalom*—variously translated as whether he comes peacefully or whether all is well. Joram's question hints that the king might have had some suspicions of political intrigue. In a threefold pattern, two soldiers, each in turn, drive out, approach Jehu, ask him השלום, "Is it *shalom*?" and then fall in behind him (v. 18, 19). In an allusion to the earlier designation of the young prophet as a madman, a sentinel, at this point, recognizes Jehu by his crazy driving (v. 20). And in a third and last attempt, Joram, unable to get any news or information about Jehu, goes out to meet him in person. Gina Hens-Piazza notes that the threefold pattern found here is utilized numerous times in 2 Kings: soldiers approach Elijah on the mount three times (2 Kgs 1:9, 11, 13); before Elijah's ascension, he makes three journeys (2:2-3, 4-5, 6); the oracle of Jehu's appointment is repeated three times before Jehu and Joram's meeting; and, finally, three accounts of three deaths—those of Joram, Ahaziah, and Jezebel—immediately

king, 'Is it peace?'" Jehu answered, "What have you to do with peace? Fall in behind me." ²⁰Again the sentinel reported, "He reached them, but he is not coming back. It looks like the driving of Jehu son of Nimshi; for he drives like a maniac."

²¹Joram said, "Get ready." And they got his chariot ready. Then King Joram of Israel and King Ahaziah of Judah set out, each in his chariot, and went to meet Jehu; they met him at the property of Naboth the Jezreelite. ²²When Joram saw Jehu, he said, "Is it peace, Jehu?" He answered, "What peace can there be, so long as the many whoredoms and sorceries of your mother Jezebel continue?" ²³Then Joram reined about and fled, saying to Ahaziah, "Treason, Ahaziah!"

follow this meeting.[12] The purpose of this repeated pattern in this case, according to Hens-Piazza, is to show that the change of regime is "by the order and plan of the Lord."[13]

The role of God presented in this narrative about the assassination of Joram (and also soon thereafter, in the murders of Ahaziah and Jezebel) is also stressed in the wordplay in Joram and Jehu's conversation. Joram, not recognizing the danger, when he reaches Jehu, asks him in person whether it is שלום, *shalom*. To this question, Jehu retorts with another harangue about Joram's mother, Jezebel, utilizing a clever doublespeak on the meaning of שלום: "He answered, 'What peace can there be, so long as the many whoredoms and sorceries of your mother Jezebel continue?' " (2 Kgs 9:22). Saul Olyan argues that different connotations of שלום, a *Leitwort* of 2 Kings 9, are employed in order to present Jehu as a restorer of שלום for the community.[14] Adding to Olyan's work, the paronomasia also has a particular misogynistic purpose.

The Hebrew root שלום, *sh-l-m*, which is usually translated as "peace," is connotatively dense. It can designate a sound state of health, completeness, order, safety from war, the state of being in a right relationship with God or between individuals.[15] Playing on its different resonances, characters are depicted as deliberately speaking past each other, putting forth divergent conceptions about what constitutes שלום or peace. For Joram, peace is defined as safety for himself and also, relatedly, the stabil-

12. Hens-Piazza, *1–2 Kings*, 290.
13. Ibid., 287.
14. Saul Olyan, "*Hašālôm*: Some Literary Considerations of 2 Kings 9," *CBQ* 46 (1984): 652–68.
15. Ibid., 660.

ity that results from an uninterrupted dynastic system. Peace as defined by Jehu (and the narrator),[16] however, designates a state of communal wellbeing that comes from a right relationship between God and Israel.

These different definitions of שלום are exploited to charge Jezebel, whom Jehu singles out in his retort to Joram, with larger, more damnable offenses. If peace is centrally about the state of YHWH and Israel's relationship, and if Jezebel is the one who is said to disrupt the שלום between YHWH and his nation, then it is Jezebel, not the people, who is solely responsible for the country's current religious disorder. In this literary witch hunt, Jezebel, the outsider and foreigner, is conveniently blamed for the religious deprivation and apostasy of an entire nation![17] Additionally, as a scapegoat for the sins of Israel (and of the Omride clan), her demise is deemed absolutely necessary for national survival. She has to be killed in order for the community to have any peace or communal wellbeing. And not just killed, but as we discussed earlier, murdered in such a way so as to ensure that she will have no peace in the afterlife. Moreover, all of this is commanded by YHWH since it is his relationship with Israel that is being damaged by this foreign witch.

Hence, Jehu's definition of שלום works to deflect blame. If peace is, as Joram defines it, a sense of safety, stability, lack of war, and well-being, then Jehu shifts and places the blame for the instability (or the lack of שלום) of the nation—instability that he causes with his numerous political assassinations—on Jezebel by redefining instability to refer to the relationship between Israel and YHWH. As Olyan puts it, "Jehu is coming with violence in order to restore šalôm."[18] Jezebel thus becomes the convenient reason that justifies the violent actions Jehu takes to gain power and to restore שלום. How ironic or perhaps fitting that Jezebel, like her son, Joram, when she sees Jehu approaching, sarcastically asks the commander whether all is at peace. According to this apology of Jehu's rise, the usurper is indeed the "restorer" of שלום, as redefined by the biblical writer.[19]

Equally interesting and deflective is Jehu's accusation in verse 22 that Jezebel is a harlot (זנוני איזבל, "harlotries of Jezebel") and a sorceress (כשפיה, "and her sorceries").

---

16. See "Composition and Redaction of the Deuteronomistic History" in the introduction.

17. Claudia Camp, "1 and 2 Kings," in *The Women's Bible Commentary*, ed. Carol A. Newsom and Sharon H. Ringe (Louisville: Westminster John Knox, 1992), 110.

18. Olyan, "*Hašālôm*," 664.

19. Ibid., 668.

Excursus on the Meaning of זנה

Phyllis Bird[20] argues that a "proper understanding of the root *znh* and its usage in the Hebrew Bible requires careful and discriminating attention to linguistic, literary, and sociological factors that determine meanings." The verb זנה has been too quickly mistranslated as "acting like a harlot, whore, or prostitute" argues instead that the main meaning of the verb זנה is simply "fornication" or "extramarital" sexual relations. As such, the noun, זונה, which derives from זנה, "represents a special case of the activity denoted by the *qal* verb," that is, someone whose occupation or role is as a "professional or habitual fornicator, a promiscuous or unchaste woman, whose role and profession are defined by her sexual activity with men to whom she is not married." In short, the noun, זונה points to a particular unmarried woman's profession and therefore designates her class or status. Despite being marginalized, was accepted in Israelite society. The verb זנה, however, when used of a married woman, refers to an activity that was deemed illicit because the woman's sexuality belonged to her husband and her action therefore violated "the recognized marital rights of another male."

These words, uttered by a man who is about to murder Jezebel's sons, have contributed to establishing the queen's long-lasting reputation as a whore and a witch.[21] As evident from other literature from the Second Temple period, such as Revelation 2:20-23, 2 Baruch 62:8, and b. Sanhedrin 39B, exegetes were quite fixated on this potent image of Jezebel as a foreign temptress and sorceress.[22] Modern interpreters have been equally taken with this vision. John Gray, for example, explains Jehu's accusations of Jezebel's "harlotries" as referring to ritual prostitution and her "sorceries" as alluding to her "seductive arts."[23] As we will discuss later in our analysis, it is this reputation of Jezebel as a harlot that has led interpreters to misread Jezebel's final death scene.

20. Phyllis Bird, " 'To Play the Harlot': An Inquiry into an Old Testament Metaphor," in *Gender and Difference in Ancient Israel*, ed. Peggy Day (Minneapolis: Fortress, 1989), 78.

21. Janet Howe Gaines, "How Bad Was Jezebel?," *BRev* 16 (2000), n.p.; Tina Pippin, "Jezebel Re-Vamped," *Semeia* 69–70 (1995): 221–33.

22. Gaines, "How Bad Was Jezebel?," n.p.; David M. Hoffeditz and Gary E. Yates, "Femme Fatale Redux: Intertextual Connection to the Elijah/Jezebel Narratives in Mark 6:4-29," *BBR* 15 (2005): 199–221.

23. John Gray, *I and II Kings*, OTL (Philadelphia: Westminster, 1970), 547.

Contrary to this reading, however, the biblical text presents no evidence of infidelity on the part of Jezebel. Indeed, considering the hatred with which the biblical writer regarded Jezebel, it is certain that he would have loudly and repeatedly damned Jezebel with such offenses had there been any hint of sexual misbehavior. Rather, the picture we get of Jezebel in the biblical narrative is of someone devoted to her husband.

Excursus on Jezebel and Other First Ladies

Mary Joan Winn Leith argues that it is Jezebel and Ahab—not God and Israel—that present a model of a healthy marriage in the biblical text.[24] Leith compares Jezebel to Eleanor Roosevelt and Nancy Reagan:

> Think of Jezebel along the lines of an American first lady—say Eleanor Roosevelt or Nancy Reagan. Even before their marriages, all three women shared something in common with their husbands: Eleanor Roosevelt came from the same New York political family as her husband; Nancy Davis was a Hollywood actress; Princess Jezebel of Tyre, like Prince Ahab of Israel, grew up in a palace. The reference to the prophets who ate "at Jezebel's table" in 1 Kings 18:19 shows Jezebel, like Mrs. Roosevelt, supervising a personal household staff—not to undermine but to further her husband's work. (Court prophets worked for the royal family.) When her husband was disheartened about Naboth's vineyard (in 1 Kings 21:4-7), Jezebel was solicitous, encouraging and practical, just like Mrs. Roosevelt with her polio-stricken husband.

> Moreover, this biblical first lady was trusted by her husband—she was a partner in power, neither a subordinate nor a scheming manipulator. Jezebel's use of Ahab's royal seal in 1 Kings 21:8 displays her husband's confidence in her and willingness to let his wife promote an unpopular political policy, just as we know Roosevelt did with the controversial issue of civil rights. Unlike Adam in the Garden, Ahab doesn't "pass the buck" and blame his wife when Elijah lights into him at the vineyard. Ahab also tolerated his wife's religious beliefs (supporting Baal and Asherah); did President Reagan make a fuss about Mrs. Reagan's astrologers? And like Mrs. Reagan, Jezebel was absolutely loyal to her husband and her husband's legacy. Rather than fleeing, Jezebel

---

24. Mary Joan Winn Leith, "First Lady Jezebel," *BRev* 20 (2004): n.p.

went to her death to defy the usurper of her family's throne. We come away from the contemplation of this couple with the impression of mutual support, respect and loyalty.

In the end, that Jezebel and Ahab have better marriage skills than Israel and Yahweh should sensitize us to the Bible's ambiguity on the subject of marriage.[25]

It is likely that the biblical writer, in this charge against the queen, is utilizing the well-beloved comparison that connects idolatry and apostasy with sexual offenses, such as adultery, promiscuity, and fornication (Hos 1–2; Jer 3; Ezek 16 and 23).[26] Hence, it is Jezebel's piety and dedication to her own god, Baal, that has been pejoratively revamped and denounced by the Deuteronomistic writer as harlotry.

The accusation of Jezebel's harlotry, however, with its potent misogynistic and xenophobic undertones, will have lasting consequences for the legacy and *Nachleben* ("afterlife" or, in this case, the postbiblical traditions) of this figure. Tina Pippin shows that similar sexist and now racist connotations still underlie the current use of the word "jezebel" to designate a "sexually dangerous African American slave woman."[27] Elucidating the dangerous repercussions of sexist and xenophobic misreadings of the biblical text, Pippin traces the ways in which this sexualized vision of Jezebel conveniently went hand in hand with racist efforts to control and justify slavery of African Americans in the United States.[28] White slave owners justified and explained their sexual abuse of enslaved black women by characterizing these women as "jezebels" or temptresses who were "just asking for it." Hence, the lingering colonial effects of this propaganda against Jezebel persist as she comes to symbolize that which is the Other.[29] Like a curse that is never fulfilled, the accusation made against Jezebel by her assassin perseveres, exploited by later interpreters to continue to disempower women, especially female minorities.

25. Leith, "First Lady Jezebel," n.p.
26. Ibid.
27. Pippin, "Jezebel Re-Vamped," 224.
28. Ibid., 224–25.
29. Ibid., 228.

The Assassinations of Joram and Ahaziah (9:24-29)

Yet before Jezebel can be fully neutralized and killed off, the text builds to this climax by first murdering the kings of Israel and Judah. Joram, when he hears Jehu's retort about his mother and שלום, recognizes that a coup has taken place and attempts to flee (v. 23). He is, however, immediately shot and killed by an arrow from Jehu (v. 24). Joram's body is then thrown on the ground that used to belong to Naboth in Jezreel (v. 25). Jehu, at this point, reiterates Elijah's curse on Ahab, which he received after his acquisition of Naboth's garden in Jezreel: "for remember, when you and I rode side by side behind his father Ahab how the LORD uttered this oracle against him: 'For the blood of Naboth and for the blood of his children that I saw yesterday, says the LORD, I swear that I will repay you on this very plot of ground'" (2 Kgs 9:26).

The narrative again tarries to emphasize the fulfillment of Elijah's oracle and to enjoy the demise of an Omride (vv. 25-26). Yet Jehu's reiteration of Elijah's oracle, which he claims he heard when he was riding beside Ahab, is not exact; it resembles but does not replicate Elijah's prophecy against Ahab in 1 Kings 21. While Jehu's retelling of Elijah's oracle emphasizes the blood of Naboth and his children (2 Kgs 9:26), Elijah's original prophecy in 1 Kings 21 focuses on the demise of Ahab and the king's descendants (vv. 21-22, 24). While Jehu's reiteration stresses the "very plot of ground," that is, Jezreel, as the place of punishment, 1 Kings 21 emphasizes a different locale. First Kings 21:19 states that dogs will lick Ahab's blood in the same place where dogs licked up Naboth's blood (v. 19), that is, outside of the city where he is illegally stoned (21:13). According to the original oracle, the walls of Jezreel are the place where Jezebel is predicted to die and be consumed by dogs (1 Kgs 21:23). Also, in the original prophecy, Ahab's descendants are cursed to be devoured by dogs or birds no matter where they are buried (1 Kgs 21:23).

The small changes in Jehu's retelling of Elijah's earlier oracle against Ahab serves to validate and explain his violent actions, especially his cold-blooded assassination of Israel's king, Joram. By incorrectly paraphrasing Elijah's prophesy, Jehu justifies his act of treason—his spilling of blood—by shifting the reader's attention to that of a different murder. It is Naboth's innocent blood spilled earlier by Ahab, not the royal blood just spilled by Jehu, that is made the focus of the "new" oracle. Similarly motivated is Jehu's emphasis on the demise of Naboth's children in his retelling (2 Kgs 11:26), something wholly unmentioned in Elijah's original prophecy in 1 Kings 21. By focusing on Naboth's children, the

24Jehu drew his bow with all his strength, and shot Joram between the shoulders, so that the arrow pierced his heart; and he sank in his chariot. 25Jehu said to his aide Bidkar, "Lift him out, and throw him on the plot of ground belonging to Naboth the Jezreelite; for remember, when you and I rode side by side behind his father Ahab how the LORD uttered this oracle against him: 26'For the blood of Naboth and for the blood of his children that I saw yesterday, says the LORD, I swear I will repay you on this very plot of ground.' Now therefore lift him out and throw him on the plot of ground, in accordance with the word of the LORD."

27When King Ahaziah of Judah saw this, he fled in the direction of Beth-haggan. Jehu pursued him, saying, "Shoot him also!" And they shot him in the chariot at the ascent to Gur, which is by Ibleam. Then he fled to Megiddo, and died there. 28His officers carried him in a chariot to Jerusalem, and buried him in his tomb with his ancestors in the city of David.

29In the eleventh year of Joram son of Ahab, Ahaziah began to reign over Judah.

mass murder of Ahab's descendants (as well as his friends, relatives, and wife), which Jehu gleefully undertakes in the next couple of verses, can be deflected and explained. Jehu is justified in murdering Ahab's children because Ahab earlier murdered Naboth's children. Look at the innocent blood of Naboth and his children, not the about-to-be-spilled blood of Ahab and his children, the narrative exclaims.

The same political purpose underlies the shift in locales in Jehu's retelling of the prophecy. Not only has Jehu just assassinated a king (and will assassinate many more members of the royal family), but he also disrespectfully commands that Joram's body be thrown on the ground and not be given a proper burial. Joram, however, is not Ahab or Jezebel, and so Jehu's disgraceful treatment of the king's corpse has to be explicated. Jehu's reiteration of Elijah's oracle attempts to do so by showing how Jehu's disrespectful actions were not something he, Jehu, decided to do but something that God ordained as a fitting punishment for Ahab's theft of Naboth's plot. The message of Jehu's revamped oracle is that since Ahab stole Naboth's garden, so Elijah foretold how YHWH will repay Ahab on the very same plot of land (2 Kgs 9:26). That is the reason why Joram's body had to be unceremoniously dumped there.

Joram will be the first in what will be a steadily growing pile of bodies. Next to die is Ahaziah of Judah who flees, presumably at the same moment as Joram. He too is pursued and wounded by one of Jehu's men. Ahaziah is, however, able to hang on until he reaches Megiddo, perishing there. As evident in the preceding chapter, Ahaziah too was disliked by YHWH as he was also related to and intermarried into the family of Ahab. His mother, the infamous Athaliah, will soon get her comeuppance in the next few chapters. As he is the king of Judah and, therefore, a legitimate heir of the beloved David with whom YHWH has a covenant (2 Sam 7), the writers allow Ahaziah to be given a proper burial, and his body is interred in the family tomb in the city of David (2 Kgs 9:27-28).

The Assassination of Queen Jezebel (9:30-37)

Predictably, Jezebel, the main target of the narrative's wrath, will not be so lucky. The lack of proper burial for Joram was mere appetizer for the literal coming meal that is the demise of Jezebel, the "wickedest of women."[30] Indeed, the biblical narrative of Jezebel's death is so saturated with misogynistic subtext that trying to understand this figure is akin to a grisly postmortem identification of a femicide victim for whom only the palms, feet, and skull remain. The text expresses a desire for the total erasure of the queen: The last lines of Jezebel's story in 2 Kings 9 is about her transformation into dog food and then into dung. Turned into excrement, she cannot be identified—cannot be known, understood, or empathized with.

Who was this woman who made the biblical writers foam at the mouth? Can her story even be pieced together from a narrative written by her murderers? Feminist interpreters, sensitive to the patriarchal wrath that underlies the overtly negative portrayal of this figure, have attempted to reread, rehabilitate, and reinterpret Jezebel. Instead of out-right and immediate rejection, they attempt to look beneath and around the text to illuminate the complex and ambivalent persona underneath. Some, such as Janet Gaines, propose a counter-reading from the queen's "vantage point."[31] Other commentators attempt to elucidate the biased motivations and strategies of the Deuteronomistic author in the creation and telling of Jezebel's story.[32] Still others argue that we should look at the complicity of the modern interpreter in the continual "Othering" of

---

30. Gaines, "How Bad Was Jezebel?," n.p.

31. Ibid.

32. Camp, "1 and 2 Kings," 109–10; Phyllis Trible, "Exegesis for Storytellers and Other Strangers," *JBL* 114 (1995): 3–19.

³⁰When Jehu came to Jezreel, Jezebel heard of it; she painted her eyes, and adorned her head, and looked out of the window. ³¹As Jehu entered the gate, she said, "Is it peace, Zimri, murderer of your master?" ³²He looked up to the window and said, "Who is on my side? Who?" Two or three eunuchs looked out at him. ³³He said, "Throw her down." So they threw her down; some of her blood spattered on the wall and on the horses, which trampled on her. ³⁴Then he went in and ate and drank; he said, "See to that cursed woman and bury her; for she is a king's daughter." ³⁵But when they went to bury her, they found no more of her than the skull and the feet and the palms of her hands. ³⁶When they came back and told him, he said, "This is the word of the LORD, which he spoke by his servant Elijah the Tishbite, 'In the territory of Jezreel the dogs shall eat the flesh of Jezebel; ³⁷the corpse of Jezebel shall be like dung on the field in the territory of Jezreel, so that no one can say, This is Jezebel.'"

and concomitant violence against female characters, such as Jezebel, in the biblical text.[33] Regardless of the strategy adopted, different readings stemming from feminist approaches have added greatly to our knowledge of this reviled figure.

Jezebel is damned in the biblical narrative from the very beginning. Her introduction into the Deuteronomistic text in 1 Kings 16:3 identifies her as the wife of Ahab and the daughter of Ethbaal of Sidon. Bookended by her relationship to men, she "enters Israel in an arrangement between males."[34] Her introduction immediately designates her as a cultural and religious Other—"the Sidonian daughter of a Baal worshipper, a Phoenician woman, a foreigner who would go on to entertain Baal . . . clearly a danger, a woman to watch."[35] Denigrating her further, and likely alluding to the conclusion of her story in 2 Kings 9, her name is deliberately pointed in the Hebrew so that it sounds like the word for "dung" (זבל). In Phoenician, the name has a loftier meaning. Phyllis Trible, among others, argue that her name in her native tongue means, "Where is the Prince?"—that is, Prince Baal—and that it is a liturgical phrase that "anticipates the return of fertility."[36] In one culture, she is called a piece of excrement; in another, her name is a line of hymnic praise. The biblical writer's feelings about this figure are unequivocal.

33. See McKinlay, "Negotiating the Frame," 320.
34. Trible, "Exegesis for Storytellers," 4.
35. McKinlay, "Negotiating the Frame," 310.
36. Trible, "Exegesis for Storytellers," 4.

So why did they hate her so much? According to the biblical writer, aside from the fact that she was an active, outspoken, powerful foreign woman, Jezebel's main problem was that she was religiously devoted to her god, Baal. Moreover, adding insult to injury, she might also have participated in the cult of Asherah (on Asherah, see commentary on 2 Kgs 13).[37] Not just a devotee, Jezebel might even have served as the priestess of either the cult of Baal or Astarte, the principal Phoenician goddess for whom her father, Ethbaal, served as high priest.[38] As we noted previously, one theme of the books of Kings is the rivalry between YHWH and Baal in their masculine fight to be designated the true god of fertility and life. In this literary combat, Jezebel becomes the cursed avatar for Baal—or at least something like his female consort, and, as such, she has little chance of getting a fair hearing in this narrative.

As a symbol of the Other, she is portrayed as an opposing twin or shadow of Elijah, the representative of YHWH who is appropriately named "YHWH is my God" (אליהו). As Elijah is zealous for YHWH, so Jezebel matches his religious fervor. Jezebel promotes her faith, feeds her prophets (1 Kgs 18:19), and kills off the prophets of the rival deity, YHWH (1 Kgs 18:4). Elijah, tit for tat, does the same—promotes his faith, feeds his people (1 Kgs 17), and kills off the prophets of YHWH's rival, Baal, after the Carmel incident (1 Kgs 18:40). Jezebel, in turn, threatens to kill Elijah (1 Kgs 19:2). Elijah, in response, announces his own death threat against the queen in the form of an oracle after the Naboth incident (1 Kgs 21:23)—a death threat, which, as we will have seen, is repeated *ad nauseam* by Jehu as verbal justification for his coup. A vivid quote in the LXX and Old Latin attributed to Jezebel highlights her twin-like relationship to Elijah: "If you are Elijah, then I am Jezebel."[39]

Though their piety is parallel and equivalent, it is not portrayed as such by the narrator. Rather, their similarities are transformed into contrasts as their characteristics are dichotomized, and their analogous actions are imbued with opposing meanings:

---

37. On Jezebel's participation in the Asherah cult, see Susan Ackerman, "The Queen Mother and the Cult in Ancient Israel," *JBL* 112 (1993): 385–401, esp. 392–98; idem, "At Home with the Goddess," in *Symbiosis, Symbolism, and the Power of the Past: Canaan, Ancient Israel and Their Neighbors from the Late Bronze Age through Roman Palaestina*, ed. Seymore Gitin and William G. Dever (Winona Lake, IN: Eisenbrauns, 2003), 460–61; Ilona Rashkow, *Taboo or Not Taboo: Sexuality and Family in the Hebrew Bible* (Minneapolis: Fortress, 2000), 51–52.

38. Gaines, "How Bad Was Jezebel?," n.p.

39. Trible, "Exegesis for Storytellers," 8.

> She is female and foreign; he, male and native. She comes from the coastlands; he, from the highlands. She thrives in a sea climate; he, in a desert climate. She belongs to husband and father; he, neither to wife nor father. She embodies royalty; he, prophecy. Both bear theophoric names that unite them in opposition: Jezebel the Baal worshiper and Elijah the YHWH worshiper.[40]

By investing the two characters with contrasting values, the various components of their identity as well as their actions and activities are likewise infused with opposing negative or positive resonances. Hence, Elijah's religion, culture, and gender are judged to be good and right. In stark contrast, Jezebel's religion, culture, and gender are deemed bad or evil. Similarly, though their religious actions are parallel, Elijah's piety is presented as something positive, while Jezebel's piety is depicted as depraved and heinous.[41] So intertwined are the two figures that Trible notes that the two characters exist in an uneasy codependent relationship. As mirror images of each other in behavior and mode, Jezebel and Elijah can never be separated. They haunt each other's narratives.[42] The repeated mention of Elijah's prophecy in this story about Jezebel's demise, especially at the conclusion, attests to their continual coexistence (2 Kgs 9:36).

Like Elijah, Jezebel too will fail to exit the narrative quietly. Despite the multiple attempts by the biblical writer to continually silence,[43] entrap, and frame her, Jezebel resists by getting a small sentence in edgewise before she is unceremoniously tossed from a window and dumped out of the story. When Jezebel hears that Jehu is approaching, she paints her eyes, adorns her hair, and looks out the window (v. 30). As Jehu enters the gates of the city, Jezebel, again utilizing the *Leitwort*, שלום, addresses him with a final pointed riposte: "Is it peace, Zimri, murderer of your master?" Jezebel is undoubtedly referring to the commander Zimri, who usurped Israel's throne only to be overthrown by the army seven days later (1 Kgs 16). In so doing, Jezebel provocatively insinuates that Jehu too will be unable to consolidate his power and establish long-term rule. According to Jezebel, in other words, Jehu is a flash in the pan. Poor Jezebel, however, as Judith McKinlay points out, in alluding to Zimri is saying more than she knows.[44] Her taunt eerily recalls another earlier

40. Ibid., 4–5.
41. Ibid., 3.
42. Ibid., 18.
43. On silencing Jezebel, see Trible, "Exegesis for Storytellers," 13.
44. McKinlay, "Negotiating the Frame," 306.

Zimri—the one who was skewered to death along with his Midianite paramour by the religiously zealous Phineas as revenge for Israelite men consorting with foreign women and, inevitably, their foreign gods in Numbers 25.

Jezebel

When Jezebel hears that Jehu has murdered her son and son-in-law and is now approaching Jezreel, her reaction is to paint her eyes, adorn her head, and look out the window (2 Kgs 9:30), awaiting Jehu's arrival. Some commentators have interpreted Jezebel's actions as an attempt to save herself by seducing Jehu. The sarcastic taunt with which she greets Jehu (2 Kgs 9:31), however, calling him Zimri, after a notorious previous usurper of the Israelite throne (see 1 Kgs 16:8-20), can hardly be considered a come-on. Since seduction is evidently not Jezebel's intent, there must be another reason she takes the time to put on makeup and adorn her hair before situating herself at the window.

Based on the descriptions in 1 Kings 16–21 of how Jezebel comports herself as queen of Israel, her reaction to the news of Jehu's approach is entirely consistent with her previous behavior. Rather than demonstrate any weakness by engaging in a display of grief or fleeing, she courageously and defiantly confronts her killer. Jezebel's final act of adorning her face and hair and facing Jehu directly reflects her determination to die with dignity, as befitting a Phoenician princess and a queen mother of Israel. Jezebel faces death the way she faced life: proud, fearless, and uncompromising.

Jezebel's framing at the window is reminiscent of Judges 5:28-30 and 2 Samuel 6:16, two other biblical texts in which women gaze out of windows. As Don Seeman has observed,[45] in all three cases the woman's gaze out the window focalizes the defeat and dissolution of a royal house, and her loss of power and progeny (or lack of progeny, in Michal's case—see 2 Sam 6:25) is directly related to the downfall and end of a regime. There might also be a suggestion of the ancient Near Eastern "woman at the window motif" in Jezebel's last act. If, as some have suggested, the woman at the window was associated with the worship of Asherah, there may well be a hint that just as her devotee Jezebel was eliminated from the land, so Asherah will be.

Hilary Lipka

---

45. Don Seeman, "The Watcher at the Window: Cultural Poetics of a Biblical Motif," *Prooftexts* 24 (2004): 1–50.

Similar charges are levied against Jezebel in the Deuteronomistic narrative. As we noted previously, Jehu's earlier charge of Jezebel's harlotry and sorcery has led some interpreters to argue that the queen was a whore and a seductress. This misunderstanding will, in turn, color the interpretation of Jezebel's final cosmetic applications: "When Jehu came to Jezreel, Jezebel heard of it; she painted her eyes, and adorned her head, and looked out of the window" (2 Kgs 9:30). In line with the view that the queen is a temptress, Simon Parker and Lloyd Barre argue that Jezebel is putting on makeup in the hopes of sexually attracting Jehu.[46] As evidence they point to biblical texts that link painting eyes and brushing hair to flirting (Isa 3:16; Jer 4:30; Ezek 23:40; Prov 6:24-26). Likewise cited by Parker is intertextual evidence from Greece, Egypt, and Sumer that depict a woman dressing her hair before seduction.[47]

Along similar lines, David M. Hoffeditz and Gary E. Yates note that a woman looking out the window was a "common ancient Near Eastern image for a prostitute."[48] They posit that the final image of Jezebel is meant to portray her as a prostitute in order to remind the reader of her "seductive influence that served her so well in carrying out her evil designs."[49] Some commentators rather gleefully connect Jezebel's cosmetic actions to her macabre conclusion. Describing Jehu's "beauty treatment" of the queen, Hoffeditz and Yates write, "Jezebel paints her eyes; Jehu has the palace walls painted with her blood. The queen, so concerned with her physical appearance in 9:30, becomes dog food and fertilizer in 9:36-37."[50]

Feminist scholars, however, challenge these interpretations of Jezebel's final grooming (as indicative of a temptress) as adding to the negative propaganda put forth by the biblical narrator. As Janet Howe Gaines notes, such interpretations paint her as callous, treacherous, and psychopathically self-interested—"she sheds familial loyalty as easily as a snake sheds its skin."[51] Several factors, however, speak against such a reading. First, Jezebel would be an aging grandmother by this point and

46. Simon B. Parker, "Jezebel's Reception of Jehu," *Maarav* 1 (1978): 67–78; Lloyd M. Barre, *The Rhetoric of Political Persuasion: The Narrative Artistry and Political Intentions of 2 Kings 9–11*, CBQMS 20 (Washington, DC: Catholic Biblical Association, 1988), 76–78.

47. Parker, "Jezebel's Reception," 67–78.

48. Hoffeditz and Yates, "Femme Fatale Redux," 212.

49. Ibid., 213.

50. Ibid.

51. Gaines, "How Bad Was Jezebel?," n.p.

would not likely have had delusions about becoming the new king's next trophy wife. Second, having been raised in the court, she would have realized that her chances of surviving the purge of a usurper who had just ruthlessly killed her son as well as the king of Judah were close to zero. Moreover, Jezebel knows that Jehu has much more to gain than to lose by killing her.[52] Finally, her taunt to Jehu that he is or will be like Zimri speaks to her seething hatred of this man who just murdered her family.

Considering this evidence, one can interpret Jezebel's application of makeup and grooming of her hair as a way of allowing her to die with dignity. Though she cannot save her life, she puts on "the female version of armor" so that she can control her last image. In so doing, she is not "callously indifferent to even her own imminent death"[53] but rather attempts to assert the little power that she has over the horrifying situation. Indeed, the power of this last image is evident in the dramatic Deuteronomistic attempt to erase and replace this final regal view of Jezebel as queen—they break her, stomp on her, cut her up, feed her to the dogs, and turn her into dung. In the literature, the image of the majestically attired, perfectly made-up and coiffured queen is overlaid and replaced with a disgusting snapshot of besmeared excrement on the ground.

Equally questionable is the argument, made by some commentators, that Jezebel's final gaze out the window alludes to her prostitution and seduction.[54] Though the woman-at-the-window motif is found in literary and material sources throughout the ancient Near East, the meaning of this motif is unclear. Indeed, the image of prostitutes looking out the window finds little support in biblical literature. Though there are women who look out of or utilize windows in the biblical text (see Sisera's mother in Judg 4:15-21; Michal in 1 Sam 6:16; Rahab in Josh 2), there is no specific mention of prostitutes being particularly associated with them in the biblical narrative.

Though we do have some material artifacts—for example, ivory plaques from different ancient Near Eastern sites, including Samaria—that depict a woman looking out a window, the identity and meaning of these pieces are debated.[55] Some have claimed that the woman pictured on the plaque is a cult prostitute. Others, however, argue for a nobler

---

52. Ibid.

53. Hoffeditz and Yates, "Femme Fatale Redux," 212.

54. Ibid., 212–13.

55. For a summary, see Susan Ackerman, *Warrior, Dancer, Seductress, Queen: Women in Judges and Biblical Israel* (New York: Doubleday, 1998), esp. 155–62.

reading and identification. Eleanor Ferris Beach, for example, who has studied ivories from Samaria featuring the woman-at-the-window motif, argues that it signifies "sensitive moments of transition for royalty."[56] If so, then the motif is utilized in 2 Kings 9 to frame the change that Jezebel, the queen, will soon undergo.

Along similar lines, scholars such as Nehama Aschkenasy, among others,[57] argue that the final image of Jezebel gazing out the window depicts her as a fertility goddess.[58] Susan Ackerman, for example, states that as the queen mother, Jezebel would have been considered the human representative or even surrogate of Asherah.[59] McKinlay adds that the coiffured hair featured on these window-framed women in the plaques associate them not just with Asherah but with the Egyptian goddess, Hathor. She argues that the emphasis on Jezebel's final hairdo shows that the Deuteronomistic writer might have deliberately overlaid Jezebel "with threatening goddess features"[60] so as to analogize her with Asherah. In so doing, the writer can simultaneously kill and expunge the hated foreign queen as well as the foreign deity she represented.[61] Peter Ackroyd, combining the prostitute and goddess interpretation, suggests that the window-framed woman might "represent the goddess as sacred prostitute."[62] He writes that, if so, Jezebel, placed in connection with this motif, might be "presented, and rejected, as the goddess herself."[63]

It is also possible that the biblical writers intended to conjure up all these associations in their last image of Jezebel. Looming large in their psyche as an avatar of their fears, it is clear that the writers had ambivalent feelings about this figure. To them, she is and remains all these

56. Eleanor Ferris Beach, "The Samaria Ivories, *Marzeah,* and the Biblical Text," *BA* 55 (1992): 135.

57. Nehama Aschkenasy, *The Woman at the Window: Biblical Tales of Oppression and Escape* (Detroit: Wayne State University Press, 1998), 13–14; Ackerman, *Warrior, Dancer, Seductress, Queen,* 155–63; Janet Everhart, "Jezebel: Framed by Eunuchs," *CBQ* 72 (2010): 690.

58. Aschkenasy, *Woman at the Window,* 12–14; Everhart, "Jezebel," 690; McKinlay, "Negotiating the Frame," 315–16.

59. Ackerman, "Queen Mother," 400.

60. McKinlay, "Negotiating the Frame," 316.

61. Ibid., 315–16.

62. Peter Ackroyd, "Goddesses, Women and Jezebel," in *Images of Women in Antiquity,* ed. Averil Cameron and Amelie Kuhrt (Detroit: Wayne State University Press, 1993), 258.

63. Ibid.

things—a common whore, a witch, a sacred prostitute, a regal queen, a foreign temptress, and a goddess. Defiant until the end, this creature of the Deuteronomistic imagination lives on in the writers' minds to taunt their dreams and to haunt their nightmares. In one light, she assumes the posture of a beckoning temptress, and in another, a devouring goddess. In writing her, the biblical writers give her everlasting life. She cannot be erased, and she does not die, no matter their expurgating efforts. As Beach notes, "The power of the woman at the window's visual image has subverted the literary intention."[64]

Desperate to eliminate her, however, the narrative builds to a frenetic finish. It dolls her up only to soil and destroy her. After Jezebel dresses, she taunts Jehu as he enters the city gates by calling him Zimri, the significance of which we noted earlier in the commentary on this chapter. Jehu, already having dispatched two monarchs, however, appears to feel little need to answer her retort or address the queen directly. Instead, he looks up at the window and asks who is on his side (v. 32). When two or three eunuchs gaze back at him—maybe a prearranged signal to assassinate the queen—he commands that they throw her down. That Jezebel's demise comes at the hands of eunuchs is fitting, considering that both they and the queen are boundary crossers who transgress normative gender roles to access power.[65] Yet unlike Jezebel, it is the eunuchs who shed "loyalty as easily as a snake sheds its skin."[66]

The text again slows at this point to luxuriate fully in the description of Jezebel's demise. Literally depicting her fall from power, the eunuchs toss their queen, Jezebel, out the window where her blood splatters on the walls. As with Elijah, the text at no point directly tells the reader that Jezebel has died. Indeed, a quick death would be a killjoy for the biblical writer who is not yet done torturing this hated woman. Yet some restraint seems to have been cautioned as textual variances hint that the stomach-turning violence enacted by Jehu might have been too over-the-top for some editors. We are told that after her blood is splattered someone or something tramples on Jezebel's flung body (v. 33). The subject of the trampling varies, however. While the MT utilizes a single verb in 2 Kings 9:33, thereby making Jehu the one who does the trampling, the LXX, Syriac, and Targum utilize a plural verb, making the horses the subject.[67]

64. Ferris Beach, "Samaria Ivories," 133.
65. Everhart, "Jezebel," 689–92.
66. Gaines, "How Bad Was Jezebel?," n.p.
67. Cogan and Tadmor, *II Kings*, 112.

Perhaps a later editor felt that depicting Jehu as running over the broken body of the queen undercut the purpose of this apology.

Regardless of who does the trampling, the narrative returns to further detailing Jezebel's gruesome demise in the next verse. While Jezebel's body remains broken on the ground, perhaps in agony—the text still refuses to give the reader the relief of knowing that she has finally passed on—the narrative stops for an intermission as her murderer goes off to dinner (v. 34). In the midst of eating, as an aside, Jehu orders that the broken body of "that cursed woman" be buried, "for she is a king's daughter" (v. 34). She is never addressed by name, and as Jehu's comment makes clear, her royal status as well as her right to be properly buried only stems from her relationship to her father. Jezebel "remains captive to the machinations of kingly men" until the end.[68] Desecration of Jezebel's body follows that of her name and identity as Jehu's servants return with news that she cannot be buried because she has been consumed by dogs. Apparently, while Jehu was inside eating, the canines outside were mimicking the actions of their new king. Only Jezebel's skull, feet, and palms remain in accordance with Elijah's early prophecy that her corpse will be like dung in Jezreel (v. 36). The narrative ends with a final attempt at a total expunction of Jezebel: "so that no one can say 'This is Jezebel'" (v. 37).

Jezebel's death scene functions as an inverted literary exorcism. Instead of expelling and expunging the queen, the text attempts to consume her. Eating, as Deborah Appler notes, is not merely about the consumption of food. Rather, like many liminal processes in which things transgress boundaries or move from one side to another, it is replete with religious significance.[69] Connected with fertility, the ability to eat—that is the abundance or lack (i.e., famine) of food—is intimately linked to ideas of divine masculinity.[70] Considering its significance, it is thus fitting that the book of Kings, with its emphasis on the rivalry between Baal and YHWH, would feature so many stories about food (1 Kgs 16, 17, 18; 2 Kgs 4, 6, 25). Jezebel, as a representative of Baal and thus illegal foreign worship, also fittingly meets her demise as canine comestible.

Appler notes that in recalling spilled blood, and a broken and consumed carcass, Jezebel functions as a type of perverted or inverted sac-

68. Trible, "Exegesis for Storytellers," 16.

69. Deborah A. Appler, "From Queen to Cuisine: Food Imagery in the Jezebel Narrative," *Semeia* 86 (1999): 55–73.

70. Cynthia Chapman, *The Gendered Language of Warfare in the Israelite-Assyrian Encounter*, HSM 62 (Winona Lake, IN: Eisenbrauns, 2004), 30–39.

rifice.[71] Instead of being properly sacrificed—that is, killed, the blood poured on the ground, cut up into pieces, and then shared and consumed by the priests (Lev 7:2-6)—her body is desecrated or sacrificed in an upside-down manner. She is thrown out of a window, her blood is splashed against the walls, her body is trampled, and her flesh is gorged upon by dogs. Both the canines who literally consume her and Jehu who symbolically eats her serve "as a priestly representative."[72] Dogs were highly regarded in Canaanite culture. Associated with funerary rites and healing, they were also linked to foreign deities, such as the Phoenician goddesses Astarte and Anat.[73] In contrast, however, the biblical writers viewed dogs as dirty and unacceptable, though they were not technically listed as unclean in Leviticus, as they were associated with the consumption of blood and dead corpses (1 Kgs 14:11; 16:14; 21:19, 23-24; 22:38; Ps 22:16, 20).[74] Hence, it is ironic that Jezebel, a Phoenician, is consumed by dogs, which, in her culture, would be associated with healing and divinity. Those things that she holds in high regard are used as a "means of disgrace."[75] Instead of being part of the heavenly meal, she becomes, in a wordplay on her name, dog feces. By connecting Jezebel to the cult of Baal or that of Asherah, this inverted sacrifice works to desacralize and desecrate these other foreign faiths with which she is associated. The message is clear: "Thus, Jezebel and her religion are excrement to be excreted."[76]

Equally significant are the parts of Jezebel that remain unconsumed by the dogs. Appler writes that the dogs, as priests, consume the fatty parts, kidneys, and life forces of Jezebel. Yet they leave her skull, hands, and feet behind. While the rabbis claim that they left these parts because Jezebel did some good with them (Pirqe R. El. 17), Danna Nolan Fewell and David Gunn instead argue that they symbolize male power.[77] In support, they note that in Hebrew, "foot" and "hand" are euphemisms for the phallus. Appler, however, raises another interesting possibility that it is not male power but female power, in particular that of the goddess

71. Appler, "From Queen to Cuisine," 66.

72. Ibid., 67.

73. Ibid., 65–66.

74. Ibid., 66.

75. Ibid.

76. Pippin, "Jezebel Re-Vamped," 227.

77. Danna Nolan Fewell and David M. Gunn, *Gender, Power, and Promise: The Subject of the Bible's First Story* (Nashville: Abingdon, 1993), 171.

Anat, that Jezebel's remains symbolize. As evidence, she points to Canaanite Baal myths in which Anat is depicted as wearing a necklace of heads/skulls and a belt of hands. She writes that the remains of Jezebel show that the queen and the foreign worship she represents were not completely expunged by the community. As a result, Jehu, after his destruction of Jezebel and the Baal cult in Israel, will continue to commit similar acts of heresy.[78] McKinlay too thinks that what remains of Jezebel symbolizes female sexuality, in particular the power of the goddess Asherah. She argues that in killing Jezebel the narrative attempts to kill the goddess that rivals YHWH.[79]

Remarkable about the conclusion of Jezebel's narrative is the fact that something remains of the queen at all. Though most of her is turned into canine dung, she is not completely annihilated. It is through this incomplete erasure that the biblical writers convey their ambivalence about this figure. It may also be a way for them to subtly acknowledge her lasting power. Indeed, this contradiction is evident in the last line of the story where it states, in a reiteration of Elijah's oracle, that the physical consumption of Jezebel and her transformation into dung was such that no one could say that this is Jezebel. Yet oddly, as we noted previously, it is this visually violent story that has allowed her to live on. We, the readers, all recognize that this is Jezebel. Indeed, we cannot get Jezebel's gruesome death out of our minds. We cannot but say, "Here lies Jezebel." Ironically, the biblical writer has given this figure everlasting life. Jezebel remains perpetually present *sous rature*. Begging the interpreter to read against the grain, to ethically reformat the text so that Jezebel can live and breathe again, she symbolizes not just the Other but the very act of counter-reading, especially of stories about women in the Bible. The things that remain of Jezebel—her hands, her skull, and her feet—in symbolizing writing (hands), speech (skull), and erotic anxieties about women (feet)[80] might point to such a meta-literary message.

78. Appler, "From Queen to Cuisine," 67–68.

79. McKinlay, "Negotiating the Frame," 218.

80. K. J. Zerbe, "'Your Feet's Too Big': An Inquiry into Psychological and Symbolic Meanings of the Foot," *Psychoanal Rev* 72 (1985): 301–14.

2 Kings 10:1-36

Regime Change and the Final Desecration of Queen Jezebel

Jehu's killing spree continues with four other episodes about his purge of the family of Ahab. After the dramatic slaughter of Jezebel, Jehu now turns his attention to Ahab's relatives and his religious supporters. First up are his heirs and descendants who pose the greatest threat to the consolidation of Jehu's power: Ahab's seventy sons (probably including relatives), who reside in Samaria. Bespeaking the complete decimation of this family, seventy, most likely, is a symbolic number connoting totality (see Judg 9:5; 12:14).[1] Next, Jehu turns his attention to the royal family of Judah who, unluckily, encounter Jehu on their journey to visit their relatives in the North. The pericope climaxes with a final bloodbath as the religious personnel of the Baal cult are slaughtered, and Baal's temple is destroyed. In an orgy of violence, Jehu consolidates his rule by decimating the house of Ahab. Reflected in this pericope is the lingering shadow of Jezebel whose religion and family are yet again ruined with relish by the biblical writer.

---

1. Mordechai Cogan and Hayim Tadmor, *II Kings: A New Translation with Introduction and Commentary*, AB 11 (Garden City, NY: Doubleday, 1988), 113.

The Purge of the Royal Families of Israel and Judah (10:1-14)

The pericope begins with Jehu's letter to the elders of Samaria to designate one of Ahab's sons as heir and to fight alongside him for the continued rule of the Ahab family (10:3). Alarmed and fearful of Jehu's speedy assumption of power, as demonstrated by his assassinations of the kings of Israel and Judah, the elders of Samaria, like Jezebel's eunuchs, quickly switch sides and submit to regime change.

Succumbing to Jehu's demands, the elders follow his instructions to behead all the relatives of Ahab and place their heads in baskets and send them to Jehu in Jezreel (10:6-7). Mimicking the Assyrians, Jehu then places the heads into two piles and lays them at the entrance of the gate (10:8).[2] Symbolizing Jehu's consolidation of power, the gruesome heaps act as a warning and deterrent to possible rebellions by Ahab's loyalists. As we noted earlier, the ease with which Jehu assumes the throne seems to hint at a growing discontent among the army, eunuchs, and elders of the rule of Omrides.

After killing Ahab's relatives in Samaria, the pericope ends with a strange declaration by Jehu that the people are innocent of the coup. Placing the blame for the murder of Ahab's family on himself, Jehu concludes with a theological statement about the fulfillment of Elijah's earlier prophecy (10:9-10). The meaning and purpose of Jehu's statement is unclear. Is he designating the people as a witness to the authenticity of God's oracle against Ahab and Jezebel?[3] Is Jehu again trying to deflect blame for his violent usurpation by claiming that it was the expressed will of God? Perhaps the statement is meant to show how he had support for his rebellion from God as well as the elders in Samaria? Or perhaps he is just trying to reassure the people that regime change will not entail retaliation against the innocent or those who just murdered Ahab's relatives? Whatever the meaning, as in the preceding accounts, stress is again placed on the actualization of Elijah's divine oracle against Jezebel and Ahab. As before, the murders and the grab for power by Jehu are justified by appeals to religion.[4]

Exemplifying his dedication to YHWH's decree to destroy the house of Ahab, Jehu next turns to Ahab's relatives in Judah who are on their way to Samaria to visit their royal relatives (10:13-14). As we noted earlier,

---

2. Burke O. Long, *2 Kings*, FOTL 10 (Grand Rapids, MI: Eerdmans, 1991), 136.
3. John Gray, *I and II Kings*, OTL (Philadelphia: Westminster, 1970), 555.
4. Gina Hens-Piazza, *1–2 Kings*, AOTC (Nashville: Abingdon, 2006), 293–96.

10:1Now Ahab had seventy sons in Samaria. So Jehu wrote letters and sent them to Samaria, to the rulers of Jezreel, to the elders, and to the guardians of the sons of Ahab, saying, 2"Since your master's sons are with you and you have at your disposal chariots and horses, a fortified city, and weapons, 3select the son of your master who is the best qualified, set him on his father's throne, and fight for your master's house." 4But they were utterly terrified and said, "Look, two kings could not withstand him; how then can we stand?" 5So the steward of the palace, and the governor of the city, along with the elders and the guardians, sent word to Jehu: "We are your servants; we will do anything you say. We will not make anyone king; do whatever you think right." 6Then he wrote them a second letter, saying, "If you are on my side, and if you are ready to obey me, take the heads of your master's sons and come to me at Jezreel tomorrow at this time." Now the king's sons, seventy persons, were with the leaders of the city, who were charged with their upbringing. 7When the letter reached them, they took the king's son and killed them, seventy persons; they put their heads in baskets and sent them to him at Jezreel. 8When the messenger came and told him, "They have brought the heads of the king's sons," he said, "Lay them in two heaps at the entrance of the gate until the morning." 9Then in the morning when he went out, he stood and said to all the people, "You are innocent. It was I who conspired against my master and killed him; but who struck down all these? 10Know then that there shall fall to the earth nothing of the word of the LORD, which the LORD spoke concerning the house of Ahab; for the LORD has done what he said through his servant Elijah." 11So Jehu killed all who were left of the house of Ahab in Jezreel, all his leaders, close friends, and priests, until he left him no survivor.

12Then he set out and went to Samaria. On the way, when he was at Beth-eked of the Shepherds, 13Jehu met relatives of King Ahaziah of Judah and said, "Who are you?" They answered, "We are kin of Ahaziah; we have come down to visit the royal princes and the sons of the queen mother." 14He said, "Take them alive." They took them alive, and slaughtered them at the pit of Beth-eked, forty-two in all; he spared none of them.

the royal families of Judah and Israel were allied through intermarriage and other family ties. Encountering Ahaziah's relatives on his journey from Jezreel, Jehu murders them as well (10:14). That Jehu happens to stumble upon Ahaziah's relatives seems too lucky to be mere coincidence. Rather, in the windfall, we are again meant to understand God's role in the rise of Jehu and the destruction of Ahab's dynasty. God again eases Jehu's rise to power by providentially allowing him to bump into

Ahab's southern relations. The theological message is clear: All who are related to Omri and Ahab are tainted and implicated in their sins and thus disfavored by YHWH.

An Encounter with Jehonadab and the Purge of the Cult of Baal (10:15-36)

The religious justification builds to a slow climax with Jehu's next lucky encounter. On his murderous journey, Jehu runs into Jehonadab, son of Rechab. Jehonadab appears to know about Jehu's coup and seems to have been on his way to meet him. Giving him his hand (10:15), Jehonadab thereby gives Jehu approval for his actions and joins him in his coup. The Rechabites, who make a lengthier appearance in Jeremiah 35, appear to have been a nomadic, ascetic group who did not farm, build houses, or drink wine. They are singled out by YHWH in Jeremiah 35 for their pious fidelity to the commandments of their forefather. Interestingly, Joseph Blenkinsopp suggests that the name of the Rechabites hints that they may have been devotees of YHWH, the "chariot god."[5] The vision of YHWH as a warrior charioteer appears several times in the stories in 2 Kings, especially in the mention of divine chariots and horsemen (2 Kgs 2:12; 6:17). The point of this second coincidental encounter with Jehonadab thus appears to further stress YHWH's blessing of Jehu's rebellion.

It also sets the scene for Jehu's final bloody purge of the adherents and officials of the Baal cult, which comes on the heels of his meeting with Jehonadab. Demonstrating his zeal for the Lord (10:16), Jehu assembles all the officials of Baal, feigning a great celebration and sacrifice for the deity as the new "royal patron and titular head of the cult"[6] (2 Kgs 10:20). Foreshadowing the destruction that follows, Burke O. Long notes that Jehu's promise "to serve" (with the root עבד) Baal sounds very similar to the word "to destroy" (with the root אבד).[7] When the religious personnel of Baal had all gathered at the temple of Baal, Jehu and Jehonadab search the gathering for any mistaken follower of YHWH. Then in a kind of sacrifice—not to Baal, but rather to YHWH—Jehu orders his soldiers to slaughter en masse the assembled Baal devotees. As in many religious

---

5. Joseph Blenkinsopp, *A History of Prophecy in Israel* (Louisville: Westminster John Knox, 1996), 61.

6. Long, *2 Kings*, 139.

7. Ibid.

[15]When he left there, he met Jehonadab son of Rechab coming to meet him; he greeted him, and said to him, "Is your heart as true to mine as mine is to yours?" Jehonadab answered, "It is." Jehu said, "If it is, give me your hand." So he gave him his hand. Jehu took him up with him into the chariot. [16]He said, Come with me, and see my zeal for the LORD." So he had him ride in his chariot. [17]When he came to Samaria, he killed all who were left to Ahab in Samaria, until he had wiped them out, according to the word of the LORD that he spoke to Elijah.

[18]Then Jehu assembled all the people and said to them, "Ahab offered Baal small service; but Jehu will offer much more. [19]Now therefore summon to me all the prophets of Baal, all his worshipers, and all his priests; let none be missing, for I have a great sacrifice to offer to Baal; whoever is missing shall not live." But Jehu was acting with cunning in order to destroy the worshipers of Baal. [20]Jehu decreed, "Sanctify a solemn assembly for Baal." So they proclaimed it. [21]Jehu sent word throughout all Israel; all the worshipers of Baal came, so that there was no one left who did not come. They entered the temple of Baal, until the temple of Baal was filled from wall to wall. [22]He said to the keeper of the wardrobe, "Bring

crusades, however, Long notes the strange, inverted irony of this final purge where, to the readers and the writers, it is the disbelievers who are the true believers of YHWH.[8] After the slaughter/sacrifice is over, Jehu and his men, for good measure, end their purge by destroying the pillar and temple of Baal so that it becomes "a latrine to this day" (10:27). As in the preceding story about the death of Jezebel, the writer adds a scatological detail to his description of Jehu's destruction.

In his violence and religious zeal, Jehu thus mirrors that of Jezebel's great nemesis, Elijah. In alluding to the prophet, the description of Jehu's purge of the Baal cult can be seen as a continuation of the story about the elimination and ruination of Jezebel. Bespeaking her powerful, ineradicable presence, the pericope, by detailing the total destruction of her beloved cult, attempts to further desecrate Jezebel and her legacy. Merely turning her into excrement in the preceding chapter was not enough. Rather, her priests have to be cut down, and her temple is turned into a latrine. Elijah, though he no longer resides on earth, has claimed final and utter victory over Jezebel through his

8. Ibid.

out the vestments for all the worshipers of Baal." So he brought out the vestments for them. ²³Then Jehu entered the temple of Baal with Jehonadab son of Rechab; he said to the worshipers of Baal, "Search and see that there is no worshiper of the Lᴏʀᴅ here among you, but only worshipers of Baal." ²⁴Then they proceeded to offer sacrifices and burnt offerings.

Now Jehu had stationed eighty men outside, saying, "Whoever allows any of those to escape whom I deliver into your hands shall forfeit his life." ²⁵As soon as he had finished presenting the burnt offering, Jehu said to the guards and to the officers, "Come in and kill them; let no one escape." So they put them to the sword. The guards and the officers threw them out, and then went into the citadel of the temple of Baal. ²⁶They brought out the pillar that was in the temple of Baal, and burned it. ²⁷Then they demolished the pillar of Baal, and destroyed the temple of Baal, and made it a latrine to this day.

²⁸Thus Jehu wiped out Baal from Israel. ²⁹But Jehu did not turn aside from the sins of Jeroboam son of Nebat, which he caused Israel to commit—the

proxy. His oracle of foretelling her gruesome demise has been fulfilled by the violent usurper, Jehu.

Yet the narrative goes too far. As the narrative progresses and becomes more prolific in its violence, it becomes increasingly difficult to empathize with Jehu. The religiously tinged bloodlust of the narrative transgresses the ethical boundaries of the modern reader. As a result, the distinction between protagonist and antagonist, hero and victim becomes increasingly and uncomfortably ambiguous. The narrative appears to sense this turning of the reader as well. For all his pious actions, a spotless summary and regnal epitaph is expected for Jehu. Instead, the story ends with a rather ambivalent note that Jehu was not granted a perpetual dynasty. His dynasty is to last for only four generations (10:30). Jehu, like the first king of the Northern Kingdom, Jeroboam, is assessed to have been incomplete in his devotion to God (10:31). Indeed, Jehu's reign concludes with the negative admission that Israel under Jehu suffered a series of heavy defeats against Hazael of Aram and that God caused Israel to lose control of many of its territories (10:32-33). For all his zeal, it does not appear that God favored Jehu for very long.

The somber final assessment of Jehu better aligns with what we know of the history of ancient Israel. Despite the textual good cheer about the demise of Jezebel and the house of Ahab, Jehu's usurpation, historically, had negative political and economic ramifications. Jezebel's death sev-

golden calves that were in Bethel and in Dan. ³⁰The LORD said to Jehu, "Because you have done well in carrying out what I consider right, and in accordance with all that was in my heart have dealt with the house of Ahab, your sons of the fourth generation shall sit on the throne of Israel." ³¹But Jehu was not careful to follow the law of the LORD the God of Israel with all his heart; he did not turn from the sins of Jeroboam, which he caused Israel to commit.

³²In those days the LORD began to trim off parts of Israel, Hazael defeated them throughout the territory of Israel: ³³from the Jordan eastward, all the land of Gilead, the Gadites, the Rubenites, and the Manassites, from Aroer, which is by the Wadi Arnon, that is Gilead and Bashan. ³⁴Now the rest of the acts of Jehu, all that he did, and all his power, are they not written in the Book of the Annals of the Kings of Israel? ³⁵So Jehu slept with his ancestors, and they buried him in Samaria. His son Jehoahaz succeeded him. ³⁶The time that Jehu reigned over Israel in Samaria was twenty-eight years.

ered the alliance between Samaria and Tyre. Moreover, Jehu's murder of the members of Judah's royal family, many of whom were related to and intermarried with the family in the North, severely weakened the ties between the two sister-nations. As the text admits in the last lines of the narrative, the battles between Aram-Damascus and Samaria continued (10:32-33). As evident in the loss of territory (10:32-33), Israel under Jehu appears to have become increasingly attenuated. Speaking to the weakened state, the Black Obelisk from Nimrud depicts Jehu, who is listed as the son of Omri,[9] kneeling and giving tribute to Shalmaneser III, the king of Assyria (858–824 BCE).[10]

The narrative of Jehu's rise raises ethical issues for the reader in its sickening gusto for violence. The repeated religious justification for Jehu's fanatical desire for murder and power raises deep questions about the relationship between violence and religion in the modern context. As Gina Hens-Piazza so astutely asks: "How do we understand a salvation history that achieves its end with violence?"[11] Moreover, what do we do with a sacred text that justifies political conflicts through appeals to

9. For an argument that Jehu was related to the family of Omri, see Tammi Schneider, "Did King Jehu Kill His Own Family? New Interpretation Reconciles Biblical Text with Famous Assyrian Inscription," *BAR* 21 (January/February 1995): 26–33, 80, 82.

10. Cogan and Tadmor, *II Kings*, 120–21.

11. Hens-Piazza, *1–2 Kings*, 293.

religion? Especially troubling is the gleeful zeal with which the writer describes the violence done against Jezebel, who symbolizes the female and the foreign. In response, some writers, such as Hens-Piazza and Judith McKinlay, have argued that the ethical act is to open our eyes to the victims, whose names and stories are littered throughout the sacred text.[12] While our job is not to rewrite and salvage their stories *per se*, we also have to be sensitive to the violence done to them, both in the text and also through our interpretation. This awareness induces us, at points, to interpret anew, to read against the grain of the text. This kind of counter-reading, moreover, has larger ramifications for how we see the world. As Hens-Piazza wisely notes, this kind of counter-reading is not just a textual act but informs our vision of the current cultural context, compelling us to reconsider those on the margins of society, those modern "Jezebels" among us who, for whatever reason, "are excoriated for their wrongdoings and are deemed undeserving of forgiveness."[13]

12. Ibid., 293–96; Judith E. McKinlay, "Negotiating the Frame for Viewing the Death of Jezebel," *BibInt* 10 (2002): 305–23, esp. 320–22.
13. Hens-Piazza, *1–2 Kings*, 296.

2 Kings 11:1-21

The Rise, Fall, and Delegitimation of Queen Athaliah

Despite being brutally murdered two chapters ago, Jezebel still lingers as a shapeshifting ghost in the narrative. In 2 Kings 11, she appears in the guise of Queen Athaliah, the only female to ever rule in ancient Israel, according to Hebrew writers. Unsurprisingly, she is drawn by the biblical writer as a Jezebel redux. In the immediate aftermath of Jehu's coup, for reasons debated by scholars, Athaliah, the mother of King Ahaziah of Judah, after learning of her son's demise (2 Kgs 9:27-29), kills all the other members of the royal family and seizes the throne. Ahaziah's sister, Jehosheba (2 Chr 22:11 presents her as the wife of the priest Jehoiada), saves one of Ahaziah's sons, Joash, by hiding him in the temple during Athaliah's murderous rampage. When the boy is seven years old, Jehoiada, the priest, stages a coup whereby he, along with his coalition, assassinates Athaliah and places the young Davidide, Joash, on the throne of Judah.

As the only (and last) female ruler of Judah, Athaliah (c. 841–835 BCE), as expected, is scorned by the biblical authors and, hence, drawn in the harshest of colors. As Judah's one and only queen, she functions as a potent symbol of the dangers that women pose to the patriarchal power structure of Judah—and to the religious ideology and organization that support it. Her story as told by the biblical authors is not only biased—how can such a figure be given a fair hearing?—but also short, succinct, and unfulfilled. Her story, in other words, as those of so many women in the biblical text, remains untold, nearly absent, and almost voided. The true story of this figure and her rule thus remains *sous rature*, barely legible in the spaces between the words of the biblical text.

The Rise of Athaliah and the Rescue of Joash (11:1-3)

The biblical text not only offers scant information about Athaliah and her reign but also has conflicting accounts of her identity.

While 2 Kings 8:18 declares Athaliah the daughter of Ahab, 2 Kings 8:26 and 2 Chronicles 22:2 refer to her as the daughter (בת) of Omri and, hence, as Ahab's sister. As בת can mean either daughter or granddaughter, some harmonize the traditions by translating בת as "granddaughter" in 2 Kings 8:26 and 2 Chronicles 22:2. Other scholars have explained this discrepancy by arguing that the reference to Athaliah as the daughter of Ahab is a later accretion. The LXX, which records her as the sister of Ahab and the daughter of Omri, scholars argue, offers the better reading.[1] Other scholars, however, offer a literary explanation, stating that the confusion in the text is the result of Athaliah, the daughter of Omri, growing up in Ahab's court, under the influence of Jezebel.[2] Whatever the case may be,[3] one of the first things that the reader finds out about this figure (2 Kgs 8:18 or 8:26), even before they encounter the account of her reign in 2 Kings 11, is that she is a princess from the hated Ahab/Omri family. This information thus helps to color the opinion of the readers, prejudicing them against her, even before they reach the story about her time on the throne.

The text sets up Athaliah as the antagonist in other ways as well. It subtly connects Athaliah to Jezebel in their characterization: first, as noted earlier, they are both said to be related to the family of Omri and Ahab; second, they are both depicted as assertive and as having improper influence on the monarchy (i.e., Jezebel's role in the seizure of Naboth's garden); and finally, both of their stories are set in the time of Jehu's

---

1. Winfried Thiel, "Athaliah," *ABD* (New York: Doubleday, 1992), 1:511.

2. Hanna J. Katzenstein, "Who Were the Parents of Athaliah?," *IEJ* 5 (1995): 197.

3. For the problems with the efforts at harmonization, see Rueven Chaim (Rudolph) Klein, "Queen Athaliah: The Daughter of Ahab or Omri?," *JBQ* 42 (2014): 11–20.

^{11:1}Now when Athaliah, Ahaziah's mother, saw that her son was dead, she set about to destroy all the royal family. ²But Jehosheba, King Joram's daughter, Ahaziah's sister, took Joash son of Ahaziah, and stole him away from among the king's children who were about to be killed; she put him and his nurse in a bedroom. Thus she hid him from Athaliah, so that he was not killed; ³he remained with her six years, hidden in the house of the LORD, while Athaliah reigned over the land.

revolt—Jezebel is murdered by Jehu, while Athaliah seizes power as the result of her son's assassination by Jehu. Patricia Dutcher-Walls argues that literary analogy as well as her characterization frame Athaliah as another Jezebel. She argues that the information given to the reader about Athaliah—that she is from the house of Ahab, a foreigner, and a queen mother—cannot but bring to mind the most famous foreign queen connected to the house of Ahab.[4] Indeed, this literary connection to Jezebel has exacerbated the question about Athaliah's identity. If Athaliah is Ahab's daughter, then she can be more directly linked to Jezebel as her literal, not just metaphoric, daughter. If so, both are denigrated together, and an easy explanation for Athaliah's behavior can be put forth: like mother, like daughter! That the biblical writer links the figures only subtly, however, hints that there was no direct connection between the two. Had Jezebel been Athaliah's mother, the biblical writer would surely have noted this fact.

As with Jezebel, however, the biblical writer works diligently to delegitimate Athaliah in other ways. The pericope about Athaliah's reign, for example, begins not with the usual Deuteronomistic regnal summary, which, among other things, gives the Deuteronomistic evaluation of the monarch's fidelity to the covenant,[5] but with a startlingly horrifying sentence: "Now when Athaliah, Ahaziah's mother, saw that her son was dead, she set about to destroy all the royal family [זרע הממלכה, 'the seed of the kingdom']" (2 Kgs 11:1). Dutcher-Walls points out that the terminology of 2 Kings 11:1 illuminates the horror of the act, creating "an aura

4. Patricia Dutcher-Walls, *Narrative Art, Political Rhetoric: The Case of Athaliah and Joash*, JSOTSup 209 (Sheffield: Sheffield Academic, 1996), 70.

5. Burke O. Long, *2 Kings*, FOTL 10 (Grand Rapids, MI: Eerdmans, 1991), 146; See also Dutcher-Walls, *Narrative Art, Political Rhetoric*, 135–39.

of evil and threat around Athaliah."[6] She notes, for example, that the terms "seed" and "kingdom" denote royal dynasty and royal authority.[7] Through the use of these particular words, the text thus depicts this woman as singlehandedly causing the near obliteration of the dynastic line of Judah founded by the famed David. More important, the description of her action conveys an implied threat to the theology associated with and underlying kingship in Judah. Known as Zion, royal, or Judean theology, it held that God promised that the descendants of David will rule Judah in perpetuity (2 Sam 7).[8] By alluding to the political and thus the concomitant theological threat posed by Athaliah, the patriarchal message and warning to the reader is clear: one assertive, power-hungry woman can nearly destroy the promise made by God to David.

As important as what is said in this first verse—that this woman set out to demolish the house of David—equally significant is what is left unstated. We are just told that she, out of the blue, started murdering everyone in her family, that is, her own children, grandchildren, and stepchildren. The text, however, never presents a motivation for Athaliah's actions.[9] It does not even state that she just wanted power. Without a reason or purpose, Athaliah cannot but be viewed by the reader as an out-of-control sociopath. Only people who are mentally deranged—and thus unfit to rule—kill without reason. By identifying her in the first verse as the mother of Ahaziah, her maternal status is utilized to emphasize more strongly her antimaternal behavior. She is a monster who kills her whole family without any justification!

Yet the lack of an explanation forces the reader to search for a more plausible, if not logical, explanation for her actions. Speculations abound as to why Athaliah tried to kill off the royal house. Josephus argues that she was simply opportunistic (*Ant.* 9.7). More sympathetically, Gina Hens-Piazza posits that Athaliah's violent actions might have stemmed from the horrors of Jehu's coup. Having just been told that her son was killed, she might have gone mad.[10] Claudia Camp takes an equally sympathetic view and argues that Athaliah, in the aftermath of her son's assassination, might have feared for her life. No longer the mother of the king, she was

6. Dutcher-Walls, *Narrative Art, Political Rhetoric*, 74.

7. Ibid., 71.

8. On the development of Zion theology, see Frank Moore Cross, *Canaanite Myth and Hebrew Epic: Essays on the History of the Religion of Israel* (Cambridge, MA: Harvard University Press, 1973), 241–73.

9. Dutcher-Walls, *Narrative Art, Political Rhetoric*, 30.

10. Gina Hens-Piazza, *1–2 Kings*, AOTC (Nashville: Abingdon, 2006), 307.

left unprotected. Her actions were probably an attempt to preserve her own life.[11] Zafira Ben-Barak similarly sees Athaliah's action as arising from fear and desperation, which is understandable in light of the recent decimation of her family in the North, including all her brothers, as well as the murder of her son in the South.[12]

Some scholars also posit that there must have been more political intrigue than the text lets on. They argue that no matter how wicked or strong willed, it would have been impossible for a single individual, let alone a woman, to have become monarch without support. Indeed, it is difficult to believe that one woman, even in the midst of a murderous rampage, can have the strength (or the time) to singlehandedly kill all the royal descendants, fending off all the palace guards, soldiers, and guardians in the process. Rather, Athaliah, as a usurper, in order to obtain the throne, would have needed the support and help of many powerful groups.[13] Some scholars even suggest that a particular pro-northern, Israelite faction facilitated her seizure of the crown. This group was later countered by another anti-Israelite priestly faction who, along with Judean nationals (the people of the land), eventually caused her fall from power.[14]

By portraying Athaliah as acting and dying alone, her coconspirators—some of whom must have later treasonously "switched sides" against her—are excused. Moreover, by portraying her as the "lone gunman," the narrative lessens her authority and power by presenting her rise to the throne as an illegal, unauthorized, nearly fatal occurrence. It also perhaps adds a sheen of dark magic to the portrayal of Athaliah. Without some evil hocus pocus, how could a woman, someone from the house of Ahab, gain the throne of Judah? The narrative thus subtly paints her as an apostate and a witch—a vision of her that becomes more clearly stressed in the later Chronistic account of her reign (2 Chr 24:7). Such a portrayal also has the added effect of linking Athaliah more closely with Jezebel—the woman whom Jehu famously accuses of sorcery (2 Kgs 9:22). As we discussed earlier, this provocative accusation, as evident by the rich afterlife it has enjoyed, has long lingered in the minds of interpreters.

11. Claudia Camp, "1 and 2 Kings" in *The Women's Bible Commentary*, ed. Carol A. Newsom and Sharon H. Ringe (Louisville: Westminster John Knox, 1992), 104.

12. Zafira Ben-Barak, "The Status and Right of the Gĕbîrâ," *JBL* 110 (1991): 28.

13. Niels-Erik A. Andreasen, "The Role of the Queen Mother in Israelite Society," *CBQ* 45 (1983): 179–94, esp. 190; Camp, "1 and 2 Kings," 111; Dutcher-Walls, *Narrative Art, Political Rhetoric*, 154.

14. Andreasen, "The Role of the Queen Mother," 190; Camp, "1 and 2 Kings," 111.

Most important, by depicting Athaliah's rise as an accidental, illegal act, induced by one psychopathic sorceress, the role of God in the political mess caused by Jehu's rebellion can be conveniently ignored. It is important to remember that Athaliah came to power because her son, the king of Judah, was assassinated by Jehu, a usurper whose rise was given divine approval in the text (2 Kgs 9:1-6). In fact, according to the narrative, it is Jehu's secret anointing by a messenger of the prophet Elisha that sets off his massacre of the entire royal family of Israel as well as large numbers of the Judean royalty (2 Kgs 9–10). If Athaliah is such an aberration, such a mistake, why does YHWH facilitate her rise to power by allowing the usurper, Jehu, to murder her son? Where is God, and what responsibility does he bear for the chaos that ensues on the heels of Jehu's rise in Judah and Israel? The narrative, of course, is conveniently silent as to the role and whereabouts of God during the whole Athaliah and Jehu debacle. As is apparent, it is much simpler to lay the blame for the political upheaval that succeeded Jehu's usurpation on one woman—the person who happens to be the only woman to ever become monarch of Judah—than it is to think deeply about the role of God in the vicissitudes of ancient Near Eastern political history.

Yet a careful consideration of Athaliah's enthronement indicates that she came to power because the political situation in the aftermath of Jehu's rebellion was in a state of chaos. How else could a woman become the first and only queen of Judah? Her rise must have been supported by powerful military, political, and religious factions in Judah—factions that were likely desperate for someone to lead them after the sudden assassination of their king and that must have felt Athaliah had the right leadership skills in politics to rule Judah judiciously. Unfortunately, Athaliah was not able to maintain power. Sadly, it is always the winners who write the histories and the winners who pick which side God has been on all along.

Athaliah's attempt to murder every royal descendant ultimately proves unsuccessful, leading to her eventual downfall. As in so many hero myths, a lone male child survives, secreted away by Ahaziah's sister, Jehosheba, to the temple where the special boy is hidden and raised by priests until he and his supporters are ready to take back the throne from the evil queen.[15]

---

15. Lowell K. Handy, "Speaking of Babies in the Temple," in *Eastern Great Lakes and Midwest Biblical Societies, Proceedings* 8 (1988): 155–65.

During this quick sequence of events, another female character is succinctly introduced, only to be hurried off the stage to make room for the male protagonists and heroes. Jehosheba's brief appearance raises questions about her identity as well as her literary purpose. Who is Jehosheba and what role does she play in the narrative? As always, the text offers sparse information. We are told that she is the daughter of King Jehoram of Judah and the sister of the recently assassinated Ahaziah (11:2). Some commentators argue that the explicit mention of her relationship to Ahaziah indicates that Jehosheba and Ahaziah shared the same mother, that is, Athaliah (see Gen 34:25; Deut 13:7).[16] If so, for reasons we will discuss shortly, the text is careful to hide the fact that the good girl of the narrative, the savior, Jehosheba, is the daughter of the hated Athaliah and that, in a psychoanalytic twist worthy of Freud, the queen mother is eventually undone by her own daughter. Her relationship to Athaliah would, in part, explain why Jehosheba is not killed along with other members of her family during Athaliah's purge.

Her rescue of Joash, moreover, indicates that she might have been more closely related to this particular member of the royal family, though the text is silent as to why Joash, instead of another prince, is saved. Equally interesting is Jehosheba's relationship to the temple, the place where she hides Joash (11:3), and, relatedly, her relationship to the priest Jehoiada, who is suddenly introduced in 2 Kings 11:4 as forming a coalition against Athaliah in order to prop up Joash on the throne. Later, Chronicles closely connects Jehosheba and Jehoiada by stating that she was his wife (2 Chr 22:11). This relationship would explain why Jehosheba places Joash in the temple for safekeeping and why the priests are so involved in the political events in the country. As evident by the high-powered marriage of Jehosheba, a Judean princess, and Jehoiada, whom Josephus names as high priest (*Ant.* 9.7), the religious and political leadership appear to have been intimately intertwined in Judah.

If so, why is the Deuteronomistic text so cagey about revealing the nature of the various relationships, such as that between Jehosheba and Jehoiada and that between Jehosheba and Athaliah? Though textual transmission issues can always be used to explain possible reasons for the incomplete information, in this case, literary explanations can also be posited. Namely, the biblical writers deliberately did not want to disclose

---

16. Mordechai Cogan and Hayim Tadmor, *II Kings: A New Translation with Introduction and Commentary*, AB 11 (Garden City, NY: Doubleday, 1988), 126.

the relationships. Direct and clear information would have revealed to the reader how much court intrigue was involved both in the rise of Athaliah and, more important, in her later demise and replacement by her grandson, Joash. Undercutting the theological message about the divinely chosen Davidic kings, a lucid picture of the ugly court politics of Judah would reveal just how similar Judah's monarchy was to others in the ancient Near East.

A clear description of the relationships among the various characters would have also undercut the androcentric message of this narrative. It is clear that the biblical writer wants to offer contrasting models of women in his presentation of Jehosheba and Athaliah, promoting one and damning the other. On the "good" side is the pious, Judean princess who is affiliated with the temple of YHWH. As a good woman, she never desires or tries to grasp political authority, which only rightly belongs to certain Israelite males. Rather, she acts as a silent facilitator and intermediary of male power by rescuing a Davidic prince and then stepping aside so that the men around her can put the right man in charge. In contrast to the good and pious Jehosheba is Athaliah, who is not just Jezebel redux but also presented by the biblical writer as an androcentric nightmare: she is an outsider, affiliated with the hated Ahab/Omri clan, and thus religiously suspect. More important, she, unlike Jehosheba, openly desires and takes power for herself instead of facilitating power among male players. She does so by doing the very opposite thing that Jehosheba and good motherly females do—she murders her own children and grandchildren in order to become queen.[17]

The open acknowledgment that Jehosheba is Athaliah's own daughter would have subverted this neat binary by revealing the close kinship between the two figures. This connection, in turn, would have disclosed other uncomfortable similarities shared by mother and daughter. The concealment of the mother-daughter relationship is related to the concealment of the relationship between the priestly husband and the royal wife. Once their relationships are known, the actions of the protagonists become much more suspect as they reveal an alternative understanding of events: Jehosheba, a Judean princess, sister to the recently slain king, raised in the court, surrounded by ambitious royal women, such as her mother, Athaliah, while her mother is trying to take and secure the crown after her brother's death, secretly hides a royal prince, entrusts him to

---

17. Robin Gallaher Branch, "Athaliah, a Treacherous Queen: A Careful Analysis of Her Story in 2 Kings 11 and 2 Chronicles 22:10–23:21," *In die Skriflig* 38 (2004): 537–59, esp. 549.

the temple, which is run by her husband, the priest. Both Jehosheba and Jehoiada then wait six years until the child is just old enough to be propped up onto the throne, at which point, the queen, his grandmother and Jehosheba's mother, is forcibly removed and assassinated by a coalition formed by the princess's husband, the priest. In such a reimagining, it is not just Athaliah who is hungry for power. Rather, Jehosheba and Jehoiada also have much to gain from their hiding of Joash and seem equally interested in getting access to the throne.

The story of Athaliah's rise and fall should be viewed not as an illegal attempt by one psychopathic woman to seize the throne but as a legitimate courtly contest between two ambitious and clever women, both bred and embedded in the political and religious systems of Judah. One woman tries to take power and hold on to it directly but eventually fails, while the other, more successfully, uses a male proxy in the form of Joash. In other words, once the relationships are disclosed it becomes clear that the apple truly does not fall far from the tree; Athaliah and Jehosheba behave similarly and are equally ambitious. They are both politicians who, like the men in the court, are willing to commit unethical acts—such as backstabbing, murdering one's family members, committing treason, or kidnapping and controlling a puppet child-king—in order to obtain power. A clear statement about the various relationships of the characters would have exposed the court intrigue underlying the events and, in so doing, would have smashed the dichotomy of good girl versus bad girl that the writer wanted to set up. It would have, in other words, exposed the complex role women played in the court politics of Israel by revealing the ways in which they too, like the men, asserted their influences, both directly and indirectly, to gain more authority and power.

The Coup and the Assassination of Athaliah (11:4-21)

The sparse account of Athaliah and Jehosheba, in setting up binary models of womanhood not only hides the ambitious activities of these women but also further victimizes them by sidelining them to the edge of the narrative. As Danna Nolan Fewell and David Gunn point out, even in contrasting the women, Jehosheba does not, in the end, emerge as the winner. Rather, it is the two males, the priest and the chosen boy, who are the true "winners" of the tale.[18] Indeed, the single-verse description

18. Danna Nolan Fewell and David M. Gunn, *Gender, Power, and Promise: The Subject of the Bible's First Story* (Nashville: Abingdon, 1993), 167.

⁴But in the seventh year Jehoiada summoned the captains of the Carites and of the guards and had them come to him in the house of the LORD. He made a covenant with them and put them under oath in the house of the LORD; then he showed them the king's son. ⁵He commanded them, "This is what you are to do: one-third of you, those who go off duty on the sabbath and guard the king's house ⁶(another third being at the gate Sur and a third at the gate behind the guards), shall guard the palace; ⁷and your two divisions that come on duty in force on the sabbath and guard the house of the LORD ⁸shall surround the king, each with weapons in hand; and whoever approaches the ranks is to be killed. Be with the king in his comings and goings."

⁹The captains did according to all that the priest Jehoiada commanded; each brought his men who were to go off duty on the sabbath, with those who were to come on duty on the sabbath, and came to the priest Jehoiada. ¹⁰The priest delivered to the captains the spears and shields that had been King David's,

of Jehosheba's actions shows an eagerness to push women out of the scene in order to bring the male players on to center stage. After this verse, the chapter focuses on the boy who is raised in the temple and most of all on Jehoiada, the priest, who, when the boy is old enough to be put forth as king, forms a conspiracy with various groups to remove Athaliah from power (2 Kgs 11:4).

Different dichotomies are put forward in the remaining male-centric narrative. The evil Omride queen who rules illegitimately is contrasted with the divinely saved, chosen, and legitimate Davidic prince who is backed by priests and the surviving members of the royal family.[19] Lowell Handy has noted that the rise of Joash fits a particular narrative type—that of the hero exposed at birth.[20] In these tales, a child of noble birth is endangered but is saved by an agent and raised by others. The child, who is then adopted by royalty, holy people, or a deity, rises to become king or a celebrated leader. The story of Moses in Exodus 1 neatly conforms to this narrative type. So also does the story in 2 Kings 11 about the boy-king Joash who is rescued and raised by a princess and a priest in the temple. By following a well-known narrative pattern, the story clarifies who it deems as the chosen hero and who, therefore, it condemns as the antagonist. By emphasizing the specialness of Joash,

19. Dutcher-Walls, *Narrative Art, Political Rhetoric*, 73.
20. Handy, "Speaking of Babies in the Temple," 155–65.

which were in the house of the LORD; [11]the guards stood, every man with his weapons in his hand, from the south side of the house to the north side of the house, around the altar and the house, to guard the king on every side. [12]Then he brought out the king's son, put the crown on him, and gave him the covenant; they proclaimed him king, and anointed him; they clapped their hands and shouted, "Long live the king!"

[13]When Athaliah heard the noise of the guard and of the people, she went into the house of the LORD to the people; [14]when she looked, there was the king standing by the pillar, according to custom, with the captains and the trumpeters beside the king, and all the people of the land rejoicing and blowing trumpets. Athaliah tore her clothes and cried, "Treason! Treason!" [15]Then the priest Jehoiada commanded the captains who were set over the army, "Bring her out between the ranks, and kill with the sword anyone who follows her." For the priest said, "Let her not be killed in the house of the LORD." [16]So they laid hands on her; she went

and by hinting that his rise is a divinely ordained event, the biblical writer can again deflect attention away from the court intrigue, especially the suspicious involvement of religious personnel, in the rescue and subsequent enthronement of Joash.

Once the story is examined in more detail, it becomes strangely apparent that Joash, though he is the chosen hero, is not discussed very much in 2 Kings 11. While this is, in part, because the history of his reign will be described in detail in the next chapter, the more apparent reason for the scant information is that, though Joash is the one who ultimately ends up as king, he is not really the main actor or protagonist of the story of the coup in 2 Kings 11. He is just seven years old and, as such, no matter how divinely chosen Joash is, he is no match for his ambitious and powerful grandmother, the queen. As a result, someone has to take the throne for him, and thus, the majority of the chapter is centered on the actions of the real protagonist of 2 Kings 11: Jehoiada, the priest, who covertly forms a coalition in order to place Joash on the throne.

As always, what is interesting and significant are the things left unstated in the narrative that the reader is forced to infer. If Jehoiada and, in all likelihood, Jehosheba, are the main leaders of a coup that replaces the current queen, Athaliah, with a new seven-year-old king, Joash, most likely it is Jehoiada and his wife who, after the enthronement, remain the true powers behind the throne. In other words, it is Jehoiada and Jehosheba who effectively control and rule Judah—that is, until the

through the horses' entrance to the king's house, and there she was put to death.

¹⁷Jehoiada made a covenant between the LORD and the king and people, that they should be the LORD's people; also between the king and the people. ¹⁸Then all the people of the land went to the house of Baal, and tore it down; his altars and his images they broke in pieces, and they killed Mattan, the priest of Baal, before the altars. The priest posted guards over the house of the Lord. ¹⁹He took the captains, the Carites, the guards, and all the people of the land; then they brought the king down from the house of the LORD, marching through the gate of the guards to the king's house. He took his seat on the throne of the kings. ²⁰So all the people of the land rejoiced; and the city was quiet after Athaliah had been killed with the sword at the king's house.

²¹Jehoash was seven years old when he began to reign.

boy-king grows up and asserts his own power, as we will see in the next chapter. The problem with clearly stating the identity of the characters in charge is that Jehoiada, as a priest, and Jehosheba, as a princess, are unfortunately not a royal male scion of the line of David. As such, their rule can be charged with the same accusations of illegitimacy as that levied against Athaliah. The dichotomy of the illegal, foreign witch-queen and the chosen, Davidic boy-king, in other words, easily breaks down when the true nature of the conspiracy is exposed.

The fact that the queenship of Athaliah is replaced by an equally illegitimate rule of a priest and a royal princess reveals the reason for the insecurity manifested in the text. This insecurity is evident in the defensive manner in which the text asserts the illegality of Athaliah's reign and, in contrast, the legitimacy of the coup. This is most apparent in the lengthiest part of the chapter, which describes the various actions that Jehoiada takes to dethrone Athaliah: after Joash comes of age, Jehoiada summons the captain of the Carites and the runners—mercenary guards who were associated with David and royal power (1 Sam 30:14; 2 Sam 8:18; 15:18; 20:7, 23)[21]—to come to the temple, where he shows them the hidden prince and makes a covenant with them to join him in the coup (v. 4). Spears and shields belonging to King David, which are stored in the temple, are handed to the members, and the young king is surrounded by soldiers and then publicly anointed and crowned king in the

21. Dutcher-Walls, *Narrative Art, Political Rhetoric*, 75; Hens-Piazza, *1–2 Kings*, 307.

temple (vv. 8-12). When Athaliah hears the noise, she goes to the temple to see what is going on and witnesses the enthronement of Joash by the pillar, a location with likely symbolic significance (vv. 13-14).[22] Despite her screams of treason, she is taken out of the temple and put to death (vv. 15-16). After the queen is murdered, Jehoiada consolidates Joash's rule by making a covenant with the Lord, the king, and the people; by letting the people of the land destroy the house of Baal and kill its priest; and, finally, by bringing the new king down to the palace and placing him on the throne (vv. 17-19).

Though initially straightforward, a deeper study of this enthronement sequence indicates the effort of the biblical writer to defend Jehoiada's actions and, hence, the legitimacy of the coup. It does so by depicting the dethronement as consisting of a series of quickly moving, spontaneous events. The narrative never describes a single thing Athaliah does as monarch; rather, she is enthroned just to be dethroned a couple of verses later. The description of her reign, in other words, has the appearance of an embarrassing mistake that the biblical writers want to skip over quickly. Moreover, adding to the legitimacy of the coup, the narrative repeats certain key terms, such as בית יהוה, "house of the Lord" (vv. 3, 4 [2x], 10, 13, 15, 18, 19), and ברת, "covenant" (vv. 4, 12, 17), and depicts the conspirators' care to preserve the sanctity of the temple: the soldiers scrupulously take Athaliah outside of the temple before assassinating her (vv. 15-16). Though Jehoiada and the other conspirators are unconcerned about the sanctity of the temple when they use it as an organizational meeting center for the coup, they now appear very concerned about defiling the space by killing Athaliah inside of it. Apparently, it is acceptable to plan to kill the queen inside the temple, but the actual killing has to be done outside.

This emphasis on the house of the Lord and the propriety of activities that take place in it is significant. According to Burke Long, sacred and profane spaces are utilized in the text to lend the conspiracy an almost divine authority and power.[23] While the coup and the members of it are depicted as sanctified, the narrative, in contrast, aligns Athaliah with Baal worship by stating that after her death the people of the land demolished the temple of Baal and killed its priest. What the text does not state directly is whether Athaliah was in any way connected to the worship of Baal. Judging by the theophoric suffix, יה (YHWH), that forms

---

22. See Dutcher-Walls, *Narrative Art, Political Rhetoric*, 81.
23. Long, *2 Kings*, 150.

part of her name as well as the absence of any direct mention of her affiliation to Baal worship in 2 Kings, Athaliah was most likely a worshiper of YHWH. By aligning the demolition of Baal's temple with the dethronement of Athaliah, the biblical writers loudly insinuate that the queen was an apostate.

TRANSLATION MATTERS

Athaliah's Name: Though the exact meaning of her name is debated, Athaliah's name speaks against the claim that she was an apostate as it contains the theophoric suffix, יה (YHWH). Moreover, if Ahab is her father and not her brother, it is telling that he names three of his children with YHWH in their name (Athaliah, Ahaziah, and Jehoram).

Adding to the propaganda, as we discussed earlier in our commentary on 2 Kings 11:1-3, the writer also takes care to depict Athaliah as isolated and alone. She begins her reign by wiping out the royal family by herself, and she ends her reign alone as no one appears to protect or side with her during the coup. In contrast, Jehoiada and his conspirators are portrayed as supported by numerous groups of people, in particular, the holy priests. Indeed, as evident by the declaration that "the people of the land rejoiced and the city was quiet after Athaliah had been killed" (v. 20), the dethronement of Athaliah is pictured as the end of a dark period of chaos, lawlessness, and impiety. The witch is dead! The enthronement of Joash, in contrast, is presented as the dawn of a new, ordered, sanctified era.

Despite the arguments put forth by the text, however, small clues in the narrative make the reader suspicious and distrustful of this overall message. First, though it appears that the rebellion is supported by a majority of Judeans, when the narrative is examined more closely, it seems to have actually enjoyed the support of only a select few. Dutcher-Walls notes that the coalition most likely consisted of the aristocratic elements of Judah, such as palace guards, clergy, members of the royal family, and landed elites, whom the biblical text misleadingly calls "the people of the land."[24] Despite the fact that the narrative describes these groups

---

24. The identity of the "people of the land" is greatly debated. For a quick overview and bibliography, see Peter R. Ackroyd, *Exile and Restoration*, OTL (Philadelphia: Westminster John Knox, 1968), 150 n. 50; Dutcher-Walls, *Narrative Art, Political Rhetoric*, 149–52.

as suddenly coming together, Dutcher-Walls notes that it would have actually taken some time to build this faction. Hence, this event is not, as the text hints, a spontaneous uprising to overthrow an illegal, horrible dictator but a reshuffling among the oligarchy that resulted in the enthronement of a more naïve, malleable puppet-king.

It is indeed strange that a coup, which is divinely sanctioned and which is presented as having so much widespread support, would be organized in secret. If Athaliah is as alone and lacking in support as the text portrays her to be, why is Jehoiada unable to plan the rebellion more openly? Additionally, if Athaliah is isolated and unsupported, why is such care needed to protect the young Joash? According to Jehoiada's directions, soldiers are to surround the young king at all times during the enthronement. They are even commanded to kill anyone who approaches the ranks (v. 8). Again, if the illegitimate Athaliah truly was deficient in all support—military, royal, and priestly—why, then, is Jehoiada so afraid that someone will hear about the rebellion and try to kill Joash? Also suspect is Jehoiada's command to kill anyone who follows the queen when she is taken out of the temple to be killed (v. 15). If the queen had no followers, why the need for the explicit command to put such people to death? Even the weapons that are utilized are telling. If the coup had the backing of large segments of the military, why does Jehoiada need to search around for and utilize ancient weaponry belonging to David, which has been stored in the temple museum (v. 10)?

Finally, while the repetition of the term ברית, "covenant," adds a sheen of legitimacy and religiosity to the coup, the number of times that cove nants are made in this narrative is odd and suspicious. Jehoiada makes all the soldiers who join in the coup agree to a covenant and makes them swear an oath in the temple (v. 4). During the coup, Jehoiada presents the just-crowned Joash—who, we must remember, is merely seven years old—with a covenant (v. 12). And finally, after Athaliah is murdered and Joash is enthroned, Jehoiada makes a covenant between YHWH and the king and the people, and a second covenant between the king and the people (v. 17). Why is Jehoiada always making agreements? Moreover, what do these covenants entail? What is everyone agreeing to?

Though we cannot know for sure, it is undeniable that there is a lot of wheeling and dealing going on before, during, and after Jehoiada's coup. This would make sense if the coup, as we argued, entailed a reshuffling among the oligarchy of Judah. Agreements would have been needed before the coup to determine the benefits each group of supporters would receive for joining it and, after the event, to divide up the various parts of Judah for a particular faction to manage. These covenants also probably entailed a loyalty or fidelity agreement to the new king—that is, to the priest and princess who were advising the new, docile, young monarch.

Sadly, Athaliah is allowed only a single chance in the narrative to voice her interpretation of events, which, unsurprisingly, is quite different from the one put forth by the text. When Athaliah enters the temple and sees Joash enthroned, she twice cries out treason before she is unceremoniously led outside of the temple to be assassinated (v. 14). Her cries clearly indicate that, despite the argument asserted in the narrative, in her viewpoint, she rules legitimately. She is the rightful monarch, and, in assassinating her, Jehoiada and his colleagues are committing treason. The numerous attempts in the narrative to delegitimate her—"Neither by birth origin (foreign) nor gender (female) nor religious sentiment (intimation of her connection with the Baal temple in Jerusalem) is Athaliah permitted to assume the throne in Judah"[25]—actually have the effect of lending some support to her claims. These efforts hint that her interpretation of events might ultimately be true.

Despite being forcibly silenced by the text, Athaliah's moderately long six-year reign and the lack of mention of any societal upheaval or military loss during her time in power suggest that she was not an altogether bad monarch. Indeed, the fact that it takes an amassing of numbers of soldiers and divinely tinged groups of men, who represent the masculinity of YHWH (i.e., priests, prophets, and the divinely anointed king), to overthrow Athaliah speaks to her power, strength, and endurability. While the intent of this narrative is to convey an androcentric warning about the secret power held and potentially abused by ambitious women, the irony is that such a portrayal expresses a different, contradictory message. Though lacking direct power—or killed and damned for wanting it—the biblical writers, out of their fears, depict these women as powerful, almost unstoppable goddesses. By silencing her, an even larger, more formidable vision of Athaliah is thus created, perpetually lingering in the text to offer her own powerful and compelling counter history.

---

25. See Dutcher-Walls, *Narrative Art, Political Rhetoric*, 112.

The Naming
of the Queen Mother

A unique feature of 1–2 Kings is the naming of the king's mother for the kingdom of Judah. Beginning with the split of the monarchy, 1–2 Kings introduces the Judean and Israelite kings through regnal formulas, which provide biographical and political information for their reigns. Included in this information for Judah is the name of the queen mother. The formulas name the mother of the king for seventeen of nineteen kings. These women are more than mothers of the king; they hold an official position, the highest for a woman and quite possibly the second most powerful position in the kingdom, under the literal title of the "Great Lady" (גבירה), most commonly translated as "queen mother."

Four of the Judean queen mothers and one Israelite queen mother function outside of their naming in the formulas. Asa removes Maacah (1 Kgs 15:2, 10, 13) from being queen mother for fashioning an image for Asherah. Athaliah (2 Kgs 8:18, 26; 11:1-15) exerts her influence as queen mother to become a ruler herself. Upon the death of her son, Ahaziah, she secures power by ordering the deaths of his sons. One son, Joash, escapes and stays hidden in the temple for six years until the high priest Jehoiada orchestrates a coup and orders Athaliah's assassination. Nehushta (2 Kgs 24:8, 12, 15) marches outside of Jerusalem with her son Jehoiachin to surrender to Nebuchadnezzar, who will exile her along with her son and additional important people in powerful or economic positions. Jeremiah passes judgment on her and her son twice, blaming both of them for the downfall of Judah (Jer 13:18; 22:24-27).

While Hamutal (2 Kgs 23:31; 24:18) appears only by name in 2 Kings, in Ezekiel 19:1-14 she is castigated for scheming to place two sons upon the throne and teaches them to act wickedly. Jezebel (1 Kgs 22:51; 2 Kgs 3:1), the lone queen mother named in the north, acts in her capacity as a queen mother during two of her sons' reigns, whom the text evaluates in light of Ahab's and Jezebel's ways. Jehu is tasked with destroying the house of Ahab, Jezebel included, for their slaughter of innocents and prophets and conspires with her eunuchs to throw her from her window, where she is trampled by his horses (2 Kgs 9:30-37).

The Hebrew Bible characterizes negatively all appearances of the queen mothers of the divided monarchy. In 1–2 Kings, when the queen mother functions outside of the regnal formulas, she is removed from power through demotion, death, or exile. A certain *mythos* surrounds the queen mother of the divided monarchy: she is inherently wicked. The other queen mothers who appear in the Hebrew Bible receive positive characterizations, even foreign queen mothers. Once Solomon becomes king, he bows to Bathsheba, and she sits beside him on a throne (1 Kgs 2:19). Proverbs 31:1-9 records the words of King Lemuel's mother, a foreign queen mother, teaching him how to rule wisely. Even a Babylonian queen mother has the wisdom to recognize that Daniel can divine the mysterious hand writing on the wall (Dan 5:10-12). The wicked queen mothers wield their power much differently, in ways that are liabilities to their son and liabilities to the nation. As the regnal formulas carry wave after wave of guilt on the Judean kings, the formulas also carry the queen mothers along, placing blame on them as well. As the second most powerful person in the kingdom, the queen mother contributes to the spiraling downfall of the nation.

Ginny Brewer-Boydston

2 Kings 12:1-21

The Reign and Mysterious Death of King Joash in Judah

Befitting a king who was divinely chosen and saved in the preceding chapter, the reign of Joash (alternatively spelled, Jehoash, in some translations) in the Southern Kingdom of Judah centers on the renovation of the house of the Lord—the sacred locale where he was hidden, raised, and first enthroned in 2 Kings 11. The depiction of the renewal of the temple as the centerpiece of Joash's reign perfectly fits his earlier portrayal in 2 Kings 11 where he was rescued as a baby from the deathly purge of his grandmother, Athaliah. The dramatic manner in which the text describes his ascent to the throne in the preceding chapters—a coup led by the priest, Jehoiada, which results in the assassination of the queen—sets high expectations for a glorious tenure. Yet while Joash's reign begins well with his pious refurbishment of the temple, it ends on a dissonantly negative note: Joash is forced to pillage the temple that he has just refurbished to buy off the Arameans. More calamitously, his reign abruptly ends when he is assassinated by his officials (2 Kgs 12:20). Joash will not be the last righteous monarch in the book of Kings to suffer an ignominious conclusion after an inspired beginning—indeed, his death is the first in a line of ever-increasing incongruous incidents, including his son, Amaziah, as well as Hezekiah and Josiah. As we will observe, inconsistent depiction of his reign hints not only at court intrigue but, more important, at the complex writing process that undergirds the text of the Deuteronomistic History.[1]

The Summary of Joash's Reign (12:1-3)

Joash's legitimacy is affirmed by his introduction in the Deuteronomistic text. Unlike Athaliah, the account of her grandson's reign begins with the typical regnal summary, noting the corresponding monarch in Israel, the length of Joash's tenure, the name of his mother, and the Deuteronomistic assessment of his fidelity to the covenant.

As expected, the reign of Joash's grandmother, Athaliah, is skipped over, and she is nowhere named in 2 Kings 12 as the preceding monarch. Small details in this beginning portion of the pericope hint at the contradictory desire on the part of the biblical writer both to erase Athaliah and to contrast Joash with his unnamed predecessor. Gina Hens-Piazza notes that it is telling that Joash's mother is so clearly named in 2 Kings 12:1 as Zibiah of Beer-sheba. She posits that this emphasis might be to signal that a new queen—that is, someone who is explicitly not Athaliah—is now in charge.[2] Unlike other regnal introductions, which begin by listing the total length of the king's name and the year of the corresponding northern monarch, in Joash's case, his reign begins by restating the age when he became king (2 Kgs 11:21).[3] The emphasis on his age, without mentioning Athaliah, subtly stresses the coup—the central event that occurred when he was seven years old—which led him to be placed on the throne of Judah.

The biblical writer thus undoubtedly considers Joash as a vast improvement on his unnamed predecessor. Interestingly, however, the same writer does not present an unequivocally positive summary of this monarch. Rather, the biblical author prepares the reader for the negative conclusion to Joash's reign by tamping down initial expectations in the introductory section. First, though Joash is given a generally positive assessment, the people are still said to have continued offering sacrifices and incense at the high places, which the king is faulted for failing to remove (2 Kgs 12:3). The removal of the high places under Hezekiah—an act that every other preceding Judean monarch, even pious ones, would fail to accomplish—will be presented as a momentous accomplishment in the eyes of the Deuteronomistic writer (2 Kgs 18:4).

---

1. See "Composition and Redaction of the Deuteronomistic History" in the introduction.

2. Gina Hens-Piazza, *1–2 Kings*, AOTC (Nashville: Abingdon, 2006), 313.

3. In some translations, the verse that appears as 2 Kings 12:1 is tacked on to the end of preceding chapter as the last verse (2 Kgs 11:21).

2 Kgs 12:1-3

¹²:¹In the seventh year of Jehu, Jehoash began to reign; he reigned forty years in Jerusalem. His mother's name was Zibiah of Beer-sheba. ²Jehoash did what was right in the sight of the LORD all his days, because the priest Jehoiada instructed him. ³Nevertheless the high places were not taken away; the people continued to sacrifice and make offerings on the high places.

Aside from the continued presence of the high places, the note at 2 Kings 12:2 that connects Joash's righteousness with the priest, Jehoiada, offers another hint of coming problems. The issue centers on the translation of the relative pronoun in this verse.

TRANSLATION MATTERS

The relative pronoun אשר in 2 Kings 12:2 can have a variety of translations. The NRSV translates the verse as follows: "Joash did what was right in the eyes of the LORD all his days, *because* the priest Jehoiada instructed him" (italics added). The NIV, however, offers a different rendering that slightly alters its meaning: "Jehoash did what was right in the eyes of the Lord all the years Jehoiada the priest instructed him." In this translation, the pronoun "that," as in "*that* Jehoiada the priest instructed him," is implied. The NIV translation is similar to the translation of this verse by the JPS: "And Jehoash did that which was right in the eyes of the Lord all his days *wherein* Jehoiada the priest instructed him" (italics added). According to the NRSV, Joash behaved righteously throughout his life because he was properly trained earlier. According to the NIV and JPS translation, however, Joash's piety was limited to those years in which he was under the tutelage of Jehoiada, the priest. This raises the question as to what happened after Jehoiada's death—a question that is taken up by the later writer of Chronicles. In the Chronicles account, after the death of Jehoiada, Joash falls under the influence of impious, corrupt officials who induce him to commit wicked acts, including the murder of Jehoiada's son, Zechariah (2 Chr 24:17-22). Some scholars even maintain that 2 Kings 12:2 might have been a marginal note qualifying Joash's righteousness, which was inserted in order to better align the Kings account with the one in Chronicles.[4]

Whatever the translation, by linking Joash's piety to Jehoiada, a pro-priestly sentiment is undeniably palpable.

---

4. Mordechai Cogan and Hayim Tadmor, *II Kings: A New Translation with Introduction and Commentary*, AB 11 (Garden City, NY: Doubleday, 1988), 137.

The Refurbishment of the Temple (12:4-21)

This version of Joash's reign, in contrast to the variant account in Chronicles, and the more negative translations of 2 Kings 12:2, attempts to give some theological coherency to this monarch's reign. It is strange that Joash's reign, which begins on such a dramatically positive note, ends so negatively with an Aramean attack and his sudden assassination. In other words, the narrative appears to be building to a different conclusion than the one that is finally presented in the narrative. As such, the story about Joash in 2 Kings feels incomplete and incongruent.

The sense of dissonance is exacerbated by the account of Joash's refurbishment of the temple. Befitting a king who was raised and hidden in the temple by a priest, King Joash, after he is introduced, gets to work by trying to improve the structure. The king commands the priests to utilize certain money donated to the temple to repair the house (vv. 4-5). The priests, however, for reasons that are unstated, disregard the king's command. Though it is unclear how much time has passed, we are told that by the twenty-third year of Joash, no repairs had been made to the temple. As a result, Joash takes more drastic measures. He calls Jehoiada and the other priests in for a meeting and asks them about their (continued) negligence. He then makes them promise not to accept more donations from the people (v. 7). They, apparently, cannot be trusted with the responsibility of collecting and utilizing the incoming donations to actually refurbish the temple. Instead, the collection, accounting, and disbursal of the money is streamlined. Jehoiada makes a donation box with a hole on the lid and places it at the entrance to the sanctuary (v. 9). The priests who guard the threshold place into this box all the money that is brought into the temple (v. 9). When the box is full, the king's secretary and the high priest empty the box and then count, store, and pay the money to the workers to repair the structure (v. 10). With these changes in the collection and distribution of money, the repairs of the temple finally get underway (vv. 9-15).

The fast pace of the narrative, which moves quickly from problem to resolution, allows little room for details or explanation. The story poses many unanswered questions. Why are the priests so negligent? If they are not utilizing the donations for the repairing of the temple, what are they doing with the money? Why does Jehoiada, the priest who coordinates the earlier coup against Athaliah, not compel the other priests to behave more responsibly? Why is it that he and the other priests so flagrantly disregard the command of the king? What were the reactions

⁴Jehoash said to the priests, "All the money offered as sacred donations that is brought into the house of the LORD, the money for which each person is assessed—the money from the assessment of persons—and the money from the voluntary offerings brought into the house of the LORD, ⁵let the priests receive from each of the donors; and let them repair the house wherever any need of repairs is discovered." ⁶But by the twenty-third year of King Jehoash the priests had made no repairs on the house. ⁷Therefore King Jehoash summoned the priest Jehoiada with the other priests and said to them, "Why are you not repairing the house? Now therefore do not accept any more money from your donors but hand it over for the repair of the house." ⁸So the priests agreed that they would neither accept more money from the people nor repair the house.

⁹Then the priest Jehoiada took a chest, made a hole in its lid, and set it beside the altar on the right side as one entered the house of the LORD; the priests who guarded the threshold put in it all the money that was brought into the house of the LORD. ¹⁰Whenever

of the priests to the donation box, which deprived them access to some of the donations? Was the relationship between the king and priests damaged because of this incident? We know that no work began on the structure until the twenty-third year into Joash's reign, but what is the precise chronology? How old was Joash when he first decided to repair the temple—he surely could not have been seven years old!—and how long does Joash wait before he calls the negligent priests in for a meeting? What is his relationship with Jehoiada like during this time? Indeed, what is the nature of the relationship between the monarchy and the temple and the cultic personnel in general?

As the text is so cagey with details, we can only speculate about the answers to these questions. Indeed, as with the preceding narratives, the silences in the text are more telling than the things that are directly stated. It is undeniable, for example, that this story about Joash's stubborn attempt to fix the temple portrays the king positively. Mario Liverani has argued that the purpose of this narrative is to justify Joash's reign. Comparing 2 Kings 12 to the inscription of Idrimi, King of Alalakh, Liverani argues that the stories of both kings serve to defend and legitimate the usurpation of the throne by monarchs whose authority might have been deemed suspicious.[5] Both Idrimi and Joash do not come to power in the

---

5. Mario Liverani, "L'Histoire de Joas," *VT* 24 (1974): 442, 451.

they saw that there was a great deal of money in the chest, the king's secretary and the high priest went up, counted the money that was found in the house of the LORD, and tied it up in bags. ¹¹They would give the money that was weighed out into the hands of the workers who had the oversight of the house of the LORD; then they paid it out to the carpenters and the builders who worked on the house of the LORD, ¹²to the masons and the stone-cutters, as well as to buy timber and quarried stone for making repairs on the house of the LORD, as well as for any outlay for repairs of the house. ¹³But for the house of the LORD no basins of silver, snuffers, bowls, trumpets, or any vessels of gold, or of silver were made from the money that was brought into the house of the LORD, ¹⁴for that was given to the workers who were repairing the house of the LORD with it. ¹⁵They did not ask an accounting from those into whose hand they delivered the money to pay out to the workers, for they dealt honestly. ¹⁶The money from the guilt offerings and the money from

usual way but are forced to hide or flee; they both are able to gain the throne only with the backing of specific groups. Interestingly, if 2 Kings 12 functions as a kind of defense of Joash, then it is clear that the preceding reign of Queen Athaliah, though deliberately absent in the account of Joash's reign, still lingers and colors the rule of her grandson.

When we consider the story in the preceding chapter concerning Joash's dramatic coronation—it is difficult not to look backward as the text itself keeps silently returning to Athaliah's reign—suspicions are raised about the description of events in Joash's reign in 2 Kings 12. Especially telling are the roles that Jehoiada and the priests play in the removal of Queen Athaliah. It is difficult to believe that these priests, after forcibly dethroning and assassinating the first queen of Judah, would just simply have handed over power to a seven-year-old boy-king. Rather, as we noted earlier, it is likely that the real powers behind the throne after Joash was enthroned would have been Jehoiada, the priest, and his wife, Jehosheba, the princess. If we read this narrative in light of the preceding account about Athaliah and her tenure, then some unsettling possible answers arise to the queries listed above.

If Jehoiada (and Jehosheba) effectively ruled Judah through the proxy child-king, Joash, for the first years of his reign, it would explain why the priests are so irresponsible about the donations coming into the temple and so inattentive to the commands of the king. Joash, if he was under the influence of Jehoiada and his aunt, Jehosheba, initially would

the sin offerings was not brought into the house of the LORD; it belonged to the priests.

¹⁷At that time King Hazael of Aram went up, fought against Gath, and took it. But when Hazael set his face to go up against Jerusalem, ¹⁸King Jehoash of Judah took all the votive gifts that Jehoshaphat, Jehoram, and Ahaziah, his ancestors, the kings of Judah, had dedicated, as well as his own votive gifts, all the gold that was found in the treasuries of the house of the LORD and of the king's house, and sent those to King Hazael of Aram. Then Hazael withdrew from Jerusalem.

¹⁹Now the rest of the acts of Joash, and all that he did, are they not written in the Book of the Annals of the Kings of Judah? ²⁰His servants arose, devised a conspiracy, and killed Joash in the house of Millo, on the way that goes down to Silla. ²¹It was Jozacar son of Shimeath and Jehozabad son of Shomar, his servants, who struck him down, so that he died. He was buried with his ancestors in the city of David; then his son Amaziah succeeded him.

not have had much authority and power over the priests. Most likely, while Joash was growing up, the priests who put him in power would have had the run of the country. The priests likely grew accustomed to managing the temple and, most important, the donations and money that came into the temple as they saw fit. When Joash got a bit older, he likely began to exert his authority by requesting that the priests repair the temple, which might have been mismanaged and thus in disrepair during his early years. Initially, the priests appear to have ignored the demands of the young monarch. The text is not clear as to how long the king waited, but it seems to have been quite a while as 2 Kings 12:6 states that nothing was done until the twenty-third year of Joash's reign. Depending on when the young king started to exert some control, we can assume that the priests ignored his charge for many years.

After waiting a lengthy amount of time and noticing the utter negligence of the priests, Joash appears to have become irritated enough to compel a meeting with the priestly group, which was led by Jehoiada. The meeting between Joash and Jehoiada, though sparsely described, undoubtedly would have been dramatic. Joash, no longer a boy and realizing his powers as king, would have forced Jehoiada—who most likely had the run of the country while Joash was a child—to take the donations out of the hands of those priests who were probably pilfering it. This almost certainly would have angered the clergy who had become accustomed to receiving the extra funds and, more important, of having control over the management of the temple. Furthermore, Jehoiada might have been the angriest of them as he had lost power not only over the temple but also seemingly over the country.

The text keeps decorously mum, refusing to fully air the court's dirty laundry. Rather, we can only speculate that Joash's attempt to exert control over the temple, the priests, and even Jehoiada likely led to problems because of the oddly negative way in which Joash's story ends. Right after telling the reader that Joash successfully accomplished the repairs to the temple, the narrative suddenly switches to say that it was all for naught. After the refurbishment is finished, King Hazael of Aram threatens to attack Jerusalem (2 Kgs 12:17), and, as a result, Joash is forced to bribe Hazael by raiding the very structure he just repaired. Poor Joash gives Hazael all the gold found in the temple as well as all the votive gifts that his predecessors had placed there. For all of Joash's attempts to make the temple grand, Joash leaves it poorer and emptier than when he began his reign.

A subtle underlying criticism of the king is thus easily detectable. Had YHWH been happy with the king's renovations of the temple, he would surely have prevented the Arameans from attacking Judah while it was under the rule of the pious Joash. Therefore, YHWH must have been unhappy with Joash about something. Since the only deed that Joash is said to have accomplished during his reign is the renovation of the temple, it must be something connected to this endeavor. As YHWH probably did not mind the repairs to his house, then his displeasure must concern the manner in which Joash accomplished this task. And as most of the narrative about the renovation centers on the king taking the donations and the management of the renovation out of the hands of the priests, the logical answer is that it was the control that Joash exerted over the priests that likely displeased the Lord. The priestly criticism, though not stated outright, is not difficult to deduce.

Aside from the account of the Aramean attack, which incidentally occurs right after the renovation of the temple, the narrative again hints of divine displeasure in its description of Joash's premature death. Immediately after plundering the temple to fend off Hazael, Joash, whose reign begins with the assassination of his grandmother, Queen Athaliah, is himself assassinated in a conspiracy. While Joash is on his way to Silla, two of his servants are said to have murdered him (vv. 20-21). The notice of Joash's untimely demise adds to the theological judgment. YHWH must have been displeased with Joash to let him be so suddenly murdered by servants.

The description of Joash's assassination also lends certain historical support to the political clashes, which would have likely ensued in the aftermath of Joash's assertion of power. Joash's attempt to assert more authority as king, especially over the management of the temple, would most likely have displeased individuals and groups that were accustomed to running the country when Joash was an impressionable young boy. This unhappy group probably would have consisted of those who had previously spearheaded the removal of Queen Athaliah, namely, the priests led by Jehoiada. Intriguingly, 2 Kings 11 notes that other groups assisted the priests in deposing the queen. 2 Kings 11:4 suggests that the priests were joined by other aristocratic elements, such as military personnel, landed elites, and palace guards, many of whom were mercenary soldiers.

Suspiciously, similar groups are tied to Joash's murder as well. Joash's own servants are said to have assassinated their king right after his renovation of the temple. Moreover, it is interesting that the king is said to have been killed by not one person but two individuals who are identified by name and paternity (v. 21). Could it be that his assassins are so specifically identified because they were prominent individuals, well known to the court? The account in Chronicles adds more detail to Joash's assassination by noting that these two men were sons of foreign women (2 Chr 24). This leads John Gray to speculate that Joash's assassins were most likely mercenary soldiers or royal retainers, many of whom were foreign.[6] As we noted earlier, mercenary palace guards are also said to have been involved in Athaliah's murder, which was primarily organized by the priests.

Tellingly, the very type of people who were hired by the aristocratic elite earlier to murder Athaliah also murder the next monarch, her grandson, Joash.[7] They do so right after Joash tries to assert a small degree of power over the priests. Adding up the clues, it appears likely that Joash's death came at the hands of the very people who placed him in power in the first place: the priests or other aristocratic elements who were probably unhappy over the king's "stringent financial control."[8] As shown by the earlier murder of Athaliah, this group would have had little compunction about killing another royal figure. As we will see, these groups likely continued their interference in palace affairs after Joash's death. Amaziah, Joash's son and heir, after reigning successfully in the beginning will also be assassinated.

---

6. John Gray, *I and II Kings*, OTL (Philadelphia: Westminster, 1970), 590.
7. Ibid.
8. Ibid.

The account in Chronicles lends further support to our reading. Though we do not have space here to discuss the complex relationship between the Deuteronomistic and Chronistic accounts, the later history is much more forthcoming about the clash between the priests and King Joash. Because of its own particular theological assumptions and purpose, the Chronistic account distances the temple repairs and the conflict between the priests and the king. The authors of Chronicles pinpoint the beginnings of Joash's trouble to the death of the king's priestly mentor, Jehoiada. After Jehoiada's death, Joash is said to have listened to wicked officials and, under their bad influence, to have begun to worship foreign gods (2 Chr 24:17-18). When Jehoiada's son, Zechariah, stands up to Joash for his impiety, the king and his wicked officials plot and murder Zechariah (2 Chr 24:20-21). In the Chronistic account, it is Joash's impious murder of Zechariah that is touted as the cause of the Aramean attack and Joash's later assassination (2 Chr 24:22-25). In other words, the Chronistic account more directly connects the king's assassination with his clashes with some members of the priestly group, namely, Zechariah. Setting aside the questions over the historicity and validity of the Chronistic narrative, this later account seems to support the conclusion that, hidden under the sparse description of Joash's rule in 2 Kings are the usual instances of ugly court politics and intrigue.

This conclusion has implications for how we read the preceding account of the reign of the one and only female monarch of Judah, Queen Athaliah. What such evidence of continuing court intrigue and priestly interference in the reign of Joash shows is that the reign of his predecessor, Athaliah, was not as illegal or unauthorized as it is described in 2 Kings 11. Despite the way that it is presented in the biblical text, it is not the case that the power-hungry, murderous witch was defeated by the pro-Davidic, pious, baby-saving priests. Rather, the same people who assassinated the queen appear to have had little qualms about also murdering the next monarch who stood in their way. In other words, as with Joash, Athaliah was also likely done in by people—namely, those in the religious establishment— who were as hungry for power and as murderous as she was.

The main difference between Athaliah and Joash is the contrasting ways in which the biblical text describes their tenure. Despite both monarchs being ruthlessly killed by certain factions within the kingdom, Athaliah's reign is portrayed as illegitimate while that of her grandson, Joash, is depicted as lawful and authorized by God. Of course the key point of difference between the two is their gender. Even though Joash angered the priests with his later assertion of monarchic power and control over the temple, the biblical writer could not dismiss his rule in the same way as he did with Athaliah because Joash was a male, Davidide heir. Though the text can hint of misgivings and mistakes on the part of Joash, it never outright delegitimates him in the same way as his predecessor. This is especially the case since, as we discussed, 2 Kings 11 vigorously attempts to contrast the legitimate, chosen, Davidic scion Joash with his illegitimate, power-hungry, grandmother Queen Athaliah. This contrast, so clearly asserted in 2 Kings 11, would be revealed as hollow if it was shown in the very next chapter that Athaliah's royal, legitimate grandson was also done in by the same religious faction that assassinated and deposed his grandmother. The text never forthrightly reveals the conflicts between monarch and priests (and possibly other aristocratic elements) that underlie the biblical text. Instead, what is conveyed is a rather incoherent story about a pious king who after renovating the temple is assassinated by his own servants. Indeed, it could be that the discordant description of Joash's reign was later found to be useful enough to be reused in other instances in the history of Judah where history butted up against theological and literary expectations. As we will see, Joash's reign will foreshadow those of other pious kings who, for some unknowable reason, suffer inexplicable ignominious ends.

2 Kings 13:1-25

The Reigns of Jehoahaz and Jehoash in Israel, and the Death of Elisha

After describing the dramatic events surrounding the monarchy in the South (Judah), the narrative in 2 Kings 13 reverts to the simultaneous unfolding situation in the North (Israel). We are told that during Joash's long forty-year reign in Judah (c. 836–796 BCE), two descendants of Jehu—Jehu's son, Jehoahaz, and Jehoahaz's own son and successor, Jehoash—rule in Israel. As we will see in the next chapter, Jehoash's term will partially overlap with that of Joash's son Amaziah. Two main occurrences mark the tenure of Jehoahaz and Jehoash. The first is the rising power of Aram-Damascus in the region during the ninth century BCE. The same kingdom that threatened Joash and forced the Judean king to strip the temple in 2 Kings 12 will also aggressively oppress Israel during the time of these two northern monarchs. The second event is the death of the prophet Elisha during Jehoash's reign. These two events—the continuation of Aramean oppression and the death of Israel's most prominent prophet—speak to the declining religious state of Samaria during this period. Elisha, however, immediately before and after his demise, will give one final gift of YHWH's procreative and life-giving powers to Israel. Though the sinfulness of the Northern Kingdom continues, YHWH's gifts of life and protection offer a relief and corrective to an otherwise dark period.

The Reign of Jehoahaz in Israel (13:1-9)

While Joash reigns in Judah, Jehoahaz, the son of Jehu, the military commander who usurped the throne of Israel and murdered Jezebel, rules in the North. As is typical of Deuteronomistic portrayals of the northern kings, Jehoahaz is said to have displeased YHWH (v. 1), continuing the sinful traditions begun by Jeroboam, the first monarch of Israel (v. 2). In particular, the biblical writer points to the existence of the sacred pole associated with the Canaanite goddess Asherah[1] as indicative of Jehoahaz's heresy (v. 6). According to the Deuteronomistic Historian, Asherah worship was championed by the wayward Jeroboam (1 Kgs 14:15, 23) and also perhaps by the hated Queen Jezebel (1 Kgs 18:19). The Asherah poles were fertility symbols, which were carved to resemble either living trees or the deity herself.[2] Though detested by the Deuteronomistic writers, the worship of Asherah was likely a part of the syncretistic religious practices in Israel, which were widespread.[3] Extrabiblical evidence speaks to the complicated relationship between YHWH and Asherah. The famous inscriptions from Kuntillet 'Ajrud and Khirbet el-Qom which speak of "YHWH and his Asherah" have led some scholars to argue that YHWH was intimately linked to this goddess, who was imagined as his divine consort or wife.[4]

1. For a thorough study of Asherah, see Saul M. Olyan, *Asherah and the Cult of Yahweh in Israel*, SBLMS 34 (Atlanta: Scholars Press, 1988).

2. Mark S. Smith, *The Early History of God: Yahweh and the Other Deities of Ancient Israel* (Grand Rapids, MI: Eerdmans, 2002), 111–18; Ellen White, "Asherah and the Asherim: Goddess or Cult Symbol," http://www.biblicalarchaeology.org/daily /ancient-cultures/ancient-israel/asherah-and-the-asherim-goddess-or-cult-symbol/.

3. Susan Ackerman, "At Home with the Goddess," in *Symbiosis, Symbolism, and the Power of the Past: Canaan, Ancient Israel and Their Neighbors from the Late Bronze Age through Roman Palaestina*, ed. Seymore Gitin and William G. Dever (Winona Lake, IN: Eisenbrauns, 2003), 455–68; William G. Dever, "Asherah, Consort of Yahweh? New Evidence from Kuntillet 'Ajrud," *BASOR* 255 (1984): 30–31; idem., *Did God Have a Wife? Archaeology and the Folk Religion in Ancient Israel* (Grand Rapids, MI: Eerdmans, 2005), 176–251; Olyan, *Asherah and the Cult of Yahweh*, 6–9; Michael Fishbane, "Israel and the 'Mothers,'" in *Garments of the Torah: Essays in Biblical Hermeneutics* (Bloomington: Indiana University Press, 1989), 56–58; Ilona Rashkow, *Taboo or Not Taboo: Sexuality and Family in the Hebrew Bible* (Minneapolis: Fortress, 2000), 49–57; Smith, *The Early History of God*, 108–11.

4. Ackerman, "At Home with the Goddess," 461; Dever, "Asherah, Consort of Yahweh?," 31; idem, *Did God Have a Wife?*, 176–251; André Lemaire, "Who or What was Yahweh's Asherah?" *BAR* 10 (1984): 42–51; Ze'ev Meshel, "Did Yahweh Have a Consort?," *BAR* 5 (1979): 24–34.; Olyan, *Asherah and the Cult of Yahweh*, 1–22, 38–61; Ephraim Stern, "Pagan Yahwism: The Folk Religion of Ancient Israel," *BAR* 27 (2001):

13:1In the twenty-third year of King Joash son of Ahaziah of Judah, Jehoahaz son of Jehu began to reign over Israel in Samaria; he reigned seventeen years. 2He did what was evil in the sight of the LORD, and followed the sins of Jeroboam son of Nebat, which he caused Israel to sin; he did not depart from them. 3The anger of the LORD was kindled against Israel, so that he gave them repeatedly into the hand of King Hazael of Aram, then into the hand of Ben-hadad son of Hazael. 4But Jehoahaz entreated the LORD, and the LORD heeded him; for he saw the oppression of Israel, how the king of Aram oppressed them. 5Therefore the LORD gave Israel a savior, so that they escaped from the hand of the Arameans; and the people of Israel lived in their homes as formerly. 6Nevertheless they did not depart from the sins of the house of Jeroboam, which he caused Israel to sin, but walked in them; the sacred pole also remained in Samaria. 7So Jehoahaz was left with an army of not more than fifty horsemen, ten chariots and ten thousand footmen; for the king of Aram had destroyed them and made them like the dust at threshing. 8Now the rest of the acts of Jehoahaz and all that he did, including his might, are they not written in the Book of the Annals of the Kings of Israel? 9So Jehoahaz slept with his ancestors, and they buried him in Samaria; then his son Joash succeeded him.

As William Dever and other scholars have convincingly shown, the "book religion" professed in the biblical text, despite its assertions as the only legitimate and legal form of worship, was not coterminus with the "folk religion" of Israel, the religion that was practiced and followed by the nonelite Israelite populace. Despite the tirade against the worship of Asherah in the biblical text, this goddess was frequently worshiped, especially by women, in the folk religious practices of Israel and Judah.[5] Dever's conclusion points to the androcentric bias that undergirds the representation of religion in the biblical text. As we have tried to show, sexist biases are evident in the subtle ways in which the biblical text legitimates and delegitimates particular persons, monarchs, deities, and modes of worship.

21–29. In contrast, John A. Emerton and Mark S. Smith argue that the asherah in the inscription from Kuntillet 'Ajrud refers to the wooden pole, not necessarily to the goddess (John A. Emerton, "New Light on Israelite Religion: The Implications of the Inscriptions from Kuntillet 'Ajrud," *ZAW* 94 [1982]: 13–14, 18; idem, " 'Yahweh and His Asherah': The Goddess or Her Symbol," *VT* 49 [1999]: 323; Smith, *The Early History of God*, 108–33).

5. Ackerman, "At Home with the Goddess," 455–68; Dever, *Did God Have a Wife?*, 176–251; Rashkow, *Taboo or Not Taboo*, 53–54.

Unsurprisingly, considering this bias, 2 Kings 13 depicts Asherah worship as wholly illegitimate. YHWH, the masculine deity of Israel, demands utter fidelity; he alone is to be worshiped, according to the biblical writer. Hence, for these religious disloyalties, YHWH expresses his frustration and anger over the impiety of the northern monarch, Jehoahaz, by letting the country be subject to military losses and foreign oppression. In this case, 2 Kings 13:2 states that YHWH handed over Israel to be subjected to the Arameans for many years. As we have seen, many of the preceding chapters of 2 Kings frequently describe interactions between Israel and Judah and their northern neighbor, Aram (modern-day Syria), during this period. YHWH's displeasure over Israel and its subjugation to Aram in 2 Kings 13:2 thus offers a theological interpretation of historical-political events occurring in the ancient Near East during the ninth century BCE, namely, the growth of power of Aram-Damascus under the reign of Hazael.

As we noted earlier, Hazael usurped the throne of Aram by assassinating the Aramean king, Ben-hadad. After taking the throne, Hazael appears to have expanded Aram's territories by trying to colonize and subject parts of Israel and Judah under his rule. Elisha weepingly foretells in 2 Kings 8 that the Aramean colonization under Hazael would lead to much misery and hardship for Judah and Israel. Indeed, the Aramean oppression is glaringly obvious by the description of the utterly weakened state of Israel's army at the end of Jehoahaz's reign. Second Kings 13:7 states that the Israelite king had almost no remaining military forces left in the country because Aram had so thoroughly destroyed them. As military might was frequently associated with masculinity and power,[6] the text depicts the emasculation of Jehoahaz—an emasculation that the text is very careful to point out was permitted by YHWH because of the sinfulness of the Israelite king (v. 3). By noting that YHWH allowed this foreign incursion, the masculine powers of the deity, which would be threatened by the oppression of his countries, are neatly reasserted and reaffirmed. YHWH purposefully permitted what looks like a decrease in his protection, might, and power in order to punish Jehoahaz.

That the northern king is damned as an apostate and is said to have earned the ire of YHWH is typical of northern kings. What is atypical, however, is that this negative summary about Jehoahaz is disrupted by

---

6. Cynthia Chapman, *The Gendered Language of Warfare in the Israelite-Assyrian Encounter*, HSM 62 (Winona Lake, IN: Eisenbrauns, 2004), 20–59.

two verses in the middle of the pericope that undermine this unfavorable tenor. Immediately after 2 Kings 13:3, which states that YHWH was incensed at Jehoahaz, the next verse (v. 4) suddenly portrays the northern king as imploring YHWH for help. Even more surprising, YHWH is said to have harkened to this king's plea. YHWH thus sends Israel an unnamed deliverer who promptly frees the country from Aramean oppression, and, as a result, the Israelites are said to have enjoyed a period of peace (v. 5). With that, the narrative pivots again and resumes the wholly negative account of Jehoahaz by noting that the king followed Jeroboam in his sinful ways, even allowing the presence of an Asherah pole (v. 6). The repetition of "Jeroboam" acts as a *Wiederaufnahme* or "resumptive repetition," which tells the reader that the narrative that began in 2 Kings 13:1-2, and was interrupted in verses 4-5, continues in verse 6.

Though it is clear that 2 Kings 13:4-5 is an insertion into the pericope of Jehoahaz, the purpose of this addition is unclear. Equally ambiguous is the larger referent of these verses. To what fuller, more complete story do the verses in 2 Kings 13:4-5 allude? Mordechai Cogan and Hayim Tadmor speculate that the referent might be the story about the famine in Samaria and the mysterious lifting of the Aramean siege in 2 Kings 6:24–7:20. They argue that both stories complement each other. Jehoahaz's "act of contrition" would explain why the siege was suddenly lifted and Samaria divinely saved.[7] The identification of Jehoahaz as the unnamed monarch of 2 Kings 13 would also elucidate more fully the portrayal of the Israelite king as irresponsible and dejected in 2 Kings 6.

Other referents have also been proposed. John W. Olley, looking at the cluster of theological motifs and vocabulary in 2 Kings 13, notes that 2 Kings 13:4-5 parallels the sin-punishment-entreaty-rescue pattern found in the book of Judges.[8] In a twist on the pattern in Judges, however, the deliverer whom YHWH raises to rescue Israel is anonymous in 2 Kings 13.[9] This has led commentators to propose a variety of possibilities for this unnamed savior, including figures who are associated with the words "deliverance" or "salvation," such as Jehoash (because of the arrow of victory or salvation in v. 17) or Jeroboam II (2 Kgs 14:27: "YHWH delivered them by the hand of Jeroboam"). Other possible figures who have been suggested are those characters who may have been responsible

---

7. Mordechai Cogan and Hayim Tadmor, *II Kings: A New Translation with Introduction and Commentary*, AB 11 (Garden City, NY: Doubleday, 1988), 144.

8. John W. Olley, "2 Kings 13: A Cluster of Hope in God," *JSOT* 36 (2011): 202.

9. Olley, "2 Kings 13," 203; Cogan and Tadmor, *II Kings*, 143.

for the withdrawal of the Arameans, such as the Assyrian king Adad-nirari II or Zakur of Hamath or even the Prophet Elisha.[10]

Olley posits, however, that the anonymity is deliberate and has a particular theological purpose. The unnamed savior in 2 Kings 13 purposefully shifts the attention of the reader from a human deliverer to a divine deliverer (i.e., YHWH).[11] Choon-Leong Seow explains the anonymity differently. He argues that the biblical writer envisioned the Aramean oppression as taking a considerable period of time. Hence, many saviors would have been needed to deliver Israel from the Aramean oppression.[12] As is clear, the two verses that discuss Jehoahaz's spiritual turnaround (2 Kgs 13:4-5) opaquely exhibit the complex writing and editing process that likely underlies the book of Kings as a whole.

The Reign of Joash in Israel (13:10-13)

Similar editorial complications are evident in the succinct account of the reign of Jehoahaz's son and successor, Joash, as king over Israel. Typical of northern monarchs, we are told that Joash took over as king after Jehoahaz and that he followed the sinful traditions of Jeroboam.

These initial statements are followed by an additional piece of information in verses 12-13 that many scholars believe is a later insertion about Joash's combative relationship with King Amaziah of Judah. As these verses are later repeated almost verbatim in the account of Amaziah's reign in 2 Kings 14:15-16, they seem to have been placed in the earlier account about Joash to better connect the two monarchs and their narratives. The stories of both Jehoahaz and his son, Joash, thus appear to show evidence of repositioning and editing.

Elisha's Death and Departing Gift (13:14-25)

The textual rearrangements are more fully evident in the concluding narrative of 2 Kings 13, which concerns the death of Elisha. Backtracking to the reign of Joash, which initially appeared to have been completed in 2 Kings 13:13 with the notice of his burial, we are told that Elisha be-

10. Cogan and Tadmor, *II Kings*, 143–44; John Gray, *I and II Kings*, OTL (Philadelphia: Westminster, 1970), 594–95; T. R. Hobbs, *2 Kings*, WBC 13 (Waco, TX: Word, 1985), 167–68.

11. Olley, "2 Kings 13," 204.

12. Choon-Leong Seow, "The First and Second Book of Kings," in *NIB*, ed. Leander E. Keck et al. (Nashville: Abingdon, 1999), 3:21.

[10]In the thirty-seventh year of King Joash of Judah, Jehoash son of Jehoahaz began to reign over Israel in Samaria; he reigned sixteen years. [11]He also did what was evil in the sight of the LORD; he did not depart from all the sins of Jeroboam son of Nebat, which he caused Israel to sin, but he walked in them. [12]Now the rest of the acts of Joash, and all that he did, as well as the might with which he fought against King Amaziah of Judah, are they not written in the Book of the Annals of the Kings of Israel? [13]So Joash slept with his ancestors, and Jeroboam sat upon his throne; Joash was buried in Samaria with the kings of Israel.

[14]Now when Elisha had fallen sick with the illness of which he was to die, King Joash of Israel went down to him, and wept before him, crying, "My father, my father! The chariots of Israel and its horsemen!" [15]Elisha said to him, "Take a bow and arrows"; so he took a

came sick during his reign and was on the verge of death (2 Kgs 13:14). In an oddly pious move, Joash, the king of Israel, who in the preceding account of his summary was assessed rather negatively by the Deuteronomistic author, is depicted as suddenly finding religion—visiting the prophet and weeping over his coming death and even going so far as to shout out the phrase exclaimed by Elisha during Elijah's ascent into heaven (2 Kgs 2:12; 13:14): "The chariots of Israel and its horsemen!" As we noted earlier in the commentary for 2 Kings 2:10-18, the meaning of this phrase is debated. One of the possibilities is that it is an honorific title for Elisha and Elijah, indicating that these prophets were representatives of God's power and divine force.[13]

Whatever the meaning, this inexplicably abrupt pious reaction of Joash leads Elisha to offer the king of Israel one final gift before he dies. The prophet tells the king to take a bow and arrow, then places his hands on the king's hands and orders the monarch to open the window facing east and shoot (vv. 15-16). When he shoots the arrow, Elisha declares, perhaps as a magical incantation,[14] that this is an arrow of victory for YHWH and an arrow of victory over Aram. Hence, the prophet declares Aram will be completely defeated at Aphek (v. 17). This sign is followed by another that Elisha now commands the king to perform. Elisha tells Joash to take arrows and to strike the ground (vv. 18-19). Joash, however, strikes the

13. See commentary on 2 Kings 2.
14. Barrick argues that this is an instance of sympathetic magic. W. Boyd Barrick, "Elisha and the Magic Bow: A Note on 2 Kings XIII 15-17," *VT* 35 (1985): 355–60, esp. 360.

bow and arrows. [16]Then he said to the king of Israel, "Draw the bow"; and he drew it. Elisha laid his hands on the king's hands. [17]Then he said, "Open the window eastward"; and he opened it. Elisha said, "Shoot"; and he shot. Then he said, "The LORD's arrow of victory, the arrow of victory over Aram! For you shall fight the Arameans in Aphek until you have made an end of them." [18]He continued, "Take the arrows"; and he took them. He said to the king of Israel, "Strike the ground with them"; he struck three times, and stopped. [19]Then the man of God was angry with him, and said, "You should have struck five or six times; then you should have struck down Aram until you had made an end of it, but now you will strike down Aram only three times."

[20]So Elisha died, and they buried him. Now bands of Moabites used to invade the land in the spring of the year. [21]As a man was being buried,

ground only three times instead of Elisha's "unstated" preference of five or six times. The incomplete striking leads to the prophet's angry declaration that, as a result, Israel will not defeat Aram completely but will be victorious over the enemy country only three times, or per the number of times Joash struck the ground with the arrow (v. 19). After this final oracle, Elisha promptly dies and is buried (v. 20), though, as we will see, this will not be the prophet's final miracle.

As Elijah ended his earthly presence with a final spectacular, magical ascent into heaven, so his protégé Elisha ends his earthly tenure with a last display of prophetic wizardry. Arrows and bows, Cogan and Tadmor explain, were frequently tied to belomancy (divination by arrows), especially in Mesopotamian prophylactic magic or prognostication.[15] Indeed, Ezekiel 21:21 seems to record an instance of belomancy being utilized by the Babylonians.[16] Samuel Iwry speculates that the double meaning of חץ as "arrowhead" and as "luck" might have something to do with the use of arrows in divination throughout the ancient Near East.[17]

15. Cogan and Tadmor, *II Kings*, 150. For the appearance of belomancy in myths, see A. W. Buckland, "Rhabdomancy and Belomancy, or Divination by the Rod and by Arrow," *Journal of the Anthropological Institute of Great Britain and Ireland* 5 (1876): 436–50.

16. T. Witton Davies, "Magic, Divination, and Demonology among the Semites," *AJSL* 14 (1898): 241–51; Paul Haupt, "Crystal-Gazing in the Old Testament," *JBL* 36 (1917): 84–92.

17. Samuel Iwry, "New Evidence for Belomancy in Ancient Palestine and Phoenicia," *JAOS* 81 (1961): 27–34, esp. 30–31.

a marauding band was seen and the man was thrown into the grave of Elisha; as soon as the man touched the bones of Elisha, he came to life and stood on his feet.

²²Now King Hazael of Aram oppressed Israel all the days of Jehoahaz. ²³But the LORD was gracious to them and had compassion on them; he turned toward them, because of his covenant with Abraham, Isaac, and Jacob, and would not destroy them; nor has he banished them from his presence until now.

²⁴When King Hazael of Aram died, his son Ben-hadad succeeded him. ²⁵Then Jehoash son of Jehoahaz took again from Ben-hadad son of Hazael the towns that he had taken from his father Jehoahaz in war. Three times Joash defeated him and recovered the towns of Israel.

While it is clear that Elisha's act is connected to magic and the otherworldly, the contours and meaning of his action as described in 2 Kings 13 remains unclear. Is Elisha divining whether Israel will overcome Aram when he commands Joash to shoot the arrow? And if so, does Elisha command the king to strike the ground only after figuring out that Israel will indeed defeat Aram so as to decipher more precisely the nature of Israel's victory—that it will be complete or somewhat incomplete? Or is it that triumph is induced through Elisha's exclamation of victory—his utterance of magical speech[18]—and not the shooting *per se*? John Gray suggests that the shooting and striking is an "act of imitative magic," which was meant to influence God through "auto-suggestion," though Gray does wonder whether these prophets really maintained such a "primitive belief."[19] Also unclear is the reason for and the effect of Elisha laying his hands on the king's hands in the first part of this act. Is this a necessary component of the belomancy or something that Elisha does to make sure Joash performs the act correctly? If the latter, could it be that Joash incorrectly performs the second part of the act—the striking—because Elisha failed to lay hands on him and help him to do it correctly as he did with the first part?

Equally ambiguous is why Elisha is not more precise in his instructions to Joash when he commands the king to strike the ground with the arrows. How is the king supposed to know that the number of times he

18. Boyd, "Elisha and the Magic Bow," 360.
19. Gray, *I and II Kings*, 599.

strikes will be equivalent to the number of victories over Aram? Is the first act of shooting the arrow supposed to show the monarch how to perform correctly the second act of striking? Moreover, why is the man of God angry at Joash for not striking the ground more than three times (v. 19) when he did not explicitly instruct him to do so? Is this just a continuation of the depiction of this prophet as ornery, which we have seen in other parts of 2 Kings (i.e., 2 Kgs 2:23-25, the killing of children by the she-bears)? Gray posits that Elisha, with his unclear directions, is testing the king to see whether he has faith in the prophet. The king's weak response, according to Gray, shows that Joash is just humoring the dying man and not taking the prophet seriously. Thus the king "revealed himself as a materialist, whose vision was limited by mere political factors," and thus he fails the test.[20]

Cogan and Tadmor argue that historical events might underlie some of the peculiar aspects of the narratives about Jehoahaz and his son, Joash.[21] As we noted earlier in the commentary for this chapter, both accounts share evidence of editing and repositioning. Most notably, the narratives of both kings are interrupted with or succeeded by sudden notices of the lessening of Aramean oppression, which the biblical text explains as the result of both monarchs' suddenly pious behaviors (see 2 Kgs 13:4-5, 14-19). Cogan and Tadmor note that extrabiblical sources indicate that Aramean hegemony in the Levant, during the time of Jehoahaz and Joash, was slowly weakened by the rise of Assyria under Adad-nirari. The Assyrian king would continue to campaign against Damascus, debilitating it so greatly that eventually, under Joash, Israel was able to defeat Aram three times at Aphek.[22]

This decline of Aram-Damascus caused by the rise of the Assyrians under Adad-nirari is given a theological explanation in the biblical narrative. The decline of Aramean oppression of Israel is the result of the northern kings' sudden changes of heart. Jehoahaz, for an unstated reason, suddenly calls out to YHWH for help against his foreign oppressors, forcing the deity to respond (2 Kgs 13:4-5), while Joash, also inexplicably, abruptly visits and weeps at the ensuing death of Elisha, prompting the prophet to give to the monarch a final parting gift of Israelite victory over Aram (2 Kgs 13:14). Perhaps sensing that the abrupt changes in the northern kings' behaviors are too jarring to be completely

20. Ibid.
21. Cogan and Tadmor, *II Kings*, 152.
22. Ibid.

persuasive in the narrative, the biblical writer, for good measure, adds another theological justification for the lessening of Aramean oppression. At the very end of 2 Kings 13, it states that though Aram oppressed Israel during Jehoahaz's reign, YHWH remained gracious and merciful to Israel because of his covenant with Abraham, Isaac, and Jacob (2 Kgs 13:23). YHWH is so gracious in fact that he even lets Jehoahaz's son, Joash, recapture some of the cities that were previously lost back from the Arameans (v. 25). By referencing the covenant with Israel's patriarchs, the biblical text thus presents another reason—albeit an unclear one—as to why Jehoahaz and Joash, though they were bad, impious, northern kings, were rewarded with a period of abatement of Aramean threats.

This is not the only theological conundrum the biblical writer attempts to address in 2 Kings 13, however. Though Elisha is depicted as a faithful prophet of YHWH until the end, the portrayal of his death may disappoint the reader when compared to how his mentor, Elijah, concludes his earthly tenure. While Elijah gets a ride to heaven from a divine convoy, Elisha just gets sick and dies. For a prophet who in preceding narratives raised a dead boy and transformed poisonous soup, getting ill seems to be a rather pedestrian end. Indeed, the presence of the cries of "the chariots of Israel and its horsemen" in both narratives about these prophets' conclusions compels the reader to compare and thus to contrast the two figures. While it is Elisha, the faithful protégé of Elijah, who cries out this sentence when Elijah dramatically ascends to heaven in 2 Kings 2, it is the unfaithful King Joash of Israel who utters it before Elisha's demise in 2 Kings 13—a rather anticlimactic ending to the life of a prophet who is said to have received double the portion of his mentor's spirit. The reader might wonder why Elisha's earthly tenure does not conclude with double the divine fireworks.

The narrator perhaps senses this unequal treatment. The biblical writer might have even felt that such a pitiful end to Elisha, the prophet of YHWH, would be theologically detrimental to the portrayal of YHWH as the deity of life, restoration, and procreative powers. Hence, in order to add more sheen to Elisha and thus, concomitantly, to reaffirm the life-giving powers of YHWH, the narrator adds another story about Elisha's demise, this time stressing the fact that despite his weak ending, the prophet, even down to his bones, still is and forever will be infused with the generative powers of YHWH, the God of reproduction and life.

Though Elisha's prophecy about Israel's victory over Aram will be the last magical act that the prophet accomplishes before his death, the grave will not prevent the prophet from performing one final postmortem miracle. In a final pericope, which Gray labels an "anecdote from the Elisha hagiology," Moabite raiders accidentally throw the body of a dead man whom they were hurriedly trying to bury into the grave of the deceased Elisha (2 Kgs 13:20). When the corpse of the man touches Elisha's bones, he comes back to life. The rejuvenating and healing powers of YHWH are so infused in his prophet Elisha that even after death the deity's reanimating powers can be passed on by the mere touch of the miracle worker's bones. With this additional story, Elisha's earthly ministry ends on a more powerful note. This narrative thus offers a more impressive conclusion to the life of Elisha. YHWH, the God of Elisha, is reaffirmed as the true and indeed only source of life, procreation, and healing.

2 Kings 14:1-29

The Reigns of Amaziah in Judah and Jehoboam II in Israel

Chapter 14 continues the account of the court history of Judah and Israel. Reverting to the political situation in the South, 2 Kings 14 resumes the story of the Davidic kings with a description of the reign of Amaziah, who comes to the throne after his father, King Joash, is assassinated in 2 Kings 12. Of special concern will be the contentious interactions between Judah and Samaria during Amaziah's reign. These hostilities will conclude with the capture of Amaziah by King Jehoash of Israel at Beth-shemesh. The chapter ends with a very brief description of the reign of Jehoash's son, Jeroboam II, in Israel who, despite the length of the account, was likely a very successful monarch. The theological dissonance created by the oppositional accounts of the two kings—the pious Judean king's unlucky reign and early demise by assassination and the impious northern king's successful tenure— reminds the reader that the Deuteronomistic History[1] is not a neutral record. Rather, it is a particular interpretation of the past with its own theological as well as gendered and socio-economic biases, preferences, and arguments.

---

1. See "Composition and Redaction of the Deuteronomistic History" in the introduction.

The Reign of Amaziah in Judah (14:1-22)

The account of Amaziah's reign begins with the typical Deuterono-mistic regnal summary, noting the corresponding king in the North, the age when the monarch begins to rule, the length of his tenure (c. 796–767 BCE) and his mother's name. Mordechai Cogan and Hayim Tadmor note that the length of reign ascribed to Amaziah—twenty-nine years (v. 1)—is oddly long and, thus, likely faulty. They argue that after Amaziah's defeat at Beth-shemesh, his son, Azariah, would probably have replaced him on the throne while Amaziah remained king in name only.[2]

Amaziah is judged positively by the Deuteronomistic writers who note that he "did what was right in the eyes of the LORD" (v. 3). Though he is not rated as commensurate with David (v. 3), and though he is faulted for not removing the high places (v. 4), he is given a favorable assessment, equal to that of his father, Joash. While this initially sounds positive, this early comparison to his father hints of darker things to come. As we saw in 2 Kings 12, Joash was also rated highly in the regnal summary. Indeed, Joash's reign, which began with the assassination of Queen Athaliah, was highly anticipated. Yet his reign ended in disappointment as he, in turn, was also assassinated by his own servants. This early comparison between Amaziah and his father lends the narrative a foreboding air and foreshadows Amaziah's equally disappointing tenure as king. Seemingly, in a case of "like father, like son," not only will Amaziah match his father's piety, but he, like his father, will also be forced to raid the temple and suffer an untimely death at the hands of assassins.

It is clear that the shadow of his father's disheartening rule lingers and shapes that of Amaziah. This is evident in one of the first acts Amaziah accomplishes after he consolidates his rule: he puts his father's murderers to death. In "a departure from customary practice,"[3] however, Amaziah is said to have been merciful with the families of the murderers, sparing their children in accordance with the law of Moses. The mention of the Mosaic prohibition (Deut 24:16) as a justification for Amaziah's leniency is odd and unclear. It is uncertain whether something called the "book of the Law of Moses" existed by the time of Amaziah or whether this is a retrojection from a later writer or editor. Cogan and Tadmor argue that, in accordance with the practice of blood revenge, it was common for the

---

2. Mordechai Cogan and Hayim Tadmor, *II Kings: A New Translation with Introduc-tion and Commentary*, AB 11 (Garden City: Doubleday, 1988), 154.

3. Ibid., 155.

¹⁴:¹In the second year of King Joash son of Joahaz of Israel, King Amaziah son of Joash of Judah, began to reign. ²He was twenty-five years old when he began to reign, and he reigned twenty-nine years in Jerusalem. His mother's name was Jehoaddin of Jerusalem. ³He did what was right in the sight of the LORD, yet not like his ancestor David; in all things he did as his father Joash had done. ⁴But the high places were not removed; the people still sacrificed and made offerings on the high places. ⁵As soon as the royal power was firmly in his hand he killed his servants who had murdered his father the king. ⁶But he did not put to death the children of the murderers; according to what is written in the book of the law of Moses, where the LORD commanded, "The parents shall not be put to death for the children, or the children be put to death for the parents; but all shall be put to death for their own sins."

⁷He killed ten thousand Edomites in the Valley of Salt and took Sela by storm; he called it Jokthe-el, which is its name to this day.

⁸Then Amaziah sent messengers to King Jehoash son of Jehoahaz, son of Jehu, of Israel, saying, "Come, let us look one another in the face." ⁹King

avenger to kill the murderer or one of his kin. In cases of usurpations, it was normal for the entirety of the royal family to be killed off in order to thwart any potential claimants or rivals.[4] Amaziah's leniency was unusual enough to be noted by the Deuteronomistic Historian.[5]

Yet as we noted earlier in the commentary on 2 Kings 12:4-21, the motivations of the assassins who murdered Amaziah's father, Joash, are unstated by the biblical writer. His murder does not appear to have been an attempt at a usurpation as Amaziah easily seems to have succeeded his father. Rather, Joash's death, as we argued earlier in the commentary on 2 Kings 12:4-21, most likely resulted from his conflict with the priests who, along with other elites in the Judean society, wanted to replace Joash with a more pliable monarch after he started to assert his authority.[6] This scenario may explain why Amaziah does not seek revenge on the families of his father's killers. Perhaps they were members of the elite or the upper class in Israel. Or perhaps the killers were hired by members of the oligarchy and/or the priests. Though Amaziah could rightfully execute those who committed the crime, he could not fully avenge his

4. Ibid.
5. Ibid.
6. So also John Gray, *I and II Kings*, OTL (Philadelphia: Westminster, 1970), 604.

Jehoash of Israel sent word to King Amaziah of Judah, "A thornbush on Lebanon sent to a cedar on Lebanon, saying, 'Give your daughter to my son for a wife'; but a wild animal of Lebanon passed by and trampled down the thornbush. [10]You have indeed defeated Edom, and your heart has lifted you up. Be content with your glory, and stay at home; for why should you provoke trouble so that you fall, you and Judah with you?"

[11]But Amaziah would not listen. So King Jehoash of Israel went up; he and

King Amaziah of Judah faced one another in battle at Beth-shemesh, which belongs to Judah. [12]Judah was defeated by Israel; everyone fled home. [13]King Jehoash of Israel captured King Amaziah of Judah son of Jehoash, son of Ahaziah, at Beth-shemesh; he came to Jerusalem, and broke down the wall of Jerusalem from the Ephraim Gate to the Corner Gate, a distance of four hundred cubits. [14]He seized all the gold and silver, and all the vessels that were found in the house of the LORD and in the treasuries of the king's house, as

father and go after their families without angering these aristocratic elements. As will become apparent at the end of this narrative, the elite members of Judean society who replaced Joash with his son, Amaziah, also seem to have grown equally tired of the son.

Amaziah, however, despite these dark hints of coming travails begins his reign successfully. Not only is he given a positive assessment by the Deuteronomistic author, but, befitting the masculine requirements of an ancient Near Eastern monarch,[7] he begins his reign with a successful military campaign, killing ten thousand Edomites (v. 7). The reason why he needed to battle the Edomites is left unstated in the text, though some scholars speculate that Edom might have been trying to take advantage of Judah's struggle with the Arameans to claim territory and trade routes.[8] Cogan and Tadmor, in contrast, suggest that it was actually Amaziah who was trying to take advantage of the political situation in the northeastern region caused by the Arameans. They argue that while Israel and Aram were engaged in combating each other, Amaziah used this time to try to reassert Judean control over the Arabah in the South (where Edom is located), which provided access to Eilat and the Red Sea.[9]

---

7. Cynthia Chapman, *The Gendered Language of Warfare in the Israelite-Assyrian Encounter*, HSM 62 (Winona Lake, IN: Eisenbrauns, 2004), 20–59.

8. Gina Hens-Piazza, *1–2 Kings*, AOTC (Nashville: Abingdon, 2006), 237; Gray, *I and II Kings*, 606.

9. Cogan and Tadmor, *II Kings*, 158.

well as hostages; then he returned to Samaria.

¹⁵Now the rest of the acts that Jehoash did, his might, and how he fought with King Amaziah of Judah, are they not written in the Book of the Annals of the Kings of Israel? ¹⁶Jehoash slept with his ancestors, and was buried in Samaria with the kings of Israel; then his son Jeroboam succeeded him.

¹⁷King Amaziah son of Joash of Judah lived fifteen years after the death of King Jehoash son of Jehoahaz of Israel. ¹⁸Now the rest of the deeds of Amaziah, are they not written in the Book of the Annals of the Kings of Judah? ¹⁹They made a conspiracy against him in Jerusalem, and he fled to Lachish. But they sent after him to Lachish, and killed him there. ²⁰They brought him on horses; he was buried in Jerusalem with his ancestors in the city of David. ²¹All the people of Judah took Azariah, who was sixteen years old, and made him king to succeed his father Amaziah. ²²He rebuilt Elath and restored it to Judah, after King Amaziah slept with his ancestors.

Gina Hens-Piazza suggests a more literary motivation behind the notice of Amaziah's triumph over the Edomites: to set up and explain Amaziah's confrontational letter that he sends to Israel's king right after the Edomite campaign.[10] Hens-Piazza's ideas align closely with the later account in 2 Chronicles. Not only is Amaziah's military power expanded and magnified by the Chronicler (2 Chr 25:1-13), but the Chronistic writer connects this victory more directly with Amaziah's disastrous conflict with Israel. According to Chronicles, after Amaziah's triumph over the Edomites, he brings their gods to Judah and incites YHWH's anger by worshiping them (2 Chr 25:14-15). This act of heresy immediately precedes Amaziah's adversarial letter to the king of Israel in Chronicles. With this sequence of events, the Chronicler strongly hints that Amaziah's military loss to Israel and his unfortunate death was the result of his impiety.

The Chronistic account of Amaziah attempts to make coherent the puzzling narrative sequence of 2 Kings 13. For unknown reasons, Amaziah, in the immediate aftermath of his military victory over the Edomites, mysteriously sends a letter to King Jehoash of Israel to request that they "meet face to face" (2 Kgs 14:8). The meaning of Amaziah's request is unclear. Perhaps it had a hostile intent or maybe it was an attempt to establish "more equitable relations with the north."[11] Cogan and Tadmor view Amaziah's

10. Hens-Piazza, *1-2 Kings*, 328.
11. Ibid.

letter as antagonistic, noting that in Mesopotamian literature the Akkadian equivalent of the Hebrew verb in 2 Kings 14:8 (N-form of *amaru*, "to see" or *nanmurru*) is occasionally utilized for confrontations with enemies.[12] Indeed, the king of Israel too seems to have taken offense at Amaziah's unprompted letter. King Jehoash dismisses Amaziah's complaint with a disparaging parable in which he compares Judah to an arrogant thistle—a plant commonly used in Mesopotamian and biblical fables and parables (see Judg 9:14-15)[13]—that tries to intermarry with a cedar (i.e., Israel) only to be trampled by a passing wild animal (v. 10). Jehoash concludes his reply by telling Amaziah that his ego has been mistakenly inflated by his recent victory over Edom. According to Jehoash, Amaziah should just be happy with the current situation and not cause unnecessary problems for his country (v. 10).

Jehoash's reply, though cryptic, is clearly adversarial and bellicose. Whatever Amaziah suggested in his letter, it was clearly rejected by Jehoash. Jehoash seems to take offense at the fact that Amaziah has even dared to send a letter in the first place. Yet it is unclear what Jehoash is rejecting or asserting in his reply because Amaziah's initial request is ambiguous. It appears from Jehoash's reply that Amaziah, in sending this letter or in his request, has overstepped his boundaries in some manner. Moreover, it seems that this overstepping entailed some kind of joint engagement or establishment of relationship as Jehoash's parable refers to a thistle pompously trying to marry a cedar. Hens-Piazza suggests that Amaziah was trying to establish more equitable relations with the more powerful Northern Kingdom[14]—a request that is roundly rejected by an offended Jehoash who compares Judah to a weak and worthless thistle, easily destroyed by a wandering beast. This reference to the weakness of Judah also hints at the possibility that perhaps Amaziah was trying to form a military alliance of equals with Israel. Jehoash not only rejects his offer but scorns it, in fact, telling Amaziah that Judah's military prowess is laughable.

The letter indicates that Amaziah failed to listen to Jehoash. Jehoash, with his harsh and patronizing response, appears to be goading Amaziah into a confrontation. His hostile and insulting reply certainly seems to heighten hostilities between the two states. This back-and-forth eventually leads to a battle between the two nations at Beth-shemesh (v. 11)

12. Cogan and Tadmor, *II Kings*, 156.
13. Ibid.
14. Hens-Piazza, *1–2 Kings*, 328.

at which Jehoash defeats Amaziah and takes him hostage. The Israelite king for good measure also breaks down a wall of Jerusalem, seizes gold, silver, and vessels from the temple of YHWH and other treasuries, and takes more hostages (vv. 13-14). Though soundly humiliated and defeated, Amaziah appears to have mysteriously remained on the throne after the confrontation as he is said to have outlived Jehoash and is eventually buried in Jerusalem. Hens-Piazza thinks that other hostages were taken as ransom for Amaziah, who was then able to return to the throne of Judah.[15]

Cogan and Tadmor again offer a more historical interpretation of the battle at Beth-shemesh. They believe that the argument and battle between the two countries was the result of Amaziah's attempt to take advantage of a period of Israelite distraction and weakness. With Israel engaged with the Arameans, Cogan and Tadmor posit that Amaziah, confident from his Edomite victory, pushed into contested border regions of the northern Shephelah. Yet Israel was not as weak or distracted as Amaziah had hoped for, and it was thus able to defeat Judah in battle at Beth-shemesh.[16]

The historical explanation, while interesting and persuasive, does not, however, alleviate the theological quandaries that this story raises. Why is the impious northern king, Jehoash—and not the righteous Davidide, Amaziah—the one proven correct in his assessment that Judah is indeed delusional about its own strength? Remember that Amaziah is given a positive assessment by the Deuteronomistic Historian, while Jehoash, like all northern kings, is judged negatively. If YHWH is pleased with Amaziah and also happy over the renovations done on the temple by Amaziah's father, Joash, why does he allow the heretical northern king, Jehoash, to defeat Judah in battle, strip the temple of its valuables, destroy a wall of Zion, and take Judah's king hostage?

The manner of Amaziah's death adds to the theological conundrum. Things go from bad to worse for this king. After the debacle with Israel, unnamed fellow Judeans conspire against Amaziah, and the king is forced to flee to Lachish. At Lachish, however, the conspirators send assassins after him who kill him there, at which point his body is brought back by horse to Jerusalem where he is buried (vv. 19-20). Many mysteries surround Amaziah's death. Who are these conspirators? Why do they so

---

15. Ibid.
16. Cogan and Tadmor, *II Kings*, 158.

badly want to kill Amaziah, and how are they so powerful or determined enough to "send after" the king in Lachish in order to assassinate him there? Hens-Piazza suspects a connection between Amaziah's murderers and those who earlier assassinated his father, Joash. She notes that the very people whom Amaziah spares in the beginning of the pericope—the family of those who murdered Joash—may be the same people who were responsible for Amaziah's later assassination.[17] Cogan and Tadmor add that the lack of reprisal by Amaziah's successor, Azariah, for his father's death indicates that the murderers were likely those of "rank and of wide following." Perhaps Azariah was even part of the conspiracy that removed and assassinated his father.[18]

Considering that Amaziah is murdered by those who were likely members of the same social class and standing as those who earlier assassinated his father, Joash, and considering Hens-Piazza's suggestion that the two groups of killers appear to be connected, it seems that Amaziah too was the victim of the same political maneuverings that undid his father earlier. As we noted in the previous chapter, Joash appears to have been placed on the throne by elite members of Judean society, only to be removed and assassinated by the same group after he came into conflict with the priests. The same groups appear to have tired of his son, Amaziah, as well—perhaps because of his heavy losses in his fight with Israel—and likely worked to remove him from the throne. Like his father, Amaziah too is thus replaced with a person whom the oligarchy prefers. Perhaps, as Cogan and Tadmor note, Amaziah's son, Azariah, participated or assisted in this conspiracy. And with this, Amaziah, who was so favorably assessed by the Deuteronomistic author in the beginning, is depicted as having a disastrous reign and a tragic demise.

The Reign of Jeroboam II in Israel (14:23-29)

The dissonant tone evident in the narrative about Amaziah is magnified by the succeeding pericope about the reign of Jeroboam II of Israel (786–746 BCE). While Amaziah is still in power, Jeroboam the son of Joash comes to the throne in the North. As with all northern kings, he is given the typical negative assessment by the Deuteronomistic author for following the sinful ways of Jeroboam I, the first king of Israel. Quickly

---

17. Hens-Piazza, *1–2 Kings*, 327.
18. Cogan and Tadmor, *II Kings*, 159.

²³In the fifteenth year of King Amaziah son of Joash of Judah, King Jeroboam son of Joash of Israel began to reign in Samaria; he reigned forty-one years. ²⁴He did what was evil in the sight of the LORD; he did not depart from all the sins of Jeroboam son of Nebat, which he caused Israel to sin. ²⁵He restored the border of Israel from Lebo-hamath as far as the Sea of Arabah, according to the word of the LORD, the God of Israel, which he spoke by his servant Jonah son of Amittai, the prophet, who was from Gath-hepher. ²⁶For the LORD saw that the distress of Israel was very bitter; there was no one left, bond or free, and no one to help Israel. ²⁷But the LORD had not said that he would blot out the name of Israel from under heaven, so he saved them by the hand of Jeroboam son of Joash.

²⁸Now the rest of the acts of Jeroboam, and all that he did, and his might, how he fought, and how he recovered for Israel Damascus and Hamath, which had belonged to Judah, are they not written in the Book of the Annals of the Kings of Israel? ²⁹Jeroboam slept with his ancestors, the kings of Israel; his son Zechariah succeeded him.

after this negative assessment, however, the pericope turns to a list of accomplishments during his reign that doubtlessly indicates that Jeroboam II, though impious, was a very successful monarch. Though there is little historical record from the time of Jeroboam II,[19] the biblical text notes that he recovered both the northern and southern borders of Israel (v. 25). Moreover, he successfully fought the Arameans like his father and even restored Damascus and Hamath (v. 28). In so doing, he effectively contained the Aramean threat and even "reinstated the original borders of the northern territories that were established under Solomon (1 Kgs 8:65)."[20]

Adding to the accomplishments, the northern king's successes are said to be "according to the word of the LORD, the God of Israel, which he spoke by his servant Jonah son of Amittai, the prophet" (v. 25). Hens-Piazza suspects that the book of Jonah may have borrowed the name for its wayward protagonist from this passage.[21] The fact that there is no record of Jonah's prophetic career or life makes him an ideal candidate for reuse in later literary works. Oddly, however, while Jonah is named, Amos and Hosea (who are said to have prophesied in Israel during the reign of Jeroboam II) are absent from the account of this monarch.

---

19. Ibid., 163.
20. Hens-Piazza, *1–2 Kings*, 331.
21. Hens-Piazza, *1–2 Kings*, 331; see also Cogan and Tadmor, *II Kings*, 161, 164.

When the Deuteronomistic assessment of the northern and southern kings are compared to their respective lists of achievements and kingly successes an odd, though not wholly unfamiliar, feeling of dissonance can be detected.[22] While Amaziah is rated highly by the historian, he is said to have been taken hostage by the northern king, Jehoash, and then assassinated. In contrast, the Israelite king, Jeroboam II, is said to have displeased the Lord but appears to have had a tremendously successful reign. Moreover, while Jehoash appears to die rather peacefully at home (2 Kgs 14:29), Amaziah, like his father, is chased after by his own countrymen and assassinated (2 Kgs 14:18-20).

There seem to be some obvious attempts in the narrative to tone down or alleviate these incongruencies. First, the writer greatly shortens the narrative of the successful northern monarch. Though Jeroboam II reigns forty-one years, the longest regnal term of any king in the North,[23] the account of his reign is very brief. It seems that the Deuteronomistic writer wanted to pass by the successes of this monarch as quickly as possible to prevent the reader from gaining a true understanding of his achievements. Second, a small theological explanation embedded in the pericope about Jeroboam II attempts to explain why God allowed Israel to prosper during the reign of this impious northern monarch. Immediately after the text states that Jeroboam II restored the borders, 2 Kings 14:26-27 abruptly and nonsensically states that YHWH saw Israel's distress and isolation and decided not to blot it out but to save it instead through the hand of Jeroboam II.

The writer evidently felt that the narrative of the prosperous rule of an impious northern king in Israel immediately after the account of a disastrous rule of a pious Davidide in Judah was rather problematic. Cogan and Tadmor explain this dissonance redactionally. They argue that the tonal misalignment is caused by the "existence of a prophetic, pre-Deuteronomistic tradition."[24] Hens-Piazza, however, looks at the impact of the tonal disharmony from a theological viewpoint. She argues that the stories of the reigns of Amaziah and Jeroboam II directly contradict and undermine Deuteronomistic ideas of divine justice. According to this theology, God rewards the righteous with long life, protection, prosperity, and healing and, in contrast, punishes evil-doers with military losses and threats, illness, and early death. These narratives, in going against this

---

22. Cogan and Tadmor, *II Kings*, 162; Hens-Piazza, *1–2 Kings*, 331.
23. Cogan and Tadmor, *II Kings*, 162.
24. Ibid., 163.

theological expectation, disturb "one's growing confidence in God and how God acts," leading the reader to question the character of God.[25] This dissonance, however, can have a positive effect as it upends one's easy understanding of how the divine interacts with humanity by showing that God can utilize both the good and the bad.[26]

Adding to Hens-Piazza's theological conclusions, an understanding of the complexity of divine-human interactions also alerts the reader to be more mindful of the unheard and unseen groups of people that lie behind the stories of these male monarchs. Behind the narrative of these kings, whom the Historian assesses with a Deuteronomistic thumbs up or thumbs down, are the stories of men, women, and children who were deeply affected by the actions of these monarchs, the vicissitudes of history, and the mysterious workings of their deity. Every battle won or lost, every divine punishment of certain nations or monarchs, and every political mistake made by these rulers had ramifications on the lives of those who remain silent, absent, and forgotten in the text.

As we have tried to show, the people whom the biblical writer blesses with voice or curses with silence depend on their respective genders, ethnicities, and socioeconomic class. As court history, these stories in 2 Kings about the reigns of various monarchs are not only theologically biased but have a gendered, ethnic, and class component. These are stories about male Israelite and Judean kings. As such, much of it concerns battles and combats that try to assert the masculinity of one king or deity over another.[27] The few women who assert a measure of power, such as Jezebel and Athaliah, are emphatically denigrated in the text. Indeed, not just powerful royal women, but other vast segments of Judean society are also rendered invisible and voiceless in 2 Kings. The book is mostly a history of the Judean court, and it does not pay attention to the poor women, men, and children that make up the general populace of Judah. A more fair and equitable reading should attempt to give voice to or at least acknowledge these silent members of society. How to go about actually recovering these unrecorded voices remains, however, a mystery or, at least, a debated predicament.

25. Hens-Piazza, *1–2 Kings*, 332.
26. Ibid., 333.
27. Chapman, *Gendered Language*, 20–59.

2 Kings 15:1-38

Political Instability and Voiceless Victims

Despite the assertion in the preceding chapter that YHWH "did not think of blotting out Israel's name from the heavens" (14:27), much of this chapter (2 Kgs 15) focuses on the nation's decline. The narrative sets the context for the approaching destruction of the Northern Kingdom by Assyria described in 2 Kings 17. The chapter, with its rundown of the ever changing monarchs of Samaria, conveys the instability that marked the Northern Kingdom before its demise. It was not instability alone, however, that led to Samaria's decimation. The nation's volatility was exacerbated by the changing political context of the ancient Mediterranean world. Namely, Assyria, under King Tiglath-pileser III (745–727 BCE), began aggressively to expand and colonize states in the ancient Near East. In so doing, King Tiglath-pileser III would forever change its landscape as well as the histories of Judah and Israel. Haunting the androcentric narratives of these monarchs, however, are the untold stories of women, children, and men who lived, died, and suffered as a result of their ambitions and actions.

The Reigns of Azariah and Jotham in Judah (15:1-7 and 15:32-38)

The chapter is sandwiched between two short accounts of the more successful Judean monarchs in the Southern Kingdom: Azariah (783–742

^{15:1}In the twenty-seventh year of King Jeroboam of Israel King Azariah son of Amaziah of Judah began to reign. ²He was sixteen years old when he began to reign, and he reigned fifty-two years in Jerusalem. His mother's name was Jecoliah of Jerusalem. ³He did what was right in the sight of the LORD, just as his father Amaziah had done. ⁴Nevertheless the high places were not taken away; the people still sacrificed and made offerings on the high places. ⁵The LORD struck the king, so that he was leprous to the day of his death, and lived in a separate house. Jotham the king's son was in charge of the palace, governing the people of the land. ⁶Now the rest of the acts of Azariah, and all that he did, are they not written in the Book of the Annals of the Kings of Judah? ⁷Azariah slept with his ancestors; they buried him with his ancestors in the city of David; his son Jotham succeeded him.

BCE) and his son, Jotham (742–735 BCE). The narrative of the reign of Azariah (also known as Uzziah in 2 Kgs 15:13, 30, 32, 34 and 2 Chr 26; 27:2; Isa 1:1; 6:1) begins with the usual regnal summary noting the age when he ascended to the throne, the length of his reign, his mother's name, and the Deuteronomistic assessment of the monarch. Like other monarchs in the South, though he is said to have failed to remove the high places (v. 4), he is nonetheless rated favorably overall as doing "what was right in the sight of the LORD" (v. 3).

Although Azariah is said to have enjoyed one of the longest reigns of the Judean kings, the Deuteronomistic Historian barely records any event during his reign except the monarch's sickness.[1] For unexplained reasons, 2 Kings 15:5 states that YHWH struck this king with leprosy and that, as a result, he resided in a separate house. Mordechai Cogan and Hayim Tadmor find it highly unlikely that a monarch would have been forced to live outside the city, however. They argue that the biblical writers mention Azariah's residence outside of Jerusalem to show their adherence to purity prohibitions mentioned elsewhere in the biblical text (Lev 13:46; 2 Kgs 7:3; cf. Num 12:14-15).[2] Mysteriously, the biblical writer never tells the reader why YHWH suddenly afflicted Azariah with this disease. Considering that this king is rated favorably by the

---

1. Mordechai Cogan and Hayim Tadmor, *II Kings: A New Translation with Introduction and Commentary*, AB 11 (Garden City, NY: Doubleday, 1988), 167.

2. Ibid., 166.

³²In the second year of King Pekah son of Remaliah of Israel, King Jotham son of Uzziah of Judah began to reign. ³³He was twenty-five years old when he began to reign and reigned sixteen years in Jerusalem. His mother's name was Jerusha daughter of Zadok. ³⁴He did what was right in the sight of the LORD, just as his father Uzziah had done. ³⁵Nevertheless the high places were not removed; the people still sacrificed and made offerings on the high places. He built the upper gate of the house of the LORD. ³⁶Now the rest of the acts of Jotham, and all that he did, are they not written in the Book of the Annals of the Kings of Judah? ³⁷In those days the LORD began to send King Rezin of Aram and Pekah son of Remaliah against Judah. ³⁸Jotham slept with his ancestors, and was buried with his ancestors in the city of David, his ancestor; his son Ahaz succeeded him.

Deuteronomistic Historian, the mention of his leprosy as the sole event of his tenure hints at underlying editorial activities.

The Chronicler also seems to have felt that the account of Azariah in 2 Kings was lacking. Also possible is that he had access to other materials about this monarch's reign. The Chronistic narrative about Azariah, which is much more detailed and extensive, more fully explains the positive assessment of Azariah. The Chronicler depicts the king as successfully waging wars against the hated Philistines with the help of God and also as engaging in several extensive building projects (2 Chr 26:6-10). Azariah's sudden bout of leprosy is also more cogently explicated as the result of his pride following his successes. When Azariah/Uzziah arrogantly tries to make an offering on the altar of incense rather than letting the priests perform the activity, God strikes him with leprosy as punishment (2 Chr 26:16-20). According to Cogan and Tadmor, the famous earthquake during the time of Uzziah, which is mentioned in Amos 1:1 and Zechariah 14:5, was envisioned in later traditions as occurring when YHWH's wrath struck the poor monarch (Josephus; *Ant.* 9.225; cf. Targum to Isa 28:21).[3]

As a result of his leprosy, 2 Kings 15:5 states that Azariah's son, Jotham, was left in charge of the palace to govern the people of the land. The reign of Jotham, which happened within the lifetime of his father, is also very succinctly described in the Deuteronomistic History (2 Kgs 15:32-38).

3. Ibid.

Jotham, like his father, after being assessed positively in the regnal summary by the Deuteronomistic Historian (2 Kgs 15:32-34), is similarly noted for a single accomplishment: he is said to have renovated the gateways of the temple (v. 35). As with Azariah, the later Chronistic account offers a more detailed assessment and narrative of Jotham's reign. In 2 Chronicles 27, he, like his father, is noted for his success in battle (v. 5) and for his construction activities (v. 3). Perhaps because Jotham's mother, as a daughter of Zadok, is said to have been affiliated with the priestly class (2 Kgs 15:33), the Chronicler specifically mentions Jotham's construction of the upper gate of the house of the Lord (2 Chr 27:3). He is even given a slightly higher overall rating than Azariah in Chronicles as he did "not invade the temple" as his father did.

The Reigns of Zechariah, Shallum, Menahem, Pekahiah, and Pekah in Israel (15:8-31)

The positive accounts of the reigns of the Judean kings, Azariah and Jotham, bookend and frame the list of the ever-changing series of northern monarchs in 2 Kings 15. The contrast between the unfavorably assessed, tumultuous sequence of northern kings and the positively rated, uninterrupted reign of the Davidides, Azariah and Jotham, in the South is clearly noticeable.[4] Though the short pericopes of these northern monarchs present little detail of a particular king's reign, taken together, they compose a picture of an unstable Israel, on the verge of complete collapse.[5] This instability, as noted earlier, was compounded by the aggressive, expansionist activities of Tiglath-pileser III of Assyria. The rise of this Assyrian monarch as well as a complex of other events would pave the way for Israel's final demise.

After the death of the successful Jeroboam II, his son, Zechariah, is able to succeed his father to the throne of Israel. Zechariah, however, is only able to reign for six short months (v. 8) before he is assassinated by a usurper, Shallum, son of Jabesh (v. 10), thus putting an end to the dynasty founded by Jehu. Shallum too, however, is quickly dispatched after only one month of rule when he is killed by another usurper, Menahem (v. 14). Menahem's takeover appears to have been particularly bloody as the text notes that Menahem sacked a town,

---

4. Gina Hens-Piazza, 1–2 Kings, AOTC (Nashville: Abingdon, 2006), 334.
5. Ibid.

⁸In the thirty-eighth year of King Azariah of Judah, Zechariah son of Jeroboam reigned over Israel in Samaria six months. ⁹He did what was evil in the sight of the LORD, as his ancestors had done. He did not depart from the sins of Jeroboam son of Nebat, which he caused Israel to sin. ¹⁰Shallum son of Jabesh conspired against him, and struck him down in public and killed him, and reigned in place of him. ¹¹Now the rest of the deeds of Zechariah are written in the Book of the Annals of the Kings of Israel. ¹²This was the promise of the LORD that he gave to Jehu, "Your sons shall sit on the throne of Israel to the fourth generation." And so it happened.

¹³Shallum son of Jabesh began to reign in the thirty-ninth year of King Uzziah of Judah; he reigned one month in Samaria. ¹⁴Then Menahem son of Gadi came up from Tirzah and came to Samaria; he struck down Shallum son of Jabesh in Samaria and killed him; he reigned in place of him. ¹⁵Now the rest of the deeds of Shallum, including the conspiracy that he made, are written in the Book of the Annals of the Kings of Israel. ¹⁶At that time Menahem sacked Tiphsah, all who were in it and its territory from Tirzah on; because they did not open it to him, he sacked it. He ripped open all the pregnant women in it.

¹⁷In the thirty-ninth year of King Azariah of Judah, Menahem son of

Tiphsah⁶ or, more likely, Tappuah,⁷ in the process even ripping open pregnant women at that locale.

Peter Dubovský⁸ notes the importance of Menahem's reign and, in particular, the mention of his violent behavior toward women. Dubovský argues that the text of 2 Kings 15 shows the buildup and evolution of Menahem's violence.⁹ According to Dubovský, the Hebrew word נכה, "to strike," is utilized three times with reference to Menahem's actions in

6. On the translational and interpretative issues with the name of this town, see Peter Dubovský, "Menahem's Reign before the Assyrian Invasion (2 Kings 15:14-16)," in *Literature as Politics, Politics as Literature*, ed. David S. Vanderhooft and Abraham Winitzer (Winona Lake, IN: Eisenbrauns, 2013), 29–45. Dubovský reads Tiphsah here and argues that Menahem was attempting to expand his territories to the Davidic-Solomonic regions (39).

7. Cogan and Tadmor, *II Kings*, 171.

8. Peter Dubovský, "Assyrian Downfall through Isaiah's Eyes (2 Kings 15–23): The Historiography of Representation," *Bib* 89 (2008): 1–16; idem, "Menahem's Reign," 29–45; idem, "Tiglath-pileser III's Campaigns in 734–732 B.C.: Historical Background of Isa 7; 2 Kgs 15–16 and 2 Chr 27–28," *Bib* 87 (2006): 153–70; idem, "Why Did the Northern Kingdom Fall According to 2 Kings 15?," *Bib* 95 (2014): 321–46.

9. Dubovský, "Menahem's Reign," 42.

Gadi began to reign over Israel; he reigned ten years in Samaria. ¹⁸He did what was evil in the sight of the LORD; he did not depart all his days from any of the sins of Jeroboam son of Nebat, which he caused Israel to sin. ¹⁹King Pul of Assyria came against the land; Menahem gave Pul a thousand talents of silver, so that he might help him confirm his hold on the royal power. ²⁰Menahem exacted the money from Israel, that is, from all the wealthy, fifty shekels of silver from each one, to give to the king of Assyria. So the king of Assyria turned back, and did not stay there in the land. ²¹Now the rest of the deeds of Menahem, and all that he did, are they not written in the Book of the Annals of the Kings of Israel? ²²Menahem slept with his ancestors, and his son Pekahiah succeeded him.

²³In the fiftieth year of King Azariah of Judah, Pekahiah son of Menahem began to reign over Israel in Samaria; he reigned two years. ²⁴He did what was evil in the sight of the LORD; he did not turn away from the sins of Jeroboam son of Nebat, which he caused Israel to sin. ²⁵Pekah son of Remaliah, his captain, conspired against him with

2 Kings 15: when he strikes and kills Shallum (v. 14), when he strikes and destroys an entire region (v. 16), and when he strikes the city and rips open pregnant women (v. 16).[10] The threefold use of this word depicts Menahem's bloody progression as he goes from striking a single person, to a region, and then, finally, to prenatal life.[11] The text thus climaxes to the king's unconscionable behavior toward women. Dubovský notes that the concentric structure of 2 Kings 15 and the inclusio (bookend framework) of the reigns of the good Judean kings in this chapter focus the reader's attention on Menahem's reign and his brutalities.[12]

The scarcity of times when the ripping open of pregnant women is mentioned in the biblical text or attested to in other ancient Near Eastern sources stresses the negative view of this act as something inhumane and utterly savage. The ripping open of pregnant women occurs three times in the Hebrew Bible, in 2 Kings 8:11-12; Amos 1:13; and Hosea 14:1, describing Arameans, Ammonites, and Assyrians, respectively, as engaging in this brutal act.[13] A few extrabiblical sources, such as a Middle Assyrian poem celebrating the victories of Tiglath-pileser I as well as

10. Ibid.
11. Ibid.
12. Dubovský, "Why Did the Northern Kingdom Fall," 337.
13. Ibid.

fifty of the Gileadites, and attacked him in Samaria, in the citadel of the palace along with Argob and Arieh; he killed him, and reigned in place of him. ²⁶Now the rest of the deeds of Pekahiah, and all that he did, are written in the Book of the Annals of the Kings of Israel.

²⁷In the fifty-second year of King Azariah of Judah, Pekah son of Remaliah began to reign over Israel in Samaria; he reigned twenty years. ²⁸He did what was evil in the sight of the LORD; he did not depart from the sins of Jeroboam son of Nebat, which he caused Israel to sin.

²⁹In the days of King Pekah of Israel, King Tiglath-pileser of Assyria came and captured Ijon, Abel-beth-maacah, Janoah, Kedesh, Hazor, Gilead, and Galilee, all the land of Naphtali; and he carried the people captive to Assyria. ³⁰Then Hoshea son of Elah made a conspiracy against Pekah son of Remaliah, attacked him, and killed him; he reigned in place of him, in the twentieth year of Jotham son of Uzziah. ³¹Now the rest of the acts of Pekah, and all that he did, are written in the Book of the Annals of the Kings of Israel.

a relief (BM 124927) of the Assyrian king Ashurbanipal's battle against Arabs, mention or portray this horrifying deed.[14]

In all cases, Dubovský notes that this behavior was seen as extreme and unacceptable.[15] The biblical writer, by portraying the Israelite king as committing this vile atrocity, damns him by aligning his behavior with barbaric and savage outsiders:[16] "King Menahem, who, like every Israelite king, was in theory supposed to guarantee order and justice, was instead promoting savage barbarity and behaving like an atrocious foreign invader."[17] Dubovský notes that Hosea prophesies a similar fate for the people of Samaria in retribution for this earlier brutality under Menahem:[18] "Samaria shall bear her guilt, because she has rebelled against her God; they shall fall by the sword, their little ones shall be dashed in pieces, and their pregnant women ripped open" (Hos 13:16). The biblical writer emphasizes the gruesome cruelty done against innocent women

14. Ibid., 42–43. See also Dubovský, P. "Ripping Open Pregnant Arab Women: Reliefs in Room L of Ashurbanipal's North Palace," *Or* 78 (2009): 394–419; and Mordechai Cogan, " 'Ripping Open Pregnant Women' in Light of an Assyrian Analogue," *JAOS* 103 (1983): 755–57.

15. Dubovský, "Menahem's Reign," 43.

16. Cogan and Tadmor, *II Kings*, 171.

17. Dubovský, "Menahem's Reign," 43.

18. Ibid.

as a means by which to show the utterly fallen state of the North. The writer offers a justification for why YHWH allows Israel to be destroyed shortly thereafter.[19] In the face of such unconscionable violence, YHWH will not—indeed cannot—continue to protect this nation. That this violence against women can have such a profound effect on the behavior of the deity presents a more favorable view of YHWH than the ones that we have seen in other accounts in the Hebrew biblical corpus.

Equally telling of the decayed state of Israel is that this violent king, Menahem, appears to have had one of the few generally stable reigns in Samaria, albeit with the help of the Assyrians whom Menahem pays off to retain his position (v. 19). He is able to hold on to power for ten years, likely through a tyrannical and bloody rule, and is even able to pass on the throne to his son, Pekahiah (v. 22). Pekahiah, however, seems to have been made of weaker stuff than his father, and he is able to reign only two years before his captain, Pekah, son of Remaliah, assassinates him and usurps the throne (v. 25). Pekah reigns for twenty years before another usurper, Hoshea, attacks and kills him (v. 30).

All these northern kings are similarly described in 2 Kings. All of them are assessed negatively by the Deuteronomistic writer. All of them, barring Menahem, are violently overthrown and killed. Moreover, except for Menahem, none of these kings' burial places are mentioned.[20] The lack of resting place is especially significant. According to Gina Hens-Piazza, the "unsettling ways each of them came to their ends" signifies the "unrest that now afflicts the whole nation."[21] Israel, testifying to its nearly dead state, appears to be run by a series of monarchs who, in the blink of an eye, transform into corpses. Indeed, symbolizing completeness, the North, at the end of 2 Kings 15, experiences seven coups d'état.[22] Moreover, the biblical writer, in referencing the particular locale of the various assassinations—first, in a public place (v. 10 with Shallum [745 BCE]), second in the capital (v. 14 with Menahem [745–737 BCE]), and, finally, in the safest place in Samaria, that is, the royal palace (v. 25 with Pekahiah [737–736 BCE])—shows the spread of instability around the kingdom. Nobody can be trusted, and no place and no one is safe.[23]

---

19. So also Dubovský, "Why Did the Northern Kingdom Fall?," 338.
20. Hens-Piazza, *1–2 Kings*, 338.
21. Ibid.
22. Dubovský, "Why Did the Northern Kingdom Fall?," 325.
23. Ibid., 328.

The narrative drives home this point by mentioning another threat looming on the horizon. While the violent men in Israel spent their energies trying to kill each other in order to become the next monarch, 2 Kings 15:28 zooms the camera away from Israel to focus on the larger situation in the ancient Near East wherein an even more violent and more dangerous power-hungry nation is shown as slowly colonizing its way toward Israel: "In the days of King Pekah of Israel, King Tiglath-pileser of Assyria came and captured Ijon, Abel-beth-maacah, Janoah, Kedesh, Hazor, Gilead, and Galilee, all the land of Naphtali; and he carried the people captive to Assyria" (v. 29). Like a beast of limitless appetite, Assyria, under Tiglath-pileser III, is depicted as slowly consuming the nations around Samaria. The Northern Kingdom, run by a series of impious, unethical usurpers, as the narrative makes clear, is next on the plate.

The instability of Samaria and the rise of Assyria will have consequences for Judah as well. Concluding the chapter, the narrative ends with the effects that this will have on Judah under its next monarch, Ahaz. 2 Kings 15:37 briefly mentions that YHWH sent King Rezin of Aram and Pekah of Israel against Judah. This verse sets the context for the account of the Syro-Ephraimite war in the next chapter, which will endanger the reign of the Davidide, Ahaz, in the South.

The Voiceless Victims in 2 Kings 15

Though this chapter, like most of the preceding accounts, focuses on the individual male kings, speedily running through their accomplishments and failures, it is important to recognize the stories of the unnamed and unmentioned women, men, and children who lie behind the androcentric biblical narrative. Behind every usurpation, every battle, every grasp for land, every colonial attempt at expansion of a country's territories, and every attempt by a ruler to gain more power are the untold sufferings of people who bear the brunt of the violence, distress, and adversity caused by these leaders and their policies. The mention of Menahem's atrocity of ripping open pregnant women gives the reader a small, horrifying glimpse into the real misery and hardships inflicted on those who, because of their gender, class, or ethnicity, are made victims of a struggle between a few, select men for power and dominance.

2 Kings 16:1-20

The Reign of Ahaz in Judah

The preceding chapter made it clear that time was quickly running out for the Northern Kingdom. The political instability caused by a series of coups d'état, the unethical activities of some of these northern monarchs, and the rise of Assyria under Tiglath-pileser III plainly indicated that Samaria was living on borrowed time. Judah and its monarchy, in contrast, was depicted as stable, pious, and, thus, safely protected by YHWH. This feeling of security would change with the account of King Ahaz's reign in 2 Kings 16. Ruling during a dangerous and tumultuous time, Ahaz is negatively assessed by the biblical writer for mishandling the nation during this perilous period. The account of his reign in 2 Kings 16, instead of clearly outlining his offenses, however, merely hints at his numerous wrongdoings. Insinuating that the king, with his infractions, set the path for Judah's downfall, the narrative prepares the reader for the climactic advent of his son, the pious Hezekiah, who will reverse this downward national trajectory. Some scholars have argued that the negative depiction of Ahaz has less to do with the historicity of events during his reign than with the attempt to set the context for the reign of Hezekiah in the following chapters.

Introductory Summary of Ahaz's Reign (16:1-4)

As with most monarchs, the account of Ahaz's reign begins with the usual summary introduction noting the corresponding northern king,

---
2 Kgs 16:1-4

16:1In the seventeenth year of Pekah son of Remaliah, King Ahaz son of Jotham of Judah began to reign. 2Ahaz was twenty years old when he began to reign; he reigned sixteen years in Jerusalem. He did not do what was right in the sight of the LORD his God, as his ancestor David had done, 3but he walked in the way of the kings of Israel. He even made his son pass through fire, according to the abominable practices of the nations whom the LORD drove out before the people of Israel. 4He sacrificed and made offerings on the high places, on the hills, and under every garden tree.

---

the age when the monarch begins to reign, the total length of his tenure, and an assessment of his piety. Hinting that something peculiar is afoot, however, the Deuteronomistic regnal summary for Ahaz in 2 Kings 16:1-4 oddly rates the Judean king unfavorably.[1]

The oddity of the assessment of Ahaz is conspicuous when we compare his rating to the four preceding Judean kings—Joash, Amaziah, Azariah, and Jotham—who are all judged positively.[2] Unlike most monarchs in Judah who are lightly criticized for the continued presence of the high places yet otherwise given approval by the Deuteronomistic author for doing "what was pleasing in the eyes of YHWH," Ahaz is blatantly said to "not do what was right in the eyes of the LORD" (v. 2). As Klaas Smelik notes, in all of 2 Kings, only Solomon in his old age (1 Kgs 11:33) and Jeroboam, the first ruler of the Northern Kingdom (1 Kgs 14:8), are appraised similarly. That Ahaz is compared to these figures is particularly telling as it is these monarchs who are viewed as responsible for the spread of idolatry in the country.[3]

An alternative form of this critique—"to do what is wrong in the eyes of the Lord"—is a frequent criticism levied at the detested northern monarchs by the Deuteronomistic Historian.[4] When applied to Judean kings, however, it is saved for the worst of the worst. The few southern monarchs who are judged equivalently are Jehoram (2 Kgs 8:18) and

---

1. Mordechai Cogan and Hayim Tadmor, *II Kings: A New Translation with Introduction and Commentary*, AB 11 (Garden City, NY: Doubleday, 1988), 190.

2. Klaas A. D. Smelik, "The Representation of King Ahaz in 2 Kings 16 and 2 Chronicles 28," in *Intertextuality in Ugarit and Israel*, ed. J. C. De Moor, OTS 40 (Leiden: Brill, 1998), 147.

3. Ibid., 148.

4. See "Composition and Redaction of the Deuteronomistic History" in the introduction.

Ahaziah (2 Kgs 8:26). The latter is said to be affiliated with and related to the hated house of Ahab. Manasseh who, as we will shortly see, is envisioned by the historian as the most despicable king in all of the Deuteronomistic History[5] is also similarly assessed. This estimation thus lumps Ahaz, a Judean king, together with the impious Israelite monarchs. The text straightforwardly parallels Ahaz with his northern royal colleagues when it states that he "followed the ways of the kings of Israel" (v. 3). The accusation that a Judean king "walked in the ways of the kings of Israel" is also applied to Jehoram in 2 Kings 8:18 and appears to be a code word for following the ways of the house of Ahab.[6] Hence, Ahaz is linked not only to the bad leaders of Israel but to the most offensive one of them all: Ahab.

Castigating him further, the writer also states that Ahaz committed numerous disturbing offenses during his tenure. Continuing the theme of royal violence against innocent people that we saw in the account of the northern king Menahem, 2 Kings 16:3 states that Ahaz "passed his son through the fire." Though there is some debate as to what this phrase means, it most likely refers to child sacrifice. As we discussed in our commentary for 2 Kings 3, though the significance of child sacrifice in the Hebrew Bible is complex and multifaceted, there appears to be some effort in the text to disassociate YHWH, the deity of life, procreation, and reproduction, with this act. By connecting child sacrifice with Ahab, the writer points to the fact that Ahaz is misaligned with YHWH, the deity of life and fertility.

The narrative further damns him by offering no reason for Ahaz's violent deed. Unlike 2 Kings 3, which portrays the Moabite king as desperately sacrificing his son in the midst of a losing battle, no reason is given for Ahaz's sacrifice of his offspring. By not stating a reason for his act, the text paints this king as randomly and wantonly violent. Like Athaliah and Menahem, this king, without reason or purpose, kills his own children.

Other passages in the Hebrew Scriptures pass negative judgment on child sacrifice. Aside from being forbidden in some biblical texts (see Lev 18:21; Deut 9:4, 18:10), the Deuteronomistic writers associate this deed

5. Smelik, "The Representation of King Ahaz," 147. The criticism is also applied to the four successors of King Josiah. This is understandable as the accounts of these monarchs who rule immediately before the exile and destruction of Judah constitute the denouement of Judean history.

6. Nadav Na'aman, "The Deuteronomist and Voluntary Servitude to Foreign Powers," *JSOT* 65 (1995): 41.

with those whom they loathe, such as King Manasseh, who is also said to have sacrificed his children (2 Kgs 21:6). Manasseh and Ahaz are further paralleled as both are said to copy the detestable practices of the Canaanites (2 Kgs 16:3; 21:2). The text directly connects Ahaz's child sacrifice with God's expulsion of the indigenous people from the land of Canaan: "He even made his son pass through fire, *according to the abominable practice of the nations whom the* Lord *drove out before the people of Israel*" (2 Kgs 16:3; emphasis added).

The biblical depiction of God commanding Joshua and the Israelites to expel and annihilate[7] the indigenous population in Syro-Palestine has deeply troubled readers.[8] More problematically, the negative effects of these narratives in Joshua have extended beyond the borders of the biblical text. Reapplied and reinterpreted, they have been used to justify acts of imperialism and wholesale destruction and enslavement of native populations in such places as the United States.[9] Carolyn Sharp warns modern faith communities against easy adoption and appropriation of these narratives. Rather, these disturbing stories should "draw contemporary communities of faith into reflection on their own subjectivity, the power dynamics that energize and fracture their common life, and their need for robust and ongoing reformation."[10]

Within the context of the biblical narrative, the violent reaction to the Canaanites speaks to the threat posed by this indigenous population to the biblical writer. According to L. Daniel Hawk, nonindigenous conquerors need to justify why they and not the indigenous residents deserve the land.[11] Frequently, as is the case with the Israelites, this justification took

---

7. On the ban in the Hebrew Bible, see Susan Niditch, *War in the Hebrew Bible* (New York: Oxford University Press, 1993), esp. 28–77.

8. Walter Brueggemann, "The God of Joshua . . . Give or Take the Land," *Int* 66 (2012): 164–75; Rivon Krygier, "Did God Command the Extermination of the Canaanites? The Rabbis Encounter with Genocide," *Conservative Judaism* 2 (2005): 78–94; Jon D. Levenson, "Is There a Counterpart in the Hebrew Bible to New Testament Antisemitism," *JES* 22 (1985): 242–59.

9. L. Daniel Hawk, "The Truth about Conquest: Joshua as History, Narrative, and Scripture," *Int* 66 (2012): 137–40; Rachel Havrelock, "The Joshua Generation: Conquest and the Promised Land," *Critical Research on Religion* 1 (2013): 308–26; Michael Prior, "The Bible and the Redeeming Idea of Colonialism," *Studies in World Christianity* 5 (1999): 129–55.

10. Carolyn Sharp, "'Are You for Us, or for Our Adversaries': A Feminist and Postcolonial Interrogation of Joshua 2–12 for the Contemporary Church," *Int* 66 (2012): 152.

11. L. Daniel Hawk, "Indigenous Helpers and Renegade Invaders: Ambivalent Characters in Biblical and Cinematic Conquest Narratives," *Journal of Religion & Film* 20 (2016): 2.

the form of "an appeal to transcendence (e.g., divine election or national destiny) or negatively rendering the indigenous people as unworthy or detrimental to the land."[12] Both the appeal to transcendence as well as the denigration of the indigenous serve to differentiate the colonialists from the conquered population and, in so doing, act as a component of identity formation. In short, the belittling of the indigenous not only justifies conquest and violence but, more importantly, reinforces and delineates what it means to be an Israelite through contradistinction.

A Postcolonial Reading of Empire in 2 Kings

Whether ancient or modern, an abiding characteristic of empire is power. In 2 Kings, specifically chapters 15–25, the workings of empire are filtered through a theological framework in which the God of Israel is the ultimate possessor and dispenser of power. Here, the kingdoms of Israel and Judah fall in and out of favor with God, the latter resulting in the retributive use of empire as an instrument of divine discipline. Yet despite this theological subtext, the effects of empire are imagined to occur on a material level—leaving their trace on bodies, objects, and spaces.

For most of the second half of 2 Kings, the Assyrian and Babylonian empires are made present in the text primarily as actors of subjugation and violence. Though Deuteronomistic theology places all empires under the sovereignty of God, there are instances in which empire acts autonomously. In chapters 18–20, the Judean king Hezekiah possesses the expected attributes of a righteous ruler and yet the Assyrian Empire remained an ever-present threat. One is left to wonder if this is not how empire actually operates, precisely as a human made socio-political phenomenon. Following this logic to its end, Hezekiah's rebellion, in turn, reflects a response against empire that appears more consistent with how colonized people maneuver under empire. In the face of Assyrian "arrogance," Hezekiah stages a resistance that is grounded in his particular cultural-religious identity. Though the Assyrian Empire would have the Judeans believe that it is a flawless and immutable force, it is from Hezekiah's resistance that empire registers its weakness as a perfect totalizing system. Hence what is striking here are the counter responses that the colonized subject manufactures separately from an "invincible" empire.

Gregory Lee Cuéllar

12. Ibid.

The formation, maintenance, and protection of Israelite identity were all the more important because the demarcation between Israelites and Canaanites was tenuous. In terms of culture and religious practice, there was little to separate the two groups.[13] Despite lingering debate on the origins of ancient Israel, many argue that Israelites emerged from native groups within Canaan.[14] The differentiation between the two groups—Israel is that which is not Canaan—is likely a deliberate fabrication, which formed the heart of Israel's sense of self. As a fabrication, however, the boundaries of Israelite identity remained fragile and in constant need of reinforcement and protection. By connecting Ahaz's practice to the abominations of the Canaanites (v. 3), the writer thus charges Ahaz with threatening to dismantle the wall that separates Israelites from the indigenous people—and, in so doing, as attempting to undo the very nature of Israel's identity. The king is leading his country to the same fate as the nations that YHWH had formerly removed from the land. Ahaz, in other words, is driving the country to ruin and leading the Judeans toward exile.[15]

Unsurprisingly, the protection of Israelite identity entailed the maintenance, defense, and surveillance of sexual boundaries. The threat posed by Canaan's indigenous population to Israel and its identity was imbued with sexual and gendered connotations. In Deuteronomy, the destruction of the Canaanites is coupled with the prohibition against intermarriage. The Israelites are instructed to decimate the indigenous people of Canaan and are also barred from marrying them lest the Canaanites tempt Israelites into worshiping other gods beside YHWH (Deut 7:1-4).[16] This

---

13. William G. Dever, *Did God Have a Wife? Archaeology and Folk Religion in Ancient Israel* (Grand Rapids, MI: Eerdmans, 2005), 266–67; idem, *Who Were the Early Israelites and Where Did They Come From* (Grand Rapids, MI: Eerdmans, 2003), 121–28; Mark S. Smith, *The Early History of God: Yahweh and the Other Deities of Ancient Israel* (Grand Rapids, MI: Eerdmans, 2002), 19–64.

14. Dever, *Who Were the Early Israelites*, 167–221; Israel Finkelstein and Neil Asher Silberman, *The Bible Unearthed: Archaeology's New Vision of Ancient Israel and the Origin of Its Sacred Text* (New York: Touchstone, 2002), 111–18; Hawk, "The Truth about Conquest," 132; Lawrence E. Stager, "Forging an Identity: The Emergence of Ancient Israel," in *The Oxford History of the Biblical World*, ed. M. D. Coogan (New York: Oxford University Press, 1998), 105.

15. Smelik, "The Representation of King Ahaz,"149.

16. Lori Rowlett, "Violent Femmes and S/M: Queering Samson and Delilah," in *Queer Commentary and the Hebrew Bible*, ed. Ken Stone, JSOTSup 334 (Cleveland: Pilgrim, 2001), 110; Dora Rudo Mbuwayesango, "Canaanite Women and Israelite Women in Deuteronomy: The Intersection of Sexism and Imperialism," in *Postcolonial Interventions: Essays in Honor of R.S. Sugirtharajah*, ed. Tat-siong Benny Liew (Sheffield: Sheffield Phoenix, 2009), 45–57.

idea that sexual and marital relationships with foreigners leads to religious infractions (Mal 2:11-16) is also reflected in the warning against the dangerous foreign seductress (Prov 5).[17] Continuing the analogy, apostasy—the worship of other gods—is frequently likened to another sexual violation, adultery, in the biblical text (Hos 1–2; Ezek 23).[18]

Fittingly, apostasy is also the final charge with which the writer concludes his regnal summary of Ahaz: the king sacrificed and made offerings on the high places, on hills, and under every green tree (v. 4). While the preceding Judean monarchs are lightly criticized for failing to remove the high places, Ahaz surpasses them all by personally making illegal offerings, not just on high places, but also on hills and under every green tree. Especially interesting is the expression "on the hills and under every green tree," which is utilized in 1 Kings 14:23 and 2 Kings 17:10 to rebuke the people of Israel for their religious degradations. Jeremiah too, among others, utilizes the phrase "under every green tree" to refer to idolatrous cult worship (see Deut 12:2; Isa 57:5; Jer 2:20; 3:6, 13; 17:2; Ezek 6:13; 2 Chr 28:4).[19] William Dever posits that this reference to trees alludes to the goddess Asherah and therefore to the folk religion, much denigrated by the Deuteronomistic author.[20] Not only does Ahaz religiously misbehave, but he goes overboard in his offenses, copying the abominations of other nations, sacrificing his son, and also practicing his apostasy anywhere and everywhere. All in all, in the eyes of the Deuteronomistic Historian, Ahaz is one of the worst Judean kings in the nation's history thus far.

Ahaz and the Syro-Ephraimite War (16:5-9)

With this highly negative appraisal of Ahaz, the narrative sets up the context for the succeeding Syro-Ephraimite War in verse 5. The narrative cryptically delineates the war as the following: "Then King Rezin of Aram and King Pekah son of Remaliah of Israel came up to wage war on Jerusalem; they besieged Ahaz but could not conquer him" (v. 5). By being secretive about the reason for Rezin and Pekah's sudden attack

---

17. On the complex portrayals of foreign women as presented in the biblical text, see Athalya Brenner-Idan, *The Israelite Women: Social Role and Literary Type in Biblical Narrative* (London: Bloomsbury T&T Clark, 2015), 115–22.

18. On the apostasy-as-fornication metaphor, see Eve Levavi Feinstein, *Sexual Pollution in the Hebrew Bible* (Oxford: Oxford University Press, 2014), 50–53.

19. Smelik, "The Representation of King Ahaz," 150.

20. Dever, *Did God Have a Wife?*, 224.

[5]Then King Rezin of Aram and King Pekah son of Remaliah of Israel came up to wage war on Jerusalem; they besieged Ahaz but could not conquer him. [6]At that time the king of Edom recovered Elath for Edom, and drove the Judeans from Elath; and the Edomites came to Elath, where they live to this day. [7]Ahaz sent messengers to King Tiglath-pileser of Assyria, saying, "I am your servant and your son. Come up, and rescue me from the hand of the king of Aram and from the hand of the king of Israel, who are attacking me." [8]Ahaz also took the silver and gold found in the house of the Lord and in the treasures of the king's house, and sent a present to the king of Assyria. [9]The king of Assyria listened to him; the king of Assyria marched up against Damascus, and took it, carrying its people captive to Kir; then he killed Rezin.

on Ahaz, the writer insinuates that this military confrontation was the result of the king's multiple offenses. Indeed, scholars note that by placing the war immediately after the critical assessment of this figure, the two events are joined in a sin-punishment pattern. The Syro-Ephraimite War is thus depicted as divine punishment for Ahaz's misbehavior.[21]

Aside from theological explanations of the Syro-Ephraimite War (735–732 BCE), the causes and purpose of this event are debated. The prevailing view, following the conclusion put forth by Joachim Begrich, is that this war was started by King Rezin of Damascus and King Pekah of Samaria when Ahaz refused to join them in an anti-Assyrian alliance. Based on Isaiah 8, it appears that Ahaz's rejection of cooperation in this coalition led the two kings to try to forcibly remove the Judean monarch in order to install a more docile puppet king.[22] In fact, Isaiah 7 offers more information about the event, describing how the two kings tried to dethrone Ahaz and replace him with another—the son of Tabeel (Isa 7:6).

Scholars of late, however, have argued for a more complex understanding of this event. Bustanay Oded, for example, lists several possible objections to Begrich's conclusion. He argues that if the objective of Damascus and Syria was to form a coalition to fend off Assyria, it would be odd that they would weaken themselves by starting a long war. More-

21. Mordecai Cogan and Hayim Tadmor, "Ahaz and Tiglath-Pileser in the Book of Kings: Historiographic Considerations," *Bib* 60 (1979): 498–99; Na'aman, "Deuteronomist and Voluntary Servitude," 41.

22. Joachim Begrich, "Der Syrisch-Ephraimitische Krieg und seine weltpolitischen Zusammenhänge," *ZDMG* 83 (1929): 213–37.

over, he states that, when one examines the political history of Syria and Palestine, wars usually arose from power struggles or disputes over territories and boundaries, not from attempts to coerce a nation to join an alliance. Finally, he argues that 2 Kings 15:37 seems to suggest that the Syro-Ephraimite War started during Jotham's tenure, that is, before Ahaz began to rule. Hence, it seems that the war had little to do with any refusal on the part of Ahaz to join the anti-Assyrian group.[23] Rather, Oded argues that the real cause behind the attack was a desire on the part of Damascus and Israel to remove Judah's hold over parts of the Transjordan.[24] Oded is joined in his conclusion by Mordechai Cogan and Hayim Tadmor, who state that tensions had risen between Judah and Samaria during this time period because of Judah's recent expansion into Gilead. They too suggest that Judah's territorial incursions as well as other rivalries might have played a part in Rezin and Pekah's challenge to Ahaz.[25]

Whatever the real cause of the Syro-Ephraimite War, the narrative in 2 Kings 16 loosely spells out what happens next: Ahaz, under threat, calls on Assyria for help so that he can remain on the throne of Judah: "Ahaz sent messengers to Tiglath-pileser of Assyria, saying, 'I am your servant and your son. Come up and rescue me from the hand of the king of Aram and from the hand of the king of Israel, who are attacking me'" (v. 7). To make sure that Tiglath-pileser responds to his call, 2 Kings 16:8 notes that Ahaz also sent along a bribe of the gold and silver that was found in the temple and palace to the Assyrian king.[26] According to Paul-Eugène Dion, who has examined the various occurrences in the Hebrew Bible when a king asks for aid from more powerful nations,

---

23. Bustanay Oded, "The Historical Background of the Syro-Ephraimite War," *CBQ* 34 (1972): 153–54.

24. Ibid., 161.

25. Cogan and Tadmor, *II Kings*, 191.

26. Smelik argues that the purpose of the bribe to the Assyrian king was to induce him to act on his behalf, not to submit to being a vassal as Judah was likely already a vassal of Assyria by this point (Klaas A. D. Smelik, "The New Altar of King Ahaz [2 Kings 16]: Deuteronomistic Re-interpretation of a Cult Reform," in *Deuteronomy and Deuteronomic Literature: Festschrift C. H. W. Brekelmans*, ed. M. Vervenne and J. Lust [Leuven: Leuven University Press/Peeters, 1997], 268–69). For the number of times when Assyria comes to the aid of a vassal and the reasons for it, see Bustanay Oded, "Ahaz's Appeal to Tiglath-Pileser III in the Context of the Assyrian Policy of Expansion," in *Studies in the Archaeology and History of Ancient Israel in Honour of Moshe Dothan*, ed. M. Heltzer, A. Segal and D. Kaufman (Haifa: Haifa University Press, 1993), 63–71.

this request for help is normal and not infrequent, but it is also usually portrayed as cowardly.[27]

Nadav Na'aman, along similar lines, argues that clues in the biblical narrative indicate that the writer is harshly critical of Ahaz's response during the Syro-Ephraimite war. For example, he notes that 2 Kings 16:5 deliberately states that Rezin and Pekah besieged Ahaz. Na'aman argues that the writer purposefully portrays the campaign as against the king, not the city or the subjects, in order to show that Ahaz's call to the Assyrians was selfishly motivated. Like Menahem, Ahaz calls on the Assyrians because he wants to save his own skin and to remain on the throne, not because he desires to save the kingdom or city.[28] Furthermore, Na'aman notes that by stating that Rezin and Pekah "could not conquer him [Ahab]" in 2 Kings 16:5, the writer insinuates that Ahaz, in panic, appealed to the Assyrians even though the attack posed no real danger to the city.

Equally derided is the manner in which Ahaz persuades Tiglath-pileser III to come to his aid. Ahaz's payment to the Assyrian king is designated as a bribe or שחד (šōḥad), a term that has a highly negative connotation in the Hebrew biblical corpus.[29] Tadmor and Cogan note: "The laws of the Pentateuch forbid it (Ex 23,8; Deut 16,19); prophets speak out against it (e.g., Isa 5,23; Ezek 22,12); and in Wisdom literature, the giving of šōḥad is considered a corrupt act, a perversion of justice (Prov 17,23; cf. Ps 15,5)."[30] By designating Ahaz's bribe as a שחד, the biblical writers make it clear that they disapprove of this king and his action.

Unsurprisingly, the list of Ahaz's misdeed continues. In addition to his earlier religious offenses and his bribe, the writer purposefully includes Ahaz's declaration to Tiglath-pileser III that he will be his servant and son in order to show that the Judean monarch freely and voluntarily submitted to Assyrian rule.[31] Equally disparaging is the emphasis on the king's voluntary payment of silver and gold from the house of YHWH and the palace treasury. Na'aman argues that while the biblical text frequently

27. Paul-Eugène Dion, "Ahaz and Other Willing Servants of Assyria," in *From Babel to Babylon: Essay on Biblical History and Literature in Honor of Brian Peckham*, ed. Joyce Rilett Wood, John E. Harvey, and Mark Leuchter (New York: T&T Clark, 2006), 133–45.

28. Na'aman, "Deuteronomist and Voluntary Servitude," 42.

29. Cogan and Tadmor, *II Kings*, 188; idem, "Ahaz and Tiglath-Pileser," 499–503; Na'aman, "Deuteronomist and Voluntary Servitude," 43.

30. Cogan and Tadmor, "Ahaz and Tiglath-Pileser," 499.

31. Na'aman, "Deuteronomist and Voluntary Servitude," 44.

utilizes the motif of taking/paying of treasures, whether forcibly as booty (1 Kgs 14:26; 2 Kgs 14:14; 24:12), as a response to a threat to the city (2 Kgs 12:19; 18:15), or as a bribe to foreign rulers (1 Kgs 16:8; Isa 30:6-7), the depiction of Ahaz as voluntarily handing over of money from the palace and temple is clearly meant to malign the king.[32]

The aftermath of Ahaz's invitation is succinctly noted in 2 Kings 16:9, where the Assyrian king, heeding Ahaz's message, marches up against Damascus and captures it, killing its king and taking its people captive. What happens to Judah's sister-country Israel is left until the next chapter to be delineated in detail. Despite the brevity with which the Assyrian response is described in 2 Kings 16, historical and textual clues provide a clearer picture of what might have occurred. The anti-Assyrian coalition without the participation of Judah seems to have confronted Tiglath-pileser III in a series of military campaigns around 734 BCE. They failed, however, to stop the encroachment of the Assyrians. As a result, Aram-Damascus was conquered and destroyed (2 Kgs 16:9) while Israel was stripped of Galilee and Gilead (2 Kgs 15:29). Hoshea son of Elah was then placed as monarch of Israel and became a vassal of Assyria (2 Kgs 15:20).[33]

Whether historical or not, Ahaz's decision to call on the Assyrians for help is portrayed in 2 Kings 16 as leading to the destruction of two countries, the deportation of large segments of their population, and the dethronement of two monarchs. Though not spelled out, Ahaz's request leads to the expulsion and death of countless women, men, and children, most of whom had little to no say in the political maneuverings of their country. Though the biblical text presents history as a parade of individual male monarchs, it is important to keep in mind that the real history of this region is composed of different untold narratives: the numerous unrecorded tales of the voiceless women, children, and men who were killed, harmed, or dislocated because of the decisions, mistakes, and acts of violence perpetrated by power-hungry male autocrats.

Ahaz's Cultic Renovations (16:10-20)

The king follows up this trail of horror with a last and final offense. For unstated reasons, 2 Kings 16:10-18 records that Ahaz went down to Damascus to meet the Assyrian king. At Damascus, Ahaz sees an altar

32. Ibid., 44–45.
33. Cogan and Tadmor, *II Kings*, 179.

¹⁰When King Ahaz went to Damascus to meet King Tiglath-pileser of Assyria, he saw the altar that was at Damascus. King Ahaz sent to the priest Uriah a model of the altar, and its pattern, exact in all its details. ¹¹The priest Uriah built the altar; in accordance with all that King Ahaz had sent from Damascus, just so did the priest Uriah build it, before King Ahaz arrived from Damascus. ¹²When the king came from Damascus, the king viewed the altar. Then the king drew near to the altar, went up on it, ¹³and offered his burnt offering, poured his drink offering, and dashed the blood of his offerings of well-being against the altar. ¹⁴The bronze altar that was before the LORD he removed from the front of the house, from the place between his altar and the house of the LORD, and put it on the north side of his altar. ¹⁵King Ahaz commanded the priest Uriah, saying, "Upon the great altar offer the morning burnt offering, and the evening grain offering, and the king's burnt offering,

(v. 10), and when the king returns to Judah, he has his priest, Uriah, create a replica of it (v. 11). When the building is complete, the monarch makes offerings and sacrifices on the new structure (2 Kgs 16:12-13, 15-16). Ahaz makes further changes to the temple complex by relocating the bronze altar (v. 14) and by stripping off and dismantling the frames of the wheeled stands, the basin, the bronze oxen, the bronze sea, and the sabbath covering (v. 18). Second Kings 16:18 ambiguously states that Ahaz stripped and dismantled all these cultic items "because of the king of Assyria."

The purpose of Ahaz's altar copying is much debated. Why did Ahaz make a duplicate of the altar he saw in Damascus? Was this altar Syrian or of a different style and design? Is this act connected to Ahaz's voluntary submission to Assyria? What does it mean that Ahaz stripped and dismantled other cultic items "because of the king of Assyria"? And is the installation of this new altar linked to the other changes at the temple complex? The argument that was widely followed in the past was that Ahaz's new altar stemmed from his obligations as a vassal to Assyria.[34] As a vassal, Ahaz was forced by the sovereign country to worship Assyrian deities at an appropriate Assyrian worship site. This conclusion,

---

34. Smelik, "The New Altar," 264. For a detailed summary about the relationship between religion and Assyrian imperial policy, see Steven Holloway, *Assur Is King! Assur Is King! Religion in the Exercise of Power in the Neo-Assyrian Empire*, Culture and History of the Ancient Near East 10 (Leiden: Brill, 2002).

and his grain offering, with the burnt offering of all the people of the land, their grain offering, and their drink offering; then dash against it all the blood of the burnt offering, and all the blood of the sacrifice; but the bronze altar shall be for me to inquire by." ¹⁶The priest Uriah did everything that King Ahaz commanded.

¹⁷Then King Ahaz cut off the frames of the stands, and removed the laver from them; he removed the sea from the bronze oxen that were under it, and put it on a pediment of stone. ¹⁸The covered portal for use on the sabbath that had been built inside the palace, and the outer entrance for the king he removed from the house of the LORD. He did this because of the king of Assyria. ¹⁹Now the rest of the acts of Ahaz that he did, are they not written in the Book of the Annals of the Kings of Judah? ²⁰Ahaz slept with the ancestors, and was buried with his ancestors in the city of David; his son Hezekiah succeeded him.

however, has been countered by scholars such as Mordechai Cogan, who argues that Assyria did not usually force its vassals to adopt the cult and religion of Assyria. Rather, once countries submitted to Assyria, it did not interfere with the local cult but, at times, even acted as a patron.[35] Cogan's conclusions are echoed by K. A. D. Smelik who lists other reasons that indicate that these cultic changes were likely unrelated to Ahaz's duties as a vassal of Assyria: the altar does not seem to be a model of an Assyrian altar as Ahaz sees it in Damascus, that is, in Syria (2 Kgs 16:10). Moreover, the altar seems to be utilized for the cult of YHWH by a priest of YHWH and not by an Assyrian priest for an Assyrian god. And finally, Ahaz's altar seems to have been used for burnt offerings, and the Assyrians did not utilize altars for burnt animal sacrifices.[36]

Especially ambiguous and important is the style of the altar that was copied. If the duplication of the altar was related to Judah's duties as an Assyrian vassal, then why does Ahaz copy an altar from Damascus? Are we to assume that it was an Assyrian altar, and if so, how did such an Assyrian altar end up in Aram? If the altar is the one used in an Aramean cult, such as at the temple of Adad-Rimmon (see 2 Kgs 5:18), why does the Judean king copy and borrow the altar used in the worship of a deity whose nation had just been defeated by another stronger state? Adding

35. Mordecai Cogan, *Imperialism and Religion: Assyria, Judah and Israel in the Eighth and Seventh Centuries B.C.E.* (Missoula, MT: Scholars Press, 1974).

36. Smelik, "The New Altar," 266–67.

to the mystery, whatever the model of the new altar, it seems that Uriah the priest who worked at the temple of YHWH in Jerusalem, and who is even lauded as a "faithful witness" in Isaiah 8:2,[37] does not raise an alarm about Ahaz's cultic innovations. Instead, 2 Kings 16:16 states that Uriah did all that Ahaz commanded.

Uriah's acquiescence to and lack of judgment about the king's cultic changes have led some scholars to argue that the biblical writers were not wholly negative in their portrayal of Ahaz, even in their description of his reduplication of the altar. Cogan and Tadmor, for example, explain the new altar as motivated "by a spirit of assimilation to the current international fashions,"[38] whereby Syrian art and styles were widely copied and followed, even by the Assyrians. Indeed, they even surmise that Ahaz's new altar was the "first wave in the larger movement of acculturation to the practices of the Assyrian empire, which . . . were heavily Aramaized."[39] Richard Nelson goes further and argues that Ahaz, like many kings in the biblical text, is depicted as having both successes and failures. Contra the prevailing opinion, Nelson argues, following Peter Ackroyd, among others,[40] that Ahaz's cultic innovations were pictured not as a misdeed but as a praiseworthy act—a cult reform or improvement along the lines of Jehoash—that served to emphasize the king's piety. As such, the renovation is not criticized by the Deuteronomistic author, and the writer does not straightforwardly declare it illegitimate. Rather, Ahaz's reign, according to Nelson, ends on a positive note, without any judgment by the biblical writers of Ahaz's plea to Assyria for help. Perhaps there is even a hint that this act by Ahaz served to preserve Judah.[41]

This conclusion has been countered by other scholars who maintain that the biblical writer, at numerous points, portrays Ahaz critically. Especially palpable is the writer's negative assessment of Ahaz's alterations at the temple complex. Smelik, for example, states that Ahaz's new altar alludes to the altar built by the detested Jeroboam at Bethel. In mimicking the apostasy of Jeroboam's cult reform, Ahaz is thus condemned by

37. Ibid., 265.

38. Cogan and Tadmor, *II Kings*, 193.

39. Ibid.

40. Peter Ackroyd, "The Biblical Interpretation of the Reigns of Ahaz and Hezekiah," in *In the Shelter of Elyon: Essays on Ancient Palestinian Life and Literature in Honor of G. W. Ahlström*, ed. W. Boyd Barrick and John R. Spencer, JSOTSup 31 (Sheffield: JSOT, 1984), 247–59.

41. Richard Nelson, "The Altar of Ahaz: A Revisionist View," *HAR* 10 (1986): 271–73.

the Deuteronomistic Historian for "walking in the ways of the kings of Israel" (v. 3).[42] Na'aman, moreover, notes that several other details in the description of Ahaz's cultic renovations also show the condemning attitude of the biblical writer. The depiction of Ahaz's relay of a priest of YHWH to the capital of a former enemy (Damascus), the emphasis on the imitation of a foreign temple, the stress on the king's participation in the cult offerings, and the removal of the Solomonic bronze altar (1 Kgs 8:64) all indicate the historian's unhappiness over the king's cultic changes.[43]

By linking Ahaz's surrender to Assyria (vv. 7-9) with the cultic innovations, which immediately follows on the heels of his plea for Assyrian aid, the writer suggests that the altar is the result of the king's capitulation.[44] The writer also telescopes Ahaz's dismantling of certain features of the temple complex (vv. 17-18) with his cultic innovations (vv. 10-16) for the same reason. Right after telling the reader about Ahaz's new altar, the writer states that Ahaz stripped and dismantled the frames of the wheeled stands, the basin, the bronze oxen, the bronze sea, and the sabbath covering in order to pay off Tiglath-pileser III. In describing the two events at the temple as occurring in succession, the two can be lumped into one big idolatrous outrage that Ahaz commits in order to pay homage and ingratiate himself with his Assyrian overlord.

The telescoping and subtle suggestions coupled with the very negative introductory summary of Ahaz in which he is criticized for all manner of religious offenses seem to indicate that the writer viewed this king rather unfavorably. Why the Deuteronomistic Historian is so subtle and indirect in his jabs and criticisms is not clear. As we noted earlier, this might be the result of a complicated redactional history of the narrative of Ahaz's reign. Equally possible is that this account served several different literary purposes: (1) it warned of the possibility of the demise of Judah and, in so doing, set forth the context for the eventual end of the nation at the conclusion of 2 Kings; (2) it not only foreshadowed but also presented theological explications of and justifications for the nation's fall; and (3) the sins of Ahaz set the stage for the triumphant reign of Ahaz's son and opposite, Hezekiah, in the next chapters. As we will see, Hezekiah's reign, like that of Josiah, will raise hopes of YHWH's deliverance and salvation of the nation.

---

42. Smelik, "The New Altar," 278; also idem, "The Representation of King Ahaz," 159.

43. Na'aman, "Deuteronomist and Voluntary Servitude," 47.

44. Ibid.

2 Kings 17:1-41

The Destruction of the Northern Kingdom of Israel

The complicated narrative in 2 Kings 17 attempts to explain why the Northern Kingdom of Israel or Samaria was destroyed and its population exiled. As the fate of the South or Judah is so deeply intertwined with its sister-nation in the North, this account is not just about Samaria but also about the destiny of both nations. In particular, 2 Kings 17 attempts to make sense of the contradiction between historical events and the theological belief system that lies at the center of both kingdoms. It does not offer a single answer but a kaleidoscope of possible reasons as to why YHWH might have allowed Samaria to be devastated. The lack of a single explication conveys the sense of theological bewilderment caused by an event, which, in the end, could not truly be explained.

The Fall of Samaria (17:1-6)

Second Kings 17 begins with the typical Deuteronomistic summary, which notes the beginning year of the monarch's reign, the corresponding king in Judah, the length of the reign, and the Deuteronomistic assessment of the ruler's piety (v. 1).

Unsurprisingly, Hoshea, as a northern king, is criticized for doing evil in the sight of YHWH (v. 2). In an unusual statement, however, which

[17:1]In the twelfth year of King Ahaz of Judah, Hoshea son of Elah began to reign in Samaria over Israel; he reigned nine years. [2]He did what was evil in the sight of the LORD, yet not like the kings of Israel who were before him. [3]King Shalmaneser of Assyria came up against him; Hoshea became his vassal, and paid him tribute. [4]But the king of Assyria found treachery in Hoshea; for he had sent messengers to King So of Egypt, and offered no tribute to the king of Assyria, as he had done year by year; therefore the king of Assyria confined him and imprisoned him.

[5]Then the king of Assyria invaded all the land and came to Samaria; for three years he besieged it. [6]In the ninth year of Hoshea the king of Assyria captured Samaria; he carried the Israelites away to Assyria. He placed them in Halah, on the Habor, the river of Gozan, and in the cities of the Medes.

serves to heighten the sense of theological tension in the chapter, Hoshea is said to have been not as bad as the kings of Israel who preceded him. With this ambivalent assessment, the reader expects a mixed record of his tenure. In the next breath, though, the biblical text describes the worst event in the history of Samaria as taking place during this monarch's reign: the destruction and exile of Israel. The demise of the North during the tenure of Hoshea, and not during that of a more impious monarch, such as Ahab, illustrates the uneasy tension between theology and history reflected in other parts of the Deuteronomistic History. This sense of disjunction will progressively increase in 2 Kings as historical events come into ever increasing conflict with the theological worldview and belief system of the biblical writers. The attempts to explain this conflict might have driven much of the redactional account of the Deuteronomist History.

After the theological summary of Hoshea, the text shifts from the usual narration of the actions and welfare of individual kings to those of the nation of Israel in general.[1] The biblical writer describes the fall of Israel as a quick succession of events: Israel, a vassal of Assyria, at some point during Hoshea's reign appears to have rebelled against Assyria's sovereignty by seeking the help of Egypt and by ceasing to pay tribute (vv. 3-4). As a result, Hoshea is imprisoned, and Assyria invades Samaria (v. 5). After holding out for some time, Israel is eventually destroyed by

1. Gina Hens-Piazza, *1–2 Kings*, AOTC (Nashville: Abingdon, 2006), 349.

Assyria, and its citizens are exiled to various places throughout the Assyrian Empire (v. 6). The speedy narration speaks to the continuing sense of horror and bewilderment that this event elicited in the minds of the biblical writers/editor. It seems that exactly how Israel was destroyed was not as important to the writer/editor as why it happened: why did YHWH allow Israel to be conquered? This quick summary of events sets the background for the longer, more detailed theological explication of the destruction that follows.

The sparseness and rather broad description of Samaria's fall make it difficult to ascertain the historical details of the events described in 2 Kings 17. One of the main questions about the fall of Israel concerns the date and nature of the Assyrian capture of Samaria. How many times was the country conquered by Assyria?[2] Queries also remain about the state of the country after Hoshea was imprisoned by the Assyrians. Unfortunately, comparative evidence from the Assyrian inscriptions offers an unclear and conflicting account of events and so does little to clarify the biblical narrative. For example, in his inscriptions, the Assyrian king, Sargon II, notes several times that he conquered Samaria.[3] Other records, such as the Babylonian Chronicle report the demolishment of Samaria by a different Assyrian king, Shalmaneser V, not Sargon II.[4] Adding to the confusion, the biblical text only mentions Shalmaneser in its account (2 Kgs 17:3). The conflicting evidence has led to several possible historical reconstructions of Samaria's last days.[5]

The one that has gained the most traction is the two-conquest theory. According to this reconstruction, two separate events were telescoped

---

2. This question has been the topic of much scholarly interest. Some major works are Hayim Tadmor, "The Campaigns of Sargon II of Assur: Chronological-Historical Study," *JCS* 12 (1958): 33–40; Nadav Na'aman, "The Historical Background to the Conquest of Samaria (720 BC)," *Bib* 71 (1990): 206–25; John H. Hayes and Jeffrey K. Kuan, "The Final Years of Samaria (730–720 BC)," *Bib* 72 (1991): 153–81; Gershon Galil, "The Last Years of the Kingdom of Israel and the Fall of Samaria," *CBQ* 57 (1995): 52–65; K. Lawson Younger, "The Fall of Samaria in Light of Recent Research," *CBQ* 61 (1999): 461–82, esp. 461–62.

3. Mordechai Cogan and Hayim Tadmor, *II Kings: A New Translation with Introduction and Commentary*, AB 11 (Garden City, NY: Doubleday, 1988), 200; Na'aman, "Historical Background," 206–7; Younger, "Fall of Samaria," 461.

4. Cogan and Tadmor, *II Kings*, 199; Na'aman, "Historical Background," 207, 210–12; Hayes and Kuan, "Final Years," 156–81; Younger, "Fall of Samaria," 461.

5. For a succinct outline of reconstructions, see Younger, "Fall of Samaria," esp. 461–62.

into one event in the biblical account of the fall of Samaria.[6] Though 2 Kings 17:6 describes one event, in reality, two different Assyrian kings conquered Samaria at two different points. According to this hypothesis, while Shalmaneser V captured Samaria, it was Sargon II who exiled the people.

Mordechai Cogan and Hayim Tadmor reconstruct the events as follows: Hoshea, who began his reign in 732/31 BCE, was a vassal of Assyria under Tiglath-pileser III. This king aggressively expanded Assyrian control over the territories west of the Mediterranean. When this monarch died in 727 BCE, various vassal nations tried to take advantage of this period of regnal transition to free themselves from Assyrian colonialism. Josephus, for example, describes in detail the unrest that followed the demise of Tiglath-pileser III (*Ant.* 9.283–87). Tiglath-pileser III's successor, Shalmaneser V, was thus forced to reconquer these territories and tamp down this unrest with a series of military campaigns. Second Kings 17:4 appears to indicate that Hoshea was among the kings who rebelled. As a result, he was taken captive and imprisoned by Shalmaneser. Though Samaria was left without a king with the imprisonment of Hoshea, the Babylonian Chronicle records that the nation withstood the Assyrian siege until eventually falling to Shalmaneser in 722 BCE. According to Cogan and Tadmor, the mention of the Egyptian pharaoh in 2 Kings 17:4 hints at Egyptian support of the rebellion against Assyria.[7]

When Shalmaneser V died, a new king, Sargon II, came to power. This period of transition led to the withdrawal of the Assyrian army from Samaria, which then joined other nations in a new rebellion. Sargon II, after he consolidated power, went out to reconquer the West, and Samaria was thus retaken. This time, the population was deported to Assyria (720 BCE). Sargon's inscriptions record the exile of many Israelites, though they do not record the places to which these deportees were relocated.[8] While the siege against Israel ended in 722/21 BCE when the state surrendered to Shalmaneser V, the death of this Assyrian monarch left the status of Israel ambiguous. His successor, Sargon II, was forced to recapture the state in 720 BCE.[9] These two conquests—one in 722/21 and a later one in 720—were telescoped into one event in the biblical record.

6. Cogan and Tadmor, *II Kings*, 199–200; Tadmor, "The Campaigns of Sargon II," 33–40;

7. Cogan and Tadmor, *II Kings*, 198–99.

8. Ibid., 199–200.

9. Ibid., 197.

Though this reconstruction is generally accepted, there is no consensus about what happened in Samaria during its last years. Nadav Na'aman, among others, cites some difficulties with the proposed idea of two campaigns. For example, the conquest of cities was in most cases an extremely destructive event. Hence, it is difficult to imagine that Samaria, after being besieged for three years and then conquered in 723/22, would so quickly rise up to promote a new rebellion.[10] Furthermore, the Assyrian inscriptions place the conquest of Samaria as one of the major events during the reign of Sargon. If all that the Assyrian king did was recapture a weak, ruined city, it would be odd that the conquest would be so highlighted in the inscriptions.[11] Na'aman also raises concerns about misreading the Babylonian Chronicle and archaeological evidence.[12] Most important, he points to the contradictory testimony provided in the biblical text of 2 Kings 17. He states that two events could have been telescoped into one only if the biblical writers who wrote about it lived so long after the historical event that they were confused or unaware of the general details. As the objections make clear, what happened in the final years of Samaria—whether it was conquered once, twice, or even many more times, and whether one or two Assyrian monarchs were involved—remains unsettled.

Despite lingering questions about the historical details of Samaria's fall, what is clear is that Israel was brutally conquered by Assyria at some point in the eighth century BCE and that some of its citizens were exiled to different parts of the Assyrian Empire. From a feminist perspective, an aspect that has not received enough attention is the status and experience of women and children during sieges and warfare. Undoubtedly, much of this deficiency results from a lack of written, epigraphic, or archaeological materials on women and children in the ancient period. Some general information, however, can be pieced together from the evidence we have. In his study of ancient sieges, Paul Bentley Kern writes that the Assyrian monarchs, in their inscriptions, frequently and graphically boasted about the brutalities and atrocities they committed during battle.[13] In gruesome accounts, the Assyrian kings proudly discuss how they flayed, impaled,

---

10. Na'aman, "Historical Background," 208.

11. Ibid.

12. Ibid., 210–11.

13. Paul Bentley Kern, *Ancient Siege Warfare* (Bloomington: Indiana University Press, 1999), 62–88. Also Erika Bleibtreu, "Grisly Assyrian Record of Torture and Dead," *BAR* 70 (1991): n.p.

burned alive, placed on stakes, mutilated, and cut off the hands, fingers, limbs, noses, and ears of their victims. To deter future rebellions, some of these monarchs made piles of severed heads or used them as decoration. At times, other body parts, such as hands and feet, adorned walls. The kings, moreover, proudly boasted of leaving no survivors of towns and of turning cities into "mounds and ruins."[14]

Archaeological and monumental evidence testify to the suffering of women and children as a result of this nauseating violence. One of the siege reliefs of the Assyrian king, Ashurnasirpal, depicts women raising their hands in terror and lamentation.

Excursus:
Gender and Iconography
from the Viewpoint of
a Feminist Biblical Scholar[15]

For the last twenty years, I have worked at the intersection of biblical texts and ancient oriental iconography, using a feminist-hermeneutic approach. Biblical texts are ambivalent in a particular way when it comes to questions of women or gender. Being a feminist biblical scholar, I generally read these texts with a "hermeneutics of suspicion." They are important documents of the (frequently opposing) history and the beliefs of women, but they are also documents of patriarchy and of androcentric perspectives.

On the one hand, as a biblical scholar and theologian, I cannot do without images as sources, because while the Bible is an important, but insufficient base for the reconstruction of ancient Israelite or early Jewish and early Christian women's history, for some periods, there are virtually no extrabiblical textual sources from Palestine/Israel, but there are image sources.[16] On the other hand, biblical texts, with their own and particular intentions and perspectives, can question, complement or elucidate the pictures and their symbolism. For the different points of touching points or distances between bible and image, image and bible, I would like to introduce three examples: goddess worship, mobility, and lamentation of the dead, which are, in my opinion, especially

---

14. Kern, *Ancient Siege Warfare*, 69.

15. Silvia Schroer, "Gender and Iconography from the Viewpoint of a Feminist Biblical Scholar," *Lectio difficilior* 2 (2008); http://www.lectio.unibe.ch/08_2/Silvia_Schroer_Gender_and_Iconography.html.

16. Images used in Schroer's article can be found at http://www.lectio.unibe.ch/08_2/Silvia_Schroer_Gender_and_Iconography.html.

elucidating with regard to gender research.

Since this article is the result of work processes which cannot be fully documented here, the impression might arise that iconography is degraded to an ancilla of exegesis and is only examined in view of biblical texts. Such an impression would be wrong. Only a well-grounded knowledge of the iconography of Palestine/Israel in the context of the picture programms [*sic*] of Israel's great neighbouring cultures allows for highlighting of the relations between images and texts (Schroer & Keel 2005).[17] If the methodical and hermeneutic treatment of images and texts can vouchsafe for their autonomy, this connection is very fertile and, for gender research, particularly worthwhile.

Though the biblical texts rarely describe the reactions and adversities of ancient women in wartime situations, these reliefs clearly indicate that women were present and suffering alongside the men during these sieges. Their reactions of horror and dismay were considered disturbing and frightening enough to be rendered by Assyrian artists for propagandistic effect.[18] Their fears were not unfounded. Women and children were not only witnesses to the violence but direct victims of it. A mass grave at Lachish, for example, likely from the Assyrian siege in 701 BCE, uncovered the bones and skulls of 665 people, which were either burned or caved in. Of these, 274 were those of women and sixty-one were of children.[19] These remnants and the injuries they reflect help to flesh out the portrait of suffering and violence experienced by these ancient victims.

Depictions of soldiers leading children and women into captivity on the Assyrian reliefs add further detail to the possible historical experience underlying 2 Kings 17. Kern writes that, though it was not standard practice, at points the Assyrians humiliated the captives by stripping their clothes and leading them away naked.[20] These sieges, with their phallic battering rams and violent penetrations of city walls, had an undeniable sexual component. Kern notes that there was a logical progression from stripping city walls to stripping off clothes of inhabitants.[21]

17. Silvia Schroer and Othmar Keel, *Die Ikonographie Palästinas/Israels und der Alte Orient, Band 1: Eine Religionsgeschichte in Bildern Band 1* (Fribourg: Academic Press, 2005).

18. Kern, *Ancient Siege Warfare*, 80–81.

19. Ibid., 81.

20. Ibid.

21. Ibid.

The sexual aspect of warfare, according to Kern, is most forcefully and clearly brought out in prophetic materials. Ezekiel, for example, saw a clear link between nakedness and vulnerability, and sex and war. In a series of disturbing prophecies much discussed by feminist scholars,[22] Ezekiel likens Jerusalem and Samaria, both of which had been destroyed and exiled, to lustful harlots who went after the Assyrians only to be stripped and humiliated by their lovers (Ezek 23–24).

Unsurprisingly, considering the connection made by the prophets between sexuality and violence, rape loomed large in their writings as a symbol and act of complete and utter violation (Isa 13:16; Zech 14:2; Lam 1:1).[23] Kern writes that rape was viewed as such a horrible act by the biblical writers—indeed, as representative of "the collapse of human culture"[24]—that it is only mentioned in prophecies of doom. The Assyrians seems to have shared this discomfort with rape. Though Assyrian sources "reveled in burning or burying people alive, impaling prisoners on stakes, slicing off heads, hands, feet, and lips, cutting out tongues, and building mounts of heads,"[25] they rarely boast about rape and say little about it in their inscriptions. Moreover, depictions of naked women are missing in Assyrian relief scenes of naked captives. This silence hints that the Assyrian writers and artists may also have felt that rape was an unacceptable violation even during times of war. Assyrian laws also list rules for how a soldier should behave with captive women whom they wish to marry (see Deut 21:11).[26] Even for the Assyrians, it seems that rape during times of warfare, though it might have occurred, was viewed as symbolic of a reprehensible, disordered, chaotic, and unlivable world.

22. For example, Peggy L. Day, "Adulterous Jerusalem's Imaged Demise: Death of a Metaphor in Ezekiel XVI," *VT* 50 (2000): 285–309; Erin Runions, "Violence and the Economy of Desire in Ezekiel 16:1-45," in *A Feminist Companion to the Prophets and Daniel*, ed. Athalya Brenner, FCB 8 (Sheffield: Sheffield Academic, 2001), 156–69; Mary E. Shields, "Multiple Exposures: Body Rhetoric and Gender Characterization in Ezekiel 16," *JFSR* 14 (1998): 5–18. For a more thorough bibliography of feminist readings of Ezekiel, see Gale A. Yee, *Poor Banished Children of Eve: Woman as Evil in the Hebrew Bible* (Minneapolis: Fortress, 2003), 111–32.

23. Kern, *Ancient Siege Warfare*, 82.

24. Ibid., 83.

25. Ibid., 82.

26. Ibid.

The Sins of Israel and Its Rejection by YHWH (17:7-23)

Second Kings 17 as a whole centers not just on rape and warfare but on an event that brings "into question the existence of any divine structure."[27] That the fall of Samaria raised theological questions about the nature of the world and of YHWH's control over it is clearly evident in the elongated explanation that follows the brief summary of the destruction of Israel in 2 Kings 17:1-6. In a lengthy list, the biblical writers painstakingly catalogue in typical Deuteronomistic language the litany of sins committed by Israel, which caused its demise at the hands of Assyria.

Starting with the umbrella charge of sinning against YHWH by following other gods (v. 7), the author details the various actions this larger apostasy entailed: the Israelites are charged with doing impious things in secret; building high places (v. 9), pillars, and sacred poles (vv. 10, 16); making offerings on the high places (v. 11); serving idols, the host of heaven, and Baal (vv. 12, 16); despising YHWH's statutes and commandments and violating their covenant (vv. 15, 16); going after false idols (v. 15); making cast images of two calves (v. 16); making their sons and daughters "pass through the fire" (v. 17); and using divination and augury (v. 17). Despite their criminal behavior, Israel's long-suffering deity, YHWH, is said to have patiently warned Israel by every prophet and every seer to turn from their orgy of sinning (v. 13). But like their ancestors, the text sadly claims, the Israelites did not listen to their God and continued in their wayward ways (v. 14).

Though the list is long and repetitive, many of the charges are familiar. Many of the same critiques were levied against the bad and evil kings of the North and South, such as Ahaz (2 Kings 17) or Ahab (1 Kgs 16:29-34). Here, however, the direction of the criticism turns from an individual monarch to the nation of Israel as a whole.[28] It appears that it was not just the kings who were acting badly; almost everyone in Israel seems to have joined in. By shifting the focus, the narrative conveys a sense of climactic progress as the weight of the sins of the northern kings, now combined with those of the Israelites, tips the scale in favor of the nation's demise. Considering this panoply of sins, how could the country not *already* have been destroyed, the narrative implies. The sense of deserved destruction helps to explain the nation's exile and, therefore, to justify the unwillingness of YHWH to stop it. By showing how the country

---

27. Ibid., 83.
28. Hens-Piazza, *1–2 Kings*, 349.

[7]This occurred because the people of Israel had sinned against the LORD their God, who had brought them up out of the land of Egypt from under the hand of Pharaoh king of Egypt. They had worshiped other gods [8]and walked in the customs of the nations whom the LORD drove out before the people of Israel, and in the customs that the kings of Israel had introduced. [9]The people of Israel secretly did things that were not right against the LORD their God. They built for themselves high places at all their towns, from watchtower to fortified city; [10]they set up for themselves pillars and sacred poles on every high hill and under every green tree; [11]there they made offerings on all the high places, as the nations did whom the LORD carried away before them. They did wicked things, provoking the LORD to anger; [12]they served idols, of which the LORD had said to them, "You shall not do this." [13]Yet the LORD warned Israel and Judah by every prophet and every seer, saying, "Turn from your evil ways and keep my commandments and my statutes, in accordance with all the law that I commanded your ancestors and that I sent to you by my servants the prophets." [14]They would not listen but were stubborn, as their ancestors had been, who did not believe in the LORD their God. [15]They despised his statutes, and his covenant that he made with their ancestors, and the warnings that he gave them. They went after false idols and became false; they followed the nations that were around them, concern-

deserved what was coming to it, doubts about the ability of YHWH to protect his nation—an aspect that, as we have discussed (see commentary for chaps. 6–7, 13, 14, 15, 16), was intimately intertwined with notions of royal and divine masculinity and power—are mitigated.

Aside from presenting a chorus of answers to the question of why Israel was exiled,[29] 2 Kings 17:7-23 also serves other complex purposes as well. The first seems to be as a message about Israel intended for Judah. Pauline Viviano writes that the "use of emphatic elements, constant repetition, and the parenetic character of the chapter"[30] seems to have a prescriptive message and function: to convince Judah to worship YHWH exclusively so as not to suffer the same outcome as the North. This chapter, in other words, is not only trying to make theological sense of the destruction of Israel,

29. Marc Brettler, "Ideology, History and Theology in 2 Kings XVII 7-23," *VT* 39 (1989): 282.

30. Pauline A. Viviano, "2 Kings 17: A Rhetorical and Form-Critical Analysis," *CBQ* 49 (1987): 559.

ing whom the LORD had commanded them that they should not do as they did. [16]They rejected all the commandments of the LORD their God and made for themselves cast images of two calves; they made a sacred pole, worshiped all the host of heaven, and served Baal. [17]They made their sons and their daughters pass through fire; they used divination and augury; and they sold themselves to do evil in the sight of the LORD, provoking him to anger. [18]Therefore the LORD was very angry with Israel and removed them out of his sight; none was left but the tribe of Judah alone.

[19]Judah also did not keep the commandments of the LORD their God but walked in the customs that Israel had introduced. [20]The LORD rejected all the descendants of Israel; he punished them and gave them into the hand of plunderers, until he had banished them from his presence.

[21]When he had torn Israel from the house of David, they made Jeroboam son of Nebat king. Jeroboam drove Israel from following the LORD and made them commit great sin. [22]The people of Israel continued in all the sins that Jeroboam committed; they did not depart from them [23]until the LORD removed Israel out of his sight, as he had foretold through all his servants the prophets. So Israel was exiled from their own land to Assyria until this day.

but is also an attempt to offer a warning and applicative message to Judah to not behave like the North. Only by reforming will Judah be delivered.

This warning, sadly, failed to change Judah's fate as it too was eventually destroyed and exiled. Several clues in 2 Kings 17 appear to indicate that the chapter was redacted to bring it into line with this later calamity. For example, Cogan and Tadmor argue that 2 Kings 17:19-20, which explains how Judah did not keep YHWH's commandments and how he, therefore, rejected all the descendants of Israel, likely is a later addition. Since the preceding verse (v. 18) states that Israel was removed from YHWH's sight but Judah remained, it seems strange that the text would suddenly switch from talking about the lone survival of Judah to a discussion about how it too was rejected by God.[31] Equally suspicious is 2 Kings 17:13, which states that YHWH sent every prophet and seer to warn Israel and Judah though Judah, at this point in the story, had not yet suffered the same calamity as Israel. These redactions suggest that this chapter was updated several times. The chapter seems to have served a variety of functions to different groups of editors and writers

---

31. Cogan and Tadmor, *II Kings*, 207.

at various points in time: to explain or justify why Israel was destroyed; to offer a warning to Judah to reform; and to foreshadow the eventual destruction and exile of the Southern Kingdom.

The Samarians as the Other (17:24-41)

The chapter concludes with a polemical story about the origins of the Samaritans (or Samarians) and their cult. After exiling the Israelite population, 2 Kings 17:24 states that the Assyrian king brought in foreigners from other nations and settled them in the cities of the North. As outsiders, they do not know how to worship YHWH properly and thus are punished with lion attacks for their improper religious activities. Cogan and Tadmor, citing 1 Kings 13:24 and 20:36, note that lions were "instruments of divine punishment against the disobedient."[32] As a result, an exiled Israelite priest is brought in to teach them "the law of the god of the land" (2 Kgs 17:27). Considering that only one priest is brought in, and that this priest is a northerner and thus likely not a pious follower of YHWH, the newly settled group continues in their syncretistic practices, serving not only YHWH, but a slew of other deities as well (vv. 29-33), a practice the biblical writer emphasizes continues "to this day." The writer ends the pericope by repetitively noting how the Samarians, even though YHWH made a covenant with them demanding exclusive reverence, continued in their wayward practice, failing to worship YHWH correctly or to follow his commandments (vv. 35-41).

Pieter van der Horst, who has examined the complex views of Samaritans in early Judaism,[33] writes that early Jewish writers, such as Josephus, believed that 2 Kings 17 described the true origins of the Samaritan cult (*Ant*. 9.227–91; b. Qidd. 75b).[34] More recently, however, scholars have focused on the blatant anti-Samaritan bias conveyed in this pericope. According to 2 Kings 17, not only do Samarians not know how to worship YHWH properly, but Yahwism "was introduced only as a superstitious gesture and then only by an illegitimate priest from one of the forbidden

---

32. Ibid., 210.

33. Pieter W. van der Horst, "Anti-Samaritan Propaganda in Early Judaism," in *Persuasion and Discussion in Early Christianity, Ancient Judaism, and Hellenism*, ed. Pieter W. van der Horst et al., CBET (Leuven: Peeters, 2003), 25–44.

34. Ibid., 27–28.

²⁴The king of Assyria brought people from Babylon, Cuthah, Avva, Hamath, and Sepharvaim, and placed them in the cities of Samaria in place of the people of Israel; they took possession of Samaria, and settled in its cities. ²⁵When they first settled there, they did not worship the LORD; therefore the LORD sent lions among them, which killed some of them. ²⁶So the king of Assyria was told, "The nations that you have carried away and placed in the cities of Samaria do not know the law of the god of the land; therefore he has sent lions among them; they are killing them, because they do not know the law of the god of the land." ²⁷Then the king of Assyria commanded, "Send there one of the priests whom you carried away from there; let him go and live there, and teach them the law of the god of the land." ²⁸So one of the priests whom they had carried away from Samaria came and lived in Bethel; he taught them how they should worship the LORD.

²⁹But every nation still made gods of its own and put them in the shrines

northern tribes."[35] Moreover, as the text keeps repeating, even after a priest is sent to Israel to retrain the people on proper religious conduct, they still continue their illegal syncretistic practices. The biblical writer stresses their wrongdoing by taking the time and space to list all the various deities (vv. 29-30) the people of Samaria continued to worship alongside YHWH. The Samaritans stubbornly cling to their wrongful ways. Even after lion attacks, reeducation and retraining by a northern priest, and the making of a new covenant with YHWH in which the Samaritans faithfully promised to not worship other gods (vv. 35-39), they still are said to have persisted in serving idols (v. 41). The message is clear: the Samaritans have been told and know the wrongfulness of their religious practices but choose to continue anyway.

The pericope tries to paint the Samaritans as outsiders who are distinct from the Israelites in the South. They are not only ethnically foreign, having been brought into Israel from other territories, but also religious outsiders, at first unable to and then later blatantly refusing to worship the deity in charge of the territory of Israel with proper and deserved respect. A more critical analysis of the pericope, however, raises doubts

---

35. Mordechai Cogan, "For We, Like You, Worship Your God: Three Biblical Portrayals of Samaritan Origins," *VT* 38 (1988): 287; Lester L. Grabbe, *Judaism from Cyrus to Hadrian*, vol. 2 (Minneapolis: Fortress, 1992), 503.

of the high places that the people of Samaria had made, every nation in the cities in which they lived; [30]the people of Babylon made Succoth-benoth, the people of Cuth made Nergal, the people of Hamath made Ashima; [31]the Avvites made Nibhaz and Tartak; the Sepharvites burned their children in the fire to Adrammelech and Anammelech, the gods of Sepharvaim. [32]They also worshiped the Lord and appointed from among themselves all sorts of people as priests of the high places, who sacrificed for them in the shrines of the high places. [33]So they worshiped the Lord but also served their own gods, after the manner of the nations from among whom they had been carried away. [34]To this day they continue to practice their former customs.

They do not worship the Lord and they do not follow the statutes or the ordinances or the law or the commandment that the Lord commanded the children of Jacob, whom he named Israel. [35]The Lord had made a cove-

---

about the accuracy of this polemical depiction. Though the biblical text makes it appear as if nearly the entire population of Israel was deported by Assyria and that an entirely new foreign group was brought into the country, it is likely that only the crème de la crème of Israelite society were exiled in the first place.[36] Most of the general populace of Israel probably remained in the land of Israel after the nation's defeat by Assyria. By relocating only those whose skills were needed in Assyria and by leaving the rest of the population intact, Assyria would have benefited both from a brain drain of the native trained talent and also the continued infusion of taxes from the rest of the populace that remained farming and working the land.[37] In other words, Assyria, as an empire, had more to gain by leaving most of the colonized citizens in place and by skimming off the top. If the majority of the population of Israel was not exiled, it seems highly unlikely that a large group of pagan foreigners were relocated into Israel, as the biblical narrative asserts. Hence, the charge that Israel, after its defeat, was suddenly emptied of native Israelites and then refilled and resettled with heretical foreigners and outsiders seems doubtful.

---

36. Yairah Amit, "The Samaritans: Biblical Considerations in the Solution of a Political Problem," in *Secularism and Biblical Studies*, ed. Roland Boer (London: Equinox, 2010), 196; van der Horst, "Anti-Samaritan Propaganda," 27.

37. Amit, "The Samaritans," 196.

nant with them and commanded them, "You shall not worship other gods or bow yourselves to them or serve them or sacrifice to them, [36]but you shall worship the LORD, who brought you out of the land of Egypt with great power and with an outstretched arm; you shall bow yourselves to him, and to him you shall sacrifice. [37]The statutes and the ordinances and the law and the commandment that he wrote for you, you shall always be careful to observe. You shall not worship other gods; [38]you shall not forget the covenant that I have made with you. You shall not worship other gods, [39]but you shall worship the LORD your God; he will deliver you out of the hand of all your enemies." [40]They would not listen, however, but they continued to practice their former custom.

[41]So these nations worshiped the LORD, but also served their carved images; to this day their children and their children's children continue to do as their ancestors did.

Equally suspect is the biblical writer's argument that the cult and religious practices of these new immigrants were especially deficient, deviant, and un-Yahwistic. Aside from the fact that the general populace of Israel likely remained intact, the illegal, syncretistic practices for which the "new" Samaritans are charged in the text, while un-Yahwistic, also appear to be a continuation of what came before. The Israelites, as we saw earlier in the chapter with the long list of their sins, are said to have been equally deficient in worshiping YHWH exclusively and correctly. Considering the impiety of the native Israelites, it seems that these resettled foreigners would have fit right in. Their impiety, in other words, looks a lot like the old impiety practiced by the preceding group who was supposedly just exiled. Indeed, the biblical account further links the practices of the exiled Israelites with the newly settled Samaritans by stating that the newcomers were religiously reeducated by a northern priest who was sent back from exile to retrain them. In short, while the biblical writer attempts to marginalize the Samaritans as ethnic and religious outsiders and foreigners who intrusively import into Israel a new, mangled, deficient cult, when the text is read more critically, the Samaritans are likely not an interloping immigrant group but a continuation of the native group that the biblical writer has chosen to redefine and recategorize. The biblical writer, in other words, for nativist reasons has transformed northerners into outsiders, into the Other.

What was the reason for this polemic? According to some scholars, the clear anti-Samaritan tone of the pericope, especially as it concerns the religious and cultic practices of the Samaritans, is less about what happened during the waning years of Samaria than about the relationship between different groups when the biblical text was being edited and assembled. The strong bias against Samaritans in this pericope seems specifically targeted at trying to delegitimate the religious practices of this group. Many scholars hold that this pericope likely is a postexilic addition to Kings, which reflects the growing animosity between the Jews and Samaritans in the Persian period.[38] The point of the story was to keep certain groups—those who had not experienced the exile—from sharing power in the running of the cult with those who returned to Palestine from exile. The sense of polemic is undeniable and gives an interesting window into the developing identity of the exilic Israelite community. A new sense of an Israelite self was needed after the destruction of the North and, as we will soon see, the South. Concomitantly needed, therefore, was the simultaneous creation of a new Other.

---

38. Amit, "The Samaritans," 193; Cogan, "For We, Like You," 288; John Gray, *I and II Kings*, OTL (Philadelphia: Westminster, 1970), 651–56.

2 Kings 18:1–20:21

The Reign of Hezekiah in Judah

hree main stories constitute the narrative of the reign of Hezekiah in Judah, one of the most important figures in the
Deuteronomistic History as well as in the history of ancient Judah. The
story of Hezekiah's reign not only appears in 2 Kings but is repeated in
First Isaiah (Isa 36–39) and again in a variant and expanded version in
2 Chronicles (chap. 32). In 2 Kings, three complicated stories involve this
figure. the story of the 701 BCE Assyrian attack, the story of Hezekiah's
illness, and the story of the visit of the Babylonian envoys. Alongside the
multiple accounts are also extrabiblical and archaeological sources from
the time of this king's reign. Unsurprisingly, considering the plethora of
historical and textual evidence, this monarch and the period of his tenure
has been the subject of much scholarly research. Gendered readings of
the narratives concerning Hezekiah are, however, few and far between,
which this chapter aims to address. As this chapter will show, these
stories about Hezekiah, like most narratives in 2 Kings, are centered on
demonstrating and defending the masculine prowess of Judah's god,
YHWH.

The Superlative Introductory Summary of Hezekiah (18:1-8)

After describing the end of Israel in the north, the narrative returns to
the situation in Judah. The account of Hezekiah's reign (715–687 BCE)

2 Kgs 18:1-8

[18:1]In the third year of King Hoshea son of Elah of Israel, Hezekiah son of King Ahaz of Judah began to reign. [2]He was twenty-five years old when he began to reign; he reigned twenty-nine years in Jerusalem. His mother's name was Abi daughter of Zechariah. [3]He did what was right in the sight of the LORD just as his ancestor David had done. [4]He removed the high places, broke down the pillars, and cut down the sacred pole. He broke in pieces the bronze serpent that Moses had made, for until those days the people of Israel had made offerings to it; it was called Nehushtan. [5]He trusted in the LORD the God of Israel; so that there was no one like him among all the kings of Judah after him, or among those who were before him. [6]For he held fast to the LORD; he did not depart from following him but kept the commandments that the LORD commanded Moses. [7]The LORD was with him; wherever he went, he prospered. He rebelled against the king of Assyria and would not serve him. [8]He attacked the Philistines as far as Gaza and its territory, from watchtower to fortified city.

begins with the typical Deuteronomistic summary noting his starting age, the length of his rule, his mother's name (Abi, daughter of Zechariah), and an assessment of his religious fidelity. In direct contrast to Ahaz, his father, Hezekiah is rated superlatively by the Deuteronomistic Historian. Certain points in the introductory summary indicate that the biblical writers believed Hezekiah to be unique and particularly significant. Hezekiah is not only said to have done what is right in the sight of YHWH but also likened to King David (2 Kgs 18:3). Considering that even the most pious Judean kings are criticized by the Deuteronomistic writer as stopping short of matching David's piety, the comparison to this beloved monarch is close to fawning praise. The importance of this comparison becomes evident when we realize that, throughout the entirety of the Deuteronomistic History, only two kings are compared to David: Hezekiah (2 Kgs 18:3) and Josiah (2 Kgs 22:2). As we will see, Josiah is the key figure underlying the writing and redaction of the Deuteronomistic History.[1] That Hezekiah is also likened to David may indicate that important redactions of the Deuteronomistic History also occurred during the reign of this monarch.[2]

1. On the redaction and writing of the Deuteronomistic History, see "Composition and Redaction of the Deuteronomistic History" in the introduction.

2. Ernest W. Nicholson, *Deuteronomy and Tradition* (Philadelphia: Fortress, 1967); Ian Provan, *Hezekiah and the Book of Kings: A Contribution to the Debate about the Com-*

The superlative assessment of Hezekiah continues in the summary of his cultic activities. Hezekiah is said to have broken down the pillars and asherahs. Most important, adding to the unparalleled appraisal, he is said to have removed the high places (v. 4). Considering that this is the one act that every other positively assessed Judean monarch has failed to accomplish previously, the removal of the high places by Hezekiah is a momentous achievement. The very thing that every good, pious Judean monarch failed to do, Hezekiah finally does.[3] As if that were not enough, the narrative mentions a detail that adds to Hezekiah's piety: the king not only follows the commandments that YHWH commanded through Moses (v. 6), but, going one step further than the great law-giver, Hezekiah even breaks into pieces the bronze serpent called the Nehushtan, which Moses made, because it had become an object of false worship (v. 4). Undoubtedly, to the Deuteronomistic writer, Hezekiah is one of the best kings that Judah has ever had. The text plainly states as much: "He trusted in the LORD the God of Israel; so that there was no one like him among all the kings of Judah after him, or among those who were before him" (2 Kgs 18:5). As we will see, the issue of trust will be one of the key themes of this narrative about Hezekiah.[4]

As a result of Hezekiah's fidelity, YHWH is said to have been with Hezekiah wherever he went, leading the king to prosper, though the manner of his prosperity and success is implied more than clearly spelled out. For example, after the text states that Hezekiah was successful because of his piety, it briefly notes that he rebelled against the king of Assyria and that he attacked the Philistines "from watchtower to fortified city" (v. 7).[5] Though not directly stated, the implied message of the sequencing is that the rebellion and the attack were the effects of the prosperity caused by God's favor. Hence, by being loyal to the masculine deity, YHWH, the king is rewarded with accolades that signify masculinity: success in battle, that is, the ability to dominate others, and protection, or the ability to protect oneself from forms of domination by other male monarchs.

---

position of the Deuteronomistic History (Berlin: de Gruyter, 1988), esp. 134–43; Baruch Halpern and David Vanderhooft, "The Editions of Kings in the 7th–6th Centuries B.C.E.," *HUCA* 62 (1991): 179–244.

3. Provan, *Hezekiah and the Book of Kings*, 82–85.

4. David Bostock, *A Portrayal of Trust: The Theme of Faith in the Hezekiah Narratives*, PBM (Milton Keynes: Paternoster, 2006).

5. John Hull, "Hezekiah—Saint and Sinner: A Conceptual and Contextual Narrative Analysis of 2 Kings 18–20" (PhD diss., Claremont Graduate School, 1994), 209.

The Destruction and Exile of Israel (18:9-12)

The utterly positive introduction to Hezekiah's reign is disjointedly followed by a gloomy summary about the fall of Samaria, which reiterates portions of the account in the preceding chapter. In the fourteenth year of Hezekiah's reign, the biblical text states that King Hoshea of Samaria was taken prisoner (v. 10) and the Israelites were exiled by Assyria (v. 11) because they transgressed God's covenant, which was commanded to them through YHWH's servant, Moses. By juxtaposing the extremely positive summary about Hezekiah with this negative account of the demise of the North, the differences between the two states are highlighted.

Hezekiah's attentiveness to God's covenant directly contrasts with the zealous transgression of YHWH's covenant by Samaria. As such, the expectation is that Judah, under the leadership of this king, will be rewarded with a contrasting fate from that of the North. As the North was destroyed because it failed to follow God's covenant, which was given through Moses, so Judah will survive and prosper because it is ruled by a king who is not only loyal to God's covenant but even goes beyond the expected fidelity by demolishing the Nehushtan made by Moses (18:4). The thrice-repeated "Moses" emphasizes this message. Hence, through the juxtaposition of the positive introduction and the depressing succeeding summary about Samaria, the message conveyed is that Judah's destiny will be different from that of the North because of Hezekiah's goodness and piety.

Theology and gender enter into this message as well. The preceding two sections strongly interweave piety, protection, power, and violence with masculinity. Proper—that is, exclusive—worship of the male god, YHWH, will lead to protection from violence as well as prosperity, protection, and life. Improper worship, which the detailed list of Samaria's sins in the preceding chapter makes clear, entails syncretistic worship or worship of other gods, and will lead to destruction, violence, death, and exile. In other words, as we noted earlier, loyalty to the male God, YHWH, will lead to those things that signify masculinity: the ability to inflict violence and overpower others in battle and protection from the same violence and subjugation from other states. Disloyalty to this male deity leads to the opposite result, that is, the suffering of violence, vulnerability, and destruction of the disloyal party.

The First Account of Sennacherib's Attack—Source A (18:13-16)

The theological message that is set forth in the previous section is immediately undermined as the succeeding narrative veers from ex-

⁹In the fourth year of King Hezekiah, which was the seventh year of King Hoshea son of Elah of Israel, King Shalmaneser of Assyria came up against Samaria, besieged it, ¹⁰and at the end of three years, took it. In the sixth year of Hezekiah, which was the ninth year of King Hoshea of Israel, Samaria was taken. ¹¹The king of Assyria carried the Israelites away to Assyria, settled them in Halah, on the Habor, the river of Gozan, and in the cities of the Medes, ¹²because they did not obey the voice of the LORD their God but transgressed his covenant—all that Moses the servant of the LORD had commanded; they neither listened nor obeyed.

¹³In the fourteenth year of King Hezekiah, King Sennacherib of Assyria came up against all the fortified cities of Judah and captured them. ¹⁴King Hezekiah of Judah sent to the king of Assyria at Lachish, saying, "I have done wrong; withdraw from me; whatever you impose on me I will bear." The king of Assyria demanded of King Hezekiah of Judah three hundred talents of silver and thirty talents of gold. ¹⁵Hezekiah gave him all the silver that was found in the house of the LORD and in the treasuries of the king's house. ¹⁶At that time Hezekiah stripped the gold from the doors of the temple of the LORD, and from the doorposts that King Hezekiah of Judah had overlaid and gave it to the king of Assyria.

pected theological assumptions. Instead of the protection and prosperity induced by the piety of Hezekiah, the opposite occurs. Judah is attacked by Assyria under King Sennacherib, and the pious Hezekiah, instead of standing up to Assyria, immediately relents and pays him tribute.

In order to pay the significant bribe requested by the Assyrian king, Hezekiah takes all the silver from the temple and the palace treasuries and, in a seemingly faithless move, even strips the gold from the doors of the temple (v. 16). Contrary to the hopeful forecast predicted by the initial summary of Hezekiah's reign (vv. 1-8), the opposite occurs: instead of divine protection, Jerusalem is attacked; instead of prosperity, there is a further loss of the wealth of Judah. Oddly, it seems that the theological message of the earlier verses, which promised that piety would lead to protection and prosperity, has been proven to be false.

As the subtitle indicates these verses do not constitute the only account of Sennacherib's attack of Jerusalem in 2 Kings 18–19. Two other varying accounts of the attack, which is dated to 701 BCE, are likely presented in these chapters. Bespeaking the significance of this event, there appears to have been several different interpretations and reports of this assault and its aftermath, some of which have been preserved in the biblical text. Because the pericope in 2 Kings 18:13-16 describes in stark, unadorned terms the actions that King Hezekiah took to protect the city, many commentators have argued that this account, Source A, is the most historically accurate and, hence, the earliest account of the 701 Assyrian attack on Jerusalem. The jerky sequencing of the account of Hezekiah's reign—the raising and deflating of expectations—hints, however, at a complicated history of writing/editing underlying the biblical narrative about Hezekiah. It is best to resist collapsing questions of historicity with those of redaction and editing.

Another Account of the 701 Assyrian Attack—Source B1 (18:17-37)

The importance of this warning becomes evident as we proceed to the next pericope in the narrative of Hezekiah's reign. Though it appears that Sennacherib's attack on Jerusalem begins and ends in 2 Kings 18:13-16 with Hezekiah's bequeathing of a bribe, the following verse (v. 17) oddly begins, not with the withdrawal of the Assyrian king and his army, but with the foreign king sending three emissaries and an army (back) to King Hezekiah in Jerusalem. As it seems unlikely that Sennacherib would return to attack Jerusalem so shortly after receiving his payment, most scholars argue that 2 Kings 18:17 begins a different, second account of the 701 attack, which presents a fuller, more descriptive narrative of the assault. This second account appears in 2 Kings 18:17–19:9a and is usually designated as Source B1.

This second account begins with Sennacherib dispatching emissaries and a "great army" to Jerusalem (v. 17). When they arrive, a shouting match ensues at the city walls where Sennacherib's emissary, the Rabshakeh, addresses the servants of Hezekiah who are at the wall as well as the people inside the city (v. 18). At this point, the camera turns to the Assyrian messenger who delivers a horrifying message to King Hezekiah from the Assyrian king. Beginning with a rhetorical question, the emissary starts by asking Hezekiah what makes him so confident (literally: "What is this trust that you trust?") (vv. 19-20) of surviving the Assyrian onslaught caused by the Judean king's rebellion. The Rabshakeh continues with rhetorical flourish that whatever source Hezekiah is trusting in to save him will prove to be unreliable and will ultimately fail. Trust is a significant *Leitwort* of these chapters.

The Rabshakeh proceeds to list these unreliable sources, striking them off one by one as incapable of withstanding the all-powerful Assyria. First up is Judah's ally, Egypt, which the emissary likens to a broken reed.

¹⁷The king of Assyria sent the Tartan, the Rabsaris, and the Rabshakeh with a great army from Lachish to King Hezekiah at Jerusalem. They went up and came to Jerusalem. When they arrived, they came and stood by the conduit of the upper pool, which is on the highway to the Fuller's Field. ¹⁸When they called for the king, there came out to them Eliakim son of Hilkiah, who was in charge of the palace, and Shebnah the secretary, and Joah son of Asaph, the recorder.

¹⁹The Rabshakeh said to them, "Say to Hezekiah: Thus says the great king, the king of Assyria: On what do you base this confidence of yours? ²⁰Do you think that mere words are strategy and power for war? On whom do you now rely, that you have rebelled against me? ²¹See, you are relying now on Egypt, that broken reed of a staff, which will pierce the hand of anyone who leans on it. Such is Pharaoh king of Egypt to all who rely on him. ²²But if you say to me, 'We rely on the LORD our God,' is it not he whose high places and altars Hezekiah has removed, saying to Judah and to Jerusalem, 'You shall worship before this altar in Jerusalem'? ²³Come now, make a wager with my master the king of Assyria: I will give you two thousand horses, if you are able on your part to set riders on them. ²⁴How then can you repulse a single captain among the least of my master's servants, when you rely on Egypt for chariots and for horsemen?

According to the Assyrian emissary, Egypt is nothing but a fractured and fragile piece of stick. The emissary implies that Hezekiah is deluded in his vision of Egypt as a strong, supportive cane and foolish to trust it as a reliable source of support. Instead, the Rabshakeh argues, Egypt, this piece of broken stick, will not only be unable to defend Judah but will actually harm the nation further just as a broken cane pierces and injures the hand of the person who leans on it for support (v. 21).

Turning from Egypt to Judah, the Rabshakeh continues his diatribe: Egypt's weakness is nothing compared to that of Judah itself, which relies on Egypt for necessary military equipment such as chariots and horsemen (v. 24). Demonstrating the utter military weakness of Judah, the emissary tauntingly offers Hezekiah two thousand horses if the king can find enough cavalry to ride on them and, presumably, utilize them to fight Assyria (v. 23). The lack of an answer to this offer clearly stresses the sad and terrible situation of the nation: Judah has little to no independent or available equipment or cavalry with which to defend itself. Driving home the point, the Rabshakeh stresses the utter weakness and vulnerability of Judah with a devastating last question

²⁵Moreover, is it without the Lᴏʀᴅ that I have come up against this place to destroy it? The Lᴏʀᴅ said to me, Go up against this land, and destroy it."

²⁶Then Eliakim son of Hilkiah, and Shebnah, and Joah said to the Rabshakeh, "Please speak to your servants in the Aramaic language, for we understand it; do not speak to us in the language of Judah within the hearing of the people who are on the wall." ²⁷But the Rabshakeh said to them, "Has my master sent me to speak these words to your master and to you, and not to the people sitting on the wall, who are doomed with you to eat their own dung and to drink their own urine?"

²⁸Then the Rabshakeh stood and called out in a loud voice in the language of Judah, "Hear the word of the great king, the king of Assyria! ²⁹Thus says the king: 'Do not let Hezekiah deceive you, for he will not be able to deliver you out of my hand. ³⁰Do not let Hezekiah make you rely on the Lᴏʀᴅ by saying, The Lᴏʀᴅ will surely deliver us, and this city will not be given into the hand of the king of Assyria.' ³¹Do not listen to Hezekiah; for thus says the king of Assyria: 'Make your peace with

and observation: If Judah cannot even muster enough riders, how can it possibly withstand Assyria's mighty, numerous army (v. 24)?

Having dispatched the myth of the reliability of Judah's ally, Egypt, as well as the strength of Judah itself, the accusations of the Rabshakeh become increasingly personal. Equally as untrustworthy as Egypt, the Rabshakeh rages, is Judah's own god who is unhappy with Hezekiah for removing the high places and altars and for centralizing worship to one locale in Jerusalem (v. 22). According to the Assyrian emissary, the religious reform undertaken by Hezekiah, the first mention of which we get in this address, has angered and displeased YHWH. As a result, not only will YHWH fail to protect Israel, but, as the Rabshakeh goes on to state a little later in his speech, YHWH is so displeased that he has personally authorized the Assyrian emperor, Sennacherib, to attack the deity's own country (v. 25). Moreover, even if YHWH wanted to save his country, the Rabshakeh asserts, he would not be able to (v. 32) as YHWH, like the deities of other conquered countries, will be unable to withstand the might of Assyria (vv. 33-35). The theme of misplaced trust thus functions as "a key link, each preceding a different view of YHWH—as the God affronted by Hezekiah, then as the God supportive of Sennacherib's attack, and finally as the God powerless before the Assyrians' might."[6]

6. Peter Machinist, "The *Rab Šaqeh* at the Wall of Jerusalem: Israelite Identity in the Face of the Assyrian 'Other,'" *HS* 41 (2000): 157.

me and come out to me; then every one of you will eat from your own vine and your own fig tree, and drink water from your own cistern, ³²until I come and take you away to a land like your own land, a land of grain and wine, a land of bread and vineyards, a land of olive oil and honey, that you may live and not die. Do not listen to Hezekiah when he misleads you by saying, The LORD will deliver us. ³³Has any of the gods of the nations ever delivered its land out of the hand of the king of Assyria? ³⁴Where are the gods of Hamath and Arpad? Where are the gods of Sepharvaim, Hena, and Ivvah? Have they delivered Samaria out of my hand? ³⁵Who among all the gods of the countries have delivered their countries out of my hand, that the Lord should deliver Jerusalem out of my hand?'"

³⁶But the people were silent and answered him not a word, for the king's command was, "Do not answer him." ³⁷Then Eliakim son of Hilkiah, who was in charge of the palace, and Shebna the secretary, and Joah son of Asaph, the recorder, came to Hezekiah with their clothes torn and told him the words of the Rabshakeh.

Considering that nothing and no one will rescue Judah, the emissary tells the good people of Judah simply to give up. Stating that Hezekiah is not to be trusted when he faithfully holds on to hope for some kind of divine deliverance (vv. 29-30), the Rabshakeh urges the Judeans to come to terms with the realities of the situation and to surrender to Assyria. Surrender, he temptingly states, will not be too bad. Yes, they will be exiled, of course, but to a land that is similar to Judah, "a land of grain and wine, a land of bread and vineyards, a land of olive oil and honey." Indeed, life will be good and peaceful for the Judeans (v. 31). Most important, however, if they would just give up and surrender, they will "live and not die" (v. 32). As scholars have noted, the Rabshakeh's promises sound disturbingly similar to the language, phrases, and ideas found in other parts of the biblical text, such as the Prophets and the book of Deuteronomy (Isa 31:1; Jer 2:27; 46:25; Ezek 29:16; Deut 30:19).[7]

The horror of the Rabshakeh's address is evident in the desperate and pitiful plea by the servants of Hezekiah who are listening at the walls of the city. The servants of the king interrupt the emissary's harangue to request that the emissary please switch from speaking in the "language

7. Hull, "Hezekiah—Saint and Sinner," 339–45; Ehud Ben Zvi, "Who Wrote the Speech of the Rabshaqeh and When," *JBL* 109 (1990): 79–92; Dominic Rudman, "Is the Rabshakeh also among the Prophets? A Study of 2 Kings XVIII 17-35," *VT* 50 (2000): 100–110.

of Judah" to Aramaic so that the people inside the city walls would be unable to understand his speech (v. 26). Unsurprisingly, this request merely emboldens the emissary. He spits back that his address is not meant for Hezekiah alone but also for those who would be most affected by this attack, to those who are doomed "to eat their own dung and to drink their own urine" (v. 27). The desperate and futile attempt by the servants to mute the Rabshakeh's speech indicates the distress and fear that this address was causing to the inhabitants of the city. Indeed, the fact that the biblical writer mentions that the Jerusalemites were silent throughout this verbal exchange *because* they had been explicitly commanded by the king to give no response clearly shows that there were people inside the city walls who desperately wanted to respond and acquiesce to the Rabshakeh's deal had they been allowed to do so (v. 36). A scene of muffled gasps, stunned silence, and utter terror is portrayed.

As noted in the preceding chapter, Assyrian texts describe the horrific acts of violence the Assyrian king inflicted on rebellious cities. Worse than a horror movie, Assyrian kings boast in these texts of committing heinous acts of torture, cruelty, and brutality on the general populace of these unlucky towns. No one, not women, children, or the elderly, was immune to the violence and destruction that ensued in the wake of Assyria's imperialistic expansion and dominance. Like all empires, its growth was fueled by blood and tears.

Though ancient sources indicate that the competition for the title of "most violent Assyrian monarch" was stiff, Sennacherib "surpassed his predecessors," at least, "in the grisly detail of his descriptions [of violence]."[8] In one of his inscriptions, Sennacherib boasts of how he slit the throat of his victims like lambs, how he made "their gullets and entrails run down upon the whole earth," and how he castrated and tore out the privates of his enemies "like the seeds of cucumbers."[9] In Sennacherib's palace at Nineveh, the Lachish reliefs depicting his conquest of this town, which was part of the same military campaign in 701 BCE that included the attack on Jerusalem, show his victims being impaled and flayed with piles of severed heads and lines of deportees and prisoners. In the face of such heinous violence, it is not difficult to imagine that the Rabshakeh's argument to choose exile and surrender would have been rather enticing to the besieged and haggard Jerusalemites.

---

8. Erika Bleibtreu, "Grisly Assyrian Record of Torture and Dead," *BAR* 70 (1991): n.p.

9. Ibid.

The Continuation of Source B1 and Hezekiah's Response (19:1-9a)

The pleas by Hezekiah's servants for the emissary to please stop speaking in "the language of Judah" (2 Kgs 18:26) and the Rabshakeh's dismissal of this request heightens the terror and the tension evident in the narrative: by all appearances, the Rabshakeh appears to be correct. There seems to be nothing that can save Jerusalem now. The biblical writer raises the stakes by next turning to the reaction of the pious Hezekiah to the Rabshakeh's address. Surely, the faithful Hezekiah will rally, confident in the power of his God, YHWH. Yet this is not how the king responds when his servants return from the walls with their clothes rent. Rather, he too puts on the garb of mourning, tears his clothes in supplication, and puts on sackcloth. Instead of giving his servant and the inhabitants a nice pep talk, the king instead sends his servants to get Isaiah the prophet (19:2). Bewailing the horror of the situation and likening it to a day when a woman about to give birth finds that she has no strength to bring forth her child, the Judean king rather unconfidently and pitifully declares that perhaps YHWH, whom he distantly calls "your God" and not "my God,"[10] might have become incensed enough by the Rabshakeh's words to respond (19:3). Cynthia Chapman notes that Hezekiah's feminizing analogy, comparing the inability of the nation "to face a military challenge" to "a woman's inability to bring forth a child," shows the utter weakness and vulnerability of the king and the nation.[11]

Surely, this is one of the low moments in this narrative. The pious king sits in his palace, hearing news that confirms his worst nightmares: his city will likely be destroyed, and he and his family will be tortured and brutally murdered. Hezekiah, unsurprisingly, is at the end of his rope, praying and hoping that the blasphemy shouted by his enemy is enough to force YHWH's hand and induce a last-minute miracle. With this, the biblical writers have shown themselves to be masterful manipulators of emotions and magnificent storytellers. Like all good writers, however, this low point is utilized to build to the climax. The careful reader should have noticed small clues in the narrative that hinted that a more optimistic ending was possible. The main clue concerns the new piece

10. Machinist, "*Rab Šaqeh*," 158.
11. Cynthia Chapman, *The Gendered Language of Warfare in the Israelite-Assyrian Encounter*, HSM 62 (Winona Lake, IN: Eisenbrauns, 2004), 83.

250   *2 Kings*

19:1When King Hezekiah heard it, he tore his clothes, covered himself with sackcloth, and went into the house of the Lord. 2And he sent Eliakim, who was in charge of the palace, and Shebna the secretary, and the senior priests, covered with sackcloth, to the prophet Isaiah son of Amoz. 3They said to him, "Thus says Hezekiah, This day is a day of distress, of rebuke, and of disgrace; children have come to the birth, and there is no strength to bring them forth. 4It may be that the LORD your God heard all the words of the Rabshakeh, whom his master the king of Assyria has sent to mock the living God, and will rebuke the words that the Lord your God has heard; therefore lift up your prayer for the remnant that is left." 5When the servants of King Hezekiah came to Isaiah, 6Isaiah said to them, "Say to your master, 'Thus says the LORD: Do not be afraid because of the words that you have heard, with which the servants of the king of Assyria have reviled me. 7I myself will put a spirit in him, so that he shall hear a rumor and return to his own land; I will cause him to fall by the sword in his own land.'"

8The Rabshakeh returned, and found the king of Assyria fighting against Libnah; for he had heard that the king had left Lachish. 9When the king heard concerning King Tirhakah of Ethiopia, "See, he has set out to fight against you,"

of information that the Rabshakeh inadvertently revealed in his address: that some kind of cult centralization occurred during the reign of Hezekiah. Considering that the Deuteronomistic Historian viewed such a reform as one of the key markers of covenant fidelity, this information raises the question as to why the narrative is so silent about this accomplishment of Hezekiah. Why did the biblical writers fail to mention this reform earlier in their list of Hezekiah's pious deeds, for example? As we will elucidate later in this chapter, this missing information might be the result of complicated redactional activities underlying the Deuteronomistic History.

With the sly mention of reform in the Rabshakeh's speech, the reader thus discovers that Hezekiah was even more pious than previously assumed. He not only destroys the idols, the asherahs, and the high places but also seems to have centralized the cult of YHWH in the nation. This enlarging of Hezekiah's reputation, however, has the effect of more forcefully raising theological questions about YHWH: if the Judean monarch is even better than we initially believed, why does YHWH allow Assyria to assault Judah under the rule of the pious Hezekiah? By raising this query, the narrative sets up and foreshadows its dramatic conclusion by contrasting the knowledge of the reader with that of the emissary. The Rabshakeh, with this accusation, seems to be theologically confused. He assumes that Hezekiah's religious reform was something distasteful to YHWH and, thus, something that made Judah weaker and more vulnerable to attack. What the reader knows, however, is that the opposite is true: YHWH is pleased by the centralization and has promised to defend and protect Judah for such acts of loyal, dedicated worship. This is one of the central theological ideas that runs throughout the Deuteronomistic History, including 2 Kings 18–19.

With this false accusation, the writer thus reveals a fissure in the Rabshakeh's and thus Assyria's armor. If the Rabshakeh is wrong about this very important and central theological detail, it strongly suggests that he is wrong about other things as well. Moreover, if Hezekiah is even more pious than we initially believed, and if the Rabshakeh's accusation about what pleases or displeases YHWH is wrong, the hope that YHWH will swoop in to save Judah at the last minute—to prove to the readers just how wrong the emissary's notion is—is raised. It seems that with the emissary's false charge the writer has set up the narrative for an unexpected ending.

And that is precisely what happens. Jerking the readers' emotions up and down, things look rather bleak and hopeless, that is, until the prophet Isaiah arrives. It appears that YHWH was indeed incensed by the mocking words of the Assyrians. Telling Hezekiah not to be afraid (v. 6), YHWH declares, through Isaiah, that Jerusalem will soon be delivered as God will put a "spirit" in the Assyrian king so that the monarch will "hear a rumor" (שמע שמועה) and return (שוב) to his own land. The punishment will not end there, however. Even when the king returns home, he will not be safe. Because of his damning words, God will further punish the Assyrian monarch by causing "him to fall by the sword in his own land" (v. 7). Hence, it will not be Hezekiah that is killed but rather the haughty Assyrian monarch, Sennacherib. Isaiah's prophecy thus promises a happy ending or at least a happier ending than that which was expected just a few short verses back. In fact, 2 Kings 19:9 seems to describe the immediate fulfillment of Isaiah's prophecy by beginning to narrate Assyria's exit: it states that Sennacherib heard (שמע) of Tirhakah's approach. The expectation thus is raised that Sennacherib will, in fulfillment of the prophecy, hear (שמע) the news of this approach and return (שוב) to his country.

Source B2 and the Conclusion to the Attack (19:9b-37)

The reader is in for a surprise, however, as the story again lurches in an unexpected direction. In the previous section, Isaiah's prophecy that Assyria will leave Jerusalem without conquering it seemed imminent, and 2 Kings 19:9a seems to begin to describe this exit. The last half of 2 Kings 19:9, however, suddenly shifts this progression by stating instead that the Assyrian king heard (שמע) and that he again sent messengers to Hezekiah.

The shift focuses on the different uses of the term שוב (*šûb*). Instead of meaning "return," שוב (*šûb*) is utilized in 2 Kings 19:9b as an indicator of repetition or to mean "again": "he [unclear who this refers to] sent messengers *again* to Hezekiah, saying . . ." (2 Kgs 19:9; emphasis added). Because of this sudden change, many scholars maintain that 2 Kings 19:9b begins a different, later account of the 701 attack on Jerusalem, which was inserted into the earlier account in 2 Kings 18:7–19:9a. As we noted previously, this earlier account is designated in most scholarly works as Source B1, the conclusion of which is found at 2 Kings 19:36, which describes Sennacherib's departure from Jerusalem. To Source B1, a later account consisting of 2 Kings 19:9b-35, 37, designated as Source B2, was added.

Aside from the apparent redactional seam at 2 Kings 19:9, other differences in the narrative distinguish Source B1 from Source B2. Overall, Source B2 is a more exaggerated and dramatic account of Sennacherib's attack.[12] For example, the Rabshakeh is even more blasphemous in Source B2. In this second address, the Assyrian king targets YHWH more directly, writing Hezekiah a letter telling the Judean king not to trust in YHWH who is deceiving him by promising salvation (2 Kgs 19:10). Remember that in B1 the target of the distrust is Hezekiah, with the Rabshakeh cautioning the Judahites against trusting their faithful king. In B2, however, the focus is more forcefully turned toward the trustworthiness and reliability of YHWH.[13] Hezekiah too is more assertively portrayed in this later source. In contrast to the rather pitiful and frightened king of Source B1 who meekly wonders aloud whether "your god" would be offended enough to act against Assyria, the Hezekiah of Source B2,

---

12. Brevard Childs, *Isaiah and the Assyrian Crisis* (London: SCM, 1967), 94–103.
13. Ibid., 98.

⁹ᵇhe sent messengers again to Hezekiah, saying, ¹⁰"Thus shall you speak to King Hezekiah of Judah: Do not let your God on whom you rely deceive you by promising that Jerusalem will not be given into the hand of the king of Assyria. ¹¹See, you have heard what the kings of Assyria have done to all lands, destroying them utterly. Shall you be delivered? ¹²Have the gods of the nations delivered them, the nations that my predecessors destroyed, Gozan, Haran, Rezeph, and the people of Eden who were in Telassar? ¹³Where is the king of Hamath, the king of Arpad, the king of the city of Sepharvaim, the king of Hena, or the king of Ivvah?"

¹⁴Hezekiah received the letter from the hand of the messengers and read it; then Hezekiah went up to the house of the LORD and spread it before the LORD. ¹⁵And Hezekiah prayed before the LORD, and said: "O LORD the God of Israel, who are enthroned above the cherubim, you are God, you alone, of all the kingdoms of the earth; you have made heaven and earth. ¹⁶Incline your ear, O LORD, and hear; open your eyes, O LORD, and see; hear the words of Sennacherib, which he has sent to mock the living God. ¹⁷Truly, O LORD, the kings of Assyria have laid waste the nations and their lands, ¹⁸and have hurled their gods into the fire, though they were no gods but the work of human hands—wood and stone—and so they were destroyed. ¹⁹So now, O LORD our God, save us, I pray you, from his hand, so that all the kingdoms of the earth may know that you, O LORD, are God alone."

²⁰Then Isaiah son of Amoz sent to Hezekiah, saying, "Thus says the LORD, the God of Israel: I have heard your prayer to me about King Sennacherib of Assyria. ²¹This is the word that the Lord has spoken concerning him:

She despises you, she scorns
> you—
virgin daughter Zion;
she tosses her head—behind your
> back,
daughter Jerusalem.
²²"Whom have you mocked and reviled?
> Against whom have you raised
> your voice
and haughtily lifted your eyes?
> Against the Holy One of Israel!
²³By your messengers you have mocked the Lord,
> and you have said, 'With my
> many chariots
I have gone up the heights of the
> mountains,
> to the far recesses of Lebanon;
I felled its tallest cedars
> its choicest cypresses;
I entered its farthest retreat,
> its densest forest.
²⁴I dug wells
> and drank foreign waters,
I dried up with the sole of my foot
> all the streams of Egypt.'
²⁵"Have you not heard
> that I determined it long ago?
I planned from days of old
> what now I bring to pass,
that you should make fortified cities
> crash into heaps of ruins,
²⁶while their inhabitants, shorn of strength,

2 Kgs 19:9b-37 (cont.)

are dismayed and confounded;
they have become like plants of
the field
and like tender grass,
like grass on the housetops,
blighted before it is grown.
[27]"But I know your rising and your
sitting,
your going out and coming in,
and your raging against me.
[28]Because you have raged
against me
and your arrogance has come
to my ears,

I will put my hook in your nose
and my bit in your mouth;
I will turn you back on the way
by which you came.
[29]"And this shall be the sign for you:
This year you shall eat what grows of
itself, and in the second year what
springs from that; then in the third
year sow, reap, plant vineyards, and
eat their fruit. [30]The surviving remnant
of the house of Judah shall again take
root downward, and bear fruit upward;
[31]for from Jerusalem a remnant shall
go out, and from Mount Zion a band

without a note of fear, enters the temple and, with no need for a prophetic intermediary, boldly prays to his god (2 Kgs 19:14-15).[14]

YHWH in this later source is also portrayed as a larger and more universal deity. In his prayer, Hezekiah asks YHWH, who is the lone God "of all the kingdoms of the earth" and who "made heaven and earth," to show the world that he is indeed "God alone" and not like the other deities of the conquered nations who are "but the work of human hands—wood and stone" by responding to the "words of Sennacherib which he has sent to mock the living God" (2 Kgs 19:17-19). Francolino Gonçalves notes that similar vocabulary and monotheistic sentiments are found in parts of the biblical texts that are dated from the exilic period and later. Thus he, among others, has suggested dating Source B2 to the same period.[15] Source B2, hence, appears to be a later, postexilic updating and reinterpretation of an earlier account of Sennacherib's attack.

Source B2, as a later retelling, attempts to finesse or "correct" the theological flaws or inconsistencies in the earlier accounts. The small theological foibles and inconsistencies in Source B1 are absent from Source B2.

14. Ibid., 100.

15. Francolino J. Gonçalves, *L'Expédition de Sennachérib en Palestine dans la littérature hébraïque ancienne*, *EBib* 7 (Paris: Gabalda, 1986), 464–66. Also see Nadav Na'aman, "New Light on Hezekiah's Second Prophetic Story (2 Kgs. 19,9b-35)," *Bib* 81 (2000): 393–401.

of survivors. The zeal of the LORD of hosts will do this.

³²"Therefore thus says the LORD concerning the king of Assyria: He shall not come into this city, shoot an arrow there, come before it with a shield, or cast up a siege ramp against it. ³³By the way that he came, by the same he shall return; he shall not come into this city, says the Lord. ³⁴For I will defend this city to save it, for my own sake and for the sake of my servant David."

³⁵That very night the angel of the LORD set out and struck down one hundred eighty-five thousand in the camp of the Assyrians; when morning dawned, they were all dead bodies. ³⁶Then King Sennacherib of Assyria left, went home, and lived at Nineveh. ³⁷As he was worshiping in the house of his god Nisroch, his sons Adrammelech and Sharezer killed him with the sword, and they escaped into the land of Ararat. His son Esar-haddon succeeded him.

The narrative of this later source proceeds in a quick and smooth fashion. To Hezekiah's bold prayer in Source B2, YHWH immediately responds by sending the prophet Isaiah to the king with a prophecy that utterly mocks the arrogance of Assyria. Stating that the virgin daughter Zion has scorned and rejected Assyria—a fascinating remark to which we will return shortly—YHWH forcefully declares that Assyria has messed with the wrong deity (19:22). Mistakenly believing that their military success resulted from their own deeds and power, YHWH declares that everything, including Assyrian victories, stem from YHWH's own will and plan (19:23-27). Assyria, in daring to speak such things about YHWH, however, has now overstepped its boundaries in its arrogance. Therefore, YHWH will treat it as a farmer treats a stupid, stubborn farm animal: YHWH will put a hook into Assyria's nose and a bit into its mouth and will force it to return (19:28). For good measure, YHWH supplements his message with a sign proving the prophecy's fulfillment (19:29) before concluding with a repetition of his promise that the king of Assyria will be utterly and totally barred from entering Jerusalem (19:32-33): "For I will defend this city to save it, for my own sake and for the sake of my servant David" (v. 34).

Not wasting another moment, the prophecy is instantly fulfilled. The dramatic account of the attack ends on an equally climactic note: with the angel of YHWH striking down 185,000 Assyrian soldiers (v. 35). Faced with a sea of dead bodies, the Assyrian king wisely decides to return home with his tail tucked between his legs (v. 36). But YHWH is not finished yet. Even at home Sennacherib is not safe, and the king is struck down by his own sons while worshiping in the house of his god (v. 37). The Lord has utterly avenged Sennacherib for his blasphemy.

The Gendered Significance of the Rabshakeh's Two Addresses in 2 Kings 18:7–19:37

These two chapters are replete with gendered significance.[16] The Rabshakeh, in his address, targets and denigrates Hezekiah and God's masculinity while aggressively asserting that of the Assyrian king. The Rabshakeh describes Sennacherib so as to stress his "royal credentials of perfected masculinity,"[17] which consist of his "unrivaled status on the battlefield, divine chosenness, and proven ability to protect and provide for one's people."[18] Sennacherib is described as exemplary in his military prowess and as the "great king, King of Assyria" (2 Kgs 18:19, 28) who was specially chosen by YHWH to attack Judah (2 Kgs 18:25). According to the Rabshakeh, Sennacherib also promises the surrendering Judeans' abundance, safety, peace, and well-being. In contrast, Hezekiah's credentials of masculinity—that is, his ability to provide for and protect his subjects and his status as a chosen royal monarch—are attacked and denigrated. The Rabshakeh states that the Judean monarch's military prowess is nil and mere talk (2 Kgs 18:20) and that, as a result, his citizens will starve to death and be compelled to drink their own urine (2 Kgs 18:27). Striking at Hezekiah's status as a divinely chosen Judean king, the emissary states that Assyria was sent by Judah's own god, YHWH, to attack it. Most important, however, the Assyrian king through his emissary tries even to outman YHWH when he asserts that YHWH, like the deities of other nations that Assyria has conquered, will be unable to save Judah from Sennacherib's power.[19]

Such severe attacks against the masculinity and power of Hezekiah and, more important, YHWH would have been intolerable to a later editor. Hence, Source B2 is a response and improved address to the critiques left unattended to in Source B1. For example, while in Source B1, the Rabshakeh urges the Judeans to surrender and eat bread, olive oil, and other good things, Source B2 responds by having Isaiah prophesy at 2 Kings 19:29 that the Judeans will indeed eat good things for three

16. See Chapman, *Gendered Language*, 76–96.
17. Ibid., 83.
18. Ibid., 82.
19. Ibid., 83.

straight uninterrupted years.[20] While in Source B1, Sennacherib declares with blatant sexual innuendo his desire to "enter" daughter Zion (2 Kgs 18:32), in Source B2, daughter Zion responds to this arrogant suitor with gestures of scorn and rejection (2 Kgs 19:21-22). Sennacherib is further rebuffed by YHWH, Zion's father figure, who denigrates Sennacherib's credentials as a suitor unworthy of his beloved city.[21]

Cynthia Chapman argues that Source B2 directly responds to the denigration of YHWH's masculinity by reversing the claims made by the arrogant Assyrian king. In direct contrast to Sennacherib's claims in Source B1 that he is the "great king" and military conqueror, Source B2 depicts Assyria, not Judah, as a rebellious underling who has arrogantly risen up against the real king, YHWH, the sole ruler of the universe (2 Kgs 19:15) and the creator of heaven and earth. As punishment for Sennacherib's arrogance and for daring to question YHWH's masculinity and power, his punishment is amplified in Source B2. While in Source B1 Sennacherib merely returns home without having conquered Jerusalem (2 Kgs 19:36), in Source B2 for attacking YHWH's masculine abilities as a warrior, YHWH, through the angel of death, goes on a killing rampage, decimating the Assyrian army and turning the camp into a field of corpses. Not yet completely satisfied, the warrior YHWH pursues the fleeing Sennacherib to his home, where the Assyrian king is assassinated. In utter denigration of Sennacherib's masculinity, 2 Kings 19:36 further states that the Assyrian king was killed by his own sons while praying in the temple of his god. As Chapman notes, the king who had the audacity to claim that YHWH could not save his own people was not able to even protect himself from his own sons while worshiping in the temple of his own god![22] Source B2 "establishes himself [YHWH] as the man with the edge in the masculine contest and manages to present Sennacherib as young, inexperienced, and arrogant in relation to the eternal and universal power of YHWH."[23]

The various accounts of Sennacherib's attack on Jerusalem, with their rollercoaster of unexpected twists and turns, create an exciting narrative, which in the end convey a theological message with an undeniable gendered component. Piety, protection, power, and violence are intimately

---

20. William Gallagher, *Sennacherib's Campaign to Judah: New Studies*, Studies in the History and Culture of the Ancient Near East 18 (Boston: Brill, 1999), 159.

21. Chapman, *Gendered Language*, 86–89.

22. Ibid., 86.

23. Ibid., 86–87.

linked with ideas of masculinity. As the narrative shows with the defeat of Sennacherib and the deliverance of Jerusalem, proper and exclusive worship, which must naturally follow a recognition of the masculine prowess of YHWH, leads to life, deliverance, and protection from violence. In contrast, doubts, questions, or outright attacks on YHWH's masculinity, whether verbal or physical, such as in the case of Sennacherib, or religious, as in the case of Samaria with their syncretistic worship, will lead to violence, destruction, and death.

The Illness and Recovery of Hezekiah (20:1-11)

Two final stories concerning Hezekiah's illness and his reception of Babylonian envoys complete the cycle of tales about this monarch in 2 Kings. As noted earlier, Isaiah 36–39 offers a very similar but not identical account of these narratives. The unexpected lurching that we have seen in the account of the 701 BCE Assyrian attack in 2 Kings 18–19 continues as we move to these last two pericopes. The first story concerning Hezekiah's illness jarringly begins on the heels of the dramatic salvation and deliverance of Jerusalem in 2 Kings 19. While the preceding pericope ended on a high note with the slaughter of the Assyrian army, the next part of the narrative oddly commences with the pious Hezekiah inexplicably getting ill and being on his death bed (2 Kgs 20:1). Hezekiah is so sick that the prophet Isaiah arrives to tell him that the Lord wants the king to set his house in order because he will not recover and will certainly die (2 Kgs 20:2).

The mystery of Hezekiah's illness is exacerbated not only by its placement after the triumphant account of the Assyrian assault but also by the generally positive portrayal of the king in preceding accounts. As we noted earlier, aside from the destruction of the asherahs and pillars, Hezekiah also removed the high places and implemented a cult reform. Indeed, according to the Deuteronomistic writer, he is a model king. Moreover, as we saw in the immediately preceding pericope, he is the king whose piety and prayer led to the intervention of YHWH and thus to the deliverance of Jerusalem from Assyria. It therefore makes little sense that such a righteous and esteemed monarch as Hezekiah would suddenly and inexplicably be struck down with a deadly illness for which YHWH offers little recourse. Certainly, a deity who just miraculously saved an entire country from the Assyrian war machine is able to deliver a righteous Judean monarch from a little illness.

Theological ideas about illnesses exacerbate the tonal dissonance. In the biblical text, sickness was usually envisioned as a mark of di-

[21:1]In those days Hezekiah became sick and was at the point of death. The prophet Isaiah son of Amoz came to him, and said to him, "Thus says the LORD: Set your house in order, for you shall die; you shall not recover." [2]Then Hezekiah turned his face to the wall and prayed to the LORD: [3]"Remember now, O LORD, I implore you, how I have walked before you in faithfulness with a whole heart, and have done what is good in your sight." Hezekiah wept bit-terly. [4]Before Isaiah had gone out of the middle court, the word of the LORD came to him: [5]"Turn back, and say to Hezekiah prince of my people, Thus says the LORD, the God of your ances-tor David: I have heard your prayer, I have seen your tears; indeed, I will heal you; on the third day you shall go up to the house of the LORD. [6]I will add fifteen years to your life. I will deliver you and this city out of the hand of the king of Assyria; I will defend this city for

vine displeasure or punishment. In Numbers 25:8, for example, plague is threatened as retribution for the marriage of an Israelite man to a Midianite woman. Moreover, God strikes the wandering Israelites with plague as punishment after Korah's rebellion in Numbers 16. Thus, Margaret Barker proposes an unstated wrongdoing on the part of Hezekiah as the cause of his sudden sickness, which she argues was a form of plague.[24] She names Hezekiah's destruction of high places and his alliance with Egypt as possible transgressions that may have induced the punishment of the illness.[25] Classical rabbinic and patristic commentators likewise claim that Hezekiah's illness resulted from an unstated transgression. For example, Clement of Alexandria (Const. ap. 2.3.22) states that Hezekiah's pride was at fault for his malady while b. Ber. 10a proposes that it was the king's refusal to have children, as the pious monarch foresaw that he would father the evil Manasseh, that led to this divinely induced malady.

Whatever the cause, the illness narrative, like the preceding account of the attack, again asserts the image of YHWH as master over life, health, well-being, and reproduction. This vision of YHWH is most clearly evident at the conclusion of the narrative when God reverses this prophecy in response to Hezekiah's prayer. Shortly after Isaiah foretells of his demise, the pious Hezekiah promptly prays to YHWH, reminding the deity of his faithfulness and his good deeds (20:3). The

24. Margaret Barker, "Hezekiah's Boil," *JSOT* 95 (2001): 31–42.
25. Ibid., 35.

my own sake and for my servant Da-vid's sake." ⁷Then Isaiah said, "Bring a lump of figs. Let them take it and apply it to the boil, so that he may recover."

⁸Hezekiah said to Isaiah, "What shall be the sign that the Lᴏʀᴅ will heal me, and that I shall go up to the house of the Lᴏʀᴅ on the third day?" ⁹Isaiah said, "This is the sign to you from the Lᴏʀᴅ, that the Lᴏʀᴅ will do the thing that he has promised: the shadow has now advanced ten intervals; shall it retreat ten intervals?" ¹⁰Hezekiah answered, "It is normal for the shadow to lengthen ten intervals; rather let the shadow re-treat ten intervals." ¹¹The prophet Isa-iah cried to the Lᴏʀᴅ; and he brought the shadow back the ten intervals, by which the sun had declined on the dial of Ahaz.

king's reminder seems to have had an instantaneous effect. YHWH, as if suddenly recalling the righteousness of this monarch, reverses course, commanding Isaiah to turn back and tell Hezekiah that God has heard his prayers and seen his tears. As a result, God promises Hezekiah will not die from his illness but be healed, so much so that in just three days he will be able to go up to the house of the Lord (20:5). YHWH explains further that Hezekiah's life will be elongated for fifteen more years and that God will deliver both the king and Jerusalem from Assyria for his own sake and also that of God's servant David—a mysterious statement to which we will shortly return (20:6). And with this, the narrative ap-pears to come to a close with Isaiah requesting a lump of figs to use as a medical application so that the king can recover (v. 7).

As in the previous story about the attack, so also here: piety, fidelity, and the recognition of YHWH's mastery and masculine powers are shown as leading to life, health, and protection. The opposite behavior, however, such as the denigration or lack of recognition of YHWH's pow-ers, as the preceding episode of the attack made clear, results in death and destruction. Just as the mere reminder to God of this equation has the immediate effect of bringing the illness to pass, Hezekiah's mention of his piety and fidelity almost instantaneously leads to YHWH's reciprocal elongation of the king's life. Confusing, however, is the strange reason given for God's decision to heal Hezekiah: "I will add fifteen years to your life. I will deliver you and this city out of the hand of the king of Assyria; I will defend this city for my own sake and for my servant Da-vid's sake" (20:6). It seems, at first, that Hezekiah's healing results from God's remembrance of David, not Hezekiah. T. R. Hobbs points out that this verse seems to disparage Hezekiah by attributing God's actions to

David.[26] Considering that earlier in the narrative Hezekiah was compared to David, it seems unlikely that this reference is intended as a jab against Hezekiah, whom God has decided a moment before to heal after being reminded of Hezekiah's, not David's, good deeds.

Since this phrase—"for the sake of the LORD's servant David"—is found mainly in 1 Kings 11 (vv. 12, 13, 32, 34) in reference to the Davidic covenant, it seems more likely that the mention of it in 2 Kings 20:6 also alludes to the promises that YHWH had made to David concerning YHWH's protection of the Davidic lineage and Jerusalem.[27] This seems almost certainly to be the case when we look more closely at 2 Kings 20:6 as a whole. This verse states not only that God will elongate Hezekiah's life but that he will also deliver the king and the city from Assyria "for the sake of David"—an event that has already happened in the preceding chapters (2 Kgs 18–19). This anachronistic reference to the salvation of Jerusalem from Assyria strongly suggests that the stories about Hezekiah were edited and rearranged. There are hints in the text, such as this anachronistic notice, that indicate that the story of the king's illness originally came before or during the 701 BCE Assyrian onslaught.[28] These stories, at some later point, were misaligned and put out of their original order. If originally Hezekiah was sick during or before the 701 BCE attack, the prophecy in 2 Kings 20:6, which links the king's illness with that of the city, can now make more sense. Hezekiah's sickness is that of the city—that is, the attack. As Hezekiah will recover, so then Jerusalem will be delivered from the Assyrian onslaught. And the reason for both recoveries is God's remembrance of the Davidic covenant, which promised divine protection for both the Davidic dynasty and the city of David (Jerusalem).

The misalignment of the order of the stories is not the only hint that the narratives of Hezekiah were redacted.[29] The most obvious indicator is the strange manner in which the story of the illness ends. As we discussed earlier, it seems that the sickness narrative is about to conclude with Isaiah's request and application of a lump of figs in 2 Kings 20:7.

26. T. R. Hobbs, *2 Kings*, WBC 13 (Waco, TX: Word, 1985), 291.

27. On Zion theology, see Frank Moore Cross, *Canaanite Myth and Hebrew Epic: Essays in the History of Religion of Israel* (Cambridge, MA: Harvard University Press, 1973), 241–73.

28. John H. Walton, "New Observations on the Date of Isaiah," *JETS* 28 (1985): 129–32.

29. For more on the theological reasons behind the redactional history of the narratives on Hezekiah, see Song-Mi Suzie Park, *Hezekiah and the Dialogue of Memory* (Minneapolis: Fortress, 2015), 84–88.

The story again lurches, however, in the next verse by backtracking the chronology. While in 2 Kings 20:7, Hezekiah appears to be on the verge of being rehabilitated, in 2 Kings 20:8, Hezekiah, who is seemingly still sick, now asks Isaiah to give him a sign validating God's promise of his forthcoming healing: "Hezekiah said to Isaiah, 'What shall be the sign that the LORD will heal me?'" (2 Kgs 20:7). Most scholars believe that 2 Kings 20:8 is the beginning of an alternate account of Hezekiah's illness, which was jarringly placed immediately after the conclusion of the first account. This second account adds a divine miracle—the regression of the sun and the retreat of its shadow on the dial of Ahaz—that reaffirms God's promise of healing. Though the process by which two stories about Hezekiah's illness and restoration came to be placed side-by-side cannot be fully elucidated, the addition of the second narrative has the effect of more strongly reasserting the image of YHWH as the deity of life, restoration, and protection. The reader now knows more definitively that piety, fidelity, and recognition of YHWH's masculine powers will lead to protection and life as it has been affirmed by a miraculous sign: the backward movement of the sun, which mirrors the backward movement of time that remains in Hezekiah's lifespan.

The Visit of the Babylonian Envoys (20:12-21)

The narratives about King Hezekiah, which began on such a high note in 2 Kings 18, conclude on a more somber tone with a final story about the visitation of Babylonian envoys. Hearing that Hezekiah is sick, King Merodach-baladan of Babylon sends envoys to Judah, along with presents and letters (v. 12). For unstated reasons, maybe to be hospitable, the newly recovered king shows the envoys all of the treasures of Judah (v. 13). The text notes that "there was nothing in his [Hezekiah] house in all his realm that Hezekiah did not show them" (v. 13). Shortly after this display, the prophet Isaiah comes to Hezekiah to deliver a very negative prophecy. After finding out that the king has shown the envoys everything in the country (vv. 14-15), the prophet prophesied the coming of the Babylonian exile when all the riches of Judah would be taken to Babylon and Hezekiah's descendants exiled and taken away to be eunuchs in the palace of the Babylonian king (v. 18). To this foreboding oracle, Hezekiah offers a strange and mysterious response: "Then Hezekiah said to Isaiah, 'The word of the LORD that you have spoken is good.' For he thought, 'Why not, if there will be peace and security in my days'" (v. 19).

2 Kgs 20:12-21

¹²At that time King Merodach-baladan son of Baladan of Babylon sent envoys with letters and a present to Hezekiah, for he had heard that Hezekiah had been sick. ¹³Hezekiah welcomed them; he showed them all his treasure house, the silver, the gold, the spices, the precious oil, his armory, all that was found in his storehouses; there was nothing in his house or in all his realm that Hezekiah did not show them. ¹⁴Then the prophet Isaiah came to King Hezekiah, and said to him, "What did these men say? From where did they come to you?" Hezekiah answered, "They have come from a far country, from Babylon." ¹⁵He said, "What have they seen in your house?" Hezekiah answered, "They have seen all that is in my house; there is nothing in my storehouses that I did not show them."

¹⁶Then Isaiah said to Hezekiah, "Hear the word of the Lord: ¹⁷Days are coming when all that is in your house, and that which your ancestors have stored up until this day, shall be carried to Babylon; nothing shall be left, says the Lord. ¹⁸Some of your own sons who are born to you shall be taken away; they shall be eunuchs in the palace of the king of Babylon." ¹⁹Then Hezekiah said to Isaiah, "The word of the Lord that you have spoken is good." For he thought, "Why not, if there will be peace and security in my days?"

²⁰The rest of the deeds of Hezekiah, all his power, how he made the pool and the conduit and brought water into the city, are they not written in the Book of the Annals of the Kings of Judah? ²¹Hezekiah slept with his ancestors; and his son Manasseh succeeded him.

This narrative is replete with unanswerable questions and mysteries. The first concerns the purpose behind Hezekiah's unfettered display of the nation's treasuries to the Babylonian envoys. Some scholars have speculated that the purpose of the Babylonian visit was politically and militarily motivated. They were sent not just to find out about Hezekiah's health but also to form an anti-Assyrian coalition. Arguing that the envoy narrative, like the preceding one about the illness, was also misaligned from a more original sequence, some scholars posit that the visit likely occurred before the 701 BCE attack. Mordechai Cogan and Hayim Tadmor, for example, put the likely date of the visit at 713 BCE, when Merodach-baladan, the monarch who sent the envoys, was securely ensconced on the throne. This period, they argue, was also when plans against Assyria were being formulated.[30] Others, such as Hans

---

30. Mordechai Cogan and Hayim Tadmor, *II Kings: A New Translation with Introduction and Commentary*, AB 11 (Garden City, NY: Doubleday, 1988), 261.

Wildberger, date the visit to right before the attack in 703 BCE when Merodach-baladan regained control of Babylon.[31] The hypothesis that the purpose of the visit was to form a military alliance is also touted in classical Jewish sources. Josephus, for example, states in *Ant.* 5.30 that the king of Babylon sent envoys to the Judean king and "invited him to become his ally and friend." If the original purpose of the visit was to create a coalition against Assyria, then Hezekiah's display can be explained as an attempt to prove his military might to potential allies. He wanted to show the Babylonians that he had the resources to function as a strong and powerful partner.

If so, then there might be reasons why Isaiah suddenly appears to deliver a negative oracle from YHWH. If the point of the visit was to get proof of Hezekiah's strength and prowess—both physically, as in his recovery from the illness, and also militarily, so as to obtain proof of Judah's defenses, resources, and supplies—then YHWH's role as the ultimate king and protector of Judah and Jerusalem is undermined. If Hezekiah and his allies are all that is needed to protect and deliver Zion, there is little need for YHWH to defend his city. Hezekiah's disclosure might have been seen as an affront to God's masculine credentials as master and defender of Zion. This is especially so since God, in the preceding story, just promised Hezekiah that he will save both Hezekiah and the city from their "illnesses." If YHWH has promised this conclusion and even affirmed it with a miraculous sign of the retreat of the shadow on the dial of Ahaz, it seems rather faithless of Hezekiah to ignore this earlier promise and attempt to form an alliance with other foreign states to thwart Assyria. Certainly, such doubting of YHWH's promises is a slur on the masculine powers of this deity.

The interaction between Isaiah and Hezekiah when the prophet arrives seems to confirm this reading. Asking about the origins of the visitors, the prophet also inquires about how much of Judah's storehouses the king has shown his visitors. To this query, Hezekiah answers that he showed them everything—that there was nothing left unseen by the Babylonians (v. 15). This emphasis on entrances, unveiling, and disclosure in the passage can be read as a sexual innuendo again emphasizing YHWH's role as the male defender and father figure of Zion who is, at points, envisioned as this deity's daughter or wife. As we noted earlier using Cynthia Chapman's work, similar sexual undertones were evident in Sennacherib's desire to enter Zion and YHWH's rebuffing of Assyria as a suitor unworthy of

---

31. Hans Wildberger, *Isaiah 28–39: A Continental Commentary*, trans. Thomas H. Trapp (Minneapolis: Fortress, 2002), 473.

"entering" his city. In other words, the ideas of unveiling and entering Jerusalem, whether by Assyria or Babylon, are intertwined with sexual meanings. Hezekiah's giving free access to the Babylonian envoys to the treasures of Judah, which he takes to be a seemingly innocent gesture, is not interpreted as such by the prophet Isaiah and, hence, by YHWH. This may explain, in part, the rather harsh prophecy that Isaiah utters to Hezekiah in response to this deed. Laying the blame for the Babylonian exile and the destruction of Zion—one of the worst disasters in Judean history—on Hezekiah's seemingly innocent display of Judah's treasures seems initially severe. This is especially so since Hezekiah is presented as one of the most righteous and pious kings of Judah.

Daughter Zion

In 2 Kings 19:21, Isaiah chastises the Assyrians who threaten Jerusalem. He invokes the image of a "virgin daughter Zion" who derisively shakes her head, scorning the arrogance of the would-be invaders. This female figure, also called "daughter Jerusalem," is an embodiment of the city and its people. The Hebrew term בתולת, translated "virgin," implies a girl on the verge of womanhood, who, in this case, is secure in the protection of her father against the advances of male adversaries. The figure of daughter Zion recurs in the Hebrew Bible yet this dynamic is often dramatically reversed. In Lamentations, Isaiah, Jeremiah, and Ezekiel, daughter Zion or the female Jerusalem is envisioned as a woman who has been abused, even sexually violated, and is accused of being responsible for her own abuse. By embodying the invasion and destruction of Jerusalem as the downfall of a woman, the city's devastation is framed in terms of the dissolution of legitimate relationships in a patrimonial society. The figure of a daughter who is no longer protected dramatizes the loss of Zion's privileged status as the chosen city and dwelling place of the deity.

The figure of daughter Zion has its roots in the genre of Mesopotamian city laments, dating from the third millennium BCE, in which a goddess mourns the destruction of her city and appeals to the gods on its behalf. This kind of direct appeal is found in the book of Lamentations. In the biblical text, daughter Zion's lament becomes a protest against God, who has allowed or has even been the agent of her suffering. She demands, "Look, O Lord, and consider! To whom have you done this?" (Lam 2:20). The unspoken answer is that God has done this to the city that once, secure in her status, had tossed her head at invaders.

Christine Neal Thomas

The gendered and sexual undertones in Hezekiah's actions might partially explain the harsh reaction by YHWH in which the king is blamed for inadvertently inducing the Babylonian exile. What to Hezekiah is an innocent gesture to YHWH is tantamount to an attack on YHWH's masculine powers. Not only is the visit, if it were for the goal of forming a coalition, a faithless disregard of YHWH's earlier promise to Hezekiah that he would deliver the country, but the display of the country's storehouses could be easily seen as a voluntary stripping and unveiling of Judah. Considering that YHWH, at different points in the biblical texts, is envisioned as Judah's husband and, as we noted in the earlier story of the Assyrian attack, as Judah's father figure, Hezekiah's display would not be viewed merely as a display. It is also an attack on YHWH's role as the true master, male protector, and father figure of Zion. In other words, Hezekiah's action is tantamount to unclothing and displaying the nakedness of YHWH's daughter/wife/ward, which is no small assault on YHWH's masculine powers! The king's act, though unwittingly done, is met with a harsh oracle of doom befitting the level of misdeed. Such unfettered access—revealing and exhibiting Judah unnecessarily and without permission—will eventually lead to a future violation of Judah by Babylon. Moreover, for attacking YHWH's masculinity by uncovering Judah's treasuries, Hezekiah's own masculinity is also attacked and denigrated. Disparaging Hezekiah's masculine powers as a progenitor and as a king, Isaiah foretells how the king's descendants will not only be taken prisoner by the Babylonian king but also be made into eunuchs. For Hezekiah's offense—for doubting and accidentally belittling God's masculine powers—the masculine powers of his descendants to procreate and reproduce will also be constrained.

To Isaiah's harsh oracle, Hezekiah gives a mysterious response. Oddly, to Isaiah's prophecy of exile, Hezekiah declares that it is something that is good "for he said, 'will there not [הלוא אם] be peace and security in my days?' " (2 Kgs 20:19). It is unclear whether Hezekiah's response should be regarded as callous selfishness and mere indifference to the plight of his future descendants[32] or a kind of pious acceptance of divine will.[33] It might even be something of both. Hezekiah, maybe somewhat now cognizant of the severity of his wrongdoing in disclosing Judah's

32. Cogan and Tadmor, *II Kings*, 262.

33. Peter Ackroyd, "An Interpretation of the Babylonian Exile: A Study of 2 Kings 20, Isaiah 38–39," *SJT* 27 (1974): 341; Bostock, *Portrayal of Trust*, 145.

storehouses to the envoys, declares the punishment as "good" because he is relieved that it will not come to pass during his life. In other words, though the punishment is harsh, if Hezekiah recognizes the severity of what he has done, that is, that he has inadvertently undermined YHWH's masculine powers, then the king might actually view this punishment as quite lenient. He could have been punished more severely for his offense. But at least he will not be alive to see the destruction that his accidental act will induce. Considering that Hezekiah nearly saw the demise of his country in 701 BCE, he might truly be thankful that he will not be around to see the nation's true final demise some time in the future.

Why is Hezekiah, a king who thus far has been presented as the face of piety, blamed for this egregious mistake of allowing the envoys unfettered access to Judah and thus inducing the exile? Why is this disaster not blamed on a more impious king? Though we cannot offer a conclusive answer, we posit that blaming the national disaster on a pious king and not an evil king more accurately captures the befuddling and difficult theological questions raised by a national catastrophe of such a magnitude. As we will see again with the narrative about Josiah (2 Kings 22–23), after the destruction of Judah, one of the questions that would have emerged in the postexilic period is why the pious deeds of the good, faithful kings of Judah were not enough to stop the nation's destruction. Later editors/redactors/writers might have felt the need to address this question by subtly slipping into the narratives of the pious kings of Judah some slight misdeed that prevented them from the perfected piety needed to prevent the upcoming calamity. Though this effort did not offer a full explanation for the exile, it might have provided some small theological relief—or at least lessened in some measure the feeling of theological dissonance.

In a similar vein, there might be another reason why this disaster was connected to the rule of Hezekiah, a good king, and not an evil king. It could be that the biblical writers by depicting Hezekiah as accidentally causing such a disaster used the stories about Hezekiah as a means by which to struggle theologically with the clash between historical events and the promises assured to them in their religious tradition. As most historians are well aware, the theological promises reflected in the biblical text did not fit with the historical experiences of Israel and Judah. This clash must have caused theological doubts and questions, especially among the educated and religious elite, such as the scribes. What better way to reflect on and struggle with such tortured queries and feelings than by portraying a very good king like Hezekiah—a king whose piety, in the preceding narrative, led to the salvation of a country—as accidentally inducing the nation's future demise.[34] The ups and downs, the unexpected twists and turns in the narratives about the good king Hezekiah indicate that for some reason he was the mirror onto which was reflected many of the theological struggles and torments faced by the nation of Judah after its downfall.

34. Park, *Hezekiah and the Dialogue*, 107–17.

2 Kings 21:1-26

The Reign of Manasseh in Judah

Veering from bad king (Ahaz) to good king (Hezekiah) to another bad king, the biblical narrative turns to discuss the reign of Manasseh (697–642 BCE),[1] the worst, most impious king of Judah. With his copious misdeeds, Manasseh's reign sets the path to Judah's eventual destruction and exile as he, more than any other monarch, is blamed by the Deuteronomistic writer for Judah's demise. As we will see, the lingering effects of his sins are such that even the cultic reformation and cleansing of the nation by his grandson, the pious King Josiah, will not be able to stop the country's slide toward annihilation.

As one of the villains of the Deuteronomistic History, Manasseh is portrayed as a completely flat, one-dimensional character.[2] Revealing little about the figure, the biblical writer presents his reign as composed entirely of a series of misdeeds. Yet Manasseh's lengthy tenure as king (fifty-five years) calls into question this negative account. The cageyness of the account in 2 Kings 22 hints that there is something to conceal. This king, for some reason, appears to have been made the scapegoat for later writers desirous of someone or something to blame for the calamitous end of the nation and the failure of YHWH to protect the country as

---

1. There are debates about the length and dates of Manasseh's reign. A possible period of co-regency with Manasseh's father, Hezekiah, has been posited.

2. Pauline Viviano, "Exhortation and Admonition in Deuteronomistic Terms: A Comparison of Second Kings 17:7-18, 34-41, Second Kings 21:2-16, and Jeremiah 7:1–8:3," *BR* 56 (2011): 42.

promised.[3] The account of King Amon, whose short reign lasted only two years, concludes the dark, disheartening chapter.

The Reign of Manasseh in Judah (21:1-18)

The account of Manasseh's reign begins with a typical regnal summary, which records his age when he assumes the throne, the total length of his reign, and his mother's name—Hephzibah—followed by the Deuteronomistic assessment of his piety (21:1). Though the introductory summary is usually followed by a list of other events during the tenure of the monarch, the account of Manasseh's reign is made up almost entirely of his numerous wrongdoings and impious infractions. We find out little about this monarch aside from the fact that he transgressed every commandment imaginable. Considering that we are told in the first verse of this chapter that Manasseh reigned fifty-five years—the longest reign of any Davidic monarch—it seems hardly plausible that sinning was the only thing this king accomplished during his long period on the throne. Other reasons need to be sought for why Manasseh is depicted so unfavorably in the Deuteronomistic History.

In part, the reason why Manasseh enjoys such a long rule is that he is only twelve when he becomes king (v. 1). Mysteriously, the text nowhere explains why he was crowned at such a young age and whether he had any older siblings who died or were bypassed for the throne. A period of co-regency with his father might provide a possible explanation. Also lacking is an explication as to why Manasseh is so intent on overturning the religious reforms of his pious father, Hezekiah. Apparently, the pious Hezekiah had little religious influence on his wayward son. Or perhaps Manasseh's actions should be viewed as an overreaction to his father's piety. The first transgression listed for Manasseh is that he rebuilt the high places that his father Hezekiah had destroyed (v. 2). The very act accomplished under Hezekiah, which no other past Davidic monarch achieved—the demolition of high places—is immediately undone by his impious son. Manasseh is portrayed as a malevolent, bitter, and hateful heir, eagerly awaiting his father's death so that he can gleefully restore the high places that his father so proudly removed.

Not just the high places, but Manasseh attempts to wholly reverse the cultic reform enacted by his father. The altars to Baal and the asherah

3. Stuart Lasine, "Manasseh as Villain and Scapegoat," in *The New Literary Criticism and the Hebrew Bible*, ed. J. Cheryl Exum and David J. A. Clines (Sheffield: JSOT Press, 1993), 163 n. 2.

²¹:¹Manasseh was twelve years old when he began to reign; he reigned fifty-five years in Jerusalem. His mother's name was Hephzibah. ²He did what was evil in the sight of the LORD, following the abominable practices of the nations that the LORD drove out before the people of Israel. ³For he rebuilt the high places that his father Hezekiah had destroyed; he erected altars for Baal, made a sacred pole, as King Ahab of Israel had done, worshiped all the host of heaven, and served them. ⁴He built altars in the house of the LORD, of which the LORD had said, "In Jerusalem I will put my name." ⁵He built altars for all the host of heaven in the two courts of the house of the LORD. ⁶He made his son pass through fire; he practiced soothsaying and augury, and dealt with mediums and with wizards. He did much evil in the sight of the LORD, provoking him to anger. ⁷The carved image of Asherah that he had made he set in the house of which the LORD said to David and to his son Solomon, "In this house, and in Jerusalem, which I have chosen out of all the tribes of Israel, I will put my name forever; ⁸I will not cause the feet of Israel to wander any more out of the

poles (on Asherah, see commentary for 2 Kings 13), are both reerected (21:3). Not stopping there, Manasseh is also said to have worshiped the heavenly hosts (21:2), that is, the sun, the moon, the stars, and the planets (Deut 4:19). Just as his father centralized the cult, so Manasseh defies the Yahwistic cult from the center outward. Starting his desecration at the very heart of YHWH worship, he builds altars to these celestial deities in the temple of YHWH (v. 4).

This depiction of Manasseh's wholesale apostasy, especially his predilection for celestial gods, should be viewed with suspicion, however. This "reverence for celestial bodies" was not as un-Israelite as the narrative suggests but a common and longstanding Semitic tradition, traceable back to the second millennium BCE.[4] Despite the attempts by the Deuteronomistic writers to demarcate the worship of YHWH cleanly from that of other celestial gods, the name and worship of Israel's deity were frequently associated with the "images of heavenly bodies."[5]

The prophet Jeremiah, for example, at Jeremiah 7:18 and 44:17-19, in remarks that provide a fascinating window into the lived religions of ancient Israelite women, condemns them for making and offering cakes,

4. Mordechai Cogan and Hayim Tadmor, *II Kings: A New Translation with Introduction and Commentary*, AB 11 (Garden City, NY: Doubleday, 1988), 266.

5. Kelly Whitcomb, "The Queen of Heaven or YHWH of Hosts: Does the God of Israel Protest (In)sufficiently in Jeremiah 44," *Conversations with the Biblical World* 33 (2013): 90.

land that I gave to their ancestors, if only they will be careful to do according to all that I have commanded them, and according to all the law that my servant Moses commanded them." ⁹But they did not listen; Manasseh misled them to do more evil than the nations had done that the LORD destroyed before the people of Israel.

¹⁰The LORD said by his servants the prophets, ¹¹"Because King Manasseh of Judah has committed these abominations, has done things more wicked than all that the Amorites did, who were before him, and has caused Judah also to sin with his idols; ¹²therefore thus says the LORD, the God of Israel, I am bringing upon Jerusalem and Judah such evil that the ears of everyone who hears of it will tingle. ¹³I will stretch over Jerusalem the measuring line for Samaria, and the plummet for the house of Ahab; I will wipe Jerusalem as one wipes a dish, wiping it and turning it upside down. ¹⁴I will cast off the remnant of my heritage, and give them into the hand of their enemies; they shall become a prey and a spoil to all their enemies, ¹⁵because they have done what is evil in my sight and have provoked me

possibly shaped to resemble a standing female figure,[6] to the Queen of Heaven—a celestial goddess.[7] Worshipers likely viewed the Queen of Heaven not as a foreign deity but as a "part of" YHWH.[8] The worship of one deity was seen as coterminous with, not a contravention of, the worship of the other. Hence, Manasseh's religious innovations might not have been as un-Israelite or as heretical as the writers suggest. Rather, his undoing of his father's reform might even be an attempt to return Judah to its more native, syncretistic religious roots—not a wholesale rejection of the one true faith of Israel, as the authors assert.

The list of Manasseh's other sins is equally suspect. His transgressions consist of a hodgepodge of different misdeeds of preceding bad kings.

---

6. William G. Dever, *Did God Have a Wife? Archaeology and Folk Religion in Ancient Israel* (Grand Rapids, MI: Eerdmans, 2005), 190–92, 230–33; Karel J.H. Vriezen, "Cakes and Figurines: Related Women's Cultic Offerings in Ancient Israel," in *On Reading Prophetic Texts: Gender-Specific and Related Studies in Memory of Fokkelien van Dijk-Hemmes*, ed. Bob Becking and Meindert Dijkstra, BibInt 18 (Leiden: Brill, 1996), 251–63.

7. On the different possible identities for the Queen of Heaven, see: Susan Ackerman, "'And the Women Knead Dough': The Worship of the Queen of Heaven in Sixth-Century Judah," in *Gender and Difference in Ancient Israel*, ed. Peggy L. Day (Minneapolis: Fortress, 1989), 110–17; Saul Olyan, "Some Observations Concerning the Identity of the Queen of Heaven," *UF* 19 (1987): 161–74.

8. Teresa Ann Ellis, "Jeremiah 44: What if 'the Queen of Heaven' Is YHWH?" *JSOT* 33 (2009): 487.

to anger, since the day their ancestors came out of Egypt, even to this day."

¹⁶Moreover Manasseh shed very much innocent blood, until he had filled Jerusalem from one end to another, besides the sin that he caused Judah to sin so that they did what was evil in the sight of the LORD.

¹⁷Now the rest of the acts of Manasseh, all that he did, and the sin that he committed, are they not written in the Book of the Annals of the Kings of Judah? ¹⁸Manasseh slept with his ancestors, and was buried in the garden of his house, in the garden of Uzza. His son Amon succeeded him.

Like Ahaz, his prototype,⁹ Manasseh too installs an illegal altar in the temple and passes his son through the fire, a likely reference to child sacrifice (2 Kgs 16:3).¹⁰ Also like Ahaz Manasseh copies the hated northern kings. His erection of the sacred poles and altars for Baal likens him to King Ahab of Israel,¹¹ who in turn is said to have been more wicked than Jeroboam.¹² That Manasseh shares a name with one of the tribal territories in the North hints of his inner northernly qualities. Francesca Stavrakopoulou posits his name might have been what attracted the Deuteronomistic writer to depict him as the ultimate villain¹³—a southern king who is actually a northerner.¹⁴

Even the hated northern kings are presented as better behaved than the detestable Manasseh. Engaging in a full bacchanalia of cultic violations, such as sorcery, soothsaying, and consulting ghosts and spirits—that is,

9. Ehud Ben Zvi, "The Account of the Reign of Manasseh in II Reg 21:1-18 and the Redactional History of the Book of Kings," *ZAW* 103 (1991): 360.

10. On prohibitions on child sacrifice in Deuteronomy, and similarities in language in Deuteronomy and the Deuteronomistic History, see Moshe Weinfeld, "The Worship of Molech and of the Queen of Heaven and Its Background," *UF* 4 (1972): 133–54.

11. On the similarities between Ahab and Manasseh, see Alison Joseph, *The Portrait of the Kings: The Davidic Prototype in Deuteronomistic Poetics* (Minneapolis: Fortress, 2015), 203; William M. Schniedewind, "History and Interpretation: The Religion of Ahab and Manasseh in the Book of Kings," *CBQ* 55 (1993): 649–61.

12. Gina Hens-Piazza, *1–2 Kings*, AOTC (Nashville: Abingdon, 2006), 377.

13. Francesca Stavrakopoulou, "The Blackballing of Manasseh," in *Good Kings and Bad Kings: The Kingdom of Judah in the Seventh Century BCE*, ed. Lester L. Grabbe (London: T&T Clark, 2005), 253. On Manasseh's name, see Francesca Stavrakopoulou, *King Manasseh and Child Sacrifice: Biblical Distortions of Historical Realities*, BZAW 338 (Berlin: de Gruyter, 2004), 116–19.

14. A. Graeme Auld, *Kings without Privilege: David and Moses in the Story of the Bible's Kings* (Edinburgh: T&T Clark, 1994), 85.

necromancy (v. 6)—Manasseh finishes his crime spree with the establishment of a pole of Asherah, a Canaanite deity who, as we noted earlier in
this commentary, might have been a consort of YHWH,[15] in the temple
of YHWH (v. 7). To underscore the magnitude of this offense, the biblical writers remind readers that the temple of YHWH is the place where
the Lord has placed his name forever.[16] By placing idols and altars to
other gods in the same space and place as that which is connected to
the name and presence of YHWH, Manasseh thus undermines claims of
YHWH's uniqueness and makes "the Lord a God among gods."[17] He,
in short, directly attacks YHWH's reputation and, in so doing, dares the
Lord to retaliate.

Manasseh's misdeeds are such that the biblical writer even brings up
the great lawgiver, Moses. Referencing the covenant between God and
Israel, 2 Kings 21:9 states that the very commandments, the keeping of
which was a necessary requirement for the Israelites' continued inhabita-
tion of the land, were being wantonly transgressed by Manasseh. This
evil king urged people to sin all the more, surpassing even the wrongdoing committed by the evil nations, which were previously tossed out
of the land by YHWH (21:9).[18] The message is clear: if YHWH merely
destroyed and evicted these preceding nations, how much more will he
do to his own country for violating their special agreement.

Yet to completely blame the misdeeds of an entire nation on just one
king, especially one who begins his rule when he might have been
twelve, seems excessive. As I noted earlier in this chapter, it is likely
that Manasseh's apostasy did not entail the introduction of foreign cults
so much as a revival of autochthonous or native Canaanite or Israelite
syncretistic practices.[19] And though Manasseh is blamed for the misdeeds
of an entire nation, his religious practices likely had wide support. The
general populace as well as members of the court, many of whom were
probably against Hezekiah's cultic reformation and its attendant strict
observances, probably welcomed Manasseh's return to prereform traditions. Seeing that Hezekiah's religious policies did little to prevent As-

15. See commentary for 2 Kings 13.
16. On "Name Theology," see Sandra Richter, *The Deuteronomistic History and the
Name Theology in the Bible and the Ancient Near East*, BZAW 318 (Berlin: de Gruyter,
2002).
17. Hens-Piazza, *1–2 Kings*, 377.
18. On Canaanites as the Other, see commentary on 2 Kings 16.
19. Morton Smith, "The Veracity of Ezekiel, the Sins of Manasseh, and Jeremiah
44:18," *ZAW* 87 (1975): 15.

syria's attack of Judah or to stem the rise of Assyria during Hezekiah's and Manasseh's reigns, Manasseh's reversal of his father's practices, though harshly disparaged by the Deuteronomistic writers, might have been welcomed by many.[20] Jeremiah 44:15-18, for example, describes a similar instance when, after the destruction of Judah, Judeans return to traditional, syncretistic worship and practices.

Groups that had been economically damaged by Hezekiah's centralization of the cult, such as the rural priests and the noncourt prophets, might have also supported Manasseh's return to more syncretistic practices. Female prophets, seers, cult officials, or artisans who because of their gender or social location were unable to gain employment in the official royal court or temple system might have been part of this group. Susan Ackerman notes, for example, that the Queen of Heaven passages from Jeremiah 7:18 and 44:17-19 show that "women of late seventh- and early sixth-century Judah and Jerusalem exercised religious power."[21] The worship of Asherah[22] might have been widespread and popular especially among women[23] because women had access to a variety of roles in the goddess cult, such as functioning as "singers, dancers, diviners, dream interpreters, mourners, and priestesses."[24]

Adding to the evidence, Mercedes L. García Bachmann, in an examination of the various types of labor engaged in by women, notes that the masculine terminology in biblical Hebrew helps to obscure the occupations of women, including those active in religious professions.[25] This is seconded by Wilda Gafney, who argues that language ambiguities conceal the presence of women prophets. Gafney maintains, however, that despite these ambiguities and despite the attempt to downplay women's roles in modern scholarship, the presence of female prophets

20. Cogan and Tadmor, *II Kings*, 273.

21. Ackerman, "'And the Women Knead Dough,'" 117–18.

22. On Asherah, see commentary on 2 Kings 13.

23. Susan Ackerman, "At Home with the Goddess," in *Symbiosis, Symbolism, and the Power of the Past: Canaan, Ancient Israel and their Neighbors from the Late Bronze Age through Roman Palaestina*, ed. Seymore Gitin and William G. Dever (Winona Lake, IN: Eisenbrauns, 2003), 455–68; William Dever, "Asherah, Consort of Yahweh? New Evidence from Kuntillet 'Ajrud," *BASOR* 255 (1984): 30–31; idem, *Did God Have a Wife?*, 176–251; Saul M. Olyan, *Asherah and the Cult of Yahweh in Israel*, SBLMS 34 (Atlanta: Scholars Press, 1988), 6; Ilona Rashkow, *Taboo or Not Taboo: Sexuality and Family in the Hebrew Bible* (Minneapolis: Fortress, 2000), 53.

24. Rashkow, *Taboo or Not Taboo*, 53.

25. Mercedes L. García Bachmann, *Women at Work in the Deuteronomistic History* (Atlanta: Society of Biblical Literature, 2013), esp. 161–76, 174.

"in each section of the canon" and in "each phase of Israelite history" clearly indicates that they "cannot be read as aberrations, but as a consistent expression of Israelite religious practice."[26]

The later description of Manasseh's tenure in 2 Chronicles 33 records a more equitable and dramatic account of his reign. Attempting to address why an evil king was allowed by God to rule for such a lengthy period, the Chronistic writer depicts the evil king as undergoing a conversion after a traumatic episode that is not recorded in 2 Kings. Though Manasseh begins his reign sinning just as fervently as in the Deuteronomistic account, in Chronicles he has a moment of transformation. Taken prisoner and shackled by the king of Assyria (2 Chr 33:11), Manasseh experiences "a personalized Babylonian deportation."[27] In dire straits, Manasseh turns to YHWH for help (2 Chr 33:12), and God, in turn, heeds Manasseh's prayers and returns him to Jerusalem. Having experienced the power of YHWH firsthand, Manasseh, throughout the rest of the chapter, is a "paradigmatic penitent."[28] The Manasseh of Chronicles thus ends his reign by effectively undoing his earlier, evil cultic innovations by getting rid of all the foreign gods, illegal altars, and images from the country. Manasseh in Chronicles serves a different symbolic purpose: as a representation of Israel's experience of exile and return.[29]

Whether historical or not,[30] the Chronistic account, which has its own theological biases and assumptions,[31] clearly shows that the Deuterono-

---

26. Wilda C. Gafney, *Daughters of Miriam: Women Prophets in Ancient Israel* (Minneapolis: Fortress, 2008), 15.

27. Gary Knoppers, "Saint or Sinner? Manasseh in Chronicles," in *Rewriting Biblical History: Essays on Chronicles and Ben Sira in Honor of Pancratius C. Beentjes*, DCLS 7, ed. Jeremy Corley and Harm van Grol (Berlin: de Gruyter, 2011), 214.

28. Ibid., 211.

29. William Schniedewind, "The Source Citations of Manasseh: King Manasseh in History and Homily," *VT* 41 (1991): 450–55.

30. Cogan and Tadmor think that the account of the kidnapping "agrees well with Assyrian activities in the West" (Cogan and Tadmor, *II Kings*, 271). Philippe Abadie disagrees, stating that the incident likely is "historically very improbable" ("From the Impious Manasseh [2 Kings 21] to the Convert Manasseh [2 Chronicles 33]: Theological Rewriting by the Chronicler," in *The Chronicler as Theologian: Essays in Honor of Ralph W. Klein*, ed. M. Patrick Graham, Steven L. McKenzie, and Gary N. Knoppers, JSOTSup 371 [London: T&T Clark, 2003], 96).

31. On the ideology, themes, and aims of the Chronicler, see Sara Japhet, *I & II Chronicles: A Commentary* (Louisville: Westminster John Knox, 1993), 43–49; idem, *The Ideology of the Book of Chronicles and Its Place in Biblical Thought* (Winona Lake, IN: Eisenbrauns, 2009).

mistic account of Manasseh's reign in 2 Kings, with its focus on delineating only Manasseh's misdeeds, is also purposefully partisan. As we will discuss in more detail in the next chapter, the utterly negative portrayal of Manasseh prepares the reader for the reign of his antithesis, Josiah, in 2 Kings 22, who will implement a reform that will in effect reverse all of Manasseh's evil deeds. The account of Manasseh's conversion and repentance in 2 Chronicles, even if it were historical, would have hindered the story of Josiah that the Deuteronomistic writer wanted to tell.[32] Josiah would have no remaining misdeeds to undo during his reform had Manasseh been shown to have gotten to them earlier. In 2 Kings, Manasseh remains evil through and through—"a cipher" who symbolizes and is blamed for the transgressions of an entire nation.[33]

Unsurprisingly, 2 Kings 21:10-15 states in no uncertain terms that YHWH has irrevocably decided to bring disaster upon Judah and Jerusalem because of Manasseh. This disaster, indeed, will be so horrifying and catastrophic that it would make the ears of those who hear about it tingle (צלל) (v. 12)—a vivid expression found in other parts of the biblical text (1 Sam 3:11 and Jer 19:3). Continuing with the lively imagery, YHWH states that he will stretch out a plumb line and a measuring line, tools utilized in construction, so as to deconstruct and undo or unbuild Judah. YHWH is pictured in these verses like an urban appraiser deciding which structures to demolish.[34] Concluding with a final image, this time of a meal, 2 Kings 21:13 promises that God will wipe out Jerusalem like a plate, even upturning it to make sure that nothing and no one remains unscathed. Sated and full, YHWH, it appears, is glutted with the sins of Judah and cannot take any more.[35]

Ending on a personal note that signifies that God has given up all hope, YHWH declares that he will abandon "the remnant of my inheritance," a poignant image alluding to the demise of the Northern Kingdom. Now only the Judeans remain as a people chosen by YHWH to be his special share (Deut 9:26, 29; 32:9; 1 Kgs 8:51, 32). Having lost all hope that the nation will behave appropriately, God will now allow enemies to besiege and plunder the only "inheritance" he has left: Judah. In so doing, YHWH appears to signal the abdication of his masculine duty of

32. Joseph, *Portrait of the Kings*, 215–23; Song-Mi Suzie Park, *Hezekiah and the Dialogue of Memory* (Minneapolis: Fortress, 2015), 236–50.

33. Viviano, "Exhortation and Admonition," 42.

34. Hens-Piazza, *1–2 Kings*, 378.

35. Cogan and Tadmor, *II Kings*, 269.

protecting his city and its people. As we have seen before, infidelity to YHWH's covenant and lack of recognition of YHWH as the sole master of Judah inevitably leads to death and destruction—the very opposite of the things promised by YHWH, the God of life, reproduction, and healing.

The dejected yet definitive tone of 2 Kings 21:10-15 has led many scholars to argue that this passage is a later, postexilic insertion.[36] Having experienced the destruction of Judah and Jerusalem, a later writer/editor added this passage to explain why the reformation of the cult by Manasseh's antithesis, Josiah, in the following chapters of 2 Kings, was ineffective in forestalling or nullifying the destruction. Manasseh's sins were so overwhelming that even the righteous action of the good king Josiah could not stop the assured exile. The exilic writer was thus able to place the blame for the destruction of the nation on the worst king of Judah, Manasseh. Manasseh's sins were so overwhelmingly bad and numerous that God had no choice but to reject his chosen nation. Thus by inserting the notice of exile in this pericope, the author can subtly offer an explanation for why the destruction happened and thus partially resolve a theological quandary raised by the nation's demise: why did YHWH, the God of Judah, fail to protect his own country?

As discussed in the preceding sections, one of the masculine credentials of YHWH is his ability to defend his nation. The destruction of Judah would have led to serious doubts and questions about the masculine prowess and power of YHWH. It might have appeared to some that YHWH had been defeated by a stronger, more manly, and more powerful deity. This passage subtly addresses such doubts by depicting YHWH as planning and thus allowing for this calamity. YHWH knew, permitted, or even caused this devastation because of the overwhelming sinfulness of his country. If YHWH allowed the destruction and knew and planned the exile of Judah, then it cannot be the case that he was defeated by another more powerful and more masculine deity. The masculinity of YHWH thus remains undamaged, salvaged by the placement of blame on the misbehavior of the Judean people and their awful king, Manasseh.

36. Ben Zvi, "Account of the Reign of Manasseh," 355–74, esp. 361–64; Cogan and Tadmor, *II Kings*, 273; Frank Moore Cross, *Canaanite Myth and Hebrew Epic: Essays in the History of the Religion of Israel* (Cambridge, MA: Harvard University Press, 1973), 278–79, 285–89; Baruch Halpern, "Why Manasseh Is Blamed for the Babylonian Exile: The Evolution of a Biblical Tradition," *VT* 48 (1998): 486, 489–92; Joseph, *Portrait of the Kings*, 190, 215; Lasine, "Manasseh as Villain and Scapegoat," 175–83; Stavrakopoulou, *King Manasseh and Child Sacrifice*, 38.

Adding to the evidence that 2 Kings 21:10-15 was likely a later insertion, the next verse (21:16), which states that Manasseh shed much blood, appears to continue the account of wrongdoing in 2 Kings 21:2-8. This may serve as the climax of the pericope.[37] Some scholars believe that this charge may refer to human sacrifice[38] while others argue that the phrase "to shed innocent blood" in prophetic literature of the late monarchic period usually refers to the oppression of the poor and the underprivileged (e.g., Jer 7:6; 22:3, 17; Ezek 22:6-7, 12-13, 25-31).[39] If the latter, it is telling that the biblical writers regard the apex of Manasseh's wrongdoings—the one sin, which was regarded as the most heinous among all the transgressions committed by Manasseh, the most evil king of Judah—as economic injustice or the maltreatment of the poor and marginalized. From a liberationist perspective, this verse would seem to suggest that the treatment of the needy was an important concern of some of the biblical writers.

This verse accusing Manasseh of "shedding innocent blood" was given a more lively interpretation in postbiblical traditions. In these legends, one of the innocent people whose blood was shed by the evil king was Isaiah, the prophet. In *The Martyrdom of Isaiah*, a pseudepigraphical Christian work from around the first century CE, the prophet is said to have been sawed in half during Manasseh's reign. Similar traditions are also recorded in classical Jewish and Christian texts, such as the *Lives of the Prophets*. For example, the rabbinic midrashim (b. Sanh. 103b; b. Yev. 49b; y. Sanh.10.28c; Targ. Isa. 66.1; Pesiq. Rab. 4:3) also attribute the murder of Isaiah to Manasseh. Some texts even argue that Manasseh, in murdering Isaiah, killed a family member since Isaiah was Manasseh's maternal grandfather (y. Sanh. 10:28c). Other later traditions further amplify the evil characterization of Manasseh by stating that this king raped married women (2 Bar. 64:2-3), committed incest by violating his own sister (b. Sanh. 103b), and routinely massacred the prophets (Josephus, *Ant.* 10.38).[40] Considering the lively postbiblical traditions as well as the varied accounts of this king in 2 Kings and 2 Chronicles, the reader is left to decide whether Manasseh was an unrepentant evildoer or an unfortunate scapegoat of the biblical writer.

37. Cogan and Tadmor, *II Kings*, 269.

38. Hens-Piazza, *1–2 Kings*, 378.

39. Ibid.

40. For more on postbiblical traditions concerning Manasseh, see Stavrakopoulou, *King Manasseh and Child Sacrifice*, 121–33.

The Short Reign of Amon in Judah (21:19-26)

The chapter concludes with a very concise account of the short, two-year reign of Manasseh's son, Amon, over Judah. Almost as an addendum, the reader is told only the age when Amon begins his reign, the length of his tenure, his mother's name, and that Amon followed in the sinful footsteps of his father before he is swiftly assassinated. Ehud Ben Zvi explains that the short description of his reign results from Amon's unfortunate location between the "two main 'players' of the dtr-H"—Manasseh and Josiah—which left Amon little role to play in the Deuteronomistic History.[41]

Bespeaking political turmoil, a feature shared by the northern monarchy before its demise, 2 Kings 21:23 states that Amon's courtiers plotted against him and killed him in the palace. The reason for the plot and the subsequent murder is unclear. Perhaps there were some who were unhappy with Manasseh's innovations to the temple and to the state cult, or perhaps Amon did something that induced the conspiracy. Abraham Malamat believes that Amon may have been assassinated by an anti-Assyrian party.[42] No matter the reason, as soon as the assassins murder Amon, they are killed in turn by the powerful people of the land. As we saw in the narratives about Athaliah and Joash (2 Kings 11), the people of the land, who seem to have some influence in the court of Judah, appear to be a faction in the country interested in the continuation of the Davidic monarchy (v. 24). After the assassination of Amon, 2 Kings 21:24 states that the people of the land set Josiah, Amon's son, on the throne, thereby concluding the short account about Amon. As with Manasseh, so also with Amon—little more is told of their story except that they were sinful.

41. Ben Zvi, "Account of the Reign of Manasseh," 361.

42. Abraham Malamat, "The Historical Background of the Assassination of Amon King of Judah," *IEJ* 3 (1953): 26–29. Cogan and Tadmor disagree with Malamat's conclusion (Cogan and Tadmor, *II Kings*, 275–76).

[19]Amon was twenty-two years old when he began to reign; he reigned two years in Jerusalem. His mother's name was Meshullemeth daughter of Haruz of Jotbah. [20]He did what was evil in the sight of the LORD, as his father Manasseh had done. [21]He walked in all the way in which his father walked, served the idols that his father served, and worshiped them; [22]he abandoned the LORD, the God of his ancestors, and did not walk in the way of the LORD.

[23]The servants of Amon conspired against him, and killed the king in his house. [24]But the people of the land killed all those who had conspired against King Amon, and the people of the land made his son Josiah king in place of him. [25]Now the rest of the acts of Amon that he did, are they not written in the Book of the Annals of the Kings of Judah? [26]He was buried in his tomb in the garden of Uzza; then his son Josiah succeeded him.

2 Kings 22:1–23:37

The Prophecy of Huldah and the Reign of Josiah in Judah

Reigning during the waning years of the Neo-Assyrian Empire, Josiah (640–609 BCE), the most important king of the Deuteronomistic History, comes to the throne of Judah. Pictured as an anti-Manasseh, Josiah reverses the cultic misdeeds and illegal innovations of his father, Manasseh, who, in turn, reversed the cultic renovations of his pious father, Hezekiah. The wavering pattern of bad king (Ahaz), good king (Hezekiah), very bad king (Manasseh), and finally very good king (Josiah) presented in the final chapters of 2 Kings culminates with the reign of Josiah. At the center of the narrative about the zealous, pious Judean king stands the figure of Huldah, the prophet, who offers an oracle about the newly discovered book of the law, which is found during the temple repairs. Standing as the interpreter of the things to come, her unfulfilled prophecy about Josiah's peaceful demise functions as a symbol of the dashed hopes of Josiah's reign.

The Beginning of Josiah's Reign and the Renovation of the Temple (22:1-7)

The account of Josiah's reign begins with a typical introductory summary noting the age when he begins his rule, the length of his reign, his

^{22:1}Josiah was eight years old when he began to reign; he reigned thirty-one years in Jerusalem. His mother's name was Jedidah daughter of Adaiah of Bozkath. ²He did what was right in the sight of the LORD, and walked in all the way of his father David; he did not turn aside to the right or to the left.

³In the eighteenth year of King Josiah, the king sent Shaphan son of Azaliah, son of Meshullam, the secretary, to the house of the LORD, saying, ⁴"Go up to the high priest Hilkiah, and have him count the entire sum of the money that has been brought into the house of the LORD, which the keepers of the threshold have collected from the people; ⁵let it be given into the hand of the workers who have the oversight of the house of the LORD; let them give it to the workers who are at the house of the LORD, repairing the house, ⁶that is, to the carpenters, to the builders, to the masons; and let them use it to buy timber and quarried stone to repair the house. ⁷But no accounting shall be asked from them for the money that is delivered into their hand, for they deal honestly."

mother's name,[1] and the Deuteronomistic assessment of his fidelity to the covenant. Josiah's rating becomes progressively superlative in the narrative.

First, Josiah is described as doing "right in the sight of the LORD," an evaluation applied to only a few kings (1 Kgs 15:11; 2 Kgs 18:30). Moreover, he is said to have "walked in all the ways of his father David" (v. 2). As remarked earlier in the commentary on 2 Kings 18:1-8, only two Judean kings—Hezekiah and Josiah—are compared to this famous monarch. Some scholars have wondered whether the subsequent description of Josiah's pious deeds paints him as even surpassing David in faithfulness and piety.[2] Finally, outperforming Hezekiah, Josiah is said "to not turn aside to the right or to the left"—a common phrase in Deuteronomy (Deut 2:27; 5:29; 17:20; 28:14)—which, when applied to a monarch, marks the figure as an ideal Israelite king.[3] A later evaluation, which directly contravenes the earlier superlative assessment given to Hezekiah, sums up Josiah's surpassing greatness: "Before him there was no king like him, who turned to the Lord with all his heart, with all his soul and with all his might, according to all the law of Moses; nor did

---

1. On the naming of the queen mothers, see the essay, "The Naming of the Queen Mothers" by Ginny Brewer-Boydston, in the commentary for 2 Kings 12.

2. Gina Hens-Piazza, *1–2 Kings*, AOTC (Nashville: Abingdon, 2006), 382.

3. Ibid., 383.

any like him arise after him" (23:25). This unique praise, which is based on Deuteronomy 6:5, appears to mimic the acclaim given to Moses in Deuteronomy 34:10, thereby placing Josiah, the unsurpassed king, on par with Moses, the unsurpassed prophet.[4]

According to 2 Kings, Josiah does not begin the renovations of the temple until the eighteenth year of his reign. Considering that Josiah was only eight years old when he assumed the throne, the delay is understandable. This ten-year lapse, however, appears to have annoyed the Chronicler, who states that, contra 2 Kings, Josiah started seeking God even as a boy (2 Chr 34:3). It might have been the case that Judah was ruled by intermediaries, perhaps from among the people of the land, while the king was a child.[5] In this, Josiah shares many features with King Joash of 2 Kings 12—another king who was installed on the throne of Judah as a child by the people of the land. The country was likely ruled by proxies until Joash came of age as well. The most important detail that the two kings share, however, is that both Joash and Josiah renovate the temple. It has been noted that verbal similarities (2 Kgs 22:5-6 and 12:12-13; 22:7 and 12:16) in the accounts of the two kings suggest that the description of Josiah's renovation in 2 Kings 22 is based on the description of the temple restoration by Joash in 2 Kings 12.[6] Unlike in Joash's case, however, where his initial attempt to renovate was unsuccessful because of the improper collection of money, in the case of the superlative Josiah, the renovations go off without a hitch. Josiah appears to be a natural manager, knowing exactly how to order the high priest to collect and distribute the money needed for the work (vv. 4-7). That Josiah surpasses Joash in the refurbishment and care of the temple is irrefutable.

The Discovery of the Book and Huldah's Prophecy (22:8-20)

In the midst of Josiah's renovations of the temple, there is a momentous discovery. Hilkiah, the high priest, informs Shaphan, the secretary, that a book of the law was found during the repairs.[7]

---

4. Mordechai Cogan and Hayim Tadmor, *II Kings: A New Translation with Introduction and Commentary*, AB 11 (Garden City, NY: Doubleday, 1988), 291.

5. Ibid., 281.

6. Ibid., 293.

7. The identity of this mysterious text has been a much-discussed question. Many scholars have long argued that the likely identity of the book was the book of

⁸The high priest Hilkiah said to Shaphan the secretary, "I have found the book of the law in the house of the LORD." When Hilkiah gave the book to Shaphan, he read it. ⁹Then Shaphan the secretary came to the king, and reported to the king, "Your servants have emptied out the money that was found in the house, and have delivered it into the hand of the workers who have oversight of the house of the LORD." ¹⁰Shaphan the secretary informed the king, "The priest Hilkiah has given me a book." Shaphan then read it aloud to the king.

¹¹When the king heard the words of the book of the law, he tore his clothes.

¹²Then the king commanded the priest Hilkiah, Ahikam son of Shaphan, Achbor son of Micaiah, Shaphan the secretary, and the king's servant Asaiah, saying, ¹³"Go, inquire of the LORD for me, for the people, and for all Judah, concerning the words of this book that has been found; for great is the wrath of the LORD that is kindled against us, because our ancestors did not obey the words of this book, to do according to all that is written concerning us."

¹⁴So the priest Hilkiah, Ahikam, Achbor, Shaphan, and Asaiah went to the prophetess Huldah the wife of Shallum son of Tikvah, son of Harhas, keeper of the wardrobe; she resided in Jeru-

By depicting the discovery as almost accidentally occurring during the temple restoration, the narrative suggests that the book had been previously misplaced and lost for many years.[8] News of the discovery of the text passes from a cultic official to a court official and, finally, to the king. When the contents are read aloud to King Josiah, he dramatically reacts by tearing his clothes in a sign of deep mourning (v. 11). By displaying Josiah's reaction before telling the reader of the book's content, the narrative sets up a mystery: what horrible things are written in this book? The resolution of the mystery—how Josiah and his crew will fix the problem—is established as the climax of the narrative.

The mystery of the book's content thickens as the ever-active Josiah sends a group on a mission to figure out a way to deter God's wrath, which the king declares has been unleashed by the continual disregard of the commands found within the newly discovered book (v. 13). The group, consisting of the high priest, Hilkiah, the secretary, Shaphan, and other court officials and priests, is sent by the king to a prophet named Huldah, who is

---

Deuteronomy or some earlier version of this text (Cogan and Tadmor, *II Kings*, 294). This hypothesis dates as far back as the early church fathers, such as Jerome (Richard Elliott Friedman, *Who Wrote the Bible?* [New York: HarperOne, 1997], 101).

8. Hens-Piazza, *1–2 Kings*, 384.

salem in the Second Quarter, where they consulted her. [15]She declared to them, "Thus says the LORD, the God of Israel: Tell the man who sent you to me, [16]Thus says the LORD, I will indeed bring disaster on this place and on its inhabitants—all the words of the book that the king of Judah has read. [17]Because they have abandoned me and have made offerings to other gods, so that they have provoked me to anger with all the work of their hands, therefore my wrath will be kindled against this place, and it will not be quenched. [18]But as to the king of Judah, who sent you to inquire of the LORD, thus shall you say to him, Thus says the LORD, the God of Israel: Regarding the words that you have heard, [19]because your heart was penitent, and you humbled yourself before the LORD, when you heard how I spoke against this place, and against its inhabitants, that they should become a desolation and a curse, and because you have torn your clothes and wept before me, I also have heard you, says the LORD. [20]Therefore, I will gather you to your ancestors, and you shall be gathered to your grave in peace; your eyes shall not see all the disaster that I will bring on this place." They took the message back to the king.

said to be the wife of Shallum, a royal official—the keeper of the wardrobe (v. 14). Considering the occupation of her husband, it appears that Huldah and her family were also affiliated with the royal administration. Moreover, though she is the only named woman prophet in the history of the Northern and Southern Kingdoms,[9] the presence of a female prophet so closely connected with the court whose prophecies were well-regarded enough to visit on such a momentous occasion suggests the existence of other unnamed female cultic or prophetic officials in ancient Israel. The text offers no special comment about Huldah being a female prophet, thus suggesting that it was not an unusual occupation for a woman to hold.[10] The presence and position of Huldah suggests that prophecy might have been considered a religious vocation that was "open to women on an equal basis with men."[11] Claudia Camp neatly summarizes the importance

9. Cogan and Tadmor, *II Kings*, 283. Huldah is one of four named female prophets in the Hebrew biblical corpus. The others are Miriam (Exod 15:20-21), Deborah (Judg 4:4-16), and Noadiah (Neh 6:14).

10. Mercedes L. García Bachmann, *Women at Work in the Deuteronomistic History* (Atlanta: Society of Biblical Literature, 2013), esp. 161–76, 174; Wilda C. Gafney, *Daughters of Miriam: Women Prophets in Ancient Israel* (Minneapolis: Fortress, 2008), 15; Hens-Piazza, *1–2 Kings*, 384.

11. Claudia Camp, "1 and 2 Kings" in *The Women's Bible Commentary*, ed. Carol A. Newsom and Sharon H. Ringe (Louisville: Westminster John Knox, 1992), 115.

of Huldah when she states that this prophet, as the first interpreter of this important document, is the one who first authorizes what will become the "core of scripture" for Judaism and Christianity.[12]

Diane Edelman, however, argues that Huldah might not originally have been so intimately connected to the worship of YHWH. Rather, Huldah might have been an important prophet associated with Asherah,[13] YHWH's consort, who is also frequently portrayed in Ugaritic myths as an intercessory figure.[14] Considering YHWH's possible wrath, it might be that Huldah was approached by the delegation to consult Asherah so that the goddess could appeal for leniency on their behalf from YHWH.[15] A postexilic writer edited Huldah's portrayal, so as to recast her as a female Jeremiah and turn her into a prophetess of YHWH when Asherah's role as YHWH's consort and coruler of heaven fell out of religious fashion.[16] Edelman's reading of Huldah points to the possible presence of not just female prophets and religious leaders affiliated with the YHWH cult but also cults in Israel dedicated to the worship of various goddesses.

Excursus: Female Prophets, Magicians, and Diviners

One should not dismiss female prophetic participation too easily, since the ancestors of prophecy are two mothers, Miriam and Deborah, and both are highly honored in their leading role as singers and musicians, like these prophets . . . there were several women closely related to music, worship, prophecy and especially to divinatory and magic practices deemed "abominable" by pure Yahwists, while others, like this widow [in 2 Kgs 4:1-7], seem to belong to a group in good standing with Yahwism. At any rate, my main point . . . is to call attention to the possible "wives of members of companies of prophets" like the starving widow saved thanks to Elisha's advice, who may have been involved in prophetic activity as part of hereditary guilds.[17]

Mercedes L. García Bachmann

---

12. Ibid.

13. On Asherah, see commentary for 2 Kings 13.

14. Diane Edelman, "Huldah the Prophet—Of Yahweh or Asherah?," in *A Feminist Companion to Samuel and Kings*, ed. Athalya Brenner, FCB 5 (Sheffield: Sheffield Academic, 1994), 231–50.

15. Ibid., 246–48.

16. Ibid., 249–50.

17. García Bachmann, *Women at Work*, 174.

According to Mordechai Cogan and Hayim Tadmor, there might be yet another reason why the delegation decided to approach a woman prophet, in particular, for the task of receiving YHWH's word about the book. They note that the rabbis believed that women prophets were more likely to give more merciful prophecies than the cheerless male prophets who normally predicted only doom and gloom (see b. Meg. 14b).[18] Aside from stereotypical ideas about women being the gentler sex,[19] there might be some historical basis for this assertion. Cogan and Tadmor state that in the seventh century BCE, particularly in the Assyrian court, women prophets often gave prophecies concerning divine protection for monarchs against their enemies.[20]

If this is the case, Huldah's prophecy does not conform to these expectations. Her prophecy is neither friendly nor favorable; it is equally as doom and gloom as the prophecies of her male contemporaries such as Jeremiah. She states that YHWH's decision to destroy Judah for abandoning him and worshiping other gods cannot be mitigated or reversed (v. 17). The demise of Judah, thus, is certain and unstoppable. YHWH apparently has had enough of the continual worship of idols and other deities by the Israelites (v. 17). Renita Weems even argues that Huldah's gender is used to emphasize "the inescapability of Judah's fate":[21] "*Even a woman* (granted, one renowned and skilled) could see . . . that the kingdom was doomed to disaster. Why couldn't the leading men see the same thing?"[22] For going through all the effort, however, Josiah is offered a consolation prize. As with Hezekiah, God promises that the pious Josiah will die before this disaster occurs, and therefore he will not be a witness to the upcoming catastrophe (v. 20). The good king instead will go to the grave in peace (v. 20)—an unfulfilled prophecy to which we will shortly return.

The odd gloominess and finality to Huldah's prophecy defies expectations, both theologically and literarily. Why does the narrative go through all the trouble to have this important book be discovered,

---

18. Cogan and Tadmor, *II Kings*, 283.

19. Renita J. Weems, "Huldah, the Prophet: Reading a (Deuteronomistic) Woman's Identity," in *A God So Near: Essays on Old Testament Theology in Honor of Patrick D. Miller*, ed. Brent A. Strawn and Nancy R. Bowen (Winona Lake, IN: Eisenbrauns, 2003), 329.

20. Cogan and Tadmor, *II Kings*, 284.

21. Weems, "Huldah, the Prophet," 330.

22. Ibid., 335. Italics are original.

read, and interpreted by Huldah only to receive a prophecy about the unstoppability of the coming destruction? Equally mysterious is Josiah's reaction to this prophecy: After the visit to Huldah, the good king begins a thorough and sweeping cultic reform of the country. Why does he begin such a reform when he has just learned of the prophet's declaration that Zion's destruction is inevitable? For these reasons, scholars argue that Huldah's prophecy has been reworked by later editors, likely after the exile of Judah had already occurred.[23] Updating the text after Zion's demise, its end is depicted as known and irrevocably decided on by YHWH. As we noted in the preceding chapter, the depiction of the exile as preordained and thus allowed by YHWH serves to mitigate theological doubts about the reliability and power of this deity. In so doing, it serves to salvage the masculinity of YHWH, which would have been questioned with the destruction of his country, Judah.

Excursus: The Forgotten Female Prophets of the Hebrew Bible

First, women engage in prophecy in all three parts of the Hebrew canon. Although oracular discourse, particularly accompanied by formulas such as "so says YHWH" and "an oracle of YHWH," is the dominant expression of prophecy, there is a broad range of activities the prophets of Israel and Judah undertake. These activities include engaging in intercessory prayer, dancing, drumming, singing, giving and interpreting laws, delivering oracles on behalf of YHWH (sometimes in ecstasy, sometimes demonstratively), resolving disputes, working wonders, mustering troops and fighting battles, archiving their oracles in writing, and experiencing visions.

Perhaps not every action undertaken by a prophet is itself prophetic, but there is still a wide range of behavior that is expressly characterized as prophetic by the use of *n-b-'*. Examples would include the following: Miriam's singing, dancing, and drumming, Ezekiel's year-long sign-action prophecy while lying on the

23. Erik Eynikel, *The Reform of King Josiah and the Composition of the Deuteronomistic History*, OtSt 33 (Leiden: Brill, 1996), 354; Steven L. McKenzie, *The Trouble with Kings: The Composition of the Book of Kings in the Deuteronomistic History*, VTSup 42 (Leiden: Brill, 1991), 112; Richard D. Nelson, *The Double Redaction of the Deuteronomistic History* (Sheffield: JSOT Press, 1981), 17; Ian Provan, *Hezekiah and the Book of Kings: A Contribution to the Debate about the Composition of the Deuteronomistic History*, BZAW 142 (Berlin: de Gruyter, 1988), 147–51.

ground, Jeremiah's soiled-loincloth-as-object-lesson, the oracles of Habakkuk and Huldah, the children conceived by Isaiah and the anonymous woman-prophet, and the mantic ecstasies of the band of prophets.

The Hebrew Scriptures are the primary written source for analysis of religious practices of the ancient Israelites; however, they represent a narrow, sectarian, and androcentric perspective. Therefore, they do not accurately reflect the religious experiences of all ancient Israelite women and men throughout the millennium the Hebrew Bible encompasses. In addition, the male focus of most of the texts has led their initial and subsequent interpreters, in separate and overlapping religious and academic bodies, to produce an interpretive tradition that is dismissive of the few women whom the Hebrew Bible designates as prophets. Androcentrism, and in some cases outright misogyny, has fostered the investigation of male prophets as the primary, if not the sole, objects of study in work on biblical prophecy.[24]

Wilda C. Gafney

Josiah's Cultic Reform (23:1-28)

Either Josiah is innocently unaware of Huldah's prophecy of unstoppable destruction or he is a fiercely determined king. If he knows about the foretold doom of his country, the description of his massive reform indicates that he will go down fighting. Ever the managerial leader, Josiah calls *all* the elders of Judah together (v. 1) and goes to the temple where they and *all* the people of Judah, *all* the Jerusalemites, priests, prophets—that is, *all* the people "great and small"—hear the content of the book of the covenant as it is read aloud (v. 2).

After the book has been read, the king leads everyone in the community to make a new a covenant with YHWH. The agreement, according to 2 Kings 23:3, is diligently accepted by *all* the people. The repeated stress on *all* indicates the totality of the community involved as well as the all-encompassing nature of Josiah's reform. By borrowing the language from the covenant-making ceremony in Deuteronomy 29:1-27 in the description of this new covenant,[25] the text presents Josiah as redoing and thereby correcting the first covenant between Israel and YHWH, which Israel has so flagrantly violated in the past. In so doing, the hope is that

---

24. Gafney, *Daughters of Miriam*, 6.
25. Hens-Piazza, *1–2 Kings*, 386.

^{23:1}Then the king directed that all the elders of Judah and Jerusalem should be gathered to him. ²The king went up to the house of the LORD, and with him went all the people of Judah, all the inhabitants of Jerusalem, the priests, the prophets, and all the people, both small and great; he read in their hearing all the words of the book of the covenant that had been found in the house of the LORD. ³The king stood by the pillar and made a covenant before the LORD, to follow the LORD, keeping his commandments, his decrees, and his statutes, with all his heart and all his soul, to perform the words of this covenant that were written in this book. All the people joined in the covenant.

⁴The king commanded the high priest Hilkiah, the priests of the second order, and the guardians of the threshold, to bring out of the temple of the LORD all the vessels made for Baal, for Asherah, and for all the host of heaven; he burned them outside Jerusalem in the fields of the Kidron, and carried their ashes to Bethel. ⁵He deposed the idolatrous priests whom the kings of Judah had ordained to make offerings in the high places at the cities of Judah and around Jerusalem; those also who made offerings to Baal, to the sun, the moon, the constellations, and all the host of the heavens. ⁶He brought out the image of Asherah from the house of the LORD, outside Jerusalem, to the Wadi Kidron, burned it at the Wadi Kidron, beat it to dust and threw the dust of it upon the graves of the common people. ⁷He broke down

the anger of YHWH directed at past contraventions of the covenant can also be undone—corrected, as it were—by this new covenant that *all* of Judah, from great to small, from laity to religious official, have now agreed assiduously to follow.

Not stopping there, Josiah demonstrates his uncompromising loyalty to YHWH by systematically destroying and removing cult personnel or items affiliated with any other deity besides YHWH. He thoroughly cleans house. He burns all the vessels for Baal, Asherah, or the hosts of heaven (v. 4); he deposes all the idolatrous priests working at the high places who are worshiping Baal or engaged in astrology (vv. 5, 8-9); he removes the male temple prostitutes (v. 7) and mediums and wizards (v. 24); he takes the images of Asherah, which Manasseh set up in the temple (2 Kgs 21), and burns them and throws their dust on the graves of common people (v. 6); he destroys the high places, the illegal altars, the asherah poles and pillars, the idols, teraphims, and other abominations (v. 24). He defiles the Topheth, where the Israelites made child sacrifice to Molech (v. 10), and removes the horses, animals that served

the houses of the male temple prostitutes that were in the house of the LORD, where the women did weaving for Asherah. ⁸He brought all the priests out of the towns of Judah, and defiled the high places where the priests had made offerings, from Geba to Beersheba; he broke down the high places of the gates that were at the entrance of the gate of Joshua the governor of the city, which were on the left at the gate of the city. ⁹The priests of the high places, however, did not come up to the altar of the LORD in Jerusalem, but ate unleavened bread among their kindred. ¹⁰He defiled Topheth, which is in the valley of Ben-hinnom, so that no one would make a son or a daughter pass through fire as an offering to Molech. ¹¹He removed the horses that the kings of Judah had dedicated to the sun, at the entrance to the house of the LORD, by the chamber of the eunuch Nathan-melech, which was in the precincts; then he burned the chariots of the sun with fire. ¹²The altars on the roof of the upper chamber of Ahaz, which the kings of Judah had made, and the altars that Manasseh had made in the two courts of the house of the LORD, he pulled down from there and broke in pieces, and threw the rubble into the Wadi Kidron. ¹³The king defiled the high places that were east of Jerusalem, to the south of the Mount of Destruction, which King Solomon of Israel had built for Astarte the abomination of the Sidonians, for Chemosh the abomination of Moab, and for Milcom the abomination of the

important cultic functions and that appear to have been utilized in sun worship (v. 11). Next, the reform turns specifically to undoing the cultic innovations of Josiah's predecessors, many of whom function as Josiah's antitheses. Altars made by Ahaz and Manasseh (v. 12), high places built by Solomon for other gods (v. 13), and the infamous altars and high places at Bethel erected by the evil king Jeroboam (v. 15) are demolished. The eradication of the cult center at Bethel is especially significant as it "reestablished Jerusalem's centrality."[26] Taking a small break, Josiah pauses at the burial site of the holy man of God who had predicted, during the reign of Jeroboam, the future rise of Josiah, and the good king commands that his bones be left intact (1 Kgs 13:1-3, 32).

As Josiah's actions at Bethel make clear, it seems that the king extends his reform beyond the boundaries of Judah to the northern region, to Samaria. Though it is unclear how much control the historical Josiah had over

---

26. Cogan and Tadmor, *II Kings*, 300.

Ammonites. [14]He broke the pillars in pieces, cut down the sacred poles, and covered the sites with human bones.

[15]Moreover, the altar at Bethel, the high place erected by Jeroboam son of Nebat, who caused Israel to sin—he pulled down that altar along with the high place. He burned the high place, crushing it to dust; he also burned the sacred pole. [16]As Josiah turned, he saw the tombs there on the mount; and he sent and took the bones out of the tombs, and burned them on the altar, and defiled it, according to the word of the Lord that the man of God proclaimed, when Jeroboam stood by the altar at the festival; he turned and looked up at the tomb of the man of God who had predicted these things.

[17]Then he said, "What is that monument that I see?" The people of the city told him, "It is the tomb of the man of God who came from Judah and predicted these things that you have done against the altar at Bethel." [18]He said, "Let him rest; let no one move his bones." So they let his bones alone, with the bones of the prophet who came out of Samaria. [19]Moreover, Josiah removed all the shrines of the high places that were in the towns of Samaria, which kings of Israel had made, provoking the Lord to anger; he did to them just as he had done at Bethel. [20]He slaughtered on the altars all the priests of the high places who were there, and burned human bones on them. Then he returned to Jerusalem.

the North during this period, in the literature, he cleans house there as well, destroying the high places and, in an act of gruesome sacrifice, slaughtering on the illegal altars the priests who served at these high places (v. 20). Solidifying the complete eradication of every non-Yahwistic cult site as well as its accompanying priests and religious accoutrements, Josiah marks the occasion with a celebration of the Passover in Jerusalem (v. 23), thus fulfilling the directive in Deuteronomy 16:5-6. The significance of this celebration becomes evident when we realize that the last celebration of this holiday occurred in Joshua 5:10-11, when the Israelites entered the land of Canaan under the leadership of Joshua![27] In referencing bygone figures such as Moses and Joshua as well as the preceding evil kings whose cultic installations were undone during the reign of Josiah, the text rewinds the narrative, traveling back through time, all the way back to the point at which Israel first received the covenant and initially entered the promised land. Through this time-traveling narrative, the text conveys the attempt of the pious king, Josiah, to re-

27. Ibid., 290.

²¹The king commanded all the people, "Keep the passover to the LORD your God as prescribed in this book of the covenant." ²²No such passover had been kept since the days of the judges who judged Israel, even during all the days of the kings of Israel and of the kings of Judah; ²³but in the eighteenth year of King Josiah this passover was kept to the LORD in Jerusalem.

²⁴Moreover Josiah put away the mediums, wizards, teraphim, idols, and all the abominations that were seen in the land of Judah and in Jerusalem, so that he established the words of the law that were written in the book that the priest Hilkiah had found in the house of the LORD. ²⁵Before him there was no king like him, who turned to the LORD with all his heart, with all his soul, and with all his might, according to all the law of Moses; nor did any like him arise after him.

²⁶Still the LORD did not turn from the fierceness of his great wrath, by which his anger was kindled against Judah, because of all the provocations with which Manasseh had provoked him. ²⁷The LORD said, "I will remove Judah also out of my sight, as I have removed Israel; and I will reject this city that I have chosen, Jerusalem, and the house of which I said, My name shall be there."

²⁸Now the rest of the acts of Josiah, and all that he did, are they not written in the Book of the Annals of the Kings of Judah?

verse the sins of Israel's ancestors who seemingly began to transgress YHWH's covenant as soon as it was ratified. By going backward to the beginning, Josiah, through his reform, is trying to turn back the great wrath of YHWH, which has been building up since the nation's origins and which appears to have been unleashed by the discovery of the book in the temple (2 Kgs 22:13).

The repetition and long-winded description of Josiah's reforms convey the totality of his religious house cleaning. Every corner of Judah, which was associated in any way with the worship of another deity aside from YHWH, is swept and cleaned. Every trace of any illegal worship in Judah and Israel is eradicated. YHWH is reinstated as the only deity that could be worshiped in Judah and Samaria, and the only place left to worship him properly—indeed, seemingly the only temple left in the entirety of the two nations—is the temple of YHWH in Jerusalem. Acting as YHWH's henchman, Josiah thus institutes strict Yahwism in the country: YHWH is the only God who can now be worshiped in Judah, and the only place in which this can be done suitably is in the temple in Jerusalem.

The fact that this reform occurs immediately after Huldah's prophecy seems to indicate that the prophet, in her original oracle, likely advocated for this cultic centralization as the means by which to stem YHWH's anger and thus stop Judah's path toward destruction. Robert Wilson believes that Huldah might have been related to northern Israelite priestly groups who were very important in encouraging and giving impetus to the reforms of Josiah and perhaps earlier to those of Hezekiah as well.[28]

The list of Josiah's accomplishments during the reform reveals an interesting window into the folk religion in Judah. Despite the arguments presented in the text that the only legitimate worship in Israel was that of YHWH, the list of other cult sites, items, and personnel, which are eradicated by Josiah, shows clearly that the people of Judah were engaged in a variety of syncretistic religious practices. They venerated a wide assortment of gods and goddesses, as shown by the destruction of the asherahs and the altars to Baal. Though the biblical text lauds Josiah's great reform, the fervor with which the king, with the support of the members of the court and the religious elite in Jerusalem, executes the purge of all folk religions, especially those practiced by women, in Judah and Israel could be disturbing for modern readers. In one fell swoop, Josiah rids the country of every other place of worship, from local shrines to regional cult centers like Bethel—places where people had been worshiping for generations. Especially disturbing is the violent manner in which the reforms are enacted. Northern priests who had loyally served in their local sanctuaries for many years are suddenly plucked out, killed, and slaughtered as a sacrifice on the altars as a means of utterly defiling their places of worship (2 Kgs 23:20). What to the biblical writer is a great reform, to the modern reader may look like the zealous, barbaric practices of the Inquisition. Indeed, considering that the main beneficiaries of this reform would have been the priests and other cultic functionaries working at the temple in Jerusalem, it is hardly surprising that the book that gives rise to this reform would be incidentally "found" by a priest during the repairs at that site. As the only legitimate religious practitioners left in the country, the priests at the Jerusalem temple would be able to lay claim to the sacrifices and religious

28. Robert R. Wilson, *Prophecy and Society in Ancient Israel* (Philadelphia: Fortress, 1980), 219–23; Cogan and Tadmor, *II Kings*, 283. For more on the northern roots of the Deuteronomistic reform, see Ernest W. Nicholson, *Deuteronomy and Tradition* (Philadelphia: Fortress, 1967).

dollars of every worshiper in the country and, as such, would have been the real winners of this cultic centralization.

The Untimely Demise of Josiah (23:29-30)

Unfortunately, as the ending to 2 Kings 23 makes clear, the intended climax of the Deuteronomistic History did not work out as expected. The succinct, sudden description of Josiah's end expresses the shock and disappointment caused by his unanticipated demise. Second Kings 23:29 briefly states that Josiah, for an unnamed reason, goes to meet the king of Egypt, Neco, in battle. Without much description or explanation, it states that Neco killed Josiah at this meeting and that the monarch's body was brought back by his servants to be buried in Jerusalem. Why did Josiah go to meet Neco? What was he trying to do, and why was he killed by the pharaoh? Moreover, what about Huldah's earlier prophecy that promised that Josiah would go to the grave in peace for his pious efforts? At the center of these questions is a larger theological quandary: Why does YHWH allow Josiah's reform and efforts to salvage the country to fail so utterly?

As to queries about the purpose of Josiah's visit and the possible motivation behind his death, most scholars offer a historical explanation about the larger geo-political situation in the ancient Near East during the end of Josiah's tenure. The Assyrian Empire, at this point, was in decline and battling the ever-increasing Babylonian threat. Egypt seems to have offered aid to Assyria to stem the rise of Babylon. Most scholars believe that Josiah went to Megiddo to stop Egypt from trying to help the Assyrians. Though the text does not state that a battle occurred, Josiah seems to have been captured and then killed by Neco during this encounter.

Whatever the historical circumstances of Josiah's unfortunate last trip, his sudden, unexpected death is a momentous turning point in the history of Judah. The brevity with which his death is discussed in the biblical text and, as we will see, the succinct manner in which the reigns of the last four monarchs of Judah are described in the final chapters of 2 Kings speak to the shock and horror felt by the biblical writer at Josiah's untimely demise. The theological issue at the center of his death is bound up with a literary concern: the preceding account of this monarch in 2 Kings 22–23 clearly is heading toward a different conclusion and climax. The triumphant narrative of the king's activities effectively readies the country to receive the blessings and protection promised by YHWH. Josiah not only alleviates the anger of YHWH caused by Manasseh's misdeed but also

[29]In his days Pharaoh Neco king of Egypt went up to the king of Assyria to the river Euphrates. King Josiah went to meet him; but when Pharaoh Neco met him at Megiddo, he killed him. [30]His servants carried him dead in a chariot from Megiddo, brought him to Jerusalem, and buried him in his own tomb. The people of the land took Jehoahaz son of Josiah, anointed him, and made him king in place of his father.

undoes Solomon's sins, which had led to the loss of Davidic control over the North. For good measure, he also remedies and reverses the numerous transgressions committed by the northern kings and populace.[29] As Baruch Halpern notes, "Josiah's reign should in prospect herald a time of extensive prosperity and of reconciliation with YHWH comparable to that of David's time, and with a leader comparable in status and in intention to Moses."[30] Yet while the narrative of Josiah's reign raises these hopes and builds to this glorious finish, this glorious ending is suddenly nullified through the short description of his death.

Adding to the theological quandary, the manner of Josiah's death seems to be flagrantly at odds with Huldah's prophecy, which had promised that the king would die in peace. Being killed by a foreign king during a confrontation can hardly be described as "in peace." The apparent contradiction has been noticed by medieval rabbinic commentators, such as Rashi, in his commentary on 2 Kings 22:20.[31] Why has Huldah's unfulfilled oracle been left unedited and intact in the narrative? One possibility is that Huldah's prophecy is fulfilled but ironically so since "in peace" can also refer to one's ally.[32] As Josiah is killed by Egypt, a country that was usually the enemy of Assyria, the monarch, by default, is killed by his ally. Thus, "Josiah died at the hands of one with whom he was in alliance."[33] Another hypothesis is that to die "in peace" does not mean the lack of war as the phrase appears to mean in Genesis 15:15 but refers to proper burial in the family tomb in Judah.[34] Since Josiah does

29. Baruch Halpern, "Why Manasseh Is Blamed for the Babylonian Exile: The Evolution of a Biblical Tradition," VT 48 (1998): 489.

30. Ibid., 489.

31. Ibid., 497.

32. Ibid., 502.

33. Ibid.

34. So Weems, "Huldah, the Prophet," 326.

indeed get a proper burial (2 Kgs 23:30), Huldah's prophecy might not be as faulty as it first appears.[35] Whatever the reason, Josiah's demise appears to have been deeply troubling to late and postbiblical writers. Writers of 2 Chronicles, 1 Esdras, Sirach, 2 Baruch; Jerome's Vulgate; the Syriac Peshitta of 2 Kings, 2 Chronicles, and 1 Esdras; the Targum and the rabbinic texts all offer various explanations for this monarch's untimely demise.[36]

The biblical narrative seems to offer its own explanation of Josiah's unfortunate end and the seeming failure of his reform. At different points in 2 Kings, it states that YHWH has definitively decided to exile and allow the destruction of Judah. After the lengthy lists of Manasseh's transgressions, YHWH promises that he will bring certain disaster on Judah for their long history of sinning (2 Kgs 21:12-15). This promise of guaranteed disaster is repeated by Huldah in 2 Kings 22:16-17 when she declares that the divine wrath unleashed by the bad behavior of the Israelites is unstoppable. In fact, immediately after the long description of Josiah's thorough religious reform and right before we are told of Josiah's meeting with Neco, the narrative abruptly and bleakly states: "Still the LORD did not turn away from the fierceness of his great wrath, by which his anger was kindled against Judah, because of all the provocations with which Manasseh had provoked him" (2 Kgs 23:26).

It seems that the biblical writer, by repeating this warning about how Zion's demise was assured, offers a hint as to why Josiah's reform failed to save his country and himself. Manasseh's sins seem to have been so overwhelming that they doomed Josiah's reform even before it began. Remarks about Judah's unstoppable destruction bookend the description of Josiah's reform, declaring it ineffective before it commences and then reaffirming its nullification after it ends. Also important is the placement of 2 Kings 23:26 right before the description of Josiah's unfortunate end. It seems that Manasseh doomed the restorative effect of Josiah's reform, and the position of 2 Kings 23:26 points to the lasting legacy of this bad king as playing some part in Josiah's early death.

35. H. D. Hoffman, *Reform und Reformen: Untersuchungen zu einem Grundthema der deuteronomistischen Geschichtsschreibung*, ATANT 66 (Zurich: Theologischer Verlag, 1980), 183–85.

36. See Steve Delamarter, "The Death of Josiah in Scripture and Tradition: Wrestling with the Problem of Evil?," *VT* 54 (2004): 29–60; Zipora Talshir, "The Three Deaths of Josiah and the Strata of Biblical Historiography," *VT* 46 (1996): 213–36.

These verses about the inevitable destruction of Zion are usually dated to a point after Judah's demise and exile. Many scholars hold that there were at least two writers/editors of the Deuteronomistic History, usually designated at Dtr1 and Dtr2. The first Deuteronomistic Historian edited and arranged the History so as to culminate with the reign of Josiah. The second historian, Dtr2, updated the History, subtly adding in passages about the assured demise of Judah, which sought to explain the destruction as partially the fault of Manasseh.[37] Though this explanation does not provide a complete explication of why YHWH allowed his country to be destroyed, it mitigates some of the dissonance between theology and historical events and partially salvages the masculinity of YHWH—a masculinity that undoubtedly came to be doubted with the end of this deity's chosen nation.

The Reigns of Jehoahaz and Jehoiakim in Judah (23:31-37)

The nation's final curtain call, however, does not immediately occur after Josiah's death. Rather, in 2 Kings 23:30 the people of the land place one of Josiah's sons, Jehoahaz, on the throne. Why this son, who is neither the oldest nor the next in line for the throne, is chosen instead of his other siblings is not stated in the text. Unlike his father, Jehoahaz is assessed as doing evil in the eyes of YHWH (v. 32), though how much evil he could have accomplished during his short three-month reign is difficult to gauge (v. 31). As soon as Jehoahaz ascends the throne, Neco, for unstated reasons, removes him from power, imprisons him, and takes him to Egypt where he eventually dies (vv. 31, 34). Neco replaces Jehoahaz with a Davidide he likes better, Eliakim, whose name the pharaoh changes to Jehoiakim (608–597 BCE), and the new king taxes the land, especially the people of the land, in order to pay Egypt's heavy tribute. As the forced name change and taxation makes clear, Judah, before its destruction, is no longer free but dominated and controlled by Egypt. The wages of Israel's sin are dramatically demonstrated: the nation that YHWH so powerfully freed from Egyptian enslavement has now returned once again to being Egypt's captive and servant. The end is not far off.

---

37. Friedman, *Who Wrote the Bible?*, 140–41; Frank Moore Cross, *Canaanite Myth and Hebrew Epic: Essays in the History of the Religion of Israel* (Cambridge, MA: Harvard University Press, 1973), 278–89.

³¹Jehoahaz was twenty-three years old when he began to reign; he reigned three months in Jerusalem. His mother's name was Hamutal daughter of Jeremiah of Libnah. ³²He did what was evil in the sight of the LORD, just as his ancestors had done. ³³Pharaoh Neco confined him at Riblah in the land of Hamath, so that he might not reign in Jerusalem, and imposed tribute on the land of one hundred talents of silver and a talent of gold. ³⁴Pharaoh Neco made Eliakim son of Josiah king in place of his father Josiah, and changed his name to Jehoiakim. But he took Jehoahaz away; he came to Egypt, and died there. ³⁵Jehoiakim gave the silver and the gold to Pharaoh, but he taxed the land in order to meet Pharaoh's demand for money. He exacted the silver and the gold from the people of the land, from all according to their assessment, to give it to Pharaoh Neco.

³⁶Jehoiakim was twenty-five years old when he began to reign; he reigned eleven years in Jerusalem. His mother's name was Zebidah daughter of Pedaiah of Rumah. ³⁷He did what was evil in the sight of the LORD, just as all his ancestors had done.

2 Kings 24:1–25:30

The End of Judah and the Deconstruction of Androcentrism

The last two chapters of 2 Kings rush through history, as if in a hurry to get past the story of Judah's gloomy end. Aside from a lack of desire to linger on the narrative of the nation's demise, the fast-paced retelling of the reigns of the last four kings of Judah seems to convey a sense of theological confusion. Can any account explicate or justify YHWH's seeming desertion and lack of defense of his country? More important, does the destruction and exile of Judah signify that, despite the claims made throughout the narrative of 2 Kings, YHWH is not the powerful masculine deity that the text asserts that he is? Does it show that YHWH has been defeated by a stronger, more powerful, more masculine god? The last two chapters of the book in positing but never fully resolving these queries and issues, in the end, provide an interesting deconstruction of the androcentric vision of this deity professed throughout 2 Kings. In so doing, the ending of the narrative, though it describes the disastrous end of the nation, might provide a way forward for a more complex, equitable vision of YHWH.

The Rise of Babylon and the End of Jehoiakim's Rule (24:1-7)

The last two chapters of 2 Kings begin with a new power player on the scene, Babylon. Befitting the usual brevity of the biblical text of 2 Kings,

24:1In his days King Nebuchadnezzar of Babylon came up; Jehoiakim became his servant for three years; then he turned and rebelled against him. 2The LORD sent against him bands of the Chaldeans, bands of the Arameans, bands of the Moabites, and bands of the Ammonites; he sent them against Judah to destroy it, according to the word of the LORD that he spoke by his servants the prophets. 3Surely this came upon Judah at the command of the LORD, to remove them out of his sight, for the sins of Manasseh, for all that he had committed, 4and also for the innocent blood that he had shed; for he filled Jerusalem with innocent blood, and the LORD was not willing to pardon. 5Now the rest of the deeds of Jehoiakim, and all that he did, are they not written in the Book of the Annals of the Kings of Judah? 6So Jehoiakim slept with his ancestors; then his son Jehoiachin succeeded him. 7The king of Egypt did not come again out of his land, for the king of Babylon had taken over all that belonged to the king of Egypt from the Wadi of Egypt to the River Euphrates.

the sudden notice that Babylon came up against Judah (2 Kgs 24:1) is the only indicator that crucial geopolitical shifts have occurred in the region.

Nebuchadnezzar II, the founder of the Neo-Babylonian Empire, a kingdom that will destroy and exile the kingdom of Judah, came to the throne around 605 BCE. After Babylon's defeat of Egypt in the battle of Carchemish (605 BCE), the nation under Nebuchadnezzar established itself as the new central imperial power in the ancient Near East. Shortly afterward, Babylon extended its control "from the Wadi of Egypt to the River Euphrates" (24:7), which included the regions in the eastern Mediterranean that had previously been under Egyptian rule. As a smaller state, Judah was caught between Egypt and Babylon in their struggle for regional power.[1] This is reflected in Judah's wavering of allegiances. Judah under Jehoiakim (608–597 BCE) became a vassal of the new overlord, Babylon. After just three years, however, the king rebelled against Babylon for untold reasons (24:1). The nature of the rebellion is not disclosed, though it might have entailed the withholding of tribute.[2] Oded Lipschits posits that Jehoiakim's rebellion may have stemmed from Egypt's return to power after a brief reprieve. This return induced

1. Abraham Malamat, "The Last Kings of Judah and the Fall of Jerusalem: An Historical—Chronological Study," *IEJ* 18 (1968): 138.

2. J. Philip Hyatt, "New Light on Nebuchadrezzar and Judean History," *JBL* 75 (1956): 279.

Jehoiakim to revert back to Egyptian control.[3] Shortly thereafter, Jehoiakim promptly died, perhaps assassinated in a palace revolt,[4] leaving his son Jehoiachin to suffer the repercussions of his act (24:6).

Before we are told of the dreadful consequences of this rebellion, the narrative prepares the reader by stating that YHWH had completely abandoned Judah. The country is besieged from all sides as YHWH sends bands of Chaldeans, Arameans, Moabites, and Ammonites against his own nation (24:2). Not only is there a new empire on the scene, but because of its transgressions and disregard of prophetic warnings, YHWH himself has turned against the nation, allowing Judah's neighbors to attack it (24:2). YHWH, as the narrative makes clear, is no longer Judah's defender but its enemy.

The description of these incessant attacks also resolves a theological problem created by the sudden death of Jehoiakim. Though viewed by the biblical writer as the worst of Judah's last four kings,[5] Jehoiakim is the only one out of the four who dies in his own country and who remains unpunished by a foreign power.[6] The writer addresses the lack of Jehoiakim's theological comeuppance by noting how God sent groups of foreign raiders to attack Judah during his tenure (24:2). According to Lipschits, the mention of these attacks during Jehoiakim's reign shows that the king did indeed suffer from divine punishment and even hints at the fact that his death was the "result of divine retribution."[7]

More important, 2 Kings 24:3 connects Jehoiakim's sins, the foreign raids, and the divinely ordained destruction of Judah with the misdeeds of Manasseh: "Surely this came upon Judah at the command of the LORD, to remove them out of his sight, for the sins of Manasseh, for all that he had committed" (24:3). This allusion to Manasseh is important because it speaks to an attempt to deflect blame away from YHWH. To ensure that YHWH is in no way accused of deserting his nation—and therefore suspected of unmanliness and powerlessness—the text repeats the reasons why Judah deserved to be divinely rejected: because of the sins of Manasseh and "also for the innocent blood that he shed" (24:3). The mention of innocent blood here is interesting and is connected to the

3. Oded Lipschits, "'Jehoiakim Slept with His Fathers . . .' (II Kings 24:6)—Did He?," *JHS* 4 (2002), http://www.jhsonline.org/cocoon/JHS/a023.html.

4. Hyatt, "New Light on Nebuchadrezzar," 279.

5. Lipschits, "'Jehoiakim Slept with His Fathers,'" 7.

6. Ibid., 8.

7. Ibid., 9.

question of the effectiveness of Josiah's reform. It may be that the writer specifically mentions this sin of innocent blood in order to show that this was the one transgression that Josiah was unable to annul through his cultic renovation. As such, the mention of innocent blood seems to provide a subtle explanation for why YHWH remained unappeased by Josiah's deeds and, hence, why Josiah failed to stop the destruction of Judah. The answer posited once again is that, despite Josiah's good deeds, Manasseh's sins were too great to cancel out or thwart their ill effects. By beginning the narrative of the demolition of the nation with such a defensive preamble, the text attempts to address doubts and insecurities about YHWH's masculinity before they arise. This preamble thus tries to frame how the reader reads the narrative that follows about Judah's end: it is not about the loss of YHWH's masculinity, prowess, and authority but merely the natural and expected outcome of a nation's sins.

The Reign of Jehoiachin in Judah (24:8-17)

As soon as the preamble concludes, the narrative turns to the short reign of Jehoiachin (597 BCE). Noting the age in which he ascends to the throne, the length of his tenure, and the name of his mother—Nehushta, who seems to have been the daughter of a high court official (Jer 26:22; 36:12, 25)[8] —Jehoiachin, like all the monarchs after Josiah, is rated unfavorably by the biblical writer. Considering his very short tenure—three months—the unfavorable assessment is, however, likely theologically and literarily motivated. How can any king, especially those who rule during Judah's declining years, ever match the superlative tenure of Josiah? A positive assessment of any of the last four of Judah's kings would have more loudly raised questions as to why YHWH allowed the destruction of his country, exacerbating doubts about YHWH's power and sovereignty.

Following the negative rating of Jehoiachin, the narrative turns to describe the devastating effects of the rebellion started by Jehoiachin's father, Jehoiakim. His rebellion against Babylon, we are told, led to a calamitous siege of Jerusalem during the reign of his son. Unlike preceding Assyrian attacks, such as the one during Hezekiah's reign in 701 BCE, no rescue was forthcoming. Rather, typical of the last two chapters

8. Volkmar Fritz, *1 & 2 Kings*, trans. Anselm Hagedorn, CC (Minneapolis: Fortress, 2003), 416.

⁸Jehoiachin was eighteen years old when he began to reign; he reigned three months in Jerusalem. His mother's name was Nehushta daughter of Elnathan of Jerusalem. ⁹He did what was evil in the sight of the LORD, just as his father had done.

¹⁰At that time the servants of King Nebuchadnezzar of Babylon came up to Jerusalem, and the city was besieged. ¹¹King Nebuchadnezzar of Babylon came to the city, while his servants were besieging it; ¹²King Jehoiachin of Judah gave himself up to the king of Babylon, himself, his mother, his servants, his officers, and his palace officials. The king of Babylon took him prisoner in the eighth year of his reign.

¹³He carried off all the treasures of the house of the LORD, and the treasures of the king's house; he cut in pieces all the vessels of gold in the temple of the LORD, which King Solomon of Israel had made, all this as the LORD had foretold. ¹⁴He carried away all Jerusalem, all the officials, all the warriors, ten thousand captives, all the artisans and the smiths; no one remained, except the poorest people of the land. ¹⁵He carried away Jehoiachin to Babylon; the king's mother, the king's wives, his officials, and the elite of the land, he took into captivity from Jerusalem to Babylon. ¹⁶The king of Babylon brought captive to Babylon all the men of valor, seven thousand, the artisans and the smiths, one thousand, all of them strong and fit for war. ¹⁷The king of Babylon made Mattaniah, Jehoiachin's uncle, king in his place, and changed his name to Zedekiah.

of 2 Kings, events are sparsely described in the text, with little detail of the duration or the effects of the siege. There is a removed, detached feeling to these chapters, and the reader hears nothing of the horrors endured by the nation.

The narrative progresses swiftly onward, informing the reader of Jehoiachin's capitulation to and imprisonment in Babylon (24:12), which puts an end to the attack. The king of Babylon replaces Jehoiachin with his uncle, Mattaniah, whose name, bespeaking the powerlessness of the country, is changed to Zedekiah (v. 17).⁹ Moreover, the crème de la crème of Judah's court, such as the members of the royal family, the officials, servants, and the elite, as well as those possessing artistic, technical, or military skills are all deported to Babylon (24:14-16) so that "no one remained, except the poorest people of the land" (24:14). The temple and

9. Not being the son of Jehoiachin, Zedekiah's legitimacy in following a direct line in the Davidic dynasty will be questioned.

the treasuries are ransacked and stripped of valuable materials. Lest the reader wonder about the whereabouts of YHWH, the protector of Judah, the narrator again reminds the reader of the reason for this disaster: "Indeed, Jerusalem and Judah so angered the LORD that he expelled them from his presence" (24:20).

The Reign of Zedekiah and the Exile of Judah (24:18–25:30)

Moving quickly toward the finish, the narrative states that Zedekiah (597–586 BCE), who is also rated unfavorably by the biblical writer, ascends the throne after Jehoiachin's removal (2 Kgs 24:18). For reasons not stated in the text, Zedekiah in his ninth year also decides to rebel against Babylon, leading to another siege of the city (2 Kgs 25:1).

Characteristic of the swift pacing in these last chapters, the deeds of Zedekiah in the preceding nine years before the siege are unaccounted for in the narrative. Jeremiah 52, however, records a nearly identical account of the end of Judah as the one found in 2 Kings 25. Jeremiah, who prophesied during the last years before the destruction, and the book associated with this prophet provide an alternative window into the period of Zedekiah's reign and the last years of Judah. The book of Jeremiah more clearly indicates that Zedekiah wavered between "subservience to Babylon and open revolt" throughout his reign (Jer 25–27).[10] Though the exact cause of Zedekiah's rebellion against Babylon is unknown, his vacillating action appears to be characteristic of this king.

One explanation for Zedekiah's mysterious rebellion is that the turmoil inside the Babylonian Empire might have led a coalition of eastern Mediterranean states to try to overthrow Babylonian control (see Jer 27:2-4 and 11).[11] It could be that Zedekiah joined this coalition. It is also possible that he was influenced by a pro-Egyptian faction inside his government to rebel against Babylon and to ally Judah with Egypt (Jer 37:5).[12] Egypt likely offered support to this pro-Egyptian faction in an effort to instigate a revolt against Babylon.[13] Jeremiah's warnings about the unreliability of Egypt went unheeded (Jer 37:6-10).

---

10. Mordechai Cogan and Hayim Tadmor, *II Kings: A New Translation with Introduction and Commentary*, AB 11 (Garden City, NY: Doubleday, 1988), 322.

11. Shimon Bakon, "Zedekiah: The Last King of Judah," *JQR* 36 (2008): 97; Cogan and Tadmor, *II Kings*, 322.

12. Bakon, "Zedekiah," 98; Abraham Malamat, "The Last Wars of the Kingdom of Judah," *JNES* 9 (1950): 222.

13. Malamat, "The Last Wars of the Kingdom of Judah," 222.

¹⁸Zedekiah was twenty-one years old when he began to reign; he reigned eleven years in Jerusalem. His mother's name was Hamutal daughter of Jeremiah of Libnah. ¹⁹He did what was evil in the sight of the Lord, just as Jehoiakim had done. ²⁰Indeed, Jerusalem and Judah so angered the Lord that he expelled them from his presence.

Zedekiah rebelled against the king of Babylon. ^{25:1}And in the ninth year of his reign, in the tenth month, on the tenth day of the month, King Nebuchadnezzar of Babylon came with all his army against Jerusalem, and laid siege to it; they built siegeworks against it all around. ²So the city was besieged until the eleventh year of King Zedekiah. ³On the ninth day of the fourth month the famine became so severe in the city that there was no food for the people of the land. ⁴Then a breach was made in the city wall; the king with all the soldiers fled by night by the way of the gate between the two walls, by the king's garden, though the Chaldeans were all around the city. They went in the direction of the Arabah. ⁵But the army of the Chaldeans pursued the king, and overtook him in the plains of Jericho; all his army was scattered, deserting him. ⁶Then they captured the king and brought him up to the king of Babylon at Riblah, who passed sentence on him. ⁷They slaughtered the sons of Zedekiah before his eyes, then put out the eyes of Zedekiah; they bound him in fetters and took him to Babylon.

⁸In the fifth month, on the seventh day of the month—which was the nineteenth year of King Nebuchadnezzar, king of Babylon—Nebuzaradan, the captain of the bodyguard, a servant of the king of Babylon, came to Jerusalem. ⁹He burned the house of the Lord, the king's house, and all the houses of Jerusalem; every great house he burned down. ¹⁰All the army of the Chaldeans who were with the captain of the guard broke down the walls around Jerusalem. ¹¹Nebuzaradan the captain of the guard carried into exile the rest of the people who were left in the city and the deserters who had defected to the king of Babylon— all the rest of the population. ¹²But the captain of the guard left some of the poorest people of the land to be vinedressers and tillers of the soil.

¹³The bronze pillars that were in the house of the Lord, as well as the stands and the bronze sea that were in the house of the Lord, the Chaldeans broke in pieces, and carried the bronze to Babylon. ¹⁴They took away the pots, the shovels, the snuffers, the dishes for incense, and all the bronze vessels used in the temple service, ¹⁵as well as the firepans and the basins. What was made of gold the captain of the guard took away for the gold, and what was made of silver, for the silver. ¹⁶As for the two pillars, the one sea, and the stands, which Solomon had made for the house of the Lord, the bronze of all these vessels was beyond weighing. ¹⁷The height of the one pillar was eighteen cubits, and on it was a bronze capital; the height of the capital was three cubits; latticework and pomegranates, all of bronze, were on the

capital all around. The second pillar had the same, with the latticework.

¹⁸The captain of the guard took the chief priest Seraiah, the second priest Zephaniah, and the three guardians of the threshold; ¹⁹from the city he took an officer who had been in command of the soldiers, and five men of the king's council who were found in the city; the secretary who was the commander of the army who mustered the people of the land; and sixty men of the people of the land who were found in the city. ²⁰Nebuzaradan the captain of the guard took them, and brought them to the king of Babylon at Riblah. ²¹The king of Babylon struck them down and put them to death at Riblah in the land of Hamath. So Judah went into exile out of its land.

²²He appointed Gedaliah son of Ahikam son of Shaphan as governor over the people who remained in the land of Judah, whom King Nebuchadnezzar of Babylon had left. ²³Now when all the captains of the forces and their men heard that the king of Babylon had appointed Gedaliah as governor, they came with their men to Gedaliah at Mizpah, namely, Ishmael son of Nethaniah, Johanan son of Kareah, Seraiah son of Tanhumeth

Though the narrative is silent and cagey, the painful death throes of Judah are evident to the reader. In addition to the text, there is also epigraphic evidence such as the Lachish letters or Lachish ostraca. These clay bullae, consisting of communications between military officials, describe the panic that beset the country in its final moments.[14] The siege, like many others, seems to have induced a devastating famine. It is the famine that might have impelled the final fall of the city (Jer 37:21).[15] As the starving mothers in 2 Kings 6 so vividly showed, the most vulnerable in society, such as women, the poor, the elderly, and children, were likely the first to succumb to the harrowing ravages of this scarcity. Though the text does not describe in detail the horrors experienced by those inside the city, the terror is still manifest in the redundant statement in 2 Kings 25:3 that "there was no food for the people of the land." The land is pictured as emptied of any and all things that support life. For disobeying YHWH, the masculine deity of life, fecundity, and reproduction, Judah's end is characterized by the very opposite features: extreme hunger, violence, death, and expulsion.

14. Ibid., 225.
15. Malamat, "The Last Kings of Judah," 155.

the Netophathite, and Jaazaniah son of the Maacathite. ²⁴Gedaliah swore to them and their men, saying, "Do not be afraid because of the Chaldean officials; live in the land, serve the king of Babylon, and it shall be well with you." ²⁵But in the seventh month, Ishmael son of Nethaniah son of Elishama, of the royal family, came with ten men; they struck down Gedaliah so that he died, along with the Judeans and Chaldeans who were with him at Mizpah. ²⁶Then all the people, high and low, and the captains of the forces set out and went to Egypt; for they were afraid of the Chaldeans.

²⁷In the thirty-seventh year of the exile of King Jehoiachin of Judah, in the twelfth month, on the twenty-seventh day of the month, King Evil-merodach of Babylon, in the year that he began to reign, released King Jehoiachin of Judah from prison; ²⁸he spoke kindly to him, and gave him a seat above the other seats of the kings who were with him in Babylon. ²⁹So Jehoiachin put aside his prison clothes. Every day of his life he dined regularly in the king's presence. ³⁰For his allowance, a regular allowance was given him by the king, a portion every day, as long as he lived.

The situation is so desperate that Zedekiah and his soldiers attempt to flee when the Babylonians finally breach the city walls (2 Kgs 25:4). The king and his crew do not make it very far, however, and the king is captured and brought to the king of Babylon to face sentence for his rebellion (25:6). In an act of total emasculation, Zedekiah's sons—the royal heirs who represent the continuation of Zedekiah's lineage and, thus, his reproductive success as king—are killed before his eyes (25:7). To make certain that this appalling scene is the last thing that the unfortunate king witnesses, Zedekiah is then blinded, a common punishment for rebellious slaves.[16] Juha Pakkala, who doubts the historicity of the biblical account of Zedekiah's flight and ignominious conclusion, argues that the point of his flight is to denigrate this king as a selfish, fearful coward and a failed leader.[17]

Going from emasculation of a king to that of a country and its deity, the Babylonians next turn to decimate the city and the temple within.

16. Cogan and Tadmor, *II Kings*, 318.

17. Juha Pakkala, "Zedekiah's Fate and the Dynastic Succession," *JBL* 128 (2006): 451. Pakkala notes further that in this humiliating depiction of Judah's last king, an anti-Zedekiah polemic is evident and points to an exilic dispute about the legitimacy of the dynastic line (450).

The palace, the temple, and every great house are burned (v. 9), the walls around Jerusalem are broken (v. 10), and another group of Judahites are exiled, leaving only "the poorest of the land" (v. 12). Slowing to tell of the demolition of the great temple of YHWH, the text describes in detail the artifacts in the abode that were taken, stripped, or destroyed by the Babylonians: the bronze pillars, stands, bronze sea, stands, pots, shovel, snuffers, dishes, fire pans, and basins (vv. 13-17). All the things that symbolized the magnificence, power, and protection—the masculine prowess—of YHWH are looted or wrecked by the Babylonians. The religious personnel suffer the same fate as those of the cultic items: the chief priest, the second priest, and the guardians of the threshold are put to death alongside other community leaders, such as the city's commanding officer, members of the king's council, and men from among the prominent people of the land (vv. 18-20). Left without any who can lead and deserted by its god, the narrative states Judah "went into exile out of its land" (v. 21).[18]

Into this leadership vacuum, the Babylonians place Gedaliah,[19] an important Jerusalemite, as governor, though his official title and status remain unclear (v. 23).[20] Gedaliah, who is mentioned in various parts of the book of Jeremiah, seems to have been an influential Judahite with a distinguished lineage. His grandfather was the scribe Shaphan, who was part of the cohort sent to the prophet Huldah during Josiah's reign. A seal found in the Lachish excavations stamped with the word *lgdlyhw*

---

18. The portrayal of Judah as utterly devastated and emptied of population during the Babylonian conquest—"the myth of the empty land"—is a fabrication according to some scholars. Instead, they argue that life in Judah largely continued as before, that the Babylonians did not wholly desolate the country, and that the deportations of the Judeans were rather minimal. See Hans M. Barstad, "After the 'Myth of the Empty Land': Major Challenges in the Study of Neo-Babylonian Judah," in *Judah and Judeans in the Neo-Babylonian Period*, ed. Oded Lipschits and Joseph Blenkinsopp (Winona Lake, IN: Eisenbrauns, 2003), 3–20; idem, *The Myth of the Empty Land: A Study of the History and Archaeology of Judah during the "Exilic" Period*, SO 28 (Oslo: Scandinavian University Press, 1996); Robert P. Carroll, "The Myth of the Empty Land," *Semeia* 59 (1992): 79–93.

19. The dates for Gedaliah, including the length of his reign and the year of his death, are unknown. See Joseph Blenkinsopp, *David Remembered: Kingship and National Identity in Ancient Israel* (Grand Rapids, MI: Eerdmans, 2013), 52.

20. Joseph Blenkinsopp argues that the Babylonians placed Gedaliah, who might have had Benjaminite origins, as a client king (ibid., 49–50).

'sr 'l hbyt may indicate that Gedaliah was a steward of the palace.[21] More important, Gedaliah was supported by and supportive of the prophet Jeremiah, whom Gedaliah rescues from a threatening mob in Jeremiah 26:24. Gedaliah's appointment was thus viewed favorably by the prophet (Jer 39:14; 40:1-6) as well as the general populace remaining in the land who saw it as a last chance for the country to obtain some measure of peace and stability after the horrific desolation of the city.

This hope for stability is quickly dashed, however, as Gedaliah is assassinated by members of the royal family of Judah and a group of other high-ranking Judeans. Contra Volkmar Fritz,[22] Mordechai Cogan and Hayim Tadmor posit that his assassination was not an act of rebellion against Babylon by the royalty but an act of "vendetta against a collaborator with the Chaldean enemy carried out by extremists."[23] They note that many exiles in Babylon viewed Gedaliah's assassination "as the death blow to national existence" and thereby fasted and mourned his death (Zech 7:5; 8:19).[24] As is so often the case, a bloody act by a few radicals leads to devastating consequences for the innocent populace. Fearful of Babylonian retaliation, the remaining Judeans self-exile by fleeing to Egypt (2 Kgs 25:26). Among this group, as we find out in the book of Jeremiah, is the prophet himself (Jer 43:4-5). The "un-exodus" of which Deuteronomy 17:16 and 28:68 forewarns has come to pass,[25] and the Israelites go backward "to the very place where in the course of salvation history they were once oppressed as slaves."[26] Jeremiah 44–45 shows that the writer of Jeremiah too viewed this flight to Egypt as a backward step in the salvation history of Israel, greatly condemned by YHWH who promises that he will pursue those fleeing to Egypt to enact his revenge through the Babylonians (Jer 44:8-14).

The book of Kings, however, ends on a slightly more hopeful note than the dismal conclusion found in the prophetic book of Jeremiah. It states that when a new Babylonian king, the unfortunately named Evil-merodach, comes to power, the exiled and imprisoned king Jehoiachin is pardoned and released (2 Kgs 25:27). Even more favorable, Jehoiachin is treated with consideration by the Babylonian emperor who grants him a

21. Blenkinsopp, *David Remembered*, 43; Fritz, *1 & 2 Kings*, 424.
22. Fritz, *1 & 2 Kings*, 424.
23. Cogan and Tadmor, *II Kings*, 327.
24. Ibid.
25. Richard Nelson, *First and Second Kings*, IBC (Atlanta: John Knox, 1987), 264.
26. Gina Hens-Piazza, *1–2 Kings*, AOTC (Nashville: Abingdon, 2006), 400.

regular allowance and permits him to eat in the Babylonian monarch's presence.

These last couple of verses about the welfare of Jehoiachin have intrigued scholars who debate whether they merely give a neutral update about the status of the last Judean monarch, as Martin Noth argues,[27] or hold out the promise of the return of the Davidic monarchy, as Gerhard von Rad posits.[28] Modern scholars have veered between these two positions, perhaps with some slight leaning toward von Rad's more positive reading.[29] Some scholars see the concluding verses as neither one nor the other but ambiguous or ambivalent.[30]

More recently, some scholars have proposed that these verses reflect the ways in which Judah's theology came to be adapted in the new diasporic environment. Jon Levenson, along with Ronald Clements, argues that these last verses show how the Davidic promise was updated in the exilic period to reflect a new conditional messianism or a "chastened royal theology."[31] Or as Ronald Clements puts it, these last

---

27. Martin Noth, *The Deuteronomistic History*, JSOTSup 15 (Sheffield: JSOT Press, 1981), 97–99.

28. Gerhard von Rad, *Studies in Deuteronomy*, SBT 9 (London: SCM, 1953), 74–91; idem, *Old Testament Theology* (New York: Harper & Row, 1962), 334–47.

29. Fritz, *1 & 2 Kings*, 426; Samantha Joo argues that, "considering the communal significance of food, the epilogue about Jehoiachin's dining habits is indeed a hopeful message" (Samantha Joo, "A Fine Balance between Hope and Despair: The Epilogue to 2 Kings [25:27-30]," *BibInt* 20 [2012]: 239).

30. Bob Becking, "Jehoiachin's Amnesty, Salvation for Israel? Notes on 2 Kings 25, 27-30," in *Pentateuchal and Deuteronomistic Studies: Papers Read at the XIIIth IOSOT Congress, Leuven 1989*, ed. C. Brekelmans and J. Lust (Leuven: Leuven University Press, 1990), 283–93; Christopher Begg, "The Significance of Jehoiachin's Release: A New Proposal," *JSOT* 36 (1986): 49–56; Jan Jaynes Granowski, "Jehoiachin at the King's Table: A Reading of the Ending of the Second Book of Kings," in *Reading between Texts: Intertextuality and the Hebrew Bible*, ed. Danna Nolan Fewell (Louisville: Westminster John Knox, 1992), 173–88: David Janzen, "An Ambiguous Ending: Dynastic Punishment in Kings and the Fate of the Davidides in 2 Kings 25:27-30," *JSOT* 33 (2008): 39–58; Donald F. Murray, "Of All the Years the Hopes—Or Fears? Jehoiachin in Babylon (2 Kings 25:27-30)," *JBL* 120 (2001): 245–65; Nelson, *First and Second Kings*, 268; Jeremy Schipper, " 'Significant Resonances' with Mephisbosheth in 2 Kings 25:27-30: A Response to Donald F. Murray," *JBL* 124 (2005): 521–29.

31. Jon D. Levenson, "The Last Four Verses in Kings," *JBL* 103 (1984): 357–61; Ronald E. Clements, "A Royal Privilege: Dining in Presence of the Great King (2 Kings 25.27-30)" in *Reflection and Refraction: Studies in Biblical Historiography in Honour of A. Graeme Auld*, ed. Robert Rezetko, Timothy H. Lim, and W. Brian Aucker, VTSup 113 (Boston: Brill, 2007), 62–66.

verses function as a bridge, showing the transition from "the old monarchic order" with its promise of the perpetual rule of the Davidides in Jerusalem to "the new order . . . a world of exile and dispersion among the nations."[32] Kari Latvus, in his postcolonial reading, goes further and states that the conclusion of 2 Kings reflects the "inner colonization of the writer" in which the main concern is "good relations between empire and subordinate" as a means of survival in the new diasporic context.[33]

Whatever the purpose of this concluding remark about Jehoiachin, a sense of theological unease remains at the end of 2 Kings. Though the narrative, at points, attempts to quell the theological doubts and questioning of the whereabouts and power of YHWH, it is not wholly successful. Can Manasseh or even the evils of the Judahites—can anything really—be so bad as to warrant the desertion of Judah by YHWH? Despite the small notices in the text that try to preserve and uphold YHWH's masculine prowess by justifying Judah's destruction as well-deserved and forewarned, it is difficult not to read into this conclusion a darker, more ambivalent message. If 2 Kings is centered on this question of whether YHWH is powerful and manly enough to defend, provide for, and give life to Judah, the conclusion sadly appears to point to a negative answer—or at least a very ambiguous one. As the text shows, it is not clear whether YHWH is actually virile enough to be the god of life, fertility, and reproduction for Judah. Even if the people are disloyal and sinful, the assertive masculinity on which the fidelity and worship of this particular deity is centered, in the end, appears to be upended. In presenting such an ambivalent vision of YHWH, the book of 2 Kings, with its muddled vision of this deity's masculinity, deconstructs the androcentric vision of God so aggressively asserted in much of the Deuteronomistic History. The conclusion of 2 Kings thus clearly demonstrates that such an androcentric vision of God might be ultimately unsustainable. And in so doing, the text compels the reader to begin the process of decolonizing the images of God so forcibly asserted in the preceding account of Israel and Judah's history in 2 Kings.

32. Clements, "Royal Privilege," 66.

33. Kari Latvus, "Decolonizing Yahweh: A Postcolonial Reading of 2 Kings 24–25," in *The Postcolonial Biblical Reader*, ed. Rasiah S. Sugirtharajah (Malden, MA: Blackwell, 2006), 189.

Afterword

Despite its name, the book of Kings is infused with female characters as well as issues relating to women and gender. Indeed, as I have argued in this work, an issue concerning gender—whether YHWH is masculine enough to defend his country and to warrant the loyalties of its people—is the key query that runs throughout 2 Kings as a whole. While the body of 2 Kings continually asserts YHWH's masculinity, especially his military and reproductive prowess, the conclusion of the book deconstructs this assertion. In so doing, readers are left, in the end, not only without an answer to this central query but with the same query reasserted for further analysis and interpretation. The masculinity of YHWH, Israel's deity, remains a driving force—one that is continually and repeatedly asserted, and then again challenged and interrogated—propelling the unfolding history of this nation.

As is clear, gender constitutes one of the fundamental lenses through which biblical writers imagined their past and, hence, their vision of themselves and their community. Despite being called "Kings," and despite being ostensibly about male monarchs and a male deity, the constant and continual formulation and reformulation of maleness in contradistinction to the feminine lies at the heart of the narrative told in 2 Kings about Israel's monarchic past.

Works Cited

Abadie, Philippe. "From the Impious Manasseh (2 Kings 21) to the Convert Manasseh (2 Chronicles 33): Theological Rewriting by the Chronicler." In *The Chronicler as Theologian: Essays in Honor of Ralph W. Klein*, edited by M. Patrick Graham, Steven L. McKenzie, and Gary N. Knoppers, 89–104. JSOTSup 371. London: T&T Clark, 2003.

Abrams, Judith Z. "*Metzora(at) Kashaleg*: Leprosy, Challenges to Authority in the Bible." *JBQ* 21 (1993): 41–45.

Ackerman, Susan. " 'And the Women Knead Dough': The Worship of the Queen of Heaven in Sixth-Century Judah." In *Gender and Difference in Ancient Israel*, edited by Peggy L. Day, 109–24. Minneapolis: Fortress, 1989.

———. "At Home with the Goddess." In *Symbiosis, Symbolism, and the Power of the Past: Canaan, Ancient Israel and their Neighbors from the Late Bronze Age through Roman Palaestina*, edited by Seymore Gitin and William G. Dever, 455–68. Winona Lake, IN: Eisenbrauns, 2003.

———. "The Queen Mother and the Cult in Ancient Israel." *JBL* 112 (1993): 385–401.

———. *Warrior, Dancer, Seductress, Queen: Women in Judges and Biblical Israel.* New York: Doubleday, 1998.

Ackroyd, Peter. "The Biblical Interpretation of the Reigns of Ahaz and Hezekiah." In *In the Shelter of Elyon: Essays on Ancient Palestinian Life and Literature in Honor of G.W. Ahlström*, edited by W. Boyd Barrick and John R. Spencer, 247–59. JSOTSup 31. Sheffield: JSOT, 1984.

———. *Exile and Restoration.* OTL. Philadelphia: Westminster John Knox, 1968.

———. "Goddesses, Women and Jezebel." In *Images of Women in Antiquity*, edited by Averil Cameron and Amelie Kuhrt, 245–59. Detroit: Wayne State University Press, 1993.

———. "An Interpretation of the Babylonian Exile: A Study of 2 Kings 20, Isaiah 38–39." *SJT* 27 (1974): 329–52.

Amit, Yairah. "A Prophet Tested: Elisha, the Great Woman of Shunem, and the Story's Double Message." *BibInt* 11 (2003): 279–94.

———. "The Samaritans: Biblical Considerations in the Solution of a Political Problem." In *Secularism and Biblical Studies*, edited by Roland Boer, 192–203. London: Equinox, 2010.

Andreasen, Niels-Erik A. "The Role of the Queen Mother in Israelite Society." *CBQ* 45 (1983): 179–94.

Appler, Deborah A. "From Queen to Cuisine: Food Imagery in the Jezebel Narrative." *Semeia* 86 (1999): 55–71.

Aschkenasy, Nehama. *The Woman at the Window: Biblical Tales of Oppression and Escape*. Detroit: Wayne State University Press, 1998.

Auld, Graeme A. *Kings without Privilege: David and Moses in the Story of the Bible's Kings*. Edinburgh: T&T Clark, 1994.

Bakon, Shimon. "Zedekiah: The Last King of Judah." *JQR* 36 (2008): 93–101.

Barker, Margaret. "Hezekiah's Boil." *JSOT* 95 (2001): 31–42.

Barre, Lloyd M. *The Rhetoric of Political Persuasion: The Narrative Artistry and Political Intentions of 2 Kings 9–11*. CBQMS 20. Washington, DC: Catholic Biblical Association, 1988.

Barrick, W. Boyd. "Elisha and the Magic Bow: A Note on 2 Kings XIII 15–17." *VT* 35 (1985): 355–63.

———. "On the Removal of the 'High Places' in 1–2 Kings." *Bib* 55 (1974): 257–59.

Barstad, Hans M. "After the 'Myth of the Empty Land': Major Challenges in the Study of Neo-Babylonian Judah." In *Judah and Judeans in the Neo-Babylonian Period*, edited by Oded Lipschits and Joseph Blenkinsopp, 3–20. Winona Lake, IN: Eisenbrauns, 2003.

———. *The Myth of the Empty Land: A Study of the History and Archaeology of Judah during the "Exilic" Period*. SO 28. Oslo: Scandinavian University Press, 1996.

Barthes, Roland. "The Death of the Author." In *Image-Music-Text*, translated by Stephen Heath, 142–48. New York: Hill and Wang, 1977.

Barton, John. *The Theology of the Book of Amos*. Cambridge: Cambridge University Press, 2012.

Becking, Bob. "Jehoiachin's Amnesty, Salvation for Israel? Notes on 2 Kings 25, 27-30." In *Pentateuchal and Deuteronomistic Studies: Papers Read at the XIIIth IOSOT Congress, Leuven 1989*, edited by C. Brekelmans and J. Lust, 283–93. Leuven: Leuven University Press, 1990.

Beek, Martinus Adrianus. "The Meaning of the Expression the Chariots and the Horsemen of Israel (2 Kings ii 12)." *OtSt* 17 (1972): 1–10.

Begg, Christopher. "The Significance of Jehoiachin's Release: A New Proposal." *JSOT* 36 (1986): 49–56.

Begrich, Joachim. "Der Syrisch-Ephraimitische Krieg und seine weltpolitischen Zusammenhänge." *ZDMG* 83 (1929): 213–37.

Bellis, Alice Ogden. *Helpmates, Harlots, and Heroes: Women Stories in the Hebrew Bible*. Louisville: Westminster John Knox, 2007.

Ben-Barak, Zafira. "The Status and Right of the Gĕbîrâ." *JBL* 110 (1991): 23–34.

Ben Zvi, Ehud. "The Account of the Reign of Manasseh in II Reg 21:1-18 and the Redactional History of the Book of Kings." *ZAW* 103 (1991): 355–74.

———. "Who Wrote the Speech of the Rabshaqeh and When." *JBL* 109 (1990): 79–92.

Berlyn, Patricia. "The Wrath of Moab." *JBQ* 30 (2002): 216–26.

Bird, Phyllis. *Missing Persons and Mistaken Identities: Women and Gender in Ancient Israel*. Minneapolis: Fortress, 1997.

———. " 'To Play the Harlot': An Inquiry into an Old Testament Metaphor." In *Gender and Difference in Ancient Israel*, edited by Peggy Day, 75–94. Minneapolis: Fortress, 1989.

Bleibtreu, Erika. "Grisly Assyrian Record of Torture and Dead." *BAR* 70 (January/February 1991): 52–61, 75.

Blenkinsopp, Joseph. *David Remembered: Kingship and National Identity in Ancient Israel*. Grand Rapids, MI: Eerdmans, 2013.

———. *A History of Prophecy in Israel*. Louisville: Westminster John Knox, 1996.

Boling, Robert G. *Judges: Introduction, Translation, and Commentary*. AB 6A. Garden City, NY: Doubleday, 1975.

———. "Levitical History and the Role of Joshua." In *The Word of the Lord Shall Go Forth: Essays in Honor of David Noel Freedman in Celebration of His Sixtieth Birthday*, edited by Carol L. Meyers and M. O'Connor, 241–61. Winona Lake, IN: Eisenbrauns, 1983.

Bostock, David. *A Portrayal of Trust: The Theme of Faith in the Hezekiah Narratives*. PBM. Milton Keynes: Paternoster, 2006.

Branch, Robin Gallaher. "Athaliah, a Treacherous Queen: A Careful Analysis of Her Story in 2 Kings 11 and 2 Chronicles 22:10–23:21." *In die Skriflig* 38 (2004): 537–59.

Brenner, Athalya, ed. *A Feminist Companion to Samuel and Kings*. FCB 5. Sheffield: Sheffield Academic, 2000.

Brenner-Idan, Athalya. *The Israelite Women: Social Role and Literary Type in Biblical Narrative*. London: Bloomsbury T&T Clark, 2015.

Brettler, Marc. "Ideology, History and Theology in 2 Kings XVII 7-23." *VT* 39 (1989): 268–82.

Bronner, Leah. *The Stories of Elijah and Elisha as Polemics Against Baal Worship*. POS 6. Leiden: Brill, 1968.

Brueggemann, Walter. "A Brief Moment for a One-Person Remnant (2 Kings 5:2-3)." *BTB* 31 (2001): 53–59.

———. "The God of Joshua . . . Give or Take the Land." *Int* 66 (2012): 164–75.

Buckland, A. W. "Rhabdomancy and Belomancy, or Divination by the Rod and by Arrow." *Journal of the Anthropological Institute of Great Britain and Ireland* 5 (1876): 436–50.

Burnett, Joel S. " 'Going Down' to Bethel: Elijah and Elisha in the Theological Geography of the Deuteronomistic History." *JBL* 129 (2010): 281–97.

Camp, Claudia. "1 and 2 Kings." In *The Women's Biblical Commentary*, edited by Carol A. Newsom and Sharon H. Ringe, 102–16. Louisville: Westminster John Knox, 1992.

Carroll, Robert P. "The Elijah-Elisha Sagas: Some Remarks on Prophetic Succession in Ancient Israel." *VT* 19 (1969): 400–415.

———. "The Myth of the Empty Land." *Semeia* 59 (1992): 79–93.

Chapman, Cynthia. *The Gendered Language of Warfare in the Israelite-Assyrian Encounter*. HSM 62. Winona Lake, IN: Eisenbrauns, 2004.

Childs, Brevard. *Isaiah and the Assyrian Crisis*. London: SCM, 1967.

Chisholm, Robert B., Jr. "Israel's Retreat and the Failure of Prophecy in 2 Kings 3." *Bib* 92 (2011): 70–80.

———. "The 'Spirit of the Lord' in 2 Kings 2:16." In *Presence, Power, and Promise: The Role of the Spirit of God in the Old Testament*, edited by David G. Firth and Paul D. Wegner, 306–17. Downers Grove, IL: Intervarsity Press, 2011.

Clements, Ronald E. "A Royal Privilege: Dining in Presence of the Great King (2 Kings 25.27-30)." In *Reflection and Refraction: Studies in Biblical Historiography in Honour of A. Graeme Auld*, edited by Robert Rezetko, Timothy H. Lim, and W. Brian Aucker, 49–66. VTSup 113. Boston: Brill, 2007.

Cogan, Mordechai. "For We, Like You, Worship Your God: Three Biblical Portrayals of Samaritan Origins." *VT* 38 (1988): 286–92.

———. *Imperialism and Religion: Assyria, Judah and Israel in the Eighth and Seventh Centuries B.C.E.* Missoula, MT: Scholars Press, 1974.

———. "Israel in Exile—The View of a Josianic Historian." *JBL* 97 (1978): 40–44.

———. "'Ripping Open Pregnant Women' in Light of an Assyrian Analogue." *JAOS* 103 (1983): 755–57.

Cogan, Mordechai, and Hayim Tadmor. *II Kings: A New Translation with Introduction and Commentary*. AB 11. Garden City: NY: Doubleday, 1988.

———. "Ahaz and Tiglath-Pileser in the Book of Kings: Historiographic Considerations." *Bib* 60 (1979): 491–508.

Cohen, Mark R. "Feeding the Poor and Clothing the Naked: The Cairo Geniza." *The Journal of Interdisciplinary History* 35 (2005): 407–21.

Cohen, Shaye J. D. *The Beginnings of Jewishness: Boundaries, Varieties, Uncertainties*. HCS 31. Berkeley: University of California Press, 1999.

Cohn, Robert. *2 Kings*. Berit Olam. Collegeville, MN: Liturgical Press, 2000.

———. "Convention and Creativity in the Book of Kings: The Case of the Dying Monarch." *CBQ* 47 (1985): 603–16.

———. "Form and Perspective in 2 Kings." *VT* 33 (1983): 171–84.

Cross, Frank Moore. *Canaanite Myth and Hebrew Epic: Essays in the History of the Religion of Israel*. Cambridge: Harvard University Press, 1973.

Davies, T. Witton. "Magic, Divination, and Demonology among the Semites." *AJSL* 14 (1898): 278–79.

Davis, Dale Ralph. "The Kingdom of God in Transition: Interpreting 2 Kings 2." *WTJ* 46 (1984): 384–95.

Day, Peggy L. "Adulterous Jerusalem's Imaged Demise: Death of a Metaphor in Ezekiel XVI." *VT* 50 (2000): 285–309.

Dearman, Andrew, ed. *Studies in the Mesha Inscription and Moab.* ABS 2. Atlanta: Scholars Press, 1989.

Delamarter, Steve. "The Death of Josiah in Scripture and Tradition: Wrestling with the Problem of Evil?" *VT* 54 (2004): 29–60.

Delaney, Carol. *Abraham on Trial: The Social Legacy of Biblical Myth.* Princeton: Princeton University Press, 1998.

Dever, William G. "Asherah, Consort of Yahweh? New Evidence from Kuntillet 'Ajrud." *BASOR* 255 (1984): 21–37.

———. *Did God Have a Wife? Archaeology and the Folk Religion in Ancient Israel.* Grand Rapids, MI: Eerdmans, 2005.

———. *Who Were the Early Israelites and Where Did They Come From.* Grand Rapids, MI: Eerdmans, 2003.

Dietrich, Walter. *Prophetie und Geschichte: Eine redaktionsgeschichtliche Untersuchung zum deuteronomistischen Geschichtswerk.* Göttingen: Vandenhoeck & Ruprecht, 1972.

van Dijk-Hemmes, Fokkelien. "The Great Woman of Shunem and the Man of God: A Dual Interpretation of 2 Kings 4.8-37." In *A Feminist Companion to Samuel and Kings,* edited by Athalya Brenner, 218–30. FCB 5. Sheffield: Sheffield Academic, 1994.

Dion, Paul-Eugène. "Ahaz and Other Willing Servants of Assyria." In *From Babel to Babylon: Essay on Biblical History and Literature in Honor of Brian Peckham,* edited by Joyce Rilett Wood, John E. Harvey, and Mark Leuchter, 133–45. New York: T&T Clark, 2006.

Dubovský, Peter. "Assyrian Downfall through Isaiah's Eyes (2 Kings 15–23): The Historiography of Representation." *Bib* 89 (2008): 1–16.

———. "Menahem's Reign before the Assyrian Invasion (2 Kings 15.14-16)." In *Literature as Politics, Politics as Literature,* edited by David S. Vanderhooft and Abraham Winitzer, 29–45. Winona Lake, IN: Eisenbrauns, 2013.

———. "Ripping Open Pregnant Arab Women: Reliefs in Room L of Ashurbanipal's North Palace." *Or* 78 (2009): 394–419.

———. "Tiglath-pileser III's Campaigns in 734–732 B.C.: Historical Background of Isa 7; 2 Kgs 15–16 and 2 Chr 27–28." *Bib* 87 (2006): 153–70.

———. "Why Did the Northern Kingdom Fall According to 2 Kings 15?" *Bib* 95 (2014): 321–46.

Dutcher-Walls, Patricia. *Narrative Art, Political Rhetoric: The Case of Athaliah and Joash.* JSOTSup 209. Sheffield: Sheffield Academic, 1996.

Edelman, Diane. "Huldah the Prophet—Of Yahweh or Asherah?" In *A Feminist Companion to Samuel and Kings,* edited by Athalya Brenner, 231–50. FCB 5. Sheffield: Sheffield Academic, 1994.

Ellis, Teresa Ann. "Jeremiah 44: What if 'the Queen of Heaven' Is YHWH?" *JSOT* 33 (2009): 465–58.

Emerton, John A. "New Light on Israelite Religion: The Implications of the Inscriptions from Kuntillet 'Ajrud." *ZAW* 94 (1982): 2–20.

———. " 'Yahweh and His Asherah': The Goddess or Her Symbol." *VT* 49 (1999): 315–37.

Everhart, Janet. "Jezebel: Framed by Eunuchs." *CBQ* 72 (2010): 688–98.

Exum, J. Cheryl. *Fragmented Women: Feminist (Sub)versions of Biblical Narratives.* JSOTSup 163. Sheffield: JSOT Press, 1993.

Eynikel, Erik. *The Reform of King Josiah and the Composition of the Deuteronomistic History.* Leiden: Brill, 1996.

Feinstein, Eve Levavi. *Sexual Pollution in the Hebrew Bible.* New York: Oxford University Press, 2014.

Fensham, F. Charles. "A Possible Explanation of the Name Baal-Zebub of Ekron." *ZAW* 70 (1967): 361–64.

———. "Widow, Orphan, and the Poor in the Ancient Near Eastern Legal and Wisdom Literature." *JNES* 21 (1962): 129–39.

Ferris Beach, Eleanor. "The Samaria Ivories, *Marzeah,* and the Biblical Text." *BA* 55 (1992): 94–104.

Fewell, Danna Nolan, and David M. Gunn. *Gender, Power, and Promise: The Subject of the Bible's First Story.* Nashville: Abingdon, 1993.

Finkelstein, Israel, and Neil Asher Silberman. *The Bible Unearthed: Archaeology's New Vision of Ancient Israel and the Origin of its Sacred Text.* New York: Touchstone, 2002.

Fishbane, Michael. "Israel and the 'Mothers.' " In *Garments of the Torah: Essays in Biblical Hermeneutics.* Bloomington: Indiana University Press, 1989.

Freedman, David Noel, ed. *The Anchor Bible Dictionary.* 6 vols. New York: Doubleday, 1992.

Friedman, Richard Elliott. *The Exile and the Biblical Narrative: The Formation of the Deuteronomistic History and Priestly Codes.* Atlanta: Scholars Press, 1981.

———. *Who Wrote the Bible?* New York: HarperOne, 1997.

Fritz, Volkmar. *1 & 2 Kings.* Translated by Anselm Hagedorn. CC. Minneapolis: Fortress, 2003.

Gafney, Wilda C. *Daughters of Miriam: Women Prophets in Ancient Israel.* Minneapolis: Fortress, 2008.

Gaines, Janet Howe. "How Bad Was Jezebel?" *BRev* 16 (2000): 12–23.

———. *Music in the Old Bones: Jezebel through the Ages.* Carbondale: Southern Illinois University Press, 1999.

Galil, Gershon. "The Last Years of the Kingdom of Israel and the Fall of Samaria." *CBQ* 57 (1995): 52–65.

Gallagher, William. *Sennacherib's Campaign to Judah: New Studies.* Studies in the History and Culture of the Ancient Near East 18. Boston: Brill, 1999.

García Bachmann, Mercedes L. *Women at Work in the Deuteronomistic History.* Atlanta: Society of Biblical Literature, 2013.

Gilmour, Rachelle. "A Note on the Horses and Chariots of Fire at Dothan." *ZAW* 125 (2013): 308–13.

Gonçalves, Francolino J. *L'expédition de Sennachérib en Palestine dans la littérature hébraïque ancienne*. EBib 7. Paris: Gabalda, 1986.

Grabbe, Lester L. *Judaism from Cyrus to Hadrian*. Vol. 2. Minneapolis: Fortress, 1992.

Granowski, Jan Jaynes. "Jehoiachin at the King's Table: A Reading of the Ending of the Second Book of Kings." In *Reading Between Texts: Intertextuality and the Hebrew Bible*, edited by Danna Nolan Fewell, 173–88. Louisville: Westminster John Knox, 1992.

Gray, John. *I and II Kings*. OTL. Philadelphia: Westminster, 1970.

Halpern, Baruch. "Why Manasseh Is Blamed for the Babylonian Exile: The Evolution of a Biblical Tradition." *VT* 48 (1998): 473–514.

Halpern, Baruch, and David Vanderhooft. "The Editions of Kings in the 7th–6th Centuries B.C.E." *HUCA* 62 (1991): 179–244.

Hamborg, G. R. "Reasons for Judgement in the Oracles Against the Nations of the Prophet Isaiah." *VT* 31 (1981): 145–59.

Handy, Lowell K. "Speaking of Babies in the Temple." In *Eastern Great Lakes and Midwest Biblical Societies, Proceedings* 8 (1988): 155–65.

Haupt, Paul. "Crystal-Gazing in the Old Testament." *JBL* 36 (1917): 84–92.

Havrelock, Rachel. "The Joshua Generation: Conquest and the Promised Land." *Critical Research on Religion* 1 (2013): 308–26.

———. *The River Jordan*. Chicago: Chicago University Press, 2011.

Hawk, L. Daniel. "Indigenous Helpers and Renegade Invaders: Ambivalent Characters in Biblical and Cinematic Conquest Narratives." *Journal of Religion & Film* 20 (2016): 1–27.

———. "The Truth about Conquest: Joshua as History, Narrative, and Scripture." *Int* 66 (2012). 129–40.

Hayes, John H., and Jeffrey K. Kuan. "The Final Years of Samaria (730–720 BC)." *Bib* 72 (1991): 153–81.

Heller, Jan. "Tod in Topfe: 2 Kön 4:38-41." *CV* 10 (1967): 71–76.

Hens-Piazza, Gina. *1–2 Kings*. AOTC. Nashville: Abingdon, 2006.

———. "Forms of Violence and the Violence of Forms: Two Cannibal Mothers before a King (2 Kings 6:24-33)." *JFSR* 14 (1998): 91–104.

Hepner, Gerson. "There's a Crowd in Shunem: Elisha's Misconduct with the Shunamite Reflects a Polemic against Prophetism." *ZAW* 122 (2010): 387–400.

Hiers, Richard H. "Transfer of Property by Inheritance and Bequest in Biblical Law and Tradition." *Journal of Law and Religion* 10 (1993): 121–55.

Hobbs, T. R. *2 Kings*. WBC 13. Waco, TX: Word, 1985.

Hoffeditz, David M., and Gary E. Yates. "Femme Fatale Redux: Intertextual Connection to the Elijah/Jezebel Narratives in Mark 6:4-29." *BBR* 15 (2005): 199–21.

Hoffman, H. D. *Reform und Reformen: Untersuchungen zu einem Grundthema der deuteronomistischen Geschichtsschreibung.* ATANT 66. Zurich: Theologischer Verlag, 1980.

Hoffner, Harry A., Jr. "Oil in Hittite Texts." *BA* 58 (1995): 108–14.

Holloway, Steven. *Assur Is King! Assur Is King! Religion in the Exercise of Power in the Neo-Assyrian Empire.* Culture and History of the Ancient Near East 10. Leiden: Brill, 2002.

Hull, John. "Hezekiah—Saint and Sinner: A Conceptual and Contextual Narrative Analysis of 2 Kings 18–20." PhD dissertation: Claremont Graduate School, 1994.

Hyatt, J. Philip. "New Light on Nebuchadrezzar and Judean History." *JBL* 75 (1956): 277–84.

Iwry, Samuel. "New Evidence for Belomancy in Ancient Palestine and Phoenicia." *JAOS* 81 (1961): 27–34.

Janzen, David. "An Ambiguous Ending: Dynastic Punishment in Kings and the Fate of the Davidides in 2 Kings 25:27-30." *JSOT* 33 (2008): 39–58.

Japhet, Sara. *I & II Chronicles: A Commentary.* Louisville: Westminster John Knox, 1993.

———. *The Ideology of the Book of Chronicles and its Place in Biblical Thought.* Winona Lake, IN: Eisenbrauns, 2009.

Jay, Nancy. *Throughout Your Generations Forever: Sacrifice, Religion, and Paternity.* Chicago: Chicago University Press, 1992.

Joo, Samantha. "A Fine Balance between Hope and Despair: The Epilogue to 2 Kings (25:27-30)." *BibInt* 20 (2012): 226–43.

Joseph, Alison. *The Portrait of the Kings: The Davidic Prototype in Deuteronomistic Poetics.* Minneapolis: Fortress, 2015.

Katzenstein, Hanna J. "Who Were the Parents of Athaliah?" *IEJ* 5 (1995): 194–97.

Keck, Leander E., ed. *The New Interpreter's Bible.* 12 vols. Nashville: Abingdon, 1994–2004.

Kern, Paul Bentley. *Ancient Siege Warfare.* Bloomington: Indiana University Press, 1999.

Kim, Jean Kyoung. "Reading and Retelling Naaman's Story (2 Kings 5)." *JSOT* 30 (2005): 49–61.

Klein, Rueven Chaim (Rudolph). "Queen Athaliah: The Daughter of Ahab or Omri?" *JBQ* 42 (2014): 11–20.

Knoppers, Gary. "Saint or Sinner? Manasseh in Chronicles." In *Rewriting Biblical History: Essays on Chronicles and Ben Sira in Honor of Pancratius C. Beentjes,* edited by Jeremy Corley and Harm van Grol, 211–29. Berlin: de Gruyter, 2011.

Krygier, Rivon. "Did God Command the Extermination of the Canaanites? The Rabbis Encounter with Genocide." *Conservative Judaism* 2 (2005): 78–94.

LaBarbera, Robert. "The Man of War and the Man of God: Social Satire in 2 Kings 6:8–7:20." *CBQ* 46 (1984): 637–51.

Labuschagne, Casper J. "Did Elisha Deliberately Lie? A Note on II Kings 8:10." *ZAW* 77 (1965): 327–28.

Lanner, Laurel. "Cannibal Mothers and Me: A Mother's Reading of 2 Kings 6.24–7.20." *JSOT* 85 (1999): 107–16.

Lapsley, Jacqueline E., and Patricia K. Tull, eds. *After Exegesis: Feminist Biblical Theology*. Waco, TX: Baylor University Press, 2015.

Lasine, Stuart. "Jehoram and the Cannibal Mothers (2 Kings 6.24-33): Solomon's Judgement in an Inverted World." *JSOT* 50 (1991): 27–53.

———. "Manasseh as Villain and Scapegoat." In *The New Literary Criticism and the Hebrew Bible*, edited by J. Cheryl Exum and David J. A. Clines, 163–83. Sheffield: JSOT Press, 1993.

———. "The Ups and Downs of Monarchical Justice." *JSOT* 59 (1993): 37–53.

Latvus, Kari. "Decolonizing Yahweh: A Postcolonial Reading of 2 Kings 24–25." In *The Postcolonial Biblical Reader*, edited by Rasiah S. Sugirtharajah, 186–92. Malden, MA: Blackwell, 2006.

Leith, Mary Joan Winn. "First Lady Jezebel." *BRev* 20 (2004): 8, 46.

Lemaire, André. "Who or What Was Yahweh's Asherah?" *BAR* 10 (1984): 42–51.

Levenson, Jon D. *The Death and Resurrection of the Beloved Son: The Transformation of Child Sacrifice in Judaism and Christianity*. New Haven: Yale University Press, 1993.

———. "From Temple to Synagogue: 1 Kings 8." In *Traditions in Transformation: Turning Points in Biblical Faith*, edited by Jon D. Levenson and Baruch Halpern, 143–66. Winona Lake, IN: Eisenbrauns, 1981.

———. "Is There a Counterpart in the Hebrew Bible to New Testament Antisemitism." *JES* 22 (1985): 242–60.

———. "The Last Four Verses in Kings." *JBL* 103 (1984): 353–61.

———. "Who Inserted the Book of the Torah?" *HTR* 68 (1975): 203–33.

Lipschits, Oded. "'Jehoiakim Slept with his Fathers . . .' (II Kings 24:6)—Did He?" *JHS* 4 (2002). http://www.jhsonline.org/cocoon/JHS/a023.html.

Lipschits, Oded, and Joseph Blenkinsopp, eds. *Judah and Judeans in the Neo-Babylonian Period*. Winona Lake, IN: Eisenbrauns, 2003.

Liverani, Mario. "L'Histoire de Joas." *VT* 24 (1974): 438–53.

Long, Burke O. *2 Kings*. FOTL 10. Grand Rapids, MI: Eerdmans, 1991.

———. "The Shunammite Woman: In the Shadow of the Prophet?" *BRev* (1991): 12–19, 42.

Machinist, Peter. "The *Rab Šaqeh* at the Wall of Jerusalem: Israelite Identity in the Face of the Assyrian 'Other.'" *HS* 41 (2000): 151–68.

Maier, Walter A., III. "The Healing of Naaman in Missiological Perspective." *CTQ* 61 (1997): 177–96.

Malamat, Abraham. "The Historical Background of the Assassination of Amon King of Judah." *IEJ* 3 (1953): 26–29.

———. "The Last Kings of Judah and the Fall of Jerusalem: An Historical—Chronological Study." *IEJ* 18 (1968): 137–56.

———. "The Last Wars of the Kingdom of Judah." *JNES* 9 (1950): 218–27.

Margalit, Baruch. "Why King Mesha of Moab Sacrificed His Oldest Son." *BAR* 12 (1986): 62–63.

Matthews, Shelly. "Feminist Biblical Historiography." In *Feminist Biblical Studies in the Twentieth Century: Scholarship and Movement*, edited by Elisabeth Schüssler Fiorenza, 233–48. Bible and Women 9.1. Atlanta: Society of Biblical Literature, 2014.

Mbuwayesango, Dora Rudo. "Canaanite Women and Israelite Women in Deuteronomy: The Intersection of Sexism and Imperialism." In *Postcolonial Interventions: Essays in Honor of R.S. Sugirtharajah*, edited by Tat-siong Benny Liew, 45–57. Sheffield: Sheffield Phoenix, 2009.

McCarter, Kyle. *I Samuel: A New Translation, Introduction, and Commentary.* AB 8. Garden City, NY: Doubleday, 1980.

McKenzie, John. *A Theology of the Old Testament.* Eugene, OR: Wipf & Stock, 1974.

McKenzie, Steven L. *The Trouble with Kings: The Composition of the Book of Kings in the Deuteronomistic History.* VTSup 42. Leiden: Brill, 1991.

McKinlay, Judith E. "Negotiating the Frame for Viewing the Death of Jezebel." *BibInt* 10 (2002): 305–23.

Menn, Esther M. "A Little Girl Shall Lead Them: The Role of the Little Israelite Servant Girl (2 Kings 5:1-19)." *CurTM* 35 (2008): 340–48.

Meshel, Ze'ev. "Did Yahweh Have a Consort?" *BAR* 5 (1979): 24–34.

Mobley, Gregory. *Samson and the Liminal Hero in the Ancient Near East.* New York: T&T Clark, 2006.

———. "The Wild Man in the Bible and the Ancient Near East." *JBL* 116 (1997): 217–33.

Moinier, Bernard M., and Tilman B. Drueke. "Aphrodite, Sex and Salt—from Butterfly to Man." *Nephrology Dialysis Transplantation* 23 (2008): 2154–61.

Murray, Donald F. "Of All the Years the Hopes—Or Fears? Jehoiachin in Babylon (2 Kings 25:27-30)." *JBL* 120 (2001): 245–65.

Na'aman, Nadav. "The Deuteronomist and Voluntary Servitude to Foreign Powers." *JSOT* 65 (1995): 37–53.

———. "The Historical Background to the Conquest of Samaria (720 BC)." *Bib* 71 (1990): 206–25.

———. "New Light on Hezekiah's Second Prophetic Story (2 Kgs. 19,9b-35)." *Bib* 81 (2000): 393–402.

Nelson, Richard. "The Altar of Ahaz: A Revisionist View." *HAR* 10 (1986): 267–76.

———. *The Double Redaction of the Deuteronomistic History.* Sheffield: JSOT Press, 1981.

———. *First and Second Kings.* IBC. Atlanta: John Knox, 1987.

Newsom, Carol A., and Sharon H. Ringe, eds. *The Women's Bible Commentary.* Louisville: Westminster John Knox, 1992.

Ngan, Lai Ling Elizabeth. "2 Kings 5." *RevExp* 94 (1997): 589–97.

Nicholson, Ernest W. *Deuteronomy and Tradition.* Philadelphia: Fortress, 1967.

Niditch, Susan. *My Brother Esau Is a Hairy Man: Hair and Identity in Ancient Israel.* New York: Oxford University Press, 2008.

———. *War in the Hebrew Bible: A Study of the Ethics of Violence.* New York: Oxford University Press, 1993.

Noth, Martin. *The Deuteronomistic History.* JSOTSup 15. Sheffield: JSOT, 1981.

Nwaoru, Emmanuel O. "The Story of Naaman (2 Kings 5:1-19): Implication for Mission Today." *Swedish Missiological Themes* 96 (2008): 27–41.

O'Brien, D. P. " 'Is This the Time to Accept . . . ?' (2 Kings V 26B): Simply Moralizing (LXX) or an Ominous Foreboding of Yahweh's Rejection of Israel (MT)?" *VT* 46 (1996): 448–57.

Oded, Bustanay. "Ahaz's Appeal to Tiglath-Pileser III in the Context of the Assyrian Policy of Expansion." In *Studies in the Archaeology and History of Ancient Israel in Honour of Moshe Dothan*, edited by M. Heltzer, A. Segal, and D. Kaufman, 63–71. Haifa: Haifa University Press, 1993.

———. "The Historical Background of the Syro-Ephraimite War." *CBQ* 34 (1972): 153–65.

Olley, John W. "2 Kings 13: A Cluster of Hope in God." *JSOT* 36 (2011): 199–218.

Olyan, Saul M. *Asherah and the Cult of Yahweh in Israel.* SBLMS 34. Atlanta: Scholars Press, 1988.

———. "*Hašālôm*: Some Literary Considerations of 2 Kings 9." *CBQ* 46 (1984): 652–68.

———. "Some Observations Concerning the Identity of the Queen of Heaven." *UF* 19 (1987): 161–74.

Overholt, Thomas. *Prophecy in Cross-Cultural Perspective: A Sourcebook for Biblical Researchers.* SBLSBS 17. Atlanta: Scholars Press, 1986.

Pakkala, Juha. "Zedekiah's Fate and the Dynastic Succession." *JBL* 128 (2006): 443–52.

Park, Song-Mi Suzie. *Hezekiah and the Dialogue of Memory.* Minneapolis: Fortress, 2015.

Parker, Julie Faith. *Valuable and Vulnerable: Children in the Hebrew Bible, Especially the Elisha Cycle.* BJS 355. Providence, RI: Brown University Press, 2013.

Parker, Simon B. "Jezebel's Reception of Jehu." *Maarav* 1 (1978): 67–78.

Pippin, Tina. "Jezebel Re-Vamped." *Semeia* 69–70 (1995): 221–33.

Pressler, Carolyn. "Wives and Daughters, Bond and Free: Views of Women in the Slave Laws of Exodus 21.2-11." In *Gender and Law in the Hebrew Bible and the Ancient Near East*, edited by Victory H. Matthews, Bernard M. Levinson, and Tikva Frymer-Kensky, 147–72. Sheffield: Sheffield Academic, 1998.

Prior, Michael. "The Bible and the Redeeming Idea of Colonialism." *Studies in World Christianity* 5 (1999): 129–55.

Provan, Ian W. *1 and 2 Kings.* NIBCOT. Peabody, MA: Hendrickson; Carlisle: Paternoster, 1995.

———. *Hezekiah and the Book of Kings: A Contribution to the Debate about the Composition of the Deuteronomistic History.* Berlin: de Gruyter, 1988.

Pyles, David. "A Double Portion of Thy Spirit." http://www.bcbsr.com/survey/eli.html.

Quint, David. *Epic and Empire: Politics and General Form from Virgil to Milton.* Princeton, NJ: Princeton University Press, 1993.

von Rad, Gerhard. *Old Testament Theology.* New York: Harper & Row, 1962.

———. *Studies in Deuteronomy.* SBT 9. London: SCM, 1953.

Rashkow, Ilona. *Taboo or Not Taboo: Sexuality and Family in the Hebrew Bible.* Minneapolis: Fortress, 2000.

Richter, Sandra. *The Deuteronomistic History and the Name Theology in the Bible and the Ancient Near East.* BZAW 318. Berlin: de Gruyter, 2002.

Römer, Thomas, and Albert de Pury. "Deuteronomistic Historiography (DH): History of Research and Debated Issues." In *Israel Constructs its History: Deuteronomistic Historiography in Recent Research,* edited by Albert de Pury, Thomas Römer, and Jean-Daniel Macchi, 24–141. Sheffield: Sheffield Academic, 2000.

Roncace, Mark. "Elisha and the Woman of Shunem: 2 Kings 4.8-37 and 8.1-6 Read in Conjunction." *JSOT* 91 (2000): 109–27.

Rowlett, Lori. "Violent Femmes and S/M: Queering Samson and Delilah." In *Queer Commentary and the Hebrew Bible,* edited by Ken Stone, 106–15. JSOTSup 334. Cleveland: Pilgrim Press, 2001.

Rudman, Dominic. "Is the Rabshakeh also among the Prophets? A Study of 2 Kings XVIII 17-35." *VT* 50 (2000): 100–110.

Runions, Erin. "Violence and the Economy of Desire in Ezekiel 16:1-45." In *A Feminist Companion to the Prophets and Daniel,* edited by Athalya Brenner, 156–69. FCB 8. Sheffield: Sheffield Academic, 2001.

Sakenfield, Katharine Doob, ed. *The New Interpreter's Dictionary of the Bible.* 5 vols. Nashville: Abingdon, 2006–2009.

Satterthwaite, Philip. "The Elisha Narratives and Coherence of 2 Kings 2–8." *TynBul* 49 (1998): 1–28.

Schipper, Jeremy. "'Significant Resonances' with Mephisbosheth in 2 Kings 25:27-30: A Response to Donald F. Murray." *JBL* 124 (2005): 521–29.

Schneider, Tammi. "Did King Jehu Kill His Own Family? New Interpretation Reconciles Biblical Text with Famous Assyrian Inscription." *BAR* 21 (1995): 26–33, 80, 82.

Schniedewind, William M. "History and Interpretation: The Religion of Ahab and Manasseh in the Book of Kings." *CBQ* 55 (1993): 646–61

———. "The Source Citations of Manasseh: King Manasseh in History and Homily." *VT* 41 (1991): 450–61.

Schroer, Silvia. "Gender and Iconography from the Viewpoint of a Feminist Biblical Scholar." *Lectio difficilior* 2 (2008). http://www.lectio.unibe.ch/08_2/Silvia_Schroer_Gender_and_Iconography.html.

Schroer, Silvia, and Othmar Keel. *Die Ikonographie Palästinas/Israels und der Alte Orient, Band 1: Eine Religionsgeschichte in Bildern Band 1.* Fribourg: Academic Press, 2005.

Schüssler Fiorenza, Elisabeth. *But She Said: Feminist Practices of Biblical Interpretation.* Boston: Beacon Press, 1992.

Seeman, Don. "The Watcher at the Window: Cultural Poetics of a Biblical Motif." *Prooftexts* 24 (2004): 1–50.

Seow, Choon-Leong. "The First and Second Book of Kings." In *NIB*, edited by Leander E. Keck et al., 3:1–295. Nashville: Abingdon, 1999.

Sharp, Carolyn. " 'Are You for Us, or for Our Adversaries': A Feminist and Postcolonial Interrogation of Joshua 2–12 for the Contemporary Church." *Int* 66 (2012): 141–52.

Shemesh, Yael. "Elisha and the Miraculous Jug of Oil (2 Kgs 4:1-7)." *JHS* 8 (2008). http://www.jhsonline.org/Articles/article_81.pdf.

Shields, Mary E. "Multiple Exposures: Body Rhetoric and Gender Characterization in Ezekiel 16." *JFSR* 14 (1998): 5–18.

———. "Subverting a Man of God, Elevating a Woman: Role and Power Reversals in 2 Kings 4." *JSOT* 58 (1993): 59–69.

Siebert-Hommes, Jopie. "The Widow of Zarephath and the Great Woman of Shunem: A Comparative Analysis of Two Stories." In *A Feminist Companion to the Bible: Samuel and Kings*, edited by Athalya Brenner, 231–50. FCB 7. Sheffield: Sheffield Academic, 2000.

Smelik, Klaas A. D. "The New Altar of King Ahaz (2 Kings 16): Deuteronomistic Re-interpretation of a Cult Reform." In *Deuteronomy and Deuteronomic Literature: Festschrift C. H. W. Brekelmans*, edited by M. Vervenne and J. Lust, 263–78. Leuven: Leuven University Press/Peeters, 1997.

———. "The Representation of King Ahaz in 2 Kings 16 and 2 Chronicles 28." In *Intertextuality in Ugarit and Israel*, edited by J. C. De Moor, 141–85. OTS 40. Leiden: Brill, 1998.

Smend, Rudolf. "Das Gesetz und die Völker: Ein Beitrag zur deuteronomistischen Redaktionsgeschichte." In *Probleme biblischer Theologie. Gerhard von Rad zum 70. Geburtstag*, edited by H. W. Wolff, 494–509. Munich: Kaiser, 1971.

———. "The Law and the Nations: A Contribution to Deuteronomistic Tradition History." In *Reconsidering Israel and Judah: Recent Studies on the Deuteronomistic History*, edited by Gary N. Knoppers and J. Gordon McConville, 95–110. Translated by P. T. Daniels. Winona Lake, IN: Eisenbrauns, 2000.

Smith, Jonathan Z. "Differential Equations: On Constructing the Other." In *Relating Religion: Essays in the Study of Religion*, 230–50. Chicago: University of Chicago Press, 2004.

———. "What a Difference a Difference Makes." In *Relating Religion: Essays in the Study of Religion*, 251–302. Chicago: University of Chicago Press, 2004.

Smith, Mark S. *The Early History of God: Yahweh and the Other Deities of Ancient Israel.* Grand Rapids, MI: Eerdmans, 2002.

Smith, Morton. "The Veracity of Ezekiel, the Sins of Manasseh, and Jeremiah 44:18." *ZAW* 87 (1975): 11–16.

Smith, W. Alan. "Naaman and Elisha: Healing, Wholeness, and the Task of Religious Education." *RelEd* 89 (1994): 205–19.

Sprinkle, Joe M. "2 Kings 3: History or Historical Fiction?" *BBR* 9 (1999): 247–70.

———. "Deuteronomic 'Just War' (Deut 20,10-20) and 2 Kings 3,27." *ZABR* 6 (2000): 285–301.

Stager, Lawrence E. "Forging an Identity: The Emergence of Ancient Israel." In *The Oxford History of the Biblical World*, edited by M. D. Coogan, 122–75. New York: Oxford University Press, 1998.

Stavrakopoulou, Francesca. "The Blackballing of Manasseh." In *Good Kings and Bad Kings: The Kingdom of Judah in the Seventh Century BCE*, edited by Lester L. Grabbe, 248–63. London: T&T Clark, 2005.

———. *King Manasseh and Child Sacrifice: Biblical Distortions of Historical Realities.* BZAW 338. Berlin: de Gruyter, 2004.

Stern, Ephraim. "Pagan Yahwism: The Folk Religion of Ancient Israel." *BAR* 27 (2001): 21–29.

Stiebert, Johanna. *Fathers and Daughters in the Hebrew Bible.* Oxford: Oxford University Press, 2013.

Strimple, Cheryl, and Ovidiu Creangă. "'And His Skin Returned Like a Skin of a Little Boy': Masculinity, Disability and the Healing of Naaman." In *Men and Masculinity in the Hebrew Bible and Beyond*, edited by Ovidiu Creangă, 110–26. Sheffield: Sheffield Phoenix, 2010.

Tadmor, Hayim. "The Campaigns of Sargon II of Assur: Chronological-Historical Study." *JCS* 12 (1958): 22–40.

Talshir, Zipora. "The Three Deaths of Josiah and the Strata of Biblical Historiography." *VT* 46 (1996): 213–36.

Tangberg, Arvid. "A Note on Ba'al-Zebub in 2 Kgs 1:2, 3, 6, 16." *SJOT* 6 (1992): 293–96.

Tarlin, Jan. "Toward a 'Female' Reading of the Elijah Cycle: Ideology and Gender in the Interpretation of 1 Kings 17–19, 21 and 2 Kings 1–2.18." In *Feminist Companion to Samuel and Kings*, edited by Athalya Brenner, 208–17. FCB 5. Sheffield: Sheffield Academic, 1994.

Thiel, Winfried. "Athaliah." In *ABD*, 1:511. New York: Doubleday, 1992.

Tiemeyer, Leon-Sofia. "Prophecy as a Way of Cancelling Prophecy—The Strategic Uses of Foreknowledge." *ZAW* 117 (2005): 329–50.

Todd, Judith A. "The Pre-Deuteronomistic Elijah Cycle." In *Elijah and Elisha in Socio-Literary Perspective*, edited by Robert B. Coote, 1–35. Atlanta: Scholars Press, 1992.

Toorn, Karel van der. "Baal-Zebub." In *NIDB*, edited by Katharine Doob Sakenfeld et al., 1:373–74. Nashville: Abingdon, 2009.

Trible, Phyllis. "Exegesis for Storytellers and Other Strangers." *JBL* 114 (1995): 3–19.

van der Horst, Pieter W. "Anti-Samaritan Propaganda in Early Judaism." In *Persuasion and Discussion in Early Christianity, Ancient Judaism, and Hellenism,* edited by Pieter W. van der Horst, M. J. J. Menken, J. F. M. Smit, and G. van Oyen, 25–44. Leuven: Peeters, 2003.

Van Seters, John. *The Edited Bible: The Curious History of the "Editor" in Biblical Criticism.* Winona Lake, IN: Eisenbrauns, 2006.

Veijola, Timo. *Die Ewige Dynastie: David und die Entstehung seiner Dynastie nach der deuteronomistischen Darstellung.* Helsinki: Suomalainen Tiedeakatemia, 1975.

———. *Das Königtum in der Beurteilung der deuteronomistischen Historiographie: Eine redaktionsgeschichtliche Untersuchung.* Helsinki: Suomalainen Tiedeakatemia, 1977.

Viviano, Pauline A. "2 Kings 17: A Rhetorical and Form-Critical Analysis." *CBQ* 49 (1987): 548–59.

———. "Exhortation and Admonition in Deuteronomistic Terms: A Comparison of Second Kings 17:7-18, 34-41, Second Kings 21:2-16, and Jeremiah 7:1–8:3." *BR* 56 (2011): 35–54.

Vriezen, Karel J. H. "Cakes and Figurines: Related Women's Cultic Offerings in Ancient Israel." In *On Reading Prophetic Texts: Gender-Specific and Related Studies in Memory of Fokkelien van Dijk-Hemmes,* edited by Bob Becking and Meindert Dijkstra, 251–63. Leiden: Brill, 1996.

Walton, John H. "New Observations on the Date of Isaiah." *JETS* 28 (1985): 129–32.

Weems, Renita J. "Huldah, the Prophet: Reading a (Deuteronomistic) Woman's Identity." In *A God So Near: Essays on Old Testament Theology in Honor of Patrick D. Miller,* edited by Brent A. Strawn and Nancy R. Bowen, 321–39. Winona Lake, IN: Eisenbrauns, 2003.

Weinfeld, Moshe. "The Worship of Molech and of the Queen of Heaven and its Background." *UF* 4 (1972): 133–54.

Weippert, Manfred. "Fragen des israelitischen Geschichtsbewusstseins." *VT* 23 (1973): 417–42.

Wentz, Richard. *The Contemplation of Otherness: The Critical Vision of Religion.* Macon, GA: Mercer University Press, 1984.

Westbrook, Raymond. "Elisha's True Prophecy in 2 Kings 3." *JBL* 124 (2005): 530–32.

Westbrook, Raymond, and Bruce Wells. *Everyday Law in Biblical Israel: An Introduction.* Louisville: Westminster John Knox, 2009.

Whitcomb, Kelly. "The Queen of Heaven or YHWH of Hosts: Does the God of Israel Protest (In)sufficiently in Jeremiah 44." *Conversations with the Biblical World* 33 (2013): 82–97.

White, Ellen. "Asherah and the Asherim: Goddess or Cult Symbol." https://www.biblicalarchaeology.org/daily/ancient-cultures/ancient-israel/asherah-and-the-asherim-goddess-or-cult-symbol/.

Wiesel, Elie. *Messengers of God: Biblical Portraits and Legends.* Translated by Marion Wiesel. New York: Random House, 1976.

———. *The Trial of God.* Translated by Marion Wiesel. New York: Schocken Books, 1979.

Wildberger, Hans. *Isaiah 28–39: A Continental Commentary.* Translated by Thomas H. Trapp. Minneapolis: Fortress, 2002.

Wills, Lawrence M. *Not God's People: Insiders and Outsiders in the Biblical World.* Lanham, MD: Rowman & Littlefield, 2008.

Wilson, Robert R. *Prophecy and Society in Ancient Israel.* Philadelphia: Fortress, 1980.

Woods, Fred E. "Elisha and the Children: The Question of Accepting Prophetic Succession." *BYU Studies* 32 (1992): 47–58.

Wright, J. Edward. "Whither Elijah? The Ascension of Elijah in Biblical and Extrabiblical Traditions." In *Things Revealed: Studies in Early Jewish and Christian Literature in Honor of Michael E. Stone,* edited by Esther G. Chazon, David Satran, and Ruth A. Clements, 123–38. JSJSup 89. Leiden: Brill, 2004.

Yee, Gale A. *Poor Banished Children of Eve: Woman as Evil in the Hebrew Bible.* Minneapolis: Fortress, 2003.

Younger, K. Lawson. "The Fall of Samaria in Light of Recent Research." *CBQ* 61 (1999): 461–82.

Zerbe, K. J. " 'Your Feet's Too Big': An Inquiry into Psychological and Symbolic Meanings of the Foot." *Psychoanal Rev* 72 (1985): 301–14.

Zucker, David. "Elijah and Elisha: Part I; Moses and Joshua." *JQR* 40 (2012): 225–30.

Index of Scripture References and Other Ancient Writings

Genesis

15:15	298
18:5	51
18:14	47
19	80
19:30-38	3
21	55
24:12	72 n. 40
26	51
31:47	xxxv n. 45
34:25	149

Exodus

1	152
2	63
3:14	xxxiv
7:14-25	33
7:21	33
8–12	37
13:8	xvii
15:20-21	287 n. 9
21:2-11	43 n. 15
21:7	43
22:15	44
22:16	44
23:8	216

Leviticus

7:2-6	133
13:46	198
14:7	68
14:16	68
14:27	68
14:51	68
18:21	209

Numbers

6:1-21	6
12:14-15	198
16	259
25	127
25:8	259
27:8-11	95
27:18	19
36:1-12	95

Deuteronomy

2:27	284
4:19	271
5:29	284
6:5	285
7:1-4	212
9:4	209

9:26	277
9:29	277
12:2	213
13:7	149
16:5-6	294
16:19	216
17:16	313
17:20	284
18:10	209
20:14	61
20:10-20	35 n. 20, 36
20:19-20	31
21:10-14	61
21:11	230
22:28	44
22:29	44
23:3	3
24:16	186
25:11	51
28:14	284
28:56-57	84
28:68	313
29:1-27	291
30:19	247
32:9	277
34:9	19

34:10	285

Joshua

2	129
2–12	210 n. 10
5:10-11	294
6:26	23
10:32	35
15:18-19	96
22:19	72 n. 40

Judges

1:1-3	28
1:13-15	96
3:10	22
3:28	35
4:14	35
4:15-21	129
5:28-30	127
6:34	22
6:36-40	28
7:2	35
8:7	35
9:5	135
9:14-15	190
11	33, 63
11:29	22
11:30-40	34 n. 14
12:14	135
13	55
13:25	22
14:6	22
15:14	22
16:28	72 n. 40
19	22
20:18-28	28

1 Samuel

1:1	55
3:11	277
6:16	129
6:18	4
10:6	22
16	110
16:13-14	22

18:30	4
19:9	22
23	72 n. 40
23:2-4	28
26	72 n. 40
26:19	72 n. 40
28:19	35
29:3	4
29:4	4
29:9	4
30:6-8	72 n. 40
30:14	154

2 Samuel

2:1	28
5:19	28
6:16	127
6:25	127
7	123, 146
8:2	106
8:12-14	106
8:12	2
8:18	154
13:14	51
15:8	72 n. 40
15:18	154
20:7	154
20:23	154
23:2	22

1 Kings

2:19	160
3:16-28	82
3:28-29	82
8	xlvi n. 18
8:32	277
8:51	277
8:64	221
8:65	193
9:16	96
11	107
11:12	261
11:13	261
11:14-22	106
11:32	261

11:33	208
11:34	261
13:1-3	293
13:24	234
13:32	293
14:8	208
14:11	133
14:15	174
14:23	174, 213
14:26	217
15:2	159
15:10	159
15:11	284
15:13	159
16	126, 132
16:14	133
16–21	127
16:3	124
16:8-20	127
16:8	217
16:29-34	231
16:31-33	28
16:34	23
17	40, 55, 125, 132
17–19	1 n. 1, 13 n. 6
17:14-16	19
17:20-22	19
18	30, 132
18:4	125
18:12	22
18:19	119, 125, 174
18:30	284
18:40	125
19:2	125
19:15-18	99
19:19	25
19:20	42
20:36	234
21	1 n. 1, 13 n. 6, 110, 121

21:4-7	119	1:15b	8		33, 34,
21:8	119	1:16	5 n. 11		35 n. 18,
21:13	121	1:17	10		37, 79, 209
21:19	121, 133	2	8, 11, 12,	3:1	159
21:21-22	121		12 n. 4,	3:1-19	29, 30
21:21-23	114		15 n. 11, 22,	3:1-27	27
21:23	121, 125		22 n. 26,	3:4-19	28
21:23-24	133		30, 40 n. 3,	3:5	2
21:24	121		41, 183	3:9	28
22:5	28	2–8	61 n. 3	3:10	29
22:24	22	2:1	12 n. 4, 22,	3:11	30
22:41-51	105		22 n. 26	3:13	29
22:51	159	2:1-2	12	3:14	29
22:47	28	2:1-6	12, 13	3:18	31
		2:1-15	11	3:20-27	31, 32
2 Kings		2:1-18	50	3:22	32
1	10, 12 n. 4,	2:2	53	3:27	27,
	68, 98	2:2-3	115		35 n. 20
1:1	2, 27	2:3	15	4	4, 15,
1:1-8	3	2:4	53		16, 39,
1:1-18	1	2:4-5	19, 115		49 n. 21,
1–2:18	1 n. 1,	2:5	15		52, 53, 54,
	13 n. 6	2:6	53, 115		55, 56, 64,
1:2	4, 5 n. 11,	2:7	15, 16		68, 74, 76,
	98	2:7-9	15, 16		94, 96, 97,
1:3	5, 5 n. 11	2:8	15, 25		132
1:9-18	7, 8	2:9	17	4:1	40, 41, 42,
1:9-12	7	2:10	17, 18, 19		43
1:13-15	7	2:10-18	20, 179	4:1-7	39, 40,
1:16-17	7	2:12	18, 20,		40 n. 2, 41,
1:3-4	6		138, 179		45, 112
1:5-8	6	2:13-14	25	4:1-44	39
1:6	5 n. 11	2:14	18	4:2	41
1:7	9	2:15	15, 18	4:4	44
1:8	25	2:15-16	15	4:5-7	44
1:9	8, 115	2:16	15 n. 14	4:6	43
1:10a	8	2:19-22	23, 24	4:7-37	39
1:10b	8	2:21	23	4:8	49, 51
1:11	8, 115	2:23	25	4:8-36	45
1:12	8	2:23-25	24, 25, 182	4:8-37	8, 45,
1:12a	8	2:43-44	19		45 n. 18,
1:12b	8	3	2, 27,		46, 52 n.
1:12-14	8		27 n. 1,		31, 53, 55,
1:13	115		28, 30, 31,		94, 94 n. 1
1:15a	8				

4:9-10	45	5:14	62, 70	6:27	82
4:12	45, 49	5:15	70, 71, 74	6:30	83
4:13	45, 94, 96	5:15-18	70, 71	6:31	83, 86
4:14	47, 96	5:16	71	6:32–7:2	86, 87
4:16	47, 49	5:18	71, 219	6:33	86
4:19	54	5:19-27	72, 73	7:1	86
4:19-20	49	5:26	72	7:2	87
4:21	69	5:27	73	7:3	89, 198
4:22-30	55	6	5 n. 11,	7:3-20	89, 90, 91,
4:24-30	69		76, 80, 94,		92
4:25-26	48		104, 132,	7:4	89
4:27	53		177, 310	7:5	89
4:28	48, 50	6–7	75, 232	7:6	91
4:30	48, 52, 53	6:1–7:20	75	7:6-7	89
4:31	50, 55	6:1-7	75, 76, 83,	7:9	90
4:34	50		112	7:15	89
4:35	68	6:6	76, 77 n. 3	7:16	90
4:36	49	6:8–7:20	79 n. 10	7:17	91
4:38-41	8, 56,	6:8-11	77	7:17-20	87
	58 n. 40	6:8-13	98	7:18-20	91
4:38-42	39	6:8-14	77, 78	8	54, 93, 94,
4:38-44	57	6:8-23	83		96, 97, 98,
4:39	56	6:10	77		102, 176
4:42-44	39, 56, 83	6:11	78	8:1	94
5	59,	6:12	78	8:1-6	52 n. 31,
	61 n. 5, 63,	6:13	78		54, 94,
	64, 68, 69,	6:15-23	79, 80, 81,		94 n. 1, 95,
	72 n. 41,		83		96
	73, 102	6:16	79	8:1-29	93
5–6	78 n. 8	6:17	20, 79, 138	8:2	94
5:1	60, 74	6:17-23	91	8:3	94, 96
5:1-4	59, 60	6:18	79	8:5	95, 96, 97
5:1-19	61 n. 5,	6:19	79	8:6	45, 95, 96
	70 n. 33	6:22	80	8:7-15	98, 99
5:1-27	59	6:24	99	8:9	98
5:2-3	61 n. 4	6:24-31	82, 83	8–9	93
5:3	62	6:24-33	82 n. 18,	8:10	100
5:4	62		83 n. 21,	8:10-13	99
5:5	98		102	8:11-12	202
5:5-7	66, 67	6:24	102	8:12	101, 103
5:8-14	68, 69	6:24–7:20	86 n. 30,	8:13	103
5:10-14	63		177	8:15	100,
5:12	68	6:25	82,		100 n. 18
5:13	69		82 n. 17	8:16	105

8:16-29	104, 105, 106	9:14-15	114	10:31	140
8:18	105, 144, 159, 208, 209	9:15	114	10:32-33	101, 140, 141
		9:16	114	11	xli, 105, 143, 150 n. 17, 152, 153, 161, 169, 170, 171, 280
		9:18	115		
8:19	105, 106	9:19	115		
8:20	106	9:20	111, 115		
8:25	105, 106	9:22	116, 117, 147		
8:26	105, 106, 144, 159, 209	9:23	121	11:1	145
8:27	105, 106, 107	9:24	121	11:1-3	144, 145, 156
		9:24-29	121, 122		
		9:25	121		
8:28	105	9:25-26	121	11:1-15	159
8:28-29	106	9:26	121, 122	11:1-21	143
8:29	105	9:27-28	123	11:2	149
9	xli, 93, 116, 116 n. 14, 123, 124, 130	9:27-29	143	11:3	149, 155
		9:30	126, 127, 128	11:4	152, 154, 155, 157, 169
		9:30-37	123, 124, 159		
9–10	148	9:31	127		
9–11	128 n. 46	9:32	131	11:4-21	151, 152, 153, 154
9:1	110	9:33	131		
9:1-6	148	9:34	132	11:8	157
9:1–10:28	105	9:35	109	11:8-12	155
9:1-13	110, 111, 112	9:36	125, 132	11:10	155, 157
		9:36-37	128	11:12	155, 157
9:1-37	109	9:37	132	11:13	155
9:2	110	10:1-14	136, 137	11:13-14	155
9:2-3	110	10:1-36	135	11:14	158
9:4	110	10:3	136	11:15	155, 157
9:5	110	10:6-7	136	11:15-16	155
9:6	110	10:8	136	11:17	155, 157
9:7	110	10:9-10	136	11:17-19	155
9:7-9	105 n. 29	10:10-11	105 n. 29	11:18	155
9:8	110	10:13-14	136	11:19	155
9:9	110	10:14	137	11:20	156
9:10	111	10:15	138	11:21	162, 162 n. 3
9:11	111, 112	10:15-36	138, 139, 140, 141		
9:11-12	111			11:26	121
9:12	111, 112	10:16	138	12	162, 165, 166, 173, 185, 186, 285
9:13	112	10:20	138		
9:14-23	114, 115, 116	10:27	139		
		10:30	140		

12:1	162, 162 n. 3	13:10-25	179, 180, 181	15–23	201 n. 8
				15–25	211
12:1-3	162, 163	13:12-13	178	15:1-7	197, 198
12:1-12	161	13:13	178	15:1-38	197
12:2	163, 164	13:14	179, 182	15:3	198
12:3	162	13:14-19	182	15:4	198
12:4-5	164	13:14-25	178	15:5	198, 199
12:4-21	164, 165, 166, 167, 187	13:15-16	179	15:8	200
		13:15-17	179 n. 14	15:8-31	200, 201, 202, 203
12:6	167	13:17	177, 179		
12:7	164	13:18-19	179	15:10	200
12:9	164	13:19	180, 182	15:13	198
12:9-15	164	13:20	180, 184	15:14	200, 202
12:12-13	285	13:23	183	15:14-16	201 n. 6
12:16	285	13:25	183	15:16	202
12:17	168	14	185, 232	15:19	204
12:19	217	14:1	186	15:20	217
12:20	161	14:1-22	186, 187, 188, 189	15:22	204
12:20-21	168			15:25	204
12:21	169	14:1-29	185	15:28	205
13	xli, xlii, 93, 125, 173, 176, 177, 177 n. 8, 178, 183, 232, 271	14:3	186	15:29	205, 217
		14:4	186	15:30	198, 204
		14:7	188	15:32	198
		14:8	189, 190	15:32-34	200
		14:10	190	15:32-38	197, 199
		14:11	190	15:33	200
		14:13-14	191	15:34	198
		14:14	217	15:35	200
13:1	174	14:15-16	178	15:37	205, 214
13:1-2	177	14:18-20	194	16	5 n. 11, 207, 208 n. 2, 214, 217, 232
13:2	174, 176	14:19-20	191		
13:1-9	174, 176	14:23-29	192, 193		
13:1-25	173	14:25	193		
13:22-25	101	14:26-27	194		
13:3	101, 176, 177	14:27	177, 197	16:1-4	207, 208, 215 n. 26
		14:28	193		
13:4	177	14:29	194	16:1-20	207
13:4-5	177, 178, 182	15	197, 200, 201, 201 n. 8, 202, 204, 232	16:2	208
				16:3	209, 210, 212, 221, 273
13:5	177				
13:6	174, 177			16:4	213
13:7	176			16:5-9	213, 214
13:10-13	178	15–16	201 n. 8		

16:5	213, 216	17:12	231	18:17-37	244, 245,
16:7	215	17:13	231, 233		246, 247
16:7-9	221	17:14	231	18:18	244
16:8	215	17:15	231	18:19	256
16:9	217, 219	17:16	231	18:19-20	244
16:10	218	17:17	231	18:20	256
16:10-16	221	17:18	233	18:21	245
16:10-18	217	17:19-20	233	18:22	246
16:10-20	217, 218,	17:24	234	18:23	245
	219	17:24-41	234, 235,	18:24	245, 246
16:11	218		236, 237	18:25	246, 256
16:12-13	218	17:27	234	18:26	248, 249
16:14	218	17:29-30	235	18:27	248, 256
16:15-16	218	17:29-33	234	18:28	256
16:16	220	17:34-41	269 n. 2	18:29-30	247
16:17-18	221	17:35-39	235	18:31	247
16:18	218	17:35-41	234	18:32	246, 247,
17	xli, 197,	17:41	235		257
	223, 225,	18–19	243, 251,	18:33-35	246
	227, 229,		258, 261	18:36	248
	231, 233,	18–20	211,	19:1-9a	249, 250
	234		241 n. 5	19:2	249
17–19	1	18:1-8	239, 240,	19:3	249
17:1	223		243, 284	19:6	251
17:1-6	223, 224,	18:1–20:21	239	19:7	251
	231	18:3	240	19:9	251, 252
17:1-41	223	18:4	162, 241,	19:9a	252
17:2	223		242	19:9b	252
17:3	225	18:5	241	19:9b-35	252
17:3-4	224	18:6	241	19:9b-37	252, 253,
17:4	226	18:7	241		254, 255
17:5	224	18:7–19:9a	252	19:14-15	254
17:6	225, 226	18:7–19:37	256	19:15	257
17:7	231	18:9-12	242	19:17-19	254
17:7-18	269 n. 2	18:9-16	243	19:21	265
17:7-23	231, 232,	18:10	242	19:21-22	257
	232 n. 29,	18:11	242	19:22	255
	233	18:13-16	242, 243,	19:23-27	255
17:8-24	53		244	19:28	255
17:9	231	18:15	217	19:29	255, 256
17:9-24	16	18:16	243	19:32-33	255
17:10	213, 231	18:17	244	19:34	255
17:11	231	18:17-35	247 n. 7	19:35	255

19:36	252, 255, 257	21:13	105 n. 29, 277	23:26	299
19:37	252, 256	21:16	279	23:29	297
20:1	258	21:19-26	280, 281	23:29-30	297, 298
20:1-11	258, 259, 260	21:23	280	23:30	299, 300
20:2	258	21:24	280	23:31	159, 300
20:3	259	22	269, 277	23:31-37	300, 301
20:5	260	22–23	267, 297	23:32	300
20:6	260, 261	22:1-7	283, 284	23:34	300
20:7	260, 261, 262	22:1–23:37	283	24–25	315 n. 33
		22:2	240, 284	24:1	304
20:8	262	22:4-7	285	24:2	305
20:12-21	262, 263	22:5-6	285	24:3	305
20:12	262	22:7	285	24:1-7	303, 304
20:13	262	22:8-20	285, 286, 287	24:1–25:30	303
20:14-15	262			24:6	305
20:15	264	22:11	286	24:7	304
20:18	262	22:13	286, 295	24:8	159
20:19	262, 266	22:14	286	24:8-17	306, 307
21	1, 16, 40 n. 3, 42, 112, 276 n. 30, 292	22:16-17	299	24:12	159, 217, 307
		22:17	289	24:14	307
		22:20	289, 298	24:14-16	307
		23:1-28	291, 292, 293, 294, 295	24:15	159
				24:17	307
21:1-18	270, 271, 272, 273, 273 n. 9	23	297	24:18	159, 308
		23:1	291	24:18–	
		23:2	291	25:30	308, 309, 310, 311
21:1-26	269	23:3	291	24:20	308
21:1	270	23:4	292	25	132, 308
21:2	210, 270, 271	23:5	292	25:1	308
		23:6	292	25:3	310
21:2-8	279	23:7	292	25:4	311
21:2-16	269	23:8-9	292	25:6	311, 313
21:3	271	23:10	292	25:7	311
21:4	271	23:11	293	25:9	312
21:6	210, 274	23:12	293	25:10	312
21:7	274	23:13	293	25:12	312
21:9	274	23:15	293	25:13-17	312
21:10-15	277, 278, 279	23:20	294, 296	25:18-20	312
		23:23	294	25:21	312
21:12	277	23:24	292	25:23	312
21:12-15	299	23:25	285	25:27	313

25:27-30	314 n. 29,	**Job**		63:14	22
	314 n. 30,	42:15	96		
	314 n. 31			**Jeremiah**	
		Psalms		2:20	213
2 Chronicles		15:5	216	2:27	247
2	239	22:16	133	3	1, 120
18:23	22	22:20	133	3:6	213
20:14	22	104:35	xxiii	3:13	213
22:2	144	173:4	72 n. 40	3:19	96
22:10–				4:30	128
23:21	150 n. 17	**Proverbs**		7:1–8:3	269 n. 2
22:11	143, 149	1:20-21	xxi	7:6	279
24	169	1:23-25	xxi	7:18	271, 275
24:7	147	5	213	10:11	xxxv n. 45
24:17-18	170	6:24-36	128	11	308
24:17-22	163	7	107	13:18	159
24:20-21	170	7:13	51	14	1
24:22-25	170	8:22-31	xxi	17:2	213
25:1-13	189	9:1-5	xxi	19:3	277
25:14-15	189	9:3-5	xxi	20:7	51
26	198	17:23	216	22:3	279
26:6-10	199	31:1-9	160	22:17	279
26:16-20	199			22:24-27	159
27	200	**Isaiah**		25–27	308
27:2	198	1:1	198	26:22	306
27–28	201 n. 8	3:16	128	26:24	313
27:3	200	5:23	216	27:2-4	308
27:5	200	6:1	198	27.11	308
28	208 n. 2	7	201 n. 8,	35	138
28:4	213		214	36:12	306
33	276,	7:6	214	36:25	306
	276 n. 30	8:2	220	37:5	308
33:11	276	9:19-20	88	37:6-10	308
33:12	276	11:2	22	37:21	310
34:3	285	13:16	230	39:14	313
		28:21	199	40:1-6	313
4 Ezra		30:6-7	217	43:4-5	313
4:7–6:18	xxxv n. 45	31:1	247	44–45	313
5:9-10	xxi	36–39	239, 258	44:8-14	313
7:12-26	xxxv n. 45	40:7	22	44:15-18	275
13:55	xxi	54	1	44:17-19	271,
14:40	xxi	57:5	213		275
23	213	59:19	22	44:18	274 n. 19

44:30	35
46:25	247
52	308

Lamentations

1:1	230
2:20	84, 265

Ezekiel

5:10	83
6:13	213
11:5	22
16	1, 120, 230 n. 22
16:1-45	230 n. 22
19:1-14	159
21:21	180
22:6-7	279
22:12	216
22:12-13	279
22:25-31	279
23	1, 120
23–24	230
23:40	128
29:16	247

Daniel

2:4–7:28	xxxv n. 45
5:10-12	160

Hosea

1–2	120, 213
1–3	1
9:3-5	72 n. 40
13:15	22
13:16	203
14:1	103, 202

Amos

1:1	199
1:13	103, 202
2:6	43
7:17	72 n. 40
8:8	43

Micah

1:14	96
2:7	22
2:9	43
3:3	88, 89

Zechariah

7:5	313
8:19	313
14:2	230
14:5	199

Malachi

2:11-16	213

Wisdom

7:22-23	xxi
7:25	xxi
8:6	xxi
10:3	xxi

Sirach

15:7-8	xxi
24:23-24	xxi
51:26	xxi

Baruch

3:9–4:4	xxi
3:12	xxi
38:2	xxi
46:4-5	xxi
62:8	118

2 Baruch

48:33	xxi
48:36	xxi
64:2-3	279

1 Enoch

42	xxi

Matthew

10:25	5
11:14	12 n. 2
11:19	xxi
11:29	xx

Mark

12:24	5
17:1-9	12 n. 2
22:1-14	xxi

Mark

3:22	5
8:31	xxi
9:2-8	12 n. 2
9:11-13	12 n. 2

Luke

1:17	12 n. 2
7:35	xxi
9:28-36	12 n. 2
11:15-19	5
14:15-24	xxi

John

1:1-18	xxi
1:10-11	xxi
20:24-29	91 n. 33

1 Corinthians

7:9	xxiii
7:1	xxiv
14:34	xxiv

Revelation

2:20-23	118
11	12 n. 2

Clement of Alexandria

Const. ap.

2.3.22	259

Hildegard of Bingen

De operatione

Dei 1.4	xxiii n. 5

Josephus's *Antiquities*

5.30	264
9.225	199
9.227-91	234
9.283-87	226

9.62	82 n. 17	*The Martyrdom of*		b. Sanh. 103b	279
9.92	100 n. 19	*Isaiah*	279	b. Meg. 14b	289
9.7	146, 149			b. Yev. 49b	279
10.38	279	**Mishnah, Talmud,**		b. Qidd. 75b	234
		Targum, and other		Pesiq. Rab. 4:3	279
Lives of the Prophets		**Rabbinic Works**		Tg. Isa. 66.1	279
	279	b. Berakot 10a	xxiii	y. Sanh.10.28c	279

Index of Subjects

Abraham, 3, 47, 51, 181, 183
Ackerman, Susan, 130, 275
Ackroyd, Peter, 130
Adad-Nirari II, 178, 182
Adad-Rimmon, 71, 219
adultery, 51, 120, 213
afterlife, 117, 120, 147
Ahab, 2, 3, 28–29, 36, 40, 42, 105–7,
    109–12, 114, 119–24, 135–41, 144–
    45, 147, 150, 156, 159, 209, 216, 224,
    231, 271–73
Ahaz, 199, 205, 207–10, 212–21, 224,
    231, 240, 260, 262, 264, 269, 273,
    283, 293
Ahaziah, 1–12, 22, 27–28, 68, 98, 101–
    2, 104–7, 111, 114–16, 121–23, 137,
    143, 145–46, 148–49, 156, 159, 167,
    175, 188–89, 209
Alalakh, 165
altar, 153–54, 165, 199, 217–21, 245–46,
    270–71, 273–74, 276, 292–94, 296
Amaziah, 161, 167, 169, 173, 178–79,
    185–92, 194, 198, 208
Amit, Yairah, 52
Ammon, 202, 294, 304–5

people of (Ammonites), 202, 294,
    304–5
Amon, 270, 273, 280–81
Amos, 193
Anat, 133–34
androcentrism, xxviii, xxxiv–xxxv,
    xxxix–xli, 12, 51, 150, 158, 175, 197,
    205, 228, 291, 303, 315
angel, 3, 5–7, 9, 155, 257
anoint, 93, 99, 109–14, 148, 153–54,
    158, 298
Aphek, 179, 180, 182
Aphrodite, 24
apostasy, 2–3, 10, 12, 117, 147, 156,
    176, 213, 220, 231, 271, 274
Appler, Deborah, 132–33
Arabah, 188
Aram, 65, 69, 98–99, 114, 141, 173,
    176, 182, 193, 214–15, 217–19, 221
people of (Arameans), 60–61, 78,
    81, 86, 89–92, 106, 115, 161, 168,
    175–76, 178, 180, 183, 188, 191,
    193, 202, 304–5
Asa, 159
Aschkenasy, Nehama, 130

Asherah (figure), 119, 125, 127, 130, 133–34, 159, 174–77, 213, 271, 274–75, 288, 292–93

asherahs or asherah poles, 174, 177, 241, 250, 258, 270, 274, 296

Ashurbanipal, 203

assassination 86, 93, 100, 102–3, 114, 116–17, 120–23, 136, 143, 145–46, 148–49, 151, 155, 158–59, 161, 164, 166, 168–71, 185–87, 191–92, 194, 204, 280, 305, 313

assimilation, 220

Assyria, 101, 136, 141, 178, 182, 197, 200, 202–5, 207, 211, 214–21, 224–31, 230, 233–36, 239–66, 274–76, 280, 283, 289, 297–98, 306
  attack (701 BCE), 229, 239, 242–63, 267, 274–75, 306
  Inscription, 101, 141, 225–27, 230, 248
  Empire, 211, 220, 225, 227, 236, 248, 283, 297
  reliefs, 228–29, 248

Astarte, 125, 133, 293

astrology, 119, 292

Athaliah, xli, 105–7, 123, 143–59, 161–62, 164, 166, 168–71, 186, 195, 209, 280

augury, 231, 233, 271

autophagy, 85

Azariah, 186, 189, 192, 197–202, 208

Baal, xlii, 1, 3–9, 12, 22, 28–31, 42, 44, 57–58, 98, 109, 119–20, 124–26, 132–35, 138–40, 154–58, 231, 233, 270–71, 273, 292, 296

Baal-Zebub, 1, 3–9, 12, 98

Baasha, 110, 112

Babylon, 24, 118, 160, 180, 211, 225–27, 235–36, 239, 258, 262–66, 276, 297, 303–4, 306–14
  Chronicle, 225–27
  empire of, 304–5, 308, 315

people of (Babylonians), 180, 264, 311–13

ban, 210

baptism, 24

Barker, Margaret, 259

Barré, Lloyd, 128

Bathsheba, xxxix, 160

Beach, Eleanor Ferris, 130–31

bears, 25–26, 31, 182

Beelzebul, *see* Baal-Zebub

Beer-sheba, 162–63, 293

Begrich, Joachim, 214

Bellis, Alice Ogden, xli

belomancy, 180–81

Ben-Barak, Zafira, 147

Ben-hadad, 82–83, 98–103, 175–76, 181

Ben Zvi, Ehud, 280

Bethel, 13, 25, 141, 220, 235, 292–94, 296

Beth-Shemesh, 185–86, 188, 190–91

Blenkinsopp, Joseph, 20, 138

blindness, 77, 79–80, 92, 311
  see also vision

blood, 17, 32–33, 36–37, 112, 121–22, 124, 128, 131–33, 135, 138, 140, 186, 218–19, 248, 273, 279, 304–6

bribe, 168, 215–17, 243–44

Bronner, Leah, 22

Brueggemann, Walter, 61–64, 66

burial, 17, 111, 122–23, 178, 204, 293, 298–99

Burnett, Joel, 25

camel, 98–99

Camp, Claudia, xliv, 85, 146, 287

Canaan, 4, 31, 44, 133, 174, 210, 212, 274, 294
  people of (Canaanites), 210, 212

cannibalism, 75, 84–86, 88–89

Carchemish, 304

Carites, 152, 154

cedar, 188, 190, 253

Chaldeans, 304–5, 309, 311, 313
  see also Babylon, people of
Chapman, Cynthia, xliii, 9, 249, 257, 264
charioteer, 21, 115, 138
chariots, 20–22, 65, 68–69, 73, 78–80, 90, 92, 105, 111, 114–16, 122, 137–39, 175, 179, 183, 245, 253, 293, 298
  of fire, 20–22, 79–80, 92
Chemosh, 34, 293
childbirth: *see* children, birth of
children, xxi–xii, xxxii, 16–17, 24–26, 31, 33–57, 59–66, 68–69, 73–75, 82–89, 92, 94, 103, 122, 145–46, 148, 150–52, 156, 166–67, 182, 186–87, 195, 197, 205, 209–10, 217, 227–29, 236–37, 248–50, 259, 273, 285, 291–92, 310
  abuse of, 36, 43–44, 61 n. 8, 103, 217, 227–29
  birth of, 17, 33–34, 47, 49–55, 94, 249–50
  enslavement of, 40–41, 43–44, 59–63, 66, 68, 73–74
  orphanage of, 43, 69
  sacrifice of, 31, 33–37, 209–10, 236, 273, 292
Chisholm, Robert, 20, 35
Christianity, xxii, xxv–xxix, xxxii–xxxv, 70, 228, 279, 288
Chronicler, 189, 199–200, 285
Clement of Alexandria, 259
Clements, Ronald, 314
Cogan, Mordecai, xliv, 2 n. 2, 13, 18, 40, 45, 70, 76, 82, 114, 177, 180, 182, 186, 188–89, 191–92, 194, 198–99, 215–16, 219–20, 226, 233–34, 263, 276 n. 30, 280 n. 42, 286 n. 7, 289, 313
colonialism, xxxi, 2–4, 27, 36–37, 56, 65, 98, 101, 103, 106, 120, 176, 197, 205, 210–12, 226, 236, 315

commandments, 240–41, 270, 274, 292
corpse, 17, 110, 122, 124, 132–33, 184, 204, 257
covenant, 123, 145, 152–55, 157–58, 162, 181, 183, 231–32, 234–35, 243, 250, 261, 274, 278, 284, 291–92, 295
Cross, Frank Moore, xlvi

Damascus, 65, 69, 98–99, 114, 141, 173, 176, 182, 193, 214–15, 217–19, 221
  see also Aram
Daniel, xx, 160
David, xxxiii, 2–3, 28–29, 51, 65, 105, 106, 110, 122–23, 143, 146, 150, 152, 154, 157, 167, 170–71, 185–89, 191, 194, 198–200, 205, 208, 219, 233, 240, 255, 259, 260–61, 270–71, 280, 284, 298, 300, 307 n. 9, 315
  city of: 106, 122, 167, 198–99, 219
  see also Jerusalem
  house of, *see* temple
death, xli, 1–12, 17, 19, 23–24, 27–28, 31–34, 37, 39, 42, 44, 52–57, 67, 73, 80–81, 83, 87–89, 91–92, 96, 98, 100–102, 105, 107, 111, 113, 115, 118, 120, 123, 125, 127, 129, 131–32, 134, 139–40, 142, 150, 154–55, 157, 159, 161, 163, 168–70, 173, 176 79, 182–84, 186–87, 189, 191–92, 194, 198, 200, 217, 230, 242, 256–60, 278, 297–300, 305, 310, 312–13
Deborah, xxxix, 287 n. 9, 288
Delaney, Carol, 36
deportation, 217, 226, 236, 248, 276, 307, 312
Deuteronomic Code, 31, 35
Deuteronomistic, xxxix, xlv–xlvi, 28, 40, 93, 107, 120, 123–24, 128, 130–31, 145, 149, 162, 170, 174, 185–88, 191–92, 194–95, 198–200, 204, 208–9, 211, 213, 215, 221, 223–24, 231, 239–41, 250–51, 258, 269–270, 273, 275, 277, 284, 297, 300, 315

History, xxxix, xlv–xlvi, 40, 128, 149, 170, 162, 185, 209, 224, 239–40, 251, 269–270, 297, 300, 315

Historian, xlv, 107, 120, 123, 130, 174, 186–88, 191–92, 194–95, 198–200, 204, 208–9, 213, 215, 221, 240–41, 250, 258, 273, 275, 277, 300

theology, 211

Dever, William, 175, 213

Dibon, 27

Dion, Paul-Eugène, 215

divination, 180, 231, 233

dog, 99, 103, 110, 112, 121, 123–24, 128–29, 132–33

donkey, 46, 82, 83, 90–91

doubling: *see* duplication

dowry, 96

   see also women, inheritance

Dubovský, Peter, 201–3

dung, 82–83, 123–24, 129, 132, 134, 246, 248

duplication, 12, 16–26, 40, 50, 52, 54, 218–20

Dutcher-Walls, Patricia, 145, 156–57

earthquake, 199

Edelman, Diane, 288

Edom, 28–30, 32, 105–6, 187–91, 214

Egypt, 37, 90, 128, 130, 224, 226, 232, 237, 244–46, 253, 259, 273, 297–98, 300–301

Eilat, 188

Ekron, 3–6, 8–9, 98

Elah, 203, 217, 224, 240, 243

Eliakim, *see* Jehoiakim

Elijah, 1–25, 30–31, 35, 40, 42, 44, 50, 52–53, 55, 73, 79, 93, 99, 110, 114–15, 118–19, 121–22, 124–26, 131–32, 134, 136–37, 139, 179–80, 183

Elisha, 4, 8, 11–65, 68–104, 110–14, 148, 173, 176, 178–84, 288, 311

emasculation, 10, 26, 178, 311

Enkidu, 7

Enoch, xxvi, 12 n. 2

enthronement, 2, 148, 153, 155–58, 161, 166, 253

Enuma Elish, 24

Ethbaal, 124–25

eunuch, 124, 131, 136, 159, 262–63, 266, 293

Evil-merodach, 311, 313

exile, xliii, xlvi, 159, 209 n. 5, 212, 223–27, 230–38, 242, 247–48, 262, 265–67, 269, 276, 278, 290, 299–300, 303–4, 308–15

exodus (event), 15, 313

family, xxiii, xxiv, 40, 42, 45, 49, 55, 62, 76, 94–96, 105–7, 112, 114, 119–20, 122–23, 129, 135–37, 141, 143–49, 151–52, 156, 187, 192, 249, 279, 287, 298, 307, 311, 313

famine, 39, 56–57, 75, 82–84, 86–92, 94–95, 102, 132, 177, 309–10

female, xvi, xxi, xxiv–vii, xxxiv, xxxix, xlv, 1, 10 n. 26, 13, 15, 17, 19, 23, 26, 33, 42, 55, 64, 69 73, 84, 98, 120, 124–26, 129, 133–34, 142–43, 149–50, 158, 170, 265, 272, 275, 287–88, 290, 317

feminine, xxiii, xlii, 1, 7, 10–12, 14, 16, 22–24, 33–34, 58, 317

feminism, xvi, xxix–xxxvi, xxxix, xli, xliv, 6, 15, 21, 33, 54, 59, 81, 109, 123–24, 128, 227–28, 230

Fensham, F. Charles, 5

fertility, 23, 58, 124–25, 128, 130, 132, 174, 209, 229, 315

Fewell, Danna Nolan, 133, 151

fire, 7–9, 20–22, 79–80, 92, 99, 101, 208–10, 231, 233, 236, 253, 271, 273, 293, 312

food, xxvii, 9, 39, 54, 56–58, 80–82, 84, 86–89, 94, 123, 128, 132, 309–10, 314 n. 29

foreigner, 59, 60, 67–68, 79, 117, 124, 145, 213, 234, 236–37

Fritz, Volkmar, 41, 50, 313

funeral, 133
    rites of, 133

Gafney, Wilda, 275, 291

Gaines, Janet Howe, 123, 128

Galilee, 203, 205, 217

García Bachmann, Mercedes L., 17, 275, 288

Gedaliah, 310–13

Gehazi, 45–49, 51, 53–55, 64, 68–69, 72–74, 94–97

ghosts, 109, 143, 273

Gilead, 106, 110–11, 114, 141, 203, 205, 215, 217

Gilgal, 13, 15, 57

Gilmour, Rachelle, 79

goddess, 125, 130–31, 133–34, 158, 174–75, 213, 228, 265, 272, 275, 288, 296

Gonçalves, Francolino, 254

graves, 181, 183–84, 229, 287, 289, 292, 297

Gray, John, 4–5, 23, 71–72, 76, 118, 169, 181–82, 184

guards, 140, 147, 152–56, 169

Gunn, David, 133, 151

Habakkuk, 291

hair, 3, 6–7, 10, 25, 126–30

Halpern, Baruch, 298

Hamath, 178, 193, 235–36, 247, 253, 301, 310

Hamutal, 159, 301, 309

Handy, Lowell, 152

harlotry, 117–18, 120, 128, 230

Hathor, 130

Hawk, L. Daniel, 210

Hazael, 98–101, 103–4, 106, 115, 140–41, 167–68, 175–76, 181

heaven, 8–9, 11, 13, 15, 18–21, 23, 25, 81, 92, 133, 179–80, 183, 193, 197, 231, 233, 253–54, 257, 271–72, 275, 288, 292

Heller, Jan, 57

Hens-Piazza, Gina, xliv, 23, 30–31, 39, 43, 56, 59, 68, 71, 76–78, 82 n. 17, 84–85, 115–16, 141–42, 162, 189–92, 194–95

Hephzibah, 270–71

Hepner, Gershon, 51–52

herem, *see* ban

hermeneutics, xxxi, 228–29

Hezekiah, xlvi n. 19, 161–62, 207, 211, 219, 221, 239–71, 274–75, 277, 283–84, 289–90, 296, 306

high place: 162–63, 186–87, 198–99, 208, 213, 231–32, 236, 240–41, 246, 250, 259, 270–71, 293–94

Hilkiah, 245–47, 284–86, 292, 295

hirsute, *see* hair

Hobbs, T. R., 260

Hoffeditz, David, 128

horses, 20, 21–22, 29, 68–69, 78–80, 90–92, 124, 131, 137–38, 154, 159, 175, 179, 183, 189, 191, 245, 292–93
    of fire, 20, 21–22, 79–80, 92

Horst, Peter von der, 234

Hosea, 193, 202–3

Hoshea, 203–4, 217, 223–26, 240, 242–43

hosts of heaven, 21 30, 271, 292

Huldah, xxxix, 283, 285–91, 297–99, 312

iconography, 228–29, 330

Idrimi, 165

imperialism, xxvii, 210, 218 n. 34, 248, 304

incest, 3, 279

indigenous, 210–12

inequities, xxi–xii, xxiv

infertility, 52, 47–48, 51, 55
    see also children, birth of

inheritance, 18, 95–96, 277
    see also women, inheritance

Inquisition, 296
intermarriage, 123, 137, 141, 190, 212
Isaac, 51, 55, 181, 183
Isaiah, 249, 250–53, 255–56, 258–66, 279, 291
Israel, xxv, xxxix, xlii–xliii, 1–4, 7, 9, 12, 15, 17, 20–22, 27–37, 41–43, 58–73, 75, 77–85, 88, 90–93, 95–96, 98–99, 101–6, 109–21, 124–27, 129, 132, 134, 136–41, 143, 146–48, 150–51, 159, 162, 174–83, 185, 187–95, 197–205, 208–17, 219, 221, 223–29, 231–43, 246, 249, 253, 259, 261, 267, 271–76, 278, 284, 287–96, 299–300, 307, 313, 315, 317
Israel (Northern Kingdom), *see* North
   see also Samaria
Israel, *see* Jacob
ivory, 129
Iwry, Samuel, 180

Jabesh, 200–201
Jacob, 181, 183, 236
Jael, xxxix
Jehoahaz, 141, 173–79, 181–83, 187, 298, 300–301
Jehoash, 154, 163, 165, 167, 173, 177, 179, 181, 185, 187–91, 194, 220
   see also Joash
Jehoiachin, 159, 304–8, 311, 313–15, 320
Jehoiada, 143, 149, 151–59, 161, 163–70
Jehoiakim, 300, 301, 303–6
Jehonadab, 138, 139–40
Jehoram, 9, 27–31, 35, 82, 93, 104–7, 111, 149, 156, 167, 208–9
Jehoshaphat, 9, 28–30, 105, 110, 115, 167
Jehosheba, 143, 145, 148–53, 166
Jehu, 93, 99, 105, 109–18, 121–22, 124–29, 131–48, 159, 163, 173–75, 187, 200–201

Jephthah, 33, 63
Jephthah's daughter, 33, 63
Jericho, 13, 21, 23, 31, 309
Jeroboam, 28–29, 110, 112, 140–41, 174–75, 177–79, 201–3, 208, 220, 233, 273, 293–94
Jeroboam II, 177, 185, 189, 192–94, 198, 200
Jerome, 286 n. 7, 299
Jerusalem, 105–6, 122, 158–59, 163, 167–68, 187–89, 191, 198–99, 213–14, 220, 230, 240, 243–65, 271–78, 281, 284, 291–98, 301, 304, 306–9, 312, 315
   temple at, *see* temple
Jezebel, xli, 16, 28–29, 36, 42, 93, 107, 109–36, 139–40, 142–45, 147, 150, 159, 174, 195
Jezreel, 106, 110, 112, 114–16, 121, 124, 127–28, 132, 136–37
Joash, 143–45, 149–93, 208, 280, 285
John the Baptist, xxi, 12 n. 2
Jonah, 193
Joram, 105–6, 109, 114–17, 121–23, 145
Jordan, 13, 15–16, 18, 20, 25, 27, 31, 65, 68–69, 76, 92, 141
Josephus, 4, 82, 100, 146, 149, 199, 226, 234, 264, 279
Joshua, 11, 15, 19, 23, 210, 293
Josiah, xlvi, 161, 209, 221, 240, 267, 269, 277–78, 280–81, 283–86, 289–301, 306, 312
Jotham, 197–200, 203, 208, 215
Judah, xxxix, xlii–xliii, xlvi, 1, 27–30, 36, 93, 101, 104–6, 110, 114–16, 121–23, 139, 135–37, 141, 143–44, 146–51, 154, 156–59, 161–62, 166–68, 171, 173–76, 178–79, 185–91, 193–95, 197–99, 201–3, 205, 207–9, 211, 215, 217–21, 223–24, 232–34, 239–54, 256–57, 262–70, 272–73, 275, 277–81, 283, 285–87, 289–300, 303–15
Judaism, xvi, xx, xxviii, 234, 288

Kern, Paul Bentley, 227, 229–30
Khirbet el-Qom, 174
Korah, 259
Kuntillet 'Ajrud, 174

LaBarbera, Robert, 79–80
Labuschagne, Casper, 100
Lachish, 189, 191–92, 229, 243, 245,
   248, 250, 310, 312
   letters (ostraca) of, 310
   reliefs of, 248
lament, 228, 265
Lapsley, Jacqueline, xli
Latvus, Kari, 315
Lemuel, 160
leprosy, 59, 60, 62–63, 65, 67, 69,
   72–74, 79, 89, 90–91, 198–99
Levenson, Jon, 34, 314
Libnah, 105–6, 250, 301, 209
Lipschits, Oded, 304–5
Liverani, Mario, 165
Long, Burke, 138, 155
Lot, 3

Maacah, 158
madman, 111–13, 115
Maier, Walter, 70
makeup, 127–29
Malamat, Abraham, 280
male, xvi–xvii, xxvii, xxxiii–xxxiv,
   xxxix–xl, xlii, xliv, 10, 15, 17, 33,
   40, 42, 49, 50, 55, 58, 62–64, 69, 73,
   85, 95, 97, 107, 112, 118, 124, 126,
   133, 148–52, 154, 171, 195, 205,
   217, 241–42, 264–66, 289, 291–93,
   317
man, 8–9, 41, 46, 50, 56–57, 67–69,
   71, 74, 76, 78, 80, 87, 92, 95–96,
   99, 110–13, 115, 118, 129, 150, 153,
   180–82, 184, 259, 293–94
   of God, 8–9, 41, 46, 50, 56–57, 69,
      71, 76, 78, 80, 87, 92, 95, 99, 180–
      82, 293–94

Manasseh, 209–10, 259, 263, 269–81,
   283, 292–93, 295, 297–300, 304–6,
   315
mantle, 15, 16, 20, 25
   of Elijah, 15, 16, 20, 25
marginalized, xxi, xxxix–xlv, 56, 63,
   66, 68–70, 77, 84, 111, 118, 237, 279
masculinity, xlii–xliii, 1–4, 7, 9–12, 14–
   17, 21–23, 25–26, 33–34, 42, 63–64,
   81, 112, 125, 132, 176, 188, 195, 232,
   239, 241–42, 256–58, 260, 262, 264,
   266–67, 275, 277–78, 290, 300, 303,
   306, 315, 317
Masoretic Text (MT), 131
Mattaniah, *see* Zedekiah
McKinlay, Judith, 113, 126, 130, 134,
   142
Mediterranean, xiii, xliv, 197, 226,
   304, 308
Megiddo, 122–23, 297–98
Menahem, 200–205, 209, 216
Menn, Esther, 65–67
mercenaries, 154
Merodach-baladan, 262–64
Mesha, 28–29, 33–34, 36–37
   Inscription, 27
messiah, 11
messianism, 314
Michal, 127, 129
Midian, 127, 259
mikveh, 24
miracles, 12, 15, 18–19, 23, 44, 54–55,
   57, 68–69, 76–77, 87–88, 97, 99, 180,
   184, 249, 262
Miriam, 287 n. 9, 288, 290
Moab, 2–4, 7, 27–37, 180, 184, 209,
   293, 304–5
   people of (Moabites), 2, 27, 31–32,
      34, 180, 304–5
Moabite stone, *see* Mesha, Inscription
Molech, 292–93
monarch, xxxiv, xxxix–xl, xlii–xliii,
   1–2, 6, 29, 42–43, 56–57, 61, 66–68,

78–79, 81, 86, 92, 94, 98–99, 101–2,
    105, 107, 110, 131, 144–45, 147–48,
    150, 155, 158–59, 161–62, 164–65,
    167, 169–71, 173–79, 182, 185–88,
    193–95, 197–200, 204–5, 207–9,
    213–14, 216–18, 223–24, 227–28,
    231, 239–41, 248, 250–51, 258–60,
    263, 269–70, 279–80, 284, 297–99,
    314, 317
monolatry, 71
Moses, xxxiv, 11, 15, 19, 23, 63, 152,
    186–87, 240–43, 272, 274, 284–85,
    294–95, 298
mothers, xxii, xxvii, 25–26, 28–30, 40,
    46–50, 55, 75, 82–83, 85–86, 88–89,
    92, 97, 100, 104, 106, 116, 121, 123,
    127–30, 137, 143, 145–46, 149–51,
    153, 159–63, 168, 171, 186–87,
    198–200, 240, 270, 280–81, 284, 288,
    306–7, 310
    see also children, birth of

Na'aman, Nadav, 216, 227
Naaman, 59–74, 76, 78, 98, 101–2
Naboth, 110, 114, 116, 119, 121–22,
    125, 144
Nebuchadnezzar II, 159, 204, 307
Neco, 297–301
necromancy, 274
Nehushta, 159, 306–7
Nehushtan, 241–42
Nelson, Richard, 5, 8, 220
New Testament, xiii–xvi, xix, xxi,
    xxvii, xxxv, 5, 11–12
Ngan, Ling Elizabeth, 72
Nile, 37
Nimrud, 141
Nimshi, 110–11, 115–16
Nineveh, 248, 255
Noadiah, 287 n. 9
North, 2–3, 28–29, 59, 66, 98, 105, 135,
    140–41, 147, 153, 159, 162, 173–74,
    176–78, 182–83, 185–86, 189–94,

197, 200, 204–5, 207–9, 218, 223–24,
    231–35, 237–39, 242, 273, 277, 280,
    287, 293–94, 296, 298
    see also Samaria
    see also Israel
Northern Kingdom of Israel, see
    North
    see also Samaria
    see also Israel
Noth, Martin, xlv, 314
Nwaoru, Emmanuel, 70–72

Obadiah, 40
Obelisk, Black, 141
O'Brien, D. P., 70
Oded, Bustanay, 214–15, 304
Old Latin, 125
Olley, John, 177–78
Olyan, Saul, 116–17
Omri, 105–6, 138, 141, 144, 150
orphan, 43, 69
oxen, 73, 218–19, 221
    bronze, 218–19, 221

Pakkala, Juha, 311
Parker, Julie Faith, xiv, 26, 33, 35–36,
    40–41, 43, 61, 63–64, 66–67
Parker, Simon, 128
Passover, xvi, 12 n. 2, 33, 37, 294–95
paternity, 52–54, 169
Pekah, 199–200, 202, 203–5, 208,
    213–16
Pekahiah, 200, 202, 203–4
people of the land, 63, 147, 153–56,
    198–99, 219, 280–81, 285, 298,
    300–301, 307, 309–10, 312
Persia, 238
    period of, 238
phallus, 54, 133, 229
Philistia, 4–5, 94–95, 199, 240–41
    people of (Philistines), 4–5, 95,
    199, 240–41
Phineas, 127

Phoenicia, 110, 114, 124–25, 127, 133
  people of (Phoenician), 110, 114,
    124–25, 127, 133
Pippin, Tina, 120
plague, 37, 259
poison, 39, 56–57, 183
poor, *see* poverty
poverty, xxvii, 39–41, 43–45, 56, 66,
    69, 75–77, 82, 84–85, 87–88, 91, 112,
    114, 195, 279, 307, 309–10, 312
Pressler, Carolyn, 43–44
priest, 50 n. 27, 125, 133, 137, 139,
    143, 147–59, 161, 163–71, 187, 192,
    199–200, 218–21, 234–37, 250, 275,
    284–86, 291–96, 310, 312
procreation, 10, 12, 15–16, 23, 25, 30,
    44, 56, 173, 183–84, 209
prophets, xxxv, 2, 4–8, 10–31, 34–57,
    59–60, 62–69, 72–81, 84–91, 93–94,
    97–98, 100–104, 110–15, 119,
    121–22, 125–26, 132, 136, 139, 148,
    158–59, 173, 178–84, 194, 203, 216,
    230–33, 247, 249–52, 254–56, 258–
    66, 271–72, 275, 279, 283, 285–92,
    294, 296–99, 304–5, 308, 312–13
prostitution, 44, 82, 118, 128–31, 292
Provan, Ian, 34

Qimhi, 76, 76 n. 3, 82
queen mother, 137, 159–60, 284 n. 1
Queen of Heaven, 272, 275
queens, xli, 42, 93, 107, 109, 114, 118,
    120, 123, 125, 127–32, 134–35, 137,
    143–62, 166, 168–71, 174, 186, 272,
    273 n. 10, 275, 284 n. 1
Quint, David, 13–14

Rabshakeh, 244–53, 256
Rad, Gerhard von, 72, 314
Rahab, 129
rain, 9, 30–31
Ramoth-Gilead, 106, 110–11, 114
rape, 43–44, 230–31, 279

Rashi, 20, 298
Ras Shamra: *see* Ugarit
Rechab, 138–40
Red Sea, 188
regeneration, 12, 15, 22–23, 44
religion, xlii, 126, 133, 135–36, 141–42,
    175, 179, 213, 219, 271, 296
  book, 175
  folk, xlii, 175, 213, 271, 296
Remaliah, 199, 202–4, 208, 213–14
reproduction, 10–12, 16, 22–24, 26, 33,
    39, 44, 49, 56–58, 183, 209, 259, 278,
    311, 315, 317
  see also children, birth of
resurrection, 50, 52, 54, 55, 91 n. 33,
    95, 96
Rezin, 199, 205, 213–16
Rimmon, 71, 219
Rizpeh, xxxix
Roncace, Mark, 52, 96–97
ruah, see spirit

salt, 23–24, 31, 187
salvation, 39, 89, 141, 177, 221, 252,
    258, 261, 268, 313
Samaria, 2–3, 25, 29, 60, 62–63, 75,
    79–84, 86–87, 92, 99–100, 105, 129–
    30, 135–37, 139, 141, 173, 175, 177,
    179, 185, 189, 193, 197, 201–5, 207,
    214–15, 223–27, 230–31, 234–38,
    242–43, 247, 258, 293–95
  see also North
  see also Israel
Samuel, 55, 110
Sargon II, 225–27
Saul, 17, 110
scapegoat, 109, 111, 117, 269, 279
Schüssler Fiorenza, Elisabeth, xxvi,
    xxxiv, xxxvi
sea, 126, 188, 193, 218–19, 221, 312
  bronze, 221, 209, 312
Seder, 12 n. 2
seductress, 128, 213

Seeman, Don, 127
Sennacherib, 242–44, 246, 248, 251–58, 264
Seow, Choon-Leong, 178
Septuagint (LXX), 2, 2 n. 2, 125, 131, 144
Shallum, 200–202, 204, 286–87
Shalmaneser III, 141
Shalmaneser V, 224–26
shalom, 115–16
Shaphan, 284–86, 310, 312
Sharp, Carolyn, 210
Shephelah, 191
Shields, Mary, 49, 51
Shunnam, 68–69, 94–97
    woman from, 68–69, 94–97
Sidon, 124, 293
siege, 82–84, 87–88, 92, 94, 99, 100, 102, 177, 213–14, 216, 224, 226–29, 243, 248, 255, 277, 305–10
sight: *see* vision
Silla, 167–68
Sisera, 129
slavery, xxiv, 40–41, 43–44, 59–63, 66, 68, 73–74, 120, 210, 300, 311, 313
Smelik, Klaas A. D., 208, 215, 219–20
Smith, W. Alan, 60, 68, 70, 62
Solomon, xx, 82, 160, 193, 201, 208, 221, 271, 293, 298, 309
soothsaying, 271, 273
sorcery, 17, 116–18, 128, 147–48, 273
soup, 39, 56, 183
South, 29, 138, 147, 153, 161, 173, 185, 188, 193–94, 197–98, 200, 205, 208, 223, 231, 234–35, 238, 273, 287, 293
    see also Judah
Southern Kingdom of Judah, *see* Judah
    see also South
spirit, xxi, 15–19, 21–23, 50, 53–54, 64, 67, 72–73, 79, 109–11, 178, 183, 220, 250–51, 273
    double share, 16–19, 21–22, 183

Sprinkle, Joe, 35
staff, 46, 50, 53–54, 119, 245
Stavrakopoulou, Francesca, 273
storm, 5, 9–10, 21–22, 30–31, 44, 58, 114, 187
sun, 32, 260, 262, 271, 292–93
syncretism, 174, 234–35, 237, 242, 258, 272, 275, 296
Syriac, 299, 131
Syro-Ephraimite war, 205, 213–16

Tabeel, 214
Tadmor, Hayim, xliv, 2 n. 2, 13, 18, 40, 45, 70, 76, 82, 114, 177, 180, 182, 186, 188–89, 191–92, 194, 198–99, 215–16, 219–20, 226, 233–34, 263, 276 n. 30, 280 n. 42, 286 n. 7, 289, 313
Tamar, xxxix
Tappuah, *see* Tiphsah
Targum, 21, 131, 199, 299
Tarlin, Jan, 1, 4, 12
Tekoa, woman of, xxxix
temple, xliii, 118, 135, 138–40, 143, 148–59, 161, 164–73, 186, 191, 200, 217–21, 233, 243, 254, 257, 271, 273–75, 280, 283, 285–86, 291–96, 307, 309, 311–12
teraphim, 292, 295
thistle, 190
Tiamat, 24
Tiglath-Pileser III, 197, 200, 202–3, 205, 207, 214–18, 221, 226
Tiphsah, 201
Tirhakah, 250–51
Todd, Judith, 18
Topheth, 292–93
Transjordan, 215
treason, 102, 110, 113, 116, 121, 147, 151, 153, 155, 158
tree, 30–32, 76, 151, 174, 208, 213, 232, 247
Trible, Phyllis, xxix n. 23, 123, 126

tribute, 27, 141, 224, 243, 300, 301, 304
Tull, Patricia, xli
Tyre, 119, 141

Ugarit, xiv, 5, 288
Uriah, 218–20
usurpation, 101–2, 109, 113–14, 117, 120, 126–27, 129, 136, 140, 147–48, 165, 174, 176, 187, 200, 204–5
Uzziah, 198–99, 203

Van Dijk-Hemmes, Fokkelien, 48, 50, 52–54
vassalage, 2, 4, 28, 215, 217–19, 224, 226, 304
vision, xxxiv, xxxvii, xl–lii, 9, 12, 20, 29, 32, 52, 74, 77–80, 88, 91, 104, 118, 120, 131, 134, 138, 142, 147, 158, 182, 245, 259, 290, 303, 315, 317
Viviano, Pauline, 232
von Rad, Gerhard, *see* Rad, Gerhard von
Vulgate, 299

warfare, xli, xliii, 27–28, 31, 35–37, 42, 65, 75, 78, 84, 103, 106, 116–17, 199, 205, 213–16, 227, 229–31, 245, 258, 298, 307
holy, *see* ban
water, xxvii, 15–16, 20, 23–25, 28–37, 65, 69, 76–77, 81, 84, 99, 107, 247, 253, 263
Weems, Renita, xxix, 289
Westbrook, Raymond, 35
whirlwind, 11, 21
widow, 16, 39–45, 52–53, 55, 66, 69, 288
Wildberger, Hans, 264
Wilson, Robert, 41, 296
windows, 4, 42, 62, 92, 124, 126–31, 133, 159, 179–80, 238, 271, 296, 308
wisdom, xv–vi, xix–xxi, xxvii–xxviii, xxxiv–xxxvii, xlv, 67, 160, 216

women, xv–vi, xix–xxxiv, xxix–xlv, 16–17, 26, 36, 40, 41–43, 45, 49–50, 55, 57, 61–63, 66, 69, 75, 82, 84–90, 92, 94–96, 99, 101, 103, 107, 109 n. 1, 112, 119–20, 123, 127, 129–30, 134, 143–44, 150–52, 158–59, 169, 175, 195, 197, 201–5, 213 n. 17, 217, 227–30, 248, 271, 275–76, 279, 287–91, 293, 296, 310, 317
enslavement of, *see* slavery
foreign, 93, 107, 113, 117–27, 130–34, 142, 145, 154, 158, 160, 213
inheritance, 95, 96
reproduction, *see* reproduction
see also children, birth of
Woods, Fred, 25

Yahwism, 1, 70, 234, 288, 295
Yates, Gary, 128
YHWH, xxxiv, xxxix, xlii–xliii, 1–17, 19, 30–31, 34–39, 42, 44, 50, 53, 56–61, 64, 67–72, 74–75, 78–81, 86–89, 91–92, 97–99, 101–2, 104, 106, 110, 112–14, 117, 122–23, 125–26, 132, 134, 136, 138–39, 148, 150, 155–58, 168, 173–74, 176–79, 182–84, 189, 191, 194, 197–99, 204–5, 207–9, 212, 216, 219–21, 223, 225, 231–35, 237, 239–42, 246, 249–52, 254–62, 264–67, 271–72, 276–78, 288–92, 295–300, 303, 305–6, 308, 310, 312–13, 315, 317
house of, 199, 250, 260, 271, 292, 295, 312
see also temple
masculinity of, *see* masculinity
reproductive/procreative abilities of, *see* reproduction *and* procreation

Zadok, 199–200
Zakur, 178

Zechariah (king), 163, 170, 193, 200–201, 240
Zechariah (prophet), 199
Zedekiah, 307–9, 311
Zelophehad, 95
    daughters of, 95

Zibiah, 162–63
Zimri, 124, 126–27, 129, 131
Zion, xliii, 146, 191, 253–55, 257, 261 n. 27, 264–66, 290, 299–300
    see also Jerusalem
Zucker, David, 15, 19

Author

Song-Mi Suzie Park (PhD, Harvard University, 2010) serves as the associate professor of Old Testament at Austin Presbyterian Theological Seminary, where she teaches courses on literary approaches to the biblical text, families, and issues of gender and sexuality. She is the author of *Hezekiah and the Dialogue of Memory* (Fortress, 2015) as well as several articles and essays.

Volume Editor

Ahida Calderón Pilarski holds a PhD in Hebrew Bible from the Lutheran School of Theology at Chicago. She is an associate professor and chair of the Theology Department at Saint Anselm College in Manchester, New Hampshire. Pilarski has written extensively on the intersection of gender and culture/ethnicity/race in the interpretation of the Bible.

Series Editor

Barbara E. Reid, OP, is a Dominican Sister of Grand Rapids, Michigan. She holds a PhD in biblical studies from The Catholic University of America and is professor of New Testament studies at Catholic Theological Union, Chicago. Her most recent publications are *Wisdom's Feast: An Invitation to Feminist Interpretation of the Scriptures* (2016) and *Abiding Word: Sunday Reflections on Year A, B, C* (3 vols.; 2011, 2012, 2013). She served as vice president and academic dean at CTU from 2009 to 2018 and as president of the Catholic Biblical Association in 2014–2015.